Jesus the Divine Teacher

Jesus the Divine Teacher

Fullness and Mediator of Biblical Revelation

Eugene Kevane

VANTAGE PRESS
New York

IMPRIMATUR
Rev. Msgr. Richard J. Burke
Vicar General, Diocese of Arlington

Cover design by Susan Thomas

FIRST EDITION

Published by Vantage Press, Inc.
516 West 34th Street, New York, New York 10001

Manufactured in the United States of America
ISBN: 0-533-14222-9

Library of Congress Catalog Card No.: 2002093924

0 9 8 7 6 5 4 3 2 1

To Our Lady of Fatima
and
Saint Thérése of Lisieux
Catechists

We did not follow cleverly devised myths when we made known to you the power and coming of our Lord Jesus Christ, but we were eyewitnesses of his majesty. For when we received honor and glory from God the Father and the voice was borne to him by the Majestic Glory, "This is my beloved Son, with whom I am well pleased," we heard this voice borne from heaven, for we were with him on the holy mountain. And we have the prophetic word made more sure.

—2 Peter 1:16–19

Contents

Foreword

About This Book . . .

Christ said, "Do not think that I have come to abolish the law and the prophets. I have come, not to abolish them, but to fulfill them. Of this much I assure you: until heaven and earth pass away, not the smallest letter of the law, not the smallest part of a letter, shall be done away with until it all comes true" (Mt. 5, 17–18).

For scholars at the time of Christ and for those who have come after, it has been reasonably clear how the teachings of Christ simply carried on and built upon the law of the prophets. However, Monsignor Kevane's work, *Jesus the Divine Teacher*, elucidates the matter in a way which has not heretofore been achieved.

As a learned and recognized Rabbi of his time among the Israelites, Jesus had put Himself into a position where He could most effectively do precisely what He had come to accomplish: to fulfill the law. *Jesus the Divine Teacher* explains how Christ, in His Divine Wisdom, systematically explained the prophecies of old, built upon them, and gradually brought them to bear upon His basic mission which was to found His church against which the gates of Hell would never prevail.

This book, *Jesus the Divine Teacher*, is the penultimate in the series of writings which Monsignor Kevane produced during his lifetime. Starting with the textbooks he authored for use at Heelan Catholic High School, Monsignor Kevane was a prolific writer: "The Lord of History," "Augustine the Educator," "Creed and Catechetics"—to name a few of his works. I believe there is a theme which lies at the foundation of all his writings and at the foundation of his own spiritual life, that God has been speaking to His people since the dawn of mankind, through His prophets, through His Divine Son, Jesus Christ, who came among us to fulfill the prophets, and through the Church which He founded to protect and pass on this Divine Message to His people until the end of time.

About the Author . . .

Monsignor Kevane brought many years of preparation into the writing of this book. Born on a farm in Northwest Iowa and raised by parents whose faith in God and dedication to the Catholic Church was both simple and profound, their faith and example were to form the foundation and the strength of his life. At the age of eighteen, he began to study for the priesthood. He studied philosophy at Loras College in Dubuque, Iowa, and received his bachelor's degree in 1933. He was sent to the North American College in Rome, Italy, for his studies of theology, returning to his Diocese of Sioux City, Iowa, in 1938.

After ten years as principal of Heelan High School in Sioux City, Iowa, the central Catholic high school which as a young priest he was commissioned to plan, coordinate and build, Monsignor Kevane was released by the Diocese of Sioux City to become a professor in the Department of Education at the Catholic University of America in Washington, D.C. He later was named Dean of the Department and became the Editor of the Catholic Educational Review. He pursued and achieved his Doctorate, and in 1969 he was appointed Founding Director of the Notre Dame Pontifical Catechetical Institute for Catechetical Instruction and quickly established a number of affiliates throughout the United States. In 1971 he was appointed Visiting Professor of Catechetics at the Angelicum University in Rome, and in 1974 Professor of Catechetics at Saint John's University in New York City.

Monsignor Kevane passed away in 1996, leaving behind this manuscript which is now being published posthumously, and another manuscript still to be published, a sequel to this one, entitled, "The Deposit of Faith."

This writer is proud to have proceeded from the same grounding in the Faith as Monsignor Kevane did, to be personally acquainted for many years with his unswerving devotion to Christ and His Church, and to witness the depth of his personal spiritual life. I am proud to be his brother.

—Raymond A. Kevane, S.T.L., J.C.D.

Preface

The publication of this book comes at a significant moment. It is that of the immense distribution of the new Catholic Catechism. For the Catechism is not only the doctrine of Jesus. It is Jesus actually teaching, through his catechists, just as he did in his public life on earth. The new Catholic Catechism is the current instrument of Jesus the Divine Teacher, teaching through his Body, which is the Church.

This book sees the Bible through the eyes of Jesus the Divine Teacher. Using the Bible constantly in his teaching, he shows us the divine authorship of the Bible, which gives it its unity and makes it the Holy Bible.

What is the context of this book? It is the massive crisis of faith that has fallen upon modern man and is even penetrating widely within the Catholic Church. This twentieth century, as I write, about to turn into the third millennium since Jesus taught and sent his Church to teach all nations, saw the rejection of the entire revelatory past, the entire Word of God from Genesis to the Book of Revelation. We are losing our grasp of the unity and holiness of the Bible, allowing it to dissolve into a disparate group of merely human writings. It follows immediately that we are losing Jesus Christ. We are unable to see Jesus accurately according to the witness of the Holy Bible to him. This has left only modern mythical imaginations about him like the blasphemous Scorsese film!

The Modernist Heresy, growing inside the Catholic Church since 1835, is the cause of this doctrinal confusion and chaos. In recent decades it has penetrated with devastating results into the programs of religious education given to Catholic children. The Modernist Heresy, to use Charles Journet's description, retains the traditional terms of Christian doctrine but only to reinterpret them. The words *creation, incarnation, redemption, real presence, transubstantiation, justification, mystical body,* and so on, take on new meanings.

We have only to recall what has become of the Apostles' Creed from the Hegelian or simply the Modernist point of view. All the words are there, like an empty husk carried about by the winds of history and ideologies at their pleasure. So Charles Journet.

One recognizes here the denial of Jesus the Divine Teacher and a rejection of the very idea of the Divine Deposit which he gave to his Apostles and their successors to be guarded by faithful teaching and explained infallibly. The Holy Spirit, who inspired the Apostolic Writings, has an emphatically different idea: "I write appealing to you to contend for the faith which was once for all delivered to the saints" (Jude 3). "Anyone who does not abide in the doctrine of Christ does not have God" (2 John 9). "O Timothy, guard the deposit" (1 Tim. 6:20).

This book is a direct confrontation with this elimination of Jesus the Divine Teacher and his Deposit of Faith and Morals. It studies the Bible in a new catechetical way that recovers and renews both the unity and divine authorship of the Holy Bible and the resulting accuracy regarding both the figure of Jesus Christ and the truth of his teaching. It sees Jesus as he actually was, the Rabbi or Teacher of the Torah in Israel who became the Redeemer and Savior of mankind.

For whom was this book written? First, for the general reader among Catholics, and also for inquirers who are seeking information about the Catholic Church, how it is rooted in the Bible, and where its Articles of Faith are to be found today, taught with the same meaning that they had when Jesus taught that meaning to his Apostles. Thus this book has in view all adults of today who are caught up one way or another in the confusions and deceptions of the times.

Second, this book is intended for all catechists who teach the Catholic Faith. These include students preparing for the Diaconate and the Priesthood, for they are to be the ordained and official catechists in the Church. But they also include all other catechists, the parents, and the CCD teachers, who need help to see what the Deposit of Faith and Morals is, how it is Jesus' own teaching, and how it is taught today with the same meaning that it had for his Apostles. It is intended, furthermore, as a resource for training volunteer catechists in parishes. Priests and directors of religious education, according to their own purposes, may wish to base courses on a chapter or combination of chapters, perhaps assigning other chapters for outside reading, as the nature of each group indicates.

Thus this book becomes a manual for Catechists according to the *General Catechetical Directory*, par. 121, exploring in the text the biblical sources of the message of salvation and giving pedagogical advice and suggestions about methods in the references. In this way they do not obtrude upon the general reader who may wish to omit them.

The approach to the Holy Bible and to Jesus the Teacher of the Bible will be explained in various places. For the present, suffice is to say that this approach is quite different from the recent aberrations in Bible study and exegesis that concentrate excessively on the human authorship as if nothing else were at hand. Here the emphasis will be the properly catechetical one, that of the divine authorship of the Bible. For this is the factor that gives the Bible its sacred character and its unity from Genesis to the Book of Revelation. This unity arises from the fact of Jesus Christ, "the Mediator and Fullness of all Revelations," as the *General Catechetical Directory* states in par. 12, citing Vatican II, *Dei Verbum*, no. 2. Catechetics is the actual contemporary mediation of this fullness, for it is the teaching that continues Jesus' mandate to teach all nations and to baptize them into his new Way of Life (see Matt. 28:16–20). In this way catechists discover their true self-image and mission.

May this survey of the Bible, especially the Gospels, from the catechetical point of view help future priests and the catechists who assist them, especially the parents of Catholic children, to imitate and to follow Jesus the Divine Teacher in their own apostolates as teachers of the Word of God.

Jesus the Divine Teacher

Part I
The Hebrew Revelation

Prophecy and Preparation

*The canonical Scripture is a Letter written by our Heavenly Father
and transmitted to the human race by the sacred writers.*
                                        —Pope Leo XIII

Chapter 1

Religion in the Life of Mankind

This "Manual for Catechists" is a source book and a guide for teaching religion. This teaching takes places in a humble way, mostly oral, in families by parents and in the various teaching programs organized by priests for pastoral care.

In the Catholic Church this specifically Catholic way of teaching religion is called catechetics, a Greek word that the Apostles used for the teaching program they had learned from Jesus their teacher. The Greek root for our words *Catechetics* and *catechesis* stands in many places of the inspired Greek text of the New Testament.

Catechetics is the study of the sacred Deposit of Divine Revelation and of the resulting Deposit of Faith and Morals. It is a practical study because it concerns the formative transmission of the divine Deposit to catechumens as their way of life. Clearly, therefore, catechetical teaching is a part of religion in the life of mankind.

Catechetics is not the same as Natural Theology, Philosophy of Religion, or the Science of Comparative Religion as taught in secular universities or even the Science of Sacred Theology as taught in Catholic higher education. It is an independent ecclesiastical science. It will need to analyze carefully its own nature and its relationship to these other disciplines.

Religion on the Human Scene

Everyone wants to know more about religion. It is the one great fascinating subject, despite all current secular indifference; religion is constantly under discussion in every kind of conversation. People take stands on it with deeply held opinions regarding it. Why is this?

It is because religion is the universal fact about mankind that exhibits our humanity, indicates our better selves, enshrines our aspirations toward God, and inspires our activities on behalf of our fellow man. Wherever one goes across the earth in space or however far back in time, religion is the constant fact on the human scene.

The study of religion, furthermore, is supremely interesting. It is also challenging because of the amount and the variety of its matter. But it is not inherently difficult. It is quite simple and most human. It studies the various ways by which human persons and human societies have related to Almighty God, seeking to know him and to bind themselves to him.

Religion is the truly worldwide fact and hence a humbling panorama. The immensity of this fact and the amount of its information give us some ideas of the greatness of God.

Above all, however, the study of religion helps us to see better the wretchedness of the human condition. We grope toward God in the dark. We become better able to appreciate the fact and the doctrine of Original Sin.

The study of religion has a special role in the life of catechists because they are persons dedicated to the handing on of religious faith by teaching. Catechists are persons of religion with a special and even official relationship to the Supreme Being of the universe, God the Father Almighty, creator of heaven and earth.

"It is impossible to please God without faith, since anyone who comes to him must believe that he exists, and that he rewards those who try to find him" (Heb. 11:6). The entire field of Catechetics is contained in this verse of the Bible. It tells us that we are concerned with a practical teaching that gives formation in the way of life that leads to God. The purpose of Catechetics, therefore, is to help others find God, come to God, and learn how to be close to him. This gives peace, happiness, self-fulfillment, and joy. All this results from helping persons know God better by means of the Articles of Faith, which catechists teach as a Divine Deposit. These Articles of Faith give divine revelation to minds and hearts, and thus their souls are illuminated. A new light shines ahead of them on the road through life. "Yahweh is my light and my salvation, whom need I fear?" (Ps. 27).

Mankind's Problem Regarding God

A popular fad in current religious literature deals with *The Problem of God*, as if there is no trouble with us human beings.[1] The fact is that the problem is in human persons individually and in mankind collectively in the various kinds and entities of social life. For there is indeed among humans a religious and therefore a moral problem of some kind. The problem is with us. It is definitely not a "problem of God." Catechetics, in fact, is the teaching that explains what God has done to solve the human problem in a definitive, effective, and final way, as the last book of the Bible teaches when it describes the Heavenly Jerusalem to come (see Rev. 21–22).

To ascertain that there is indeed a problem with mankind, one need but listen for the next siren. As in *For Whom the Bell Tolls*, the siren screams for some unfortunate human being in trouble with the law, suffering a heart attack, struck by a car, or whatever. The front page of each daily newspaper documents the fact: there is a problem with humanity. Popular literature reflects it perhaps now more than ever. Even in the more Christian times literature tended to reflect mankind's problem. In pagan antiquity literature was an evil flood bearing down upon souls, staining them and drowning them in sin. Saint Augustine describes this murky situation in unforgettable passages of his *Confessions* on the cultural flood that took him away from the Catholic religion of his mother and plunged him into spiritual and moral wretchedness. Augustine gives us theater and the stage of his time as his examples. It is the same today: one need but reflect on recreation and entertainment, enhanced now and universalized by television and the video cassette.

In a striking passage Fr. James Alberione, one of the major religious founders of the twentieth century, writes: "The apostolate of the media of communication is aimed at this intimately tormented world, where people suffer because of their erroneous ideas and thoughts, suffer because of their faithlessness, and because of their lack of the message of salvation." How could it be expressed better? One sees immediately why religion has this universal interest for people. It offers help for the human condition. This concerns catechetical teachers directly, because they teach the very program of Jesus Christ the Divine Teacher. He healed and cured people. His program for teaching the Word of God has a medicinal quality.

His teaching program heals human persons for time and especially for eternity.

One can look out on the human situation, then, in these various ways, coming to realize better that there is indeed a human problem regarding God. Nor do we need to confine ourselves to the newspapers, literature, and recreation. We meet it in dealing with people. What people? Is not our own self the first person we deal with? Here the problem with mankind comes home to each of us in person. What is the matter with us?

The problem is that we know God exists, but we do not live in his presence.[2]

It is the constant teaching of the Bible and of the Church that we have the power to know with certitude that God exists. Saint Paul says we are inexcusable if we fail to use this power (see Rom. 1:20). We know with certitude that there is a Supreme Being. It follows immediately that this entails prayer and adoration.

But what happens in practice? We become so absorbed in our earthly lives that we hardly think of God at all. We cease to pray. Adoration? Once a week? We are often too tired, we say, because of our earthly activities.

Suppose we enter the religious life, following a special vocation. Here everything is organized to permit more time for God, more reflective thought, more prayer. But even here the religious life does not automatically accomplish the presence of God: the persons must work at it. It simply provides a better environment for their effort to live in the presence of God.

Thus one comes to see better the human problem regarding God. He is absent, as if far away.

There is another aspect of the problem with us: while we can indeed know with certitude that God exists, nevertheless by our natural powers we cannot know much about him. Mostly we only know what he is not, not positively what he is. This kind of negative knowledge, which is our natural situation entirely apart from our sinfulness, is not enough to establish a close personal relationship with God. It does not provide a sufficient foundation for the interior life of prayer. Hence we see our problem still better. If we cultivate our powers of reason correctly, we can come to a knowledge that our very existence comes from God and realize that he is closer to us than we are to ourselves. Why is this? Because God is present everywhere. Hence, if he is present everywhere, then he is present in this place where I am, wherever I am. One can realize again the truth stated by Saint Paul: "In fact he is not far from any of us, since it is in him that we live, and move, and exist" (Acts 17:28). But we do not have a sense of this closeness of God. Human beings tend rather to have a sense of the absence of God. What we feel is the opposite of the truth. People tend to experience not his nearness but his distance. They even think of him vaguely as something far away, some *thing*, not *someone*. Yet they are not atheists. They say in the polls, up to 90 percent or more, that they believe in God. But their idea of God is inadequate. That is what Father Alberione meant in the passage quoted earlier: people do not think the right thoughts about God. Would it not solve the human problem regarding God if some great and even divine Teacher came with a teaching from God to cure the human situation? Here the greatness of the calling of the Catechist comes into view.

John Henry Newman, a precocious adolescent who read widely among the modern philosophers, was almost persuaded of atheism by David Hume. By the grace of God when about fifteen Newman triumphed over the atheistic thinking with the firm personal conviction that God exists which characterized the rest of his long life. In a classic passage of his *Apologia* he tells us that the social world outside shows him no evidence of God's presence and that he was constantly thrown back upon this luminous personal certitude, the grace of his teenage years.[3]

The fact is, then, that people in general do not walk with God. The world of human society reflects this fact. Spiritual writers tell us that our first parents did indeed walk in the presence of God. Then their sin intervened: they lost their privileged sense of God's nearness. This was the beginning of the practical absence of God from human persons and human society. It is a condition that grows in human history. We human beings are occupied and preoccupied with things that are not God and even with interests and activities that are not Godly. We do not relate to God. Our bond with him is missing.

The result is a propensity for idolatry.[4] The more one studies the human scene, the more visible the fact becomes that we are born idolators. We see this constantly in the Old Testament: the Prophets were in a perpetual struggle against idolatry. It lies deep in human nature. What is idolatry? It sets up an idol and worships it instead of God. Idolatry is the worship of an idol. People tend to substitute something other than God as their basic interest and purpose in life. Always this idol is the human *self* in some form. When the ancients carved idols, a bear, a crocodile, or whatever, they exhibited a simple and childlike form of idolatry. But always these idols reflected the way people wanted to live. Always the human persons turned the object of worship to fit what each one wants and against the way each one ought to be, against *what I ought to be.* Hence idolatry becomes the expression of sinfulness.

A very common form of idolatry sets up the inner flow of our own conscious states, saying "This is the voice of God," "I have an expression of the Divine," or "I perceive the Numinous." Then they teach what they perceive and thus religious ideas are propagated. But these views are only idols, profoundly mistaken ones: idols and not God. This is why Saint John of the Cross placed such stress upon faith in the Word of God: faith alone, even if it is the dark night of faith. These experiencings of "the Numinous" or "the Divine" that we hear so much about these days are the idolatries of today.

What people need, especially children and young people, is not their own experiencings but the teaching that brings them the Word of God as a Divine Deposit and not some mere human experiencing or thinking (see 1 Thess. 2:13). This is why the study of religion is fundamental: it locates that sacred Deposit and formatively explains its content. Faith always brings catechetical teachers on the scene because Catechetics is simply the teaching of the Divine Deposit accomplished in a way that helps to deepen faith in it. This is the living contract with God-near-us and God-with-us that sets aside all idols and all idolatry, whether ancient or modern.

There is a further very real and very serious dimension in this matter of idolatry and not least in its modern form of personal experiencings. There is someone else. Someone else one must say, a person indeed but not God, for he is the adversary of God who works behind this idolatrous self-deception and self-seeking done in the name of religion. The study of religion is a serious matter. It needs to be done carefully and with prayer for the divine assistance.[5]

These considerations make it clear that it is the quality of each person's own interior life that is at stake. This is the problem of us human beings regarding God. Catechetical teaching is the process of helping people avoid these idolatrous self-deceptions by bringing them to see and to know the self-revelation of God. It helps people to find God and to live in his presence. They find God by hearing his Word, which comes to them in the teaching. This is indeed quite different from an experience of the Numinous. After catechumens hear God's Word, the teaching then helps them deepen their way of life in his presence, now turned toward him. This is the repentance, the *metanoia,* the obedience in life to the Word one hears and embraces in faith. And thus the purpose of human life is seen in a new and true light: it is not confined to this earth but looks forward to the resurrection of the body and life everlasting in heaven.

The human problem, then, is one of the interior life of prayer and adoration. This problem has been with mankind since the first human pair in distant prehistory. It has been growing and indeed immensely as a social and cultural phenomenon in recent centuries.

But since we have the ability to know God by our powers of natural reason, could we not solve our human problem by cultivating these natural powers better? The effort has indeed been made and brings before us the next aspect of religion on the human scene.

Natural Theology

It is important to note that we are about to discuss Natural Theology, not Sacred Theology. Sacred Theology is a special science within the Catholic Church; in fact, it is one of the four forms of the Ministry of the Word in the Church, as *GCD* no. 17 teaches. Catechists especially, but all Christians generally, must heed this distinction carefully, because many theologies today are actually natural theologies, even though they present themselves deceptively in the terminology and from the academic chairs of Sacred Theology. Among the natural theologies, everything depends upon the concept of God that is taught. Today they frequently descend to the level of mere "philosophies of religion" and teach some form of pantheism.

Sacred Theology is quite different. It is the science proper to the People of God. It takes the Articles of Faith as its point of departure and develops its discourse about divine things in the light of those Articles. This places it into a helpful relationship with Catechetics.

Natural Theology is clearly not the same, even when it is philosophically sound; but it does indeed relate to Sacred Theology because it provides the preambles for faith by teaching its natural foundations. Natural Theology is a natural science of discipline that took its origin in the pagan philosophical schools of classical Greece. It may well be called the central and most important current in Western intellectual life from that day to the present. Hence it is an immensely large and challenging subject; here only the salient features can be sketched in brief outline from the viewpoint of their relationship to Catechetics.[6]

Natural Theology: The Aspiration of Greek Philosophy

The Greeks stand at the fountainhead of Western civilization by their *paideia,* their system of education, implemented by the Seven Liberal Arts. *Paideia,* deriving from *pais,* the Greek word for a child, is a richly expressive word that denotes both the process of education, which enculturates a young person into the social heritage of Greek humanism, and the outcome of the process, the culture by which Greek society lives. Hence the tools that shape and form the child and youth are supremely important. Without them the process cannot take place, just as the sculptor and carpenter are helpless without their specific tools for use in the practical arts. The Liberal Arts are these tools used by teachers, the set of disciplines in the curriculum of education that shape and form young people into the ideals of Greek humanism and culture.[7]

These Liberal Arts are the lasting achievement of the Greeks, not only admired but actually still taught and practiced in the cultural heritage of the West. Since the Fathers of the Church were learned in these Liberal Arts and made use of them in their catechetical apostolate, the Greek achievement relates very directly to Catechetics across the centuries. The expressive Greek word *logos,* meaning the "word" of human discourse, lives on in the names of intellectual disciplines such as "logic," "geology," "anthropology," "sociology," and, not least, "theology."

The teaching profession, accordingly, was basic in Greek life and culture. The teachers were known as Sophists, from *sophia*, wisdom. By using these Liberal Arts they were to develop young people as persons of wisdom, persons namely who possess the social heritage of Greek humanism and culture. The fact is, however, that the Sophists placed Rhetoric in the seventh position, for skill in the use of words was the key to success in the politics and business of this world. Socrates, himself a Sophist or Teacher, rose up against this merely worldly approach, which had expediency and success in practical affairs as its purpose. For Socrates and his disciples Plato and Aristotle, the Sophists were on a path that threatened the fundamental values of Greek culture. Rhetoric should not be the culminating Liberal Art. The seventh art should cultivate a love for true wisdom: it should be a *logos* or science of abiding truth, reality, and value. The Greek way of life would be strengthened in its foundations rather than undermined. Thus "philosophy," meaning "love of wisdom," was born. These Greek thinkers projected this seventh art or science as the culmination of human education by means of the study of Natural Theology.

Plato offers an idea of this aspiration in book 10 of *The Laws*, and the concept pervades his famous *Dialogues*. Aristotle developed this seventh Liberal Art further by laying the ontological basis for it in his *Metaphysics*. He projected the completion of his Ontology by a formal course in Natural Theology, the study of the Supreme Being and his attributes. If he did actually teach this course, the text of his lecture notes did not survive. His intention, however, is clear and well known. He uses the term *theology* to name the discipline he has in mind, the *logos* of God elaborated by the power of human reason. It was to be the use of systematically cultivated human reason to achieve understanding that reaches beyond sense perception. Theology was to be a systematic natural science or discipline, *metaphysical* in purpose and nature, that has God as the object of academic teaching and learning.

This aspiration to build a natural knowledge of God and divine things on the level of systematic higher education did not come to fruition among the pagan Greek thinkers, even among these greatest of the Greek philosophers whose ontological principles were open to the Supreme Being. In practice they failed to achieve a clear and accurate concept of God the Creator, upon whom the entire cosmos, man included, depends in the order of existence. Hence creaturehood was not rightly understood, nor its first obligation to the Supreme Being, prayer for help in living a moral life according to His Will and for His sake. Matter was thought to be itself eternal, and human life was confined to time and the things of the material cosmos. Thus Greek philosophy, even at its best, did not know either God or the nature of man and the material cosmos in an accurate and concretely effective way. Always, even among these most acute of the pagan thinkers, matter seemed to stand autonomous and eternal, together with whatever higher beings there might be. The doctrine of creation was missing. It was unable therefore to fulfill its own highest aspiration, that of regenerating and renewing the popular religion of the classical Greeks and Romans. Seen from this point of view, the study of Graeco-Roman philosophy is one aspect of the study of religion. It exemplifies the ultimate powerlessness of Natural Theology, by itself and in autonomous separation from revealed religion, to renew man's concept of God and to regenerate his religious heritage. The religion of the Greeks and the Romans continued to sink ever deeper into the crude polytheism, the pan-sexism and the secularization to which Saint Paul bears witness in the first chapter of his Epistle to the Romans, and which the excavations at Pompeii make visible today.[8]

Christian Philosophy: The Development of Natural Theology

Natural Theology was more a frustrated aspiration in Graeco-Roman philosophy than an actually existing and functioning academic discipline. Its articulation and development to this status had to wait, as a matter of historical fact, for the work of Christian scholars. Augustine, the founder of Christian philosophy, retained the heritage of pagan philosophy in his program for Christian higher education, but he saw it now as regenerated and renewed in the light of Divine Revelation. He calls philosophy "the science of virtue and of wisdom" and provides for its purification and regeneration, converting it to Christian use.[9]

This work of the Church Fathers in bringing the philosophical heritage of the Classical culture into the Church, culminating in

Augustine, represents the birth of Christian philosophy as a distinctive kind and mode of philosophy on the human scene. It was at home in the Schools of Christendom where this stronger and more lucid natural theology, able to rise to the doctrine of creation, was articulated as a philosophical science with right of place as the seventh Liberal Art in the programs of study. But this work, while philosophical in nature and rooted in the openness of the Greek principles, was built upon the Patristic catechetical explanations of the first Article of the Creed.[10] It was a natural knowledge of God that functioned within the Faith and actually continued and supported the childhood catechesis of young people on the level of higher education.

In the Christian times from the Early Fathers through Saint Thomas Aquinas, a thousand years in round numbers, Natural Theology flourished as never before, for it was now Christian philosophy in that position as the discipline that completed and culminated the Liberal Arts. Saint Thomas Aquinas provides its most lucid and comprehensive statement in his short treatise *On Being and Essence* and in the first twenty-six questions of his *Summa Theologiae,* the highest development of man's natural power to know God.[11]

For educated young people, this natural science of God was a personal blessing, for it provided the rational preamble, foundation, and defense of that elevated concept of God that they had learned as children in family and parish catechetics.

Modern Philosophy: The Death of Natural Theology

After Saint Thomas Aquinas the cultivation of Christian philosophy began to decline in the Schools of Christendom as educated persons turned increasingly toward the rapidly developing empirical sciences of this cosmos. The time came, about three hundred years ago and four centuries after Aquinas, when professors of philosophy began to cultivate Natural Theology in separation from the Faith, from an academic position outside the Faith. This is the distant and initially very small beginning of a schism between the academic and the catechetical orders of teaching, a matter now of direct and vital concern to every student of Catechetics and teacher of the Catholic Faith.

This ushers Descartes, the founder of modern philosophy, into view, for he introduces a fundamental change in the status of Natural Theology, one that the catechetical study of religion in modern times cannot ignore. Descartes subjected it to the process of separation that characterized his philosophizing: Natural Theology is no longer to function within religious faith but is to be autonomous, separated from it, as matter is separated from spirit, as religion itself, conceived as a realm of feeling and emotion, is separated from intellectual life and its objective scientific disciplines.

This is the origin of the modern atheism that has spread like a cancer from the campus of Western colleges and universities to every aspect of political, social, and cultural life. Spinoza, Descartes' chief follower, stands at the fountainhead of this real problem for religion and its teachers, for he taught an outright pantheism, making "God" identical with "this natural cosmos" that the natural and mathematical sciences were learning in his time to explore with a new kind of success. God, this pantheism believes, is the life that is visible in the life of trees, animals, and especially human beings. There is only one substance, the Divine, and humans are its highest and most manifest modes. One must bear in mind this portentous teaching that identifies "the Divine" with this visible cosmos and with human beings in particular. Spinoza is rightly called the Metaphysician of Modern Atheism, and his doctrine is the most basic reason that the *General Cetechetical Directory* titles its part 1 "The Reality of the Problem."

Spinoza's metaphysics, coupled with the Cartesian method, led directly to the rise and spread of philosophical atheism in modern academic life and to its reverse side, the secularization of modern social life and culture. For the atheistic intellectual revolution spread on to Hume, Comte, and Hegel and to their disciples Marx, Engels, and Nietzsche. The outcome was a rejection of the values of Western and Christian humanism in favor of a new modern secular humanism, which thought to solve all personal and social problems by the use of science and technology.

Thus Saint Pius X, the great catechist of the twentieth century, identifies the special circumstance that all Catechists must bear in mind. "An atmosphere of unbelief has been created," he writes, "which is most harmful to the interior and spiritual life. This atmosphere wages war upon any idea of a higher authority, any idea of

God, of revelation, of the life to come, and of mortification in this life. Hence parents and teachers must inculcate with the greatest care the basic truths found in the first questions given in the catechism."[12]

This process of philosophical negation subjected the religious heritage of the West, and the Bible in particular, to a peculiar hermeneutics that interprets revealed religion as necessarily mythological. It could be nothing but a collection of man-made myths, since no personal God exists who could speak to mankind in this way or in any way.

Varieties of Religion Experience

This situation evokes the figure of Emmanuel Kant to conclude this summary on the Western heritage of Natural Theology. Wincing from the scorn of these atheistic philosophers for what they termed nothing but prattle about abstractions, Kant thought to save religious faith in God by a Copernican Revolution in philosophy, as he himself termed his new approach that did away with Natural Theology altogether. Kant granted to the atheists that there is no metaphysics by which the human mind can ascend to transcendent reality. This was Kant's antiintellectualist revolt that replaced the power of human reason to know God by an appeal to a categorical imperative of felt need, emotional experience, and the so-called "reasons of the heart." Clearly this will impact upon Catechetics, for it means that religious education no longer has a doctrine to teach and must shift to some kind of experience approach.

Natural Theology has as its best known academic forum the Gifford Foundation at the University of Edinburgh, sponsor of the annual Gifford Lectures, which have become in their published form the most copious single resource for this aspect of the study of religion. For the terms of the Gifford Foundation presuppose the existence of the Science of Natural Theology as a valid study of the divine nature and attributes and of the relations of man and the universe to the personal Supreme Being. When William James, America's foremost psychologist and philsopher, a student in Germany where he became a disciple of Kant, was invited to give the

Gifford Lectures, the Kantian approach received its classic presentation in the resulting volume, *Varieties of Religious Experience.*[13] From more than one point of view, James's work represents the end of Natural Theology and the *denouement* of the modern period of Western intellectual history. For James is confined to the modern West. He represents the atheistic movement on the one hand, with its denial of the existence of an intelligent and transcendent Supreme Being who has spoken to mankind, and whose message, somehow and in some at least vestigial fashion, is taught by the religions of mankind; and on the other hand the varieties of religious experience that he describes, subjective strivings of the human spirit, are those of the Western world, indeed primarily those of Anglo-Saxon Protestantism in America.

In William James' approach there is no longer an intelligible, systematic academic discourse about the Supreme Being and his attributes. One learns much about the experience approach in religion and religious education by comparing William James' *Varieties of Religious Experience* with the first twenty-six questions of Saint Thomas' *Summa.* What mankind has been aspiring to do since the ancient Greeks is to know about God, not to have feelings about the Divine or have an experience about divine things. Always and everywhere humans aspire to knowledge about God, simply because they are born as creatures endowed with the power to reason. The human intellect is the divine image on the human brow: hence its use is broader than the academic education of the Western world. It is this that introduces the next highly interesting fact, perhaps even more significant for Catechetics, which the catechetical student of religion encounters.

Kant died in 1804, a century before his American disciple delivered these Gifford Lectures. Natural Theology had indeed fallen upon lean years across the nineteenth century, the years that elaborate the "Modern" concept of progress as a function of intellectual departure from the very idea of revealed religion. These are the very years when a new turn of events took place that bears upon the study of Catechetics, giving it the quite different and postmodern character exemplified by Christopher Dawson's Gifford Lectures of 1947.[14]

The Discovery of Religion as the Universal Human Fact

These vicissitudes of Natural Theology as an academic discipline in the curriculum of Western higher education took place in isolation from the rest of mankind. From Plato and Aristotle across twenty-five centuries to William James delivering his philosophically specialized *Varieties of Religious Experience* Western men had lived and thought in the context of their own intellectual heritage, confined to the northwest quadrant of the planet. To the north and west the ocean was an impenetrable barrier, for men dared not sail out of sight of land. To the south the Sahara Desert was equally impassable. Vaguely men knew of other humans to the east, the fabled land of Prester John, whence human storms came from time to time like Attila and his Huns and Genghis Khan and the Mongols. Somewhere farther east were India and China, known only by garbled rumor: the distance was too great for the means of travel and communications. Furthmore, Islam had sealed off the long overland route to the east since the seventh century. It was Prince Henry the Navigator in Portugal, a devout member of a Third Order motivated by a missionary's love for Christ, who circumvented the Islamic roadblock in order to carry the message of Christ to the rest of mankind in the Far East. For he opened up the conquest of the oceans by the scientific research and applied technology of his Academy of Navigation near Lisbon. Columbus and Magellan came from this school of applied science and used the navigational instruments that Prince Henry's staff of specialists had developed.

Suddenly, as a result, the Christian West was liberated from its geographical restriction in the northwest quadrant. Saint Francis Xavier sailed from Lisbon in one of the small but now accurately navigating wooden ships for India, Japan, and China. To the surprise of the West, furthermore, an entire New World of two hitherto unknown continents was discovered across the Atlantic with still another even larger ocean beyond it that did indeed reach to India and China. The shape and continental outlines of the planet Earth were suddenly understood by empirical knowledge. The impact upon the Christian culture of Western Europe was electrifying. And this not least because the new lands were peopled with the widest variety of human beings, peoples of culture, barbarian tribes, and as it were pushed to the margins of the continents, primitive savages

without the use of metal and in some cases not yet even knowing
the use of shaped stone.

The Universality of Religion in Space

Missionaries and merchants throughout the period from 1492
through the nineteenth century pushed out to all these tribes,
tongues, peoples, and nations. Voluminous reports were filled in
the Western centers of learning. A vast mass of information began
to accumulate in the West concerning the rest of mankind, the
material cultures or patterns of living, and the spiritual dimension
of thought, belief, and worship.

Nowhere was an irreligious tribe or people discovered. Everywhere the Westerners found some kind of religion, some specific
pattern for recognizing some concept of Deity, which sustained both
personal life and the social fabric of the group.

Everywhere, furthermore, there was the Man of God, a person
of the tribe set aside somehow for communion and communication
with the higher Powers, who returns to the human community as
its recognized Teacher to give it spiritual doctrine and moral leadership. Always the tribe lived by a body of doctrine received from the
past, which it handed on to its young people by teaching.

"It is the aim of . . . the Shaman," Dawson writes, "to transcend
the limits of ordinary knowledge and to attain that deeper level of
consciousness which we have described already as the natural basis
of religious experience. . . . [All primitive cultures] value the super-
normal experience of dream and vision, trance and ecstasy, and the
men who possess such experiences are the religious leaders and
the intellectual teachers of the community."[15] Every human society,
whether across the planet as explored since Prince Henry the Navigator or back in time to absolute human origins, exhibits this phenomenon of a religious class or order of men set apart for the things
of religion. Their functions are sometimes distinguished as those of
the Sacred Priests or Kings or Prophets, but the prophetic type
or "Shaman" seems to be the most original and most universal,
combining in his mission and role all three functions.

Dawson continues:

The study of primitive religion during the last century has tended to emphasize more and more the importance of primitive ideas of supernatural power which are not necessarily derived from a belief in particular gods or spirits or from the technique of the professional magician. Words like the Polynesian *Mana,* the North American *Wakan* and *Manito* . . . are found amongst very many primitive people and denote an impersonal power, "an ocean of supernatural energy" . . . which manifests itself in nature and in vision and in all events which appear portentous or miraculous. The anthropologists may describe this element as "magical," the students of comparative religion as "numinous" or "dynamistic" and the theologians as "divine," but whatever term is used the distinctive thing about it is its transcendent character. It is always felt as something outside man's common experience: an *other* world, an *other* power, an *other* being, which forcibly or mysteriously imposes itself on this world of human beings and human power as greater or more powerful or more sacred. No doubt in many cases this transcendent quality is attached to persons and things, as in the case of Mana which is associated with the person of the sacred chief in Polynesia, or as with the West African fetish and the North American "medicine bundle." But this does not detract from its transcendent character. . . . In fact, the conception of Mana can be most easily understood as a pagan analogy to the Christian conception of grace. The universality and importance of this scene of transcendence in the most primitive forms of religion can hardly be questioned. . . . [16]

Dawson gives this summary of the modern empirical discovery of the religious fact:

This primordial knowledge of God and the soul is very remote from anything that can be called Natural Theology. Primitive man is not concerned with abstract truth but with the reality and power of the forces on which his life depends, and his religion finds expression in myths and rites or sacred techniques. It is only at a later stage of culture, when social organization is sufficiently advanced to leave room for learning and study, that we can expect to find any systematic tradition of rational thought . . . This holds good of all the historic religions: everywhere revelation is regarded as the primary source of religious truth, and intuition and reason are secondary. And this is true in the sense that positive, historic religion is always primary, and philosophical or theological religion is the result of a secondary reflective activity. The concept of revelation is as old as religion itself, since the most primitive types of religion always rely on the authority of an immortal tradition and/or on some supernatural means of communication with the higher powers such as omens, divination and the visions and inspired utterances of Shamans or prophets. . . . Of course I do not mean that the concept of revelation is confined to the lower forms of culture and the more primitive types of religion. On the contrary it is universal and found in different forms at every stage of religious development, whereas the idea of Natural Theology is found in only a few cultures and there only at a relatively advanced stage of development.[17]

So much for the discovery of religion as Westerners explored the entire planet in space. All of this, of course, illuminates the place of the Bible on the human scene and the religion of the Hebrew Prophets.

The Universality of Religion in Time

The nineteenth century added a new temporal perspective to the spatial dimensions of man's varied religious life across the planet. Beginning with the discovery and deciphering of the Rosetta Stone in the Napoleonic period, the new science of Archaeology began to open up the vistas of prehistory with its excavation of ancient villages and the first cities of mankind. Babylon was unearthed, and Ur of the Chaldees whence Abraham was called, together with many less famous sites. Patterns of prehistoric culture and cultural diffusion were identified. The development of hunting tribes and agricultural villagers into peoples was reconstructed and of peoples into city-states. Finally, the empires of historic time appear, documented now by their invention of writing.

Archaeology and geology combine to produce a new knowledge of "prehistoric," the human ages that precede the invention of writing at about 4000 B.C. From sparse beginnings visible in the geological strata, human families, tribal societies, and agricultural villages increase and multiply. Always and everywhere religion is woven into the fabric of social and cultural life, no matter how far back in history scholarship has penetrated, always in the same pattern that the spatial discovery of contemporary human patterns was revealing. Always and everywhere there is a social worship by sacrifices. Amid the variety of human beliefs and religious practices certain constants began to appear in scholarly study: the idea of the holy, applied to sacred times, places, and persons. And always there was a sorry side to the picture: magic, superstition, idolatry, pansexism, perversions of all types, and man's inhumanity to man under the cloak of his religions. Always and everywhere scholarship identified the Priest, the King, ruling on behalf of the local deities, and the Shaman, the person set aside for intimacy with the higher powers and the spokesman for them to the tribe.

Sacred Writings

When historic times are reached, the sacred oral traditions that had sustained human social life in the prehistoric ages are recorded in writing and the great literatures are formed that enshrine and preserve the heritage and at the same time enculturate the oncoming younger generations. Babylon, Persia, Greece, and Rome take shape as a succession of religious cultural entities in the past, of the same type that India, China, Islam, and Western culture represent in the more recent life of mankind on earth.

There is no question, then, regarding the universality of religion as a fact. The gathering of empirical data on this fact gradually took on the ordered and systematic approach of an academic discipline. Thus the new Science of Comparative Religion, quite different from the older treatises on Natural Theology, came to be added to the curricular offerings of Western universities and the seminal works of the field began to be published.[18]

The facts regarding religion in human cultural life, then, have come to be at hand as never before. The question is the interpretation of these facts. Interpretation is the function of philosophy. Philosophies closed to God throw a quite different light upon religious facts from that which shines from a metaphysics open to the personal and transcendent Supreme Being.[19]

The facts report universal worship by prayer and sacrifice, embedded, however, in polytheism, pantheism, and idolatry. Sacrifice in particular, while universal, is corrupted by magical concepts and practices. Yet the aspirations of this mysterious worship by sacrifices is clear. Human beings offer this worship to higher beings, in gratitude and supplication, and seek in this sacrificial worship a communion with this higher order of reality and power.[20] How is this religious fact to be explained? These facts on worship by prayer and sacrifice received a truly dramatic addition at the end of the nineteenth century and across the first half of the twentieth century, which has brought the conflict in interpretations to a head. The Bible, Biblical Catechetics, and the Biblical Foundations of Catechetics are directly concerned. We turn therefore to a brief summary of these new discoveries of ethnological science.

The Discovery of the Primitives and Their Religion

As the outreach of Western colonial administrators, missionaries, and university professors continued in modern times, a surprising new fact emerged. In isolated areas of the continental land masses, secluded from the main stream of human development, true primitives were discovered who lived as simple food gatherers, without some tools. They live a mode of life in contemporary times that seems prior to the Stone Ages identified by the science of Prehistory. In fact, using only tools of wood and bone, these primitives would leave nothing of their way of life in the archaeological record.

The further immensely important fact is their elevated and pure religion, their worship of one personal Supreme Being by the sacrifice of the first fruits of their daily labor of gathering food. This simple but pure and noble form of worship, furthermore, was found by the Western observers to be substantially identical in the widely separated habitats—from Arctic North America and Siberia to Australia, to the Andaman Islands, to interior Africa, and to the southern tip of South America. It is a global phenomenon, one that quite obviously presents a special hermeneutical challenge.[21]

The Atheistic Hermeneutics

This massive discovery of hitherto unknown factual material came at the precise historical epoch when Natural Theology was suffering the vicissitudes sketched earlier and was finding itself under increasing attack by the rise and spread of philosophical atheism in the academic life of Western universities. The philosophy of Progress understood as departure from any form or practice of religion was reinforced when Darwin's theory made this atheistic philosophy seem to be a science. Evolutionism conceived as a law governing all human phenomena became the light under which these facts of religion were interpreted by the atheistic hermeneutics. Accordingly, these religious facts were moved about like chessmen and gathered into categories that exhibited a development from early crude forms of magic and superstition, conceived as proper to human beings evolving slowly from the level of the brute animals, toward more refined religious forms, higher in culture and more philosophically acceptable. Monotheism is made to appear as a late development, arising out of the aspiration toward human unification linked with the empires that appear in historical times.

In this atheistic hermeneutics, of course, the facts of religion are regarded as important for those earlier times and stages of human cultural progress, but devoid of any objective truth or validity. They cannot exhibit a relationship, however deformed, to a transcendent intelligent Being, for in the Spinozan metaphysics that underlies atheistic thought in the modern West no such dimension of objective reality exists. The religious facts discovered by Comparative Religion, however universal, are nothing but a purely human phenomenon, related to man's underdeveloped condition and readily understood as a transitory phase in mankind's passage toward fully rational adulthood.

Science and the Open Philosophical Hermeneutics

The theistic hermeneutics, interpreting these facts in openness to the Person who is the Supreme Being of the universe, sees a directly opposed perspective. The later stages of human cultural development, reflected in the great peoples and empires of historical times (since approximately 4000 B.C.), represent not an improvement in religion but rather a decline from an earlier more pure and elevated condition in man's relationship to the Supreme Being,

without later accretions of polytheism, magic, and idolatry. The simple tribes living in isolation on the margins of the continents, rediscovered by Western man in the manner already noted, appear to
be contemporary witnesses pointing toward an earlier and more
primitive stage, and their religion correlates with the prehistoric age
uncovered by the science of archaeology. Always and everywhere,
the more simple ways of life, more primitive in culture, when well
and accurately known, are discovered to possess a more elevated
religious and moral life and to worship one personal Supreme Being, addressed as the Father Almighty, by prayer and sacrifice.

The question arises immediately whether contemporary primitives are remnants of man's historical beginnings. This is the question of Primitive Monotheism, so upsetting to the pattern of
development constructed by the atheistic hermeneutics.[22] For a
common pattern of prayer and sacrifice to the Supreme Being conceived as a pure Spirit, the Father Almighty, Creator of heaven and
earth, is difficult to explain merely as an invention of human reason.
If such a qualitatively superior religion stands at human origins and
if witness is borne to it in the nineteenth and twentieth centuries
by vestigial remnants of the primitive stage in places so widely separated as the Eskimos around the North Pole, the Tierra del Fuegians
near the South Pole, and remote tribes of Australia, and the margins
of Asia, certain isolated and primitive tribes of North American Indians, and the aboriginals of Australia and Africa, then the atheistic
construct of an evolutionary development of religion out of magic
and other lower forms of earlier superstition collapses, and an open-
mindedness toward the possibility of a Primitive Revelation from
the Supreme Being to the first humans, prior to the slow Stone
Age dispersion of food-gathering tribes over the planet, becomes
an element of authentic intellectual life, open to the facts as they
are and open to the interpretation that they appear to bear within
themselves, apart from philosophical constructs imposed upon
them.

The Embarrassment of the Closed Hermeneutic

Thus a mighty question is raised by the empirical sciences themselves in this recent discovery of the primitive religion, which

younger scholars will need to pursue as the twenty-first century begins. Are the observations made by missionaries who have been living with the primitives in these recent times, the reports of explorers and merchants, and many of the findings of anthropological field research teams sent out by universities in recent decades to be discounted as a reading of Judaeo-Christian concepts into the data? Or is the atheistic hermeneutics an imposition of Western philosophy, parochial in space and time, upon the worldwide religious situation of mankind?

Younger scholars must take up the challenge, sift the factual material that has been gathered, and discern accurately what is empirical and what is Western prejudice, whether philosophical or theological.[23]

In any case, the witness of the primitive tribes themselves is clear. Without exception they attribute their tribal religion not to some human thinking, preserved in their oral traditions, but to an immensely important communication from the Supreme Reality, *in illo tempore,* at that time long ago when the tribe originated with its first ancestor. As to the atheistic interpretation of this mass of factual information on the planetary religious situation of mankind, the primitives of the earth raise up their voices, as Prof. Wilhelm Koppers writes, crying in unanimous protest: "You are on a wrong track. Your mental experiments (or rather hypotheses) will not work. The belief in a Father God, handed down by our forebears from time immemorial, cannot possibly be regarded as a final stage in human development. He must rather be the starting-point, as is shown in our creation-myths: in the beginning there was God the Creator. Is this not also the teaching of your Bible?"[24]

Revelation, Faith, and Catechetical Teaching: Mankind's Greatest Need

With this mention of the Bible, the study of religion turns to its proper object and arrives at the domain of Fundamental Catechetics. For Catechetics is the study of Divine Revelation from the viewpoint of its nature and mode: what it is, where it is found, and how it is handed on by teaching. Divine Revelation is, first, God's call to all human beings to turn away from sin and toward him in personal conversion. Then, second, it is the formative and practical teaching of Divine Revelation that helps them "deepen their conversion."[25] The purpose, content, method, and teaching personnel of catechesis will be studied in detail later in this manual. But these elements should be kept in mind throughout in order to recognize their roots in the Bible.

It is important, furthermore, to note the relationship between catechetical teaching and the immense need of mankind to hear and have the revealed Word of God, a Word that is filled with the presence and power of God to renew human nature and to reorient human life to its true and eternal purpose.

The religious situation and condition of mankind that has been sketched manifests the inability of unaided human reason to maintain that elevated concept of God with which the historic human journey apparently began. A sound and true, practically effective relationship to God in personal and social life has not in fact been maintained. The later tribes and peoples and nations exhibit the widest variety of religious opinions and practices, but the condition in historic times, when mankind has increased and multiplied, when cultural progress has been made and civic life achieved, is everywhere one and the same. Faith in God the Father Almighty, Creator of heaven and earth, has been lost. Polytheism flourishes everywhere. This visible cosmos is thought to have existed from eternity. Matter is considered to stand independent of the gods, who at most are thought perhaps to have shaped the preexisting and autonomous stuff this way or that. In practice, man is his own god, shaping his life as he decides on the basis of his own inclinations. He is in practice his own law, for he no longer is certain about any other law coming to him from on high.

The consequences are everywhere visible since about 4000 B.C. in the records of historic time: polytheism and idolatry, secularization, pan-sexism, moral corruption, and the despair of the hereafter that turns man in upon himself and his earthly pursuits. One need only think of the mute evidence of Pompeii, excavated for the twentieth century to see. Pornography is not a modern invention.

All tribes and peoples and nations and especially the cities, Babylon, Ur of the Chaldees, Athens, and pagan Rome, existed throughout historical times in the alienation from God and the moral darkness that Saint Paul describes. He writes in his Epistle to the Romans:

> The wrath of God is revealed from heaven against all ungodliness and wickedness of men who by their wickedness suppress the truth. For what can be known about God is plain to them, because God has shown it to them. Ever since the creation of the world his invisible nature, namely, his eternal power and deity, has been clearly perceived in the things that have been made. So they are without excuse; for although they knew God, they did not honour him as God or give thanks to him, but they became futile in their thinking and their senseless minds were darkened. Claiming to be wise, they became fools, and exchanged the glory of the immortal God for images resembling mortal man or birds or animals or reptiles.
>
> Therefore God gave them up in the lusts of their hearts to impurity, to the dishonouring of their bodies among themselves, because they exchanged the truth about God for a lie and worshipped and served the creature rather than the Creator, who is blessed forever! Amen.
>
> For this reason God gave them up to dishonourable passions. Their women exchanged natural relations for unnatural, and the men likewise gave up natural relations with women and were consumed with passion for one another, men committing shameless acts with men and receiving in their own persons the due penalty for their error.
>
> And since they did not see fit to acknowledge God, God gave them up to a base mind and to improper conduct. They were filled with all manner of wickedness, evil, covetousness, malice. Full of envy, murder, strife, deceit, malignity, they are gossips, slanderers, haters of God, insolent, haughty, boastful, inventors of evil, disobedient to parents, foolish, faithless, heartless, ruthless. Though they know God's decree that those who do such things deserve to die, they not only do them but approve those who practice them. (Rom 1:18–32)

Certainly this is a powerful description and indictment of the fallen condition of human nature, one that is now wonderfully corroborated by the Science of Comparative Religion. Mankind has declined in religion and morals throughout the long ages of prehistory, with these results visible in the civilized societies and empires of the present historic age.

Would the Supreme Being of the universe bend in mercy and love to this blinded and corrupted humanity? Did he as a matter of fact do so? If so, how? Did he do so as the Divine Teacher, teaching mankind the way of righteousness and salvation, the Way of Life, giving his own truth and perhaps his own life? What arrangements did he make for the secure continuation of his teaching?

Fundamental Catechetics is the systematic study of such questions and their answers. It is the study of the content and the mode of the intervention of God in human history, to teach mankind his own truth as an order of knowledge distinct from merely human science and philosophy; this higher knowledge, furthermore, is linked with divine grace and power to make the knowledge effective in the practice of human living.

The divine plan began with the call of Abraham to come out of Ur of the Chaldees, out of the corrupted Gentile condition, to found a new people for the purpose that the Hebrew Revelation records. This brings us to the Holy Bible, Holy because it has God as its primary author and Holy because it is the depository of God's Revelation to mankind.

Chapter 2
The Bible and Biblical Catechetics

The study of biblical Catechetics is perhaps best begun by taking the Holy Bible in hand. What kind of book is this? Where did it come from? Who is the author? To whom does it rightfully belong?

The Holy Bible belongs in a special way to the Jewish people. In a still more special way it belongs to the Catholic Church and the people of the New Testament. In a sense it belongs now to all the people of the earth, for it has become the world's most widely distributed book. Finally, in a most proper sense it belongs to the catechist who teaches the Catholic faith. Let us explore the authorship, for this is the factor that will throw light on these various questions and statements about the Holy Bible. In this exploration biblical Catechetics had one of its most important challenges and tasks in the late twentieth century, that of a catechetical study and use of the Bible that recovers and renews faith in its divine authorship.

The Human Authors of the Bible

To begin: when did the human authors of the Bible live and write? One must recall the recent discovery of prehistory, which was noted above as part of the background. The Bible belongs to the Age of Civilizations, which began at about 4000 B.C. with the invention of writing, the development of mankind's first cities out of the prehistoric agricultural villages, and the keeping of historical annals and records by the temple priesthoods at the central government of each city.[1] So it was in Egypt and in Mesopotamia. Prior to this key date in the life of mankind there were only the oral traditions handed down in the hunting tribes and the agricultural villages. With the invention of writing these oral traditions were committed to writing: thus the literature of the historic peoples after 4000 B.C. came into existence. The Babylonians had entire libraries, which have been excavated and deciphered. Later in this ongoing Age of the Civilizations the Greek people arose and developed their literature, which centered upon the epic poetry of Homer, saturated with the religion of the earlier oral tradition. So, too, the Roman literature, centering in a similar way upon the epic of Vergil. These literatures sustained their people, for they were the vehicle that handed on the social heritage by teaching it to the young generation. So likewise in India and China. Thus there are several bodies of sacred literature on the human scene.

This provides the general context of the Holy Bible. It is the literature of a particular people. Hence it includes the various literary genres that characterize human literatures generally: narrative history, poetry, writings that contain the wisdom and teachings of the people, and the like. It is religious in character, indeed eminently so among all the sacred books and literatures of these six thousand recent years. One needs but glance at the Book of Psalms, now the prayerbook of all mankind. Who then were its authors and when did they live? The authors were the Hebrew Prophets, beginning with Moses. They lived over a long period of time, well over 1,000 years, in the second half of that 4,000-year period in the Age of the Civilizations that led up to the coming of Christ.

John Henry Newman gives eloquent expression to the first impression made by the Holy Bible when taken initially in hand:

> I observe that Scripture is not one book; it is a great number of writings, of various persons, living at different times, put together into one, and assuming its existing form as if casually and by accident. It is as if you were to seize the papers or correspondence of leading men in any school of philosophy or science, which were never designed for publication, and bring them out in one volume. . . . The doctrines, the first principles, the rules, the objects of the school, would be taken for granted, alluded to, implied, not directly asked. You would have some trouble to get at them. . . . . Such, I conceive, with limitations presently to be noticed, is the structure of the Bible. . . . . [These are] the writings of men who had already been introduced into a knowledge of the unseen world and the society of Angels, and who reported what they had seen and heard.[2]

This from Newman introduces the second aspect of the Bible, the one that is not self-evident when it is first taken in hand and the one by which it is called the Holy Bible. The next step in biblical Catechetics, therefore, is to explore this aspect, for it will unlock the unity that binds together this multiplicity of writings and thus provides the foundation for a systematic teaching based upon the Bible. Before taking up this divine authorship of the Bible, known only by divine faith, one must summarize its prerequisite on the part of Bible readers, biblical scholars, and catechists today.

The Preambles of Faith

Faith in the Bible as the very Word of God because it has God as its Author, and is therefore "the Holy Bible," is possible only to rational human beings. Plants and the brute animals obviously cannot make acts of divine faith. These acts on the part of human persons, however, presuppose the right use of human reason. Among educated persons, furthermore, these acts presuppose a correctly educated power of human reason. If the educational process fails to accomplish this or, which is worse, systematically inculcates a philosophically unsound use of human reason, then the preambles of faith will be weakened or destroyed and catechists will face the crisis of faith, or "The Reality of the Problem," as the *GCD* terms it in the title of its part 1.

The preambles of faith, therefore, are of primary importance for biblical Catechetics. This is the catechetical reason for the contemporary renewal of Christian Philosophy in the Catholic Church: it provides educated persons with the human and Christian heritage in this right use of human reason.[3]

These preambles of faith are basically twofold, historical and philosophical. When the science of history is rightly cultivated, the Bible is recognized as a set of reports, according to the literary genres of its various writings, on what actually took place in the past. Saint Augustine speaks for all the Fathers of the Church in his second "Sermon" when he addressed his people in these words: "Before everything else, brethren, I both admonish and command that when you hear Scripture expounded as narrating what actually took place, you have faith in what was read as having taken place as you heard; otherwise, if you take away that foundation of what actually took place, you will be like persons trying to build as it were in the air."[4] The reading of Scripture on the occasion of this homily had been the account of Abraham and his son Isaac. Augustine then discusses the fact that God is the Almighty who has the power to create things from nothing and hence could easily give Abraham and Sarah this son in a way beyond the ordinary course of nature because of her advanced age.

This introduces the concept of philosophical preamble for faith. It is simply the cultivation in the process of education of the seventh among the seven Liberal Arts, namely, the Christian philosophy and its metaphysics, which Augustine and the other Fathers founded and which was taught in Catholic schools for a thousand years through the times of Saints Bonaventure and Thomas Aquinas. In this Christian philosophy the natural science of Metaphysics ascends to "the sublime truth," as Saint Thomas terms it, of the transcendent Supreme Being, the personal, intelligent, and almighty Creator.[5] This natural knowledge of God recognizes that God is a pure Spirit who exists beyond time in the eternal *Now* and beyond space in the sharp edge and point of eternity. Thus God is omnipresent, present to each and all of his creatures throughout all time and space, closer to them, as Augustine repeats many times, than they are to themselves.

This is the ascent of natural reason to the Supreme Being that was discussed earlier under the heading of "Natural Theology." Saint Augustine again provides the characteristic way of the Fathers of the Church in their approach to the Bible, an approach that already stands upon this preamble of natural reason cultivated to think correctly about the "eternal power and deity" of God (Rom. 1:20). Speaking to his people in his church at Hippo, Augustine discusses the ways by which this intelligent and transcendent Person speaks to his rational creatures:

> There are many ways by which God speaks to us. Sometimes he uses an instrument, as in the case of the books of the divine Scriptures. Or he may speak through some natural phenomenon of this world, as in his speaking to the Magi by means of the star (Matt. 2:2). For what is it to speak, if not to signify one's will? God sometimes speaks through the casting of lots, as in the case of the ordination of Matthias

to replace Judas (Acts 1:26). He speaks, furthermore, by means of the human soul when he speaks through his Prophets. God speaks through his Angels, as we know with regard to the various Patriarchs, Prophets and the Apostles. He is heard to speak by means of a created vocal sound, as for instance the voice of the Heavenly Father heard on Mount Tabor. Likewise he speaks in dreams, as one sees in Gen. 31:24 or Gen. 41:1–32, in the case of Pharaoh. Sometimes God elevates the human spirit in what the Greeks call ecstasy, as we note in Peter's vision of the net, let down from heaven . . . when Peter understood from it what God wished him to do. . . . For God is Truth Itself, and he speaks thus in many ways, some internal to the human persons, and some external.[6]

This eloquent passage is cited here for two reasons. First, it exhibits the concept of God that the Fathers of the Church had in mind, one that is open to the possibility of a message from God to his human creatures. And second, it leads directly to the recognition of the divine authorship of the Bible.

The Prophetic Light

The next step in approaching the relationship of this collection of human writings that we hold in hand and call the Holy Bible to the Supreme Being of the universe is to note that the human authors were God's Prophets in the Old Testament and his Apostles in the New Testament, men who shared in the prophetic office by their relationship to Jesus the Prophet. A human author of a writing can be the instrument of God in his writing of it by means of the prophetic light. In such a case, God himself becomes the primary author of that Scripture and his prophet is the secondary or instrumental author. This prophetic light is therefore a fundamental of biblical Catechetics. A failure to appreciate properly the nature of this prophetic light leads directly to a misconception of the Bible and its exegesis and to disarray in catechetical teaching. What, exactly, is this prophetic light? How does it relate to other forms of light? How does it relate to the Bible? To the inspiration of the Scriptures? To the Catholic faith? To the official catechism that catechists use when teaching the content of this Catholic faith? In all such questions Saint Thomas Aquinas offers basic guidance in his lapidary discussion of the four chief kinds of light.[7]

There are four kinds of light, Saint Thomas teaches. First, there is this sensory light that organic senses perceive and both man and the higher animals know by similar sense organs. The more recent discoveries in the physical sciences have given mankind an immensely improved understanding of the nature and properties of this corporeal light, relating it to the very stuff of this visible cosmos. These discoveries confirm the material and corporeal nature of this light in all its forms, from sunlight to firelight and electric light on earth.

Second, there is the intelligible light. It is quantitatively distinct from and immeasurably higher than the light of the senses. This is the light of reason, the power of the intelligence to shine upon the sensory objects with insight and understanding. It "sees with understanding," as the Bible says. This is the point where authentic philosophy takes its origin—authentic, one must say, because there is a negative kind of philosophy that denies this power of understanding, attempting to reduce it to nothing but a complex form of sense knowledge. But the fact that the human intelligence is a power of knowing distinct from the senses and related to insights and understandings "seen" in this intelligible light has been a part of the common philosophical patrimony since Socrates, Plato, and Aristotle. It is only recently, since Locke and Hume, that the negation has arisen as an aspect of the death of Natural Theology noted earlier.

Third, there is the prophetic light, a true illumination of the human mind but one that is qualitatively distinct from the intelligible light and therefore from all human philosophy even when cultivated at its best. The prophetic light stands as far above the light of human reason as its light is superior to that of the senses. It is crucially important for Catechetics to recognize that the illumination of the mind by the prophetic light exists in the order of knowledge and not in that of organismic experiencing.

"Prophetic knowledge," Saint Thomas Aquinas teaches, "is brought about by a divine light which makes possible the knowledge of all realities, whether they be human or divine, spiritual or corporeal. And so prophetic revelation extends to all such realities."[8] This prophetic light has a power all its own; it illuminates from God in a mode far superior to natural human reason and its philosophizing and can extend even to future contingencies known to God alone. This higher illumination can have repercussions upon the bodily organism of the person, called a *prophet*, who receives it.[9] But in itself and primarily it belongs to the order of knowledge, for it is a special participation in God's own knowledge. Saint Thomas Aquinas does not relate this prophetic light to organismic experiencing but rather to the corporeal reality of human discourse. "Prophecy," he teaches, "consists secondarily in utterance or speech, insofar as the prophets know what God has taught them, and they then proclaim their knowledge for the welfare of others."[10]

Clearly catechists are directly involved: the teaching that they do is related somehow to this prophetic light and to the teaching that the Prophets have given to their fellowmen. It is the task of Catechetics as an ecclesiastical science to analyze this entire matter. Biblical Catechetics naturally stands at the origin of this kind of study. For the prophets, persons called by God from among men to receive the prophetic light have a social role and function. They are teachers who teach out of this higher order of knowledge. This raises up and forms a special People of God. They formulate into the words of the ordinary human discourse in their time and place what they have come to know by the prophetic light. This is the origin of what Saint Peter calls "the prophetic word" (2 Pet. 1:19, and see both 1 and 2 Peter, *passim*). The Prophets hand this word on to their fellowmen by proclamation and explain it by teaching.

This is the reason for the solemn teaching of the Supreme Magisterium of the Catholic Church at Vatican I in a passage that establishes the charter and foundation of the field of Catechetics: "The constant consensus of the Catholic Church has also held and still holds that there is a twofold order of knowledge, distinct not only in origins but also in object. These orders are distinct in origin, because in one order we know by natural reason, in the other by divine faith. They are distinct in object, because in addition to what natural reason can attain, there are proposed for one's belief mysteries hidden in God, which cannot be known unless divinely revealed."[11]

It is impossible to overemphasize the importance of this teaching of Catechetics, because it gives the foundation for the specific difference of Catholic religious education. It removes both the so-called experience approach and the religiosity of what is called philosophical faith. Catechetics relates to this higher order of knowledge, which it gives to catechumens by its teaching. Thus revealed religion comes into view as distinct from all forms of merely natural religion.[12] It is religion, religious teaching, religious formation, and practice that come from "prophets," the authentic and true Prophets who are called by God to receive the prophetic light and then to give it to others in the words of human discourse. The Prophets are spokesmen for God. What they hand on to their fellowmen is the very Word of God. By receiving it as it truly is, the Word of God and not mere human thought and philosophy elaborated out of the intelligible light, their fellowmen become the People of God living a qualitatively distinct and higher way of life. Saint Paul makes this point explicitly in the case of his beloved Thessalonians. "We also thank God constantly for this," he writes to them, "that when you received the word of God which you heard from us, you accepted it not as the word of men but as it really is, the Word of God, which is at work in you believers" (1 Thess. 2:13).

Fourth among the kinds of light identified by Saint Thomas is the divine light. Is the prophetic light the same as the divine light? Definitely not: the vision of God and of all other things in the divine light is reserved for the blessed in heaven. Hence their happiness is called the beatific vision. The prophetic light is related to the divine light, of course, as indeed in their own proper ways the intelligible and the sensory lights are so related. The prophetic light is a special participation in the divine light but not identical with it. "The principle of all that relates to supernatural knowledge," Saint Thomas teaches, "and of all that is manifested by prophesy, is God himself, who in his essence cannot be known by the prophets."[13]

The nature of Catechetics in general and the special role of biblical Catechetics are becoming visible in these considerations. The purpose of their study is to explore and to clarify the linkages of this prophetic light with the Bible, Catechetics, and the official catechisms of the church. Clearly an openness to the existence of this higher light and the possibility that God might choose spokesmen for himself to receive it and to hand it on to others is at the very heart of the matter. This is the meaning of the preambles of faith. On the one hand, if a philosophy were to exclude this openness and this possibility, it would minister to a special kind of darkness and generate a different kind of religious education on the human scene. On the other hand, the philosophy of metaphysical openness to the transcendent personal Creator of heaven and earth establishes the possibility of the divine authorship of the Bible as the work of God's Prophets whom he called to be his instruments.[14]

The Divine Authorship of the Bible

The Jewish people, as we shall see later in the topical study of the Old Testament, always believed firmly by divine faith that they were privileged to have a revealed religion by virtue of the teaching received from their Prophets. This people, furthermore, is known in history as "the People of the Book," for it was an integral part of their faith that their Prophets committed their teaching, given to them by God through the prophetic light, to their writings. These writings were carefully preserved by the disciples of the Prophets and the priestly authority. It is clear that this literature would be like other literatures of other peoples and at the same time unlike them because of this divine factor. Jesus Christ accepted this teaching of his Jewish people about the authority of "the Chair of Moses" and its literature. Thus this same concept of revealed religion and the writings by which it is handed on from generation to generation passed forward to Jesus' Church, which has given the Holy Bible to all mankind.[15]

The fact of the divine authorship, therefore, is absolutely basic for an understanding of the nature of the Bible. It is this that makes it "the *Holy* Bible." Hence biblical Catechetics encounters here one of its most important foundations. It is in order, therefore, to review in summary the constant teaching of the Catholic Church since Jesus and his Apostles on the divine authorship of the Holy Bible.

The Council of Trent gathers up and canonizes this traditional teaching at the outset of its sessions when it states as a dogma of the Catholic faith that "the One God is the author of all the books of the Bible, both of the Old Testament and the New Testament."[16]

The First Vatican Council confirms this teaching and explicitates the consequent approach in exegesis and hermeneutics. Chapter 2 of the Constitution *Dei Filius* on Divine Revelation states in solemn definition of the Catholic faith that:

According to the faith of the universal Church, as declared by the holy Council of Trent, this supernatural revelation is contained "in written books." . . . These books of the Old and the New Testament, in their integrity and with all their parts, as they are enumerated in the decree of the same Council and in the ancient Latin editions of the Vulgate, must be accepted as sacred and canonical. The Church regards these books as sacred and canonical, not because they were composed by human industry alone and later approved by her authority; nor because they contain revelation without error; but because, written under the inspiration of the Holy Spirit, they have God as their author; and because they have been entrusted as such to the Church.[17]

Since the Holy Bible is composed of written books, written indeed long ago and in now-unfamiliar languages, the hermeneutical questions of their correct reading and exegetical interpretation will come up necessarily and has done so in the case of every heresy, from Arianism in the early Church through the Eucharistic heresies from Berengarius to Luther and Calvin and on to the contemporary Modernist Heresy. Hence Vatican I, again in solemn form, expresses the foundational position for biblical Catechetics.

The Council continues in the same place: Since some men have explained in a distorted manner the salutary norms for interpreting divine Scripture that the holy Council of Trent decreed in order to curb impudent dispositions, we reaffirm the same decree, and we declare this to be its intent: in matters of faith and morals that pertain to the substance of Christian doctrine, that sense of Sacred Scripture must be held as true which Holy Mother Church has held and still holds. She has the right to judge concerning the true sense and interpretation of the Sacred Scriptures. No one, therefore, is permitted to interpret Sacred Scripture contrary to this sense, or contrary to the unanimous sense of the Fathers.[18]

It is not surprising, therefore, that Leo XIII in *Providentissimus Deus* (November 18, 1893), the Encyclical which was occasioned by the exegetical approach of the Modernist Heresy, writes as follows on the divine authorship:

The God of all providence, who in the adorable designs of his love at first elevated the human race to the participation of the divine nature, and afterwards delivered it from universal guilt and ruin, restoring it to its primitive dignity, has, in consequence, bestowed on man a splendid gift and safeguard: making known to him, by supernatural means, the hidden mysteries of his divinity, his wisdom and his mercy.... This supernatural revelation, according to the belief of the universal Church, is contained both in the unwritten tradition and in written books, which are, therefore, called sacred and canonical because, "being written under the inspiration of the Holy Spirit, they have God for their author, and as such have been delivered to the Church" (citing Trent as above). This belief has been perpetually held and professed by the Church in regard to the Books of both Testaments; and there are well-known documents of the gravest kind, coming down to us from the earliest times, which proclaim that God, who spoke first by the Prophets, then by his own mouth, and lastly by the Apostles, composed also the canonical Scriptures, and that these are his own oracles and words: a Letter written by our Heavenly Father and transmitted by the sacred writers to the human race in its pilgrimage so far from its heavenly country.[19]

Leo XIII continues with Jesus' own use of the Scriptures in his teaching, in a passage of special significance for biblical Catechetics:

Among the reasons for which the Holy Scripture is so worthy of commendation, in addition to its own excellence and to the homage which we owe to God's Word, the chief of all is the innumerable benefits of which it is the source. According to the infallible testimony of the Holy Spirit himself, "All Scripture inspired of God is profitable to teach, to reprove, to correct, to instruct in justice: that the man of God may be perfect, furnished to every good work" (2 Tim. 3:16–17). That such was the purpose of God in giving the Scriptures to men is shown by the example of Christ our Lord and of his Apostles. For he himself . . . was accustomed in the exercise of his divine mission to appeal to the Scriptures. He uses them at times to prove that he is sent by God, and is God himself. From them he cites instructions for his disciples and confirmation of his doctrine. He vindicates them from the calumnies of objectors. He quotes them against Sadducees and Pharisees and retorts from them upon Satan himself when he dares to tempt him. At the close of his life his utterances are from the Holy Scripture, and it is the Scripture that he expounds to his disciples after his resurrection, until he ascends to the glory of his Father.[20]

The divine authorship of the Bible, then, stands at the center of the faith of the ancient Hebrews in the teaching of their Prophets as the very Word of God. It is confirmed by the doctrine and practice of Jesus when he taught and formed his Apostles. This understanding of the nature of the Holy Bible is the first principle of all interpretation of Sacred Scriptures by the Catholic Church, to which the Bible has been entrusted as a basic component of its deposit of faith.

The Catholic Hermeneutics: The Unity of the Bible

This attitude toward the Holy Bible that Jesus taught to his Apostles was handed forward to the Fathers of the Early Church and consolidated by them as the foundation for all the forms of the ministry of the Word of God, including academic teaching on the level of higher education that Saint Augustine called "doctrina christiana."[21]

The Fathers of the Church, furthermore, established the basic hermeneutic or interpretation of the Bible by giving primacy to its divine authorship and only a secondary and instrumental role to its various human authors. This provided them with the key to understanding the unity of the Bible from Genesis to the Book of Revelation. This unity is wonderful to behold when the eye of faith is rightly cultivated to see it in such a variety of literary forms used by human authors over so great a span of time—from the archaic modes of expression and teaching adopted and used by Moses in the Book of Genesis through upward of two millennia to the writing of the New Testament by Jesus' Apostles and their helpers.

It is this unity that makes the Bible different from the literatures of other peoples, including those humanly somewhat similar ones of the ancient Near East. In what does this unity consist? The answer to this question will be the concern of this work throughout its topical and analytical study of the Holy Bible. For the present, to specify the chief items for which this study will be searching, the unique concept of God that pervades the Holy Bible from beginning to end should be kept in the first place. For the Bible is the record of God's self-revelation to his Chosen People, chosen by him to be the bearer of divine revelation by their mode of life, which he gave to them as their Torah, or Law. This choice of them, furthermore, was not to be for their separate and private benefit, so to speak; they were to give it to all the other peoples of planet Earth and thus to become, as the Prophet Isaiah told them, "a Light to the Gentiles" (Is. 42:6).[22]

Closely linked with God's self-revelation is his holiness and hence his hatred of sin. The call of Abraham to come out from among the sinful Gentiles to found a new people holy in the sight of God follows directly from God's self-revelation and leads forward to the great unifying theme in the Bible of divine redemption. In all of this more is involved than a teaching of the correct concept of God. In his mercy and love God reveals himself as coming close to his people in a way gradually to be disclosed, as his Old Testament name, Emmanuel, meaning "God-with-us," indicates.

The Fathers of the Church concentrated on this divine authorship of the Bible from which its unity results. The human writings are indeed human, but investigation of the human side, the details of language, place, and time, was not uppermost in their interest. They were content to understand the meaning that the human authors had in mind when they wrote, for this meaning is precisely the truth that God conveyed to them by the prophetic light. One should not conclude, therefore, that the Fathers of the Church were indifferent to accurate knowledge of the human side of these writings. The contrary is true. Saint Augustine, for example, by common admission the greatest of the Fathers of the Church, with voluminous commentaries and sermons on the Scriptures, did not know the Semitic languages, and his knowledge of Greek was limited. But he was concerned to have the best available translation of the sacred text, as one sees in his constant contact with Saint Jerome. Saint Jerome was the Father of the Church who moved from Rome to Bethlehem in order to master the Hebrew language and who accomplished the translation of the Bible into Latin, called the *Vulgate,* which is official in the Catholic Church to this day. It has been updated constantly in the light of the ongoing accumulation of new knowledge about the biblical languages and their use at the various times and places of the human authors, as the recent new editions of the recent popes bear witness.[23]

In a word, the Fathers of the Church did not have access to the weight of historical and linguistic scholarship regarding the human

authors and their literary genres that has become available especially in the recent times of progress in the historical, archaeological,
and linguistic sciences. But they did not need this human knowledge
in order to recognize the unity of the Bible as a whole that results
from its divine authorship. This is an abiding principle of the Catholic hermeneutics, which has come to have a particular significance
for Catechetics for reasons that will be discussed later.

The academic teaching developed this Catholic hermeneutics
across the thousand years, in round numbers, that saw the monastery and cathedral schools of the Christian times after the Fathers
of the Church develop into the universities of Western civilization.
Perhaps no one has expressed this unity of the Bible better than
Saint Bonaventure, professor at the University of Paris in the thir-
teenth century. Addressing the professors and student body, he
called their attention to the unity of all knowledge in the light of
the Sacred Scriptures, a light that comes from Jesus, who is Wisdom
Incarnate and the center of the unity of the Bible because he is
Emmanuel, God-with-us, the redeemer of mankind from sin.[24] Each
branch of human knowledge, from the making of artifacts to metaphysics itself, results from a particular light of understanding. Then
there is a higher light "not acquired by human research, for it comes
down from the 'Father of Light,' and which is one . . . by its literal
meaning . . . , which illumines the mind for the understanding of
saving truth."[25]

This unity of the Bible, the consequences of its divine authorship, and visible in the concept of God reflected variously in every
book of the Bible, is a principle of hermeneutics or interpretation
that depends on the foundation of the Natural Theology that expresses metaphysical openness to the transcendent and personal
Supreme Being, the Almighty Creator who is able to speak his Word
to his human creatures. Hence the sketch of Natural Theology in
chapter 1 becomes crucially important, for it is the human prerequisite for recognizing the divine authorship and hence the unifying
redemptive purpose of the Bible as a whole. It is here that the
loss of Christian philosophy and its metaphysics in modern times,
resulting in that "Death of Natural Theology" noted earlier, affects
the interpretation and exegesis of the Bible. For if there is no such
intelligent and transcendent Supreme Being, "who declares to man
what is his thought" as the Prophet Amos says (Amos 4:13), what

will happen to the Bible? Will it not become immediately a mere set of human writings with only a problematical unity in the natural life of a particular people of antiquity? Biblical Catechetics would be challenged obviously at its very heart and threatened with a substantial change in its nature and purpose. It would become merely another form of natural religious education. Some brief attention must therefore be given to the loss of the heritage of Metaphysics and its role as a preamble of faith for recognizing the true nature of the Holy Bible.

The Atheistic Hermeneutics of the Bible

The General Catechetical Directory calls the attention of biblical Catechetics to this strange recent development in Western intellectual life that is rightly called the Death of Natural Theology. The rise and spread of philosophical atheism in the colleges and universities of the West is a phenomenon that catechists cannot overlook, for it generates what the title of part 1 of the *Directory* calls "The Reality of the Problem." Why is this? Because it generates a pattern of thinking that obscures the transcendent reality of the personal Supreme Being. This pattern of thinking causes people:

> to feel that God is less present, and less needed. . . . Hence a religious crisis can easily arise. . . . In times past, faulty opinions and errors about faith and the Christian way of life generally reached a comparatively small number of people, and were to a greater extent than is so today confined within groups of intellectuals. Now, however, human progress and the instruments of social communication are having this effect: faulty opinions are being spread abroad with greater speed and are exerting an ever-wider influence among the faithful, young adults especially, who suffer grave crises and are not infrequently driven to adopt ways of acting and thinking that are hostile to religion. This situation calls for pastoral remedies that are truly adapted to the circumstances.[26]

The *Directory* goes on to specify that circumstance that bears directly upon biblical hermeneutics: "Many baptized persons have withdrawn so far from their religion that they profess a form of indifferentism or something close to atheism. Many of our contemporaries recognize in no way this intimate and vital link with God, or else they explicitly reject it. Thus atheism must be accounted among the most serious problems of this age, and must be subjected to closer examination."[27]

This is not the place for this closer examination, which belongs properly to the second volume of this manual in its chapter on the philosophical and theological foundations of Catechetics. Here one need but draw attention to the salient features of this recent phenomenon as it impacts upon the Holy Bible as such.

This impact can be summarized briefly as the removal of the idea of the "Holy" from the Bible, with its resulting reduction to nothing but a collection of merely human writings coming from a distant past and an archaic stage of culture. When this reduction takes place, the divine authorship is no longer recognized and the human authors spread across the two millennia of the literature receive all the attention.

The origin of this novel approach to the Sacred Scriptures dates from Descartes and Spinoza, who introduced a new kind of philosophy into Western higher education, replacing that metaphysics of openness to the personal Supreme Being which had been cultivated in the Schools of Christendom for a thousand years after the Fathers of the Church.[28] It is Spinoza who formulated explicitly this new metaphysics or view of the nature of ultimate reality when he identified "God" with "Nature," namely, with this visible cosmos. There is no tremendous Supreme Person, the Creator of the cosmos, able to communicate divine revelation, his own Word, to his rational creatures.

This substitution of a new inner-cosmic metaphysics immediately begets the atheistic hermeneutics. For upon this preamble of unbelief the Bible must be reinterpreted. Wherever it speaks of an intervention from a higher order of reality above and beyond this visible cosmos, it must undergo the explanation given by the new atheistic worldview: such passages are nothing but reflections of the mythological thinking of those intellectually underdeveloped times prior to the advent of this new Modern Philosophy as conceived and propagated by Descartes and Spinoza.

Spinoza, a Jew whom his synagogue had excommunicated when he was twenty-four, did not venture to apply his hermeneutics to the New Testament. He did so, however, to the Old Testament. In due time, as this intellectual fall from the sound heritage of philosophical openness to God as an intelligent and transcendent Supreme Person, distinct from the cosmos that is his creature, reached its maturity in Kant, Comte, and Hegel, the application to the New Testament was made by Christians imbued with this new metaphysical thinking. The net result, accomplished by Liberal Protestantism and Catholic Modernism, was the reduction of Jesus Christ to nothing but "an ordinary and mere man," to use the words of Saint Pius X in *Pascendi,* his Encyclical on Modernism.

While this perverse and perverted metaphysical view of ultimate reality was being substituted in the area of the seventh Liberal Art, the domain of philosophy, a parallel development was taking place in the natural sciences and disciplines that form the first six of these same Liberal Arts, the core of Western education since the Greeks. This is the famous Copernican Revolution, usually understood as the unsettling transition from the geocentric cosmology due to the invention of the telescope. It is wider than that one discovery, however, for it included a set of far-reaching developments, already noted, in the sciences of geology, archaeology, history, and linguistics that led to a corresponding revolution in mankind's natural knowledge of human origins and development on this planet.

It is at this point that biblical Catechetics becomes directly and deeply involved. For these developments in the historical sciences are immensely beneficial to biblical studies when they are used properly. The reason is the fact that they assist greatly in determining the intention of the human authors of the Bible in its various literary genres. This ministers to accurate knowledge of the divine authorship because that intention, which the human authors were teaching and expressing by virtue of the prophetic light, is the very Word of God to mankind.[29]

At the same time, these developments in the various historical and natural sciences, in themselves good and the result of the use of human reason, which is the divine image impressed on the brow of man by his Creator, are subject to abuse. This abuse takes place when these sciences are put to work in exegesis without careful exclusion of any taint from the atheistic hermeneutics. Carelessness here or even emulation begets an ambiguity that begins to infect biblical studies and thence theology itself. This infection is visible from the time of Schleiermacher, the disciple of Kant, in his many disciples across the nineteenth century to the present.

The Purely Rational Exegesis

Thus was born that approach to the Bible known as the "purely rational exegesis." It takes texts in isolation from that meaning of the Bible as a whole, coming from the divine authorship. It seeks to understand isolated texts, segments, and even entire books of the Bible simply by themselves in the light of the new tools that give the more detailed knowledge of the life, the language, and the culture of the human authors. Thus the new knowledge is abused instead of used, for it no longer ministers to knowing more accurately how the text or literary genre relates to the meaning of the Bible in its divine authorship.

Clearly this opens up a large question that the study of biblical Catechetics must keep in mind. For it is at this point that the recent academic reading and study of the Bible becomes different from what we may call the catechetical approach to reading and studying of the Bible. In this catechetical approach, the heritage from the Fathers of the Early Church is maintained in place: the divine authorship and its unifying light receive the primacy of interest and study. At the same time, the developments in the historical sciences are used properly in the way mentioned earlier. And the abuses that result from the purely rational exegesis are avoided.

In this challenge for catechists, the negative side can be illustrated in the unfortunate career of Fr. Alfred Loisy, professor of biblical exegesis at the Institut Catholique in Paris. His deviation into the purely rational exegesis was the occasion for the Encyclical *Providentissimus Deus* (November 18, 1893) of Leo XIII. Loisy had allowed his mind to become imbued with the inner-cosmic metaphysics of Spinoza and Auguste Comte. Thus Loisy came to see the Bible as nothing but a collection of merely human writings. It comes as no surprise, therefore, that his death in 1940 found him in a state of complete atheism and in apostasy both from his Catholic faith and from the heritage in the open metaphysics that his Church was attempting to renew in all her institutions of higher education.

Because of its contemporary bearing, it seems that one should point out another illustration of the negative side. May it serve to alert students of biblical Catechetics regarding the discernment that is needed with regard to contemporary writings on the Bible. It is the approach of Fr. Raymond E. Brown, S.S., a prolific writer in the field of New Testament exegesis, who stated in his keynote address, "Catechetics in an Age of Theological Change," delivered to teachers of Catholic faith at the NCEA Convention in New Orleans on April 23, 1973. "Modern theological discussion," he writes, "is not focused on marginal questions but on a contemporary reunderstanding of the *fundamental* teachings of Christianity" (his emphasis).[30] Since Catechetics is a formative teaching of the Articles of Faith, this seems to raise the question whether these Articles are to be understood by Christians today in the same meaning that they had for the Apostles.[31] The question persists in Father Brown's use of the terminology of the political order, with no hint that he recognizes the Articles of Faith as belonging, together with the Holy Bible from which the authority of the Church has derived them, to the higher order of the prophetic light. Using the terms *swing to the left* and *ultra-conservative or fundamentalist Catholics*, he observes that "these Catholic fundamentalists denounce as heretical the freer Catholic positions which have emerged from Vatican II. . . . Our great assurance for the future is that the real organs of Catholic theological education are solidly in the hands of those who accept modern insights."[32] Father Brown presents himself as occupying a calm and reasonable position between two forms of extremism. Yet his use of these political categories, "right vs. left," "conservative vs. liberal," is a signal to biblical Catechetics that careful analysis is needed that is done in the light of the Church's contemporary renewal of the heritage of metaphysics open to the prophetic light. For these political categories are out of place when the Sacred Deposit of the Articles of Faith is concerned. He seems unaware that these Articles exist or that the atheistic hermeneutics has created a problem both for them and for the Bible. What does Father Brown mean by "serious theology"?[33] Does he mean the Sacred Theology that takes its point of departure and the light of its discourse from the Articles of Faith understood as the Apostles understood them? Or is he being ambiguous about the new hermeneutics that has arisen in modern academic life since Spinoza? In biblical Catechetics one may not indulge in superficial or ambiguous discussion that proceeds in a make-believe world, as if the Articles of Faith do not really exist. For these Articles do indeed exist. They summarize for catechetical teachers the biblical Word of God. Jesus himself entrusted these Articles of Faith to his Apostles and their Successors as a Deposit of Faith to be taught to all nations always in the same meaning that he himself had given to them by his teaching. They are not to be politicized, for they stand above political categories such as "liberal" and "conservative." One cannot but be on guard regarding Father Brown's prediction. "I venture to predict," he writes, "that this period into which we are now entering will be taken up with the impact of biblical criticism on the Roman Catholic understanding of doctrine."[34] Unfortunately, Father Brown leaves undefined the precise philosophical light under which he sees "biblical criticism." Others in the Church, however, including those who speak with the authority of the Holy See, have become increasingly concerned to preserve the divine authorship of the Bible from the philosophical negation arising from a purely rational exegesis of its human authorship. This, too, concerns biblical Catechetics, as the following summary will show.

The Holy See and the Catechetical Approach to the Bible

The documents and guidelines of the Holy See on the Bible in recent times offer the positive side in these matters, for they manifest constantly a twofold concern: first, the primacy of the divine authorship of Sacred Scripture and second, the proper use of the progress in the historical, archaeological, and linguistic sciences. Students of biblical Catechetics should study the full text of these documents from the viewpoint of this twofold concern. Here only brief attention can be drawn to them and to their larger context, the renewal of Catholic intellectual life since Vatican I.

This larger context is the program for the renewal of Catholic intellectual life, an edifice of academic teaching in theology and biblical exegesis that rests on its own foundation of Christian philosophy. If this foundation is replaced by some form of modern philosophy closed to the personal and transcendent Supreme Being, the edifice of doctrine will be like a building on sand. This is true above all in exegesis, where the divine authorship will recede and exclusive emphasis on the human authorship will become the norm. Hence, with the atheistic hermeneutics explicitly in mind, the Catholic Church in the century since Vatican I has been renewing the teaching of Christian philosophy with its metaphysics of openness to the God who can speak his Word to mankind. In practice, the Church requires a thorough grounding in Christian philosophy before students take up the study of theology and then biblical exegesis. One can say, therefore, that the program for the renewal of Christian philosophy is itself an expression of the concern for the divine authorship of the Bible, eclipsed in recent times by the Spinozan Metaphysics and its atheistic hermeneutics. It follows that this philosophical renewal should be basic in catechetical institutes, not least because it relates directly to biblical Catechetics. The intellectual life of the Catholic Church is a seamless robe of doctrine in which each branch of study correlates with the others and all branches rest on the same foundation, this heritage of the metaphysics that is open to the personal Supreme Being and thus to the possibility of the prophetic light. The documents and actions of the Holy See regarding the Bible are intelligible only in this large context, for they presuppose these philosophical foundations of the Catholic intellectual life as a whole.

The first of these biblical documents is the *Providentissimus Deus* (November 18, 1893), mentioned sufficiently earlier. In connection with it and its problematic, the presence of the Modernist Heresy, Pope Leo XIII set up a biblical commission of recognized biblical scholars to bring out the weight of human learning to identify the right use of the historical sciences and to guard the body of Catholics from the effects of their abuse. This commission, as one would expect, has been much maligned and opposed. Biblical Catechetics, however, can well feel kindly toward these measures of the Holy See, for the average catechist cannot be a specialist in the sciences but must depend with gratitude upon the authorized translations of the Scriptures, often with explanatory notes, done under the auspices of these scholars who unite specialized scientific competence with general metaphysical and religious soundness.[35] Otherwise the idea spreads that the Bible is the exclusive domain of specialists in the human sciences, an idea that gradually eliminated the catechetical teaching of a content of doctrine deriving from the divine authorship. The reason is clear. The purely rational exegesis, concentrating on texts in isolation from the meaning of the Bible as a whole, has the effect of suppressing its unity, the meaning that comes from its divine authorship. It is this meaning that provides catechetical teaching with its content.

Next come two major Encyclicals of the Holy See, *ex professo* on the Holy Bible. The *Spiritus Paraclitus* (September 15, 1920) of Benedict XV is increasingly timely in view of the recovery of the approach of the Fathers of the Church to the Holy Bible that characterizes the most recent leadership of the See of Saint Peter, to be discussed later. *Spiritus Paraclitus* centers upon Saint Jerome, the great patristic biblical scholar who upheld the divine authorship and consequently the holiness and unity of meaning of the Bible. Then it turns to "Modern Views Incompatible with Tradition and with Christ's Method," an illuminating discussion that bears upon the atheistic hermeneutics and its effect "even upon children of the Catholic Church, and what is a peculiar sorrow to us, even clerics and professors of sacred learning, who in their own concert either openly repudiate or at least attack in secret the Church's teaching."[36]

The second Encyclical, the *Divino afflante Spiritu* (September 30, 1943) of Pius XII, was published, significantly, on the feast of Saint Jerome, whom the Pope calls "the greatest Doctor in the exposition of the Sacred Scriptures." The union and communion of this document with those of Leo XIII and Benedict XV will be evident when all three are studied comparatively in their full texts. This is important in the case of *Divino afflante* because it concerns primarily the proper use of the natural and historical sciences with regard to the human authorship of the Bible. As has been noted, those who suffer from the overemphasis on this aspect of Sacred Scripture, one must expect, tend to cite selectively from this Encyclical. It is clear from its conclusion that biblical Catechetics and its catechetical approach to the Bible are directly concerned, for again it is the divine authorship that is primary. It is the factor that unifies these three major Encyclicals in the contemporary life of the Church.[37]

Perhaps the best illustration of the truly necessary vigilance of the biblical commission is its *Instructions on the Historicity of the Gospels* (April 21, 1964).[38] This again concerns biblical Catechetics at its most vital point, because "Catechesis must necessarily be Christocentric."[39]

Finally, there is the passage in the Encyclical *Humani Generis* (August 12, 1950), the major document of Pius XII, which analyzes the ongoing problem of philosophical abuse of the natural and historical sciences by minds more or less infected by the Modernist Heresy. It is given here because of its special relevance to biblical Catechetics, its awareness of the prophetic light, and its concern for that use of human science that ministers to understanding better the Word of God that the human authors intend to convey:

> Just as in the biological and anthropological sciences, so also in history there are those who boldly flout the limits and safeguards set up by the Church. Deplorable in particular is a certain fashion of interpreting too freely the historical books of the Old Testament. . . . The first eleven chapters of Genesis, although they do not properly conform to the rules of historical composition used by the great Greek and Latin historians, or by the historians of our time, do nevertheless pertain to history in a true sense to be further studied and determined by exegetes . . . these chapters contain, in simple and metaphorical language adapted to the mentality of a people of low culture, the principal truths fundamental for our eternal salvation and a popular description of the origin of the human race and the chosen people. For the rest, if the ancient human authors (of the Bible) have taken anything from popular narratives (and this may be conceded), we must not forget that they did so with the help of divine inspiration which preserved them from error in selecting and appraising these documents. In any case, whatever of popular narratives have found a place in the Sacred Scriptures must in no way be considered on a par with myths or other such things; these are more the product of an exuberant imagination than of that striving for truth and simplicity which is so apparent in the Sacred Books, also of the Old Testament, that its human author must be regarded as decidedly superior to the profane writers of antiquity.[40]

Renewal of the Patristic Approach

With this reference to the distinctive character of the Holy Bible, deriving from its divine authorship and the prophetic light shining in the minds of its human authors, biblical Catechetics can turn to the most recent leadership of the Holy See. This is the conscious recovery and renewal of the Patristic approach to the Bible. It is exemplified by the work of Msgr. John McCarthy at the Holy See in transcending the inadequacies on "Form Criticism" and the purely rational exegesis generally.[41]

Cardinal Joseph Ratzinger supports this same recent recovery and renewal of the approach of the Fathers of the Church to the Holy Bible. "An exegesis which lives and understands the Bible no longer with the living organism of the Church," he writes, "becomes archaeology, a museum of past things. Concretely, this is seen in the fact that the Bible falls apart as Bible, to become nothing more than a collection of heterogeneous books."[42] This is exactly the loss of the divine authorship, on the one hand, and, on the other hand, the exclusive concentration of the human authorship seen through the colored glasses of unsound philosophical hermeneutics.

Cardinal Ratzinger returns *ex professo* to the unsound philosophical base of the typical modern exegesis now dominant in the academic order of teaching with his penetrating lecture in New York of January 27, 1988.[43] Urbanely he points out the philosophical error that underlies the recent theories that attempt to remove the doctrine of the Church as an "impediment to a correct understanding of the Bible, . . . which have increased and multiplied and separated one from another, and become a veritable fence which blocked access to the Bible for all the uninitiated. Those who were initiated were no longer reading the Bible anyway, but were dissecting it into the various parts from which it had to have been composed. . . . Finally they turn into a jungle of contradictions. In the end, one no longer learns what the text says, but what it should have said."[44] Thus a philosophical dogma derived from the inner-cosmic metaphysics of the modern period in philosophy is imposed upon the human authors and their writing. Cardinal Ratzinger illustrates by the case of Rudolf Bultmann, who "uses the philosophy of Martin Heidegger as a vehicle to represent the biblical word. . . . In the end, are we listening to Jesus, or to Heidegger, with this kind of approach to biblical understanding?"[45]

Central to Ratzinger's analysis is his call for foundational work by younger scholars in the coming years. "We must get beyond disputes over details," he writes, "and press on to the foundations. What we need might be called a criticism of criticism."[46] "The real philosophic presupposition of the whole system [of the Bultmannian exegesis] seems to me to lie in the philosophic turning point proposed by Immanuel Kant. According to him the voice of being in itself cannot be heard by human beings."[47] They are confined, Ratzinger points out, to Kant's subjective categories of the human self and thus to the empirical order of the so-called exact sciences, "which by definition excludes the appearance of what is 'wholly other,' or the one who is wholly other. . . . It is with this basic conviction that Bultmann, with the majority of modern exegetes, reads the Bible. . . . The real question before us, then, is: Can one read the Bible any other way? Or perhaps better, must one agree with the philosophy which requires this kind of reading? At its core, the debate about modern exegesis is not a dispute among historians: it is rather a philosophical debate."[48]

Cardinal Ratzinger and with him Pope John Paul II and the Holy See are challenging younger scholars to take another look at the program of the Catholic Church for the renewal of Christian philosophy and its natural metaphysics of mankind. For it was this metaphysics that functioned in the linguistic usage of the human authors of the Bible and provides the bond of meaningful understanding between them and their writings and their readers today. As everyone knows, it was the Spinozan Metaphysics and the Kantian subjective or transcendental idealism that led the Church to launch this philosophical renewal, in order to preserve the meaning of both the Bible and of the Deposit of Faith and Morals in the pastoral care of souls.

"In the last one hundred years," Ratzinger concludes, "exegesis has had many great achievements, but it has brought forth great errors as well. These latter have in some measure grown to the stature of academic dogmas. To criticize them at all would be taken by many as tantamount to sacrilege, especially if it were done by a non-exegete."[49] Hence Ratzinger turns for the last word to the truly great exegete Heinrich Schlier, originally a disciple of Bultmann but who, discovering the more solid and more human philosophical foundation, became a convert to the Catholic Church: "The first presupposition of all exegesis is that it accepts the Bible as a book. . . . It identifies this particular literature as the product of a coherent history, and this history as the proper space for coming to understanding. . . . It acknowledges the faith of the Church as a hermeneutic, the space for understanding, which does not do dogmatic violence to the Bible, but precisely allows the solitary possibility for the Bible to be itself."[50]

With this new attitude of exegetical openness to the unity of the Bible running through its various literary genres and through the many centuries of history in its writing one can conclude this review of the catechetical approach to the Bible upheld by the Holy See consistently throughout modern times. For this approach renews the perception of the divine authorship of the Bible and restores it as the Holy Bible to the People of God generally and to catechists in particular as the basis for teaching the Deposit of Faith and Morals.

The Catechetical Study of the Bible

This chapter on the Bible and biblical Catechetics began by taking the Bible in hand and asking what kind of literature it is and who the people are to whom it belongs. It has been noted how the vicissitudes suffered by Natural Theology at the hands of the inner-cosmic metaphysics carried over to the sufferings of the Bible from the atheistic hermeneutics. The renewal of Christian philosophy liberates Catholic intellectual life and the teaching of the Deposit of Faith and Morals from dogmatic violence at the hands of philosophy. Catechists are free once more to take the Bible in hand as rightfully their own, reading it, studying it, and teaching on the basis of it in the catechetical way as distinct from this particular and parochial way described by Cardinal Ratzinger, now receding into a dated past.

It remains to ask what this "catechetical way" is now and how it is done. Only the most salient points need be given here to be kept in mind in the coming chapters of biblical Catechetics. They will be enlarged upon in volume 2 of this manual for catechists.

To begin, biblical Catechetics is not "philosophy." It takes its stand with the Church in its renewal of the natural metaphysics of mankind, grateful for it and recognizing that it is the bond of intellectual unity between people today and the human authors of the Bible in their times early in this Age of Civilizations. But it does not do a study of that renewal, which has its own place in the curriculum.

Biblical Catechetics, furthermore, is not exegesis of the Bible in the specialized sense of applying the human sciences of history, archaeology, and linguistics to the human authorship. It accepts the versions of the Bible that the Church proposes, done by scientists and sometimes bearing their copious notes as in the case for example of the Jerusalem Bible. The primary concern of biblical Catechetics is not the human authorship but rather the divine authorship that gives the Bible its unity and meaning as the object of study.

What, then, is "Catechetics"? It is the practical ecclesiastical science that studies divine revelation in itself and how it is handed on by teaching. It specifies the purpose of this apostolic activity and determines who the persons are who carry it out with authority.

And what is "biblical Catechetics"? It is that initial branch of Catechetics that locates divine revelation in the call of God to his Prophets to receive his prophetic light and to teach it to his people. Hence this is a "Chosen People," chosen to be the bearer of divine revelation as a light for their own way of life and through them a "light to the Gentiles."[51] Biblical Catechetics, accordingly, will accept the Bible as the literature of this people that records the plan and purpose of God revealing his word to mankind. Thus it will study the Bible by a set of topics that give emphasis to its divine authorship, manifesting first the nature and purpose of Moses' revelation and its preparatory Testament and second its relationship to Jesus, the expected Messiah, and his New Testament. For he is the one whom that special Prophet, John the Baptist, pointed out to his own followers as "him of whom Moses in the Law and also the Prophets wrote" (John 1:45).

These topics will analyze in the Bible itself, in both the Old Testament and the New Testament, those basic components of Catechetics in general noted earlier: the practical study of revelation in itself and as a content of teaching handed on formatively so as to raise up a People of God. Thus the catechists of today will be assisted in forming their authentic self-image from the doctrine and practice of the Hebrew Prophets and from the fulfilling doctrine and practice of Jesus, the last and greatest of the Prophets and the Divine Teacher of mankind.

What, then, is the formal object or orientation of this study, the light under which it proceeds? It is its emphasis upon the divine authorship in the patristic mode, a mode that is neither "medieval" nor "ancient." For it stands on the natural metaphysics of mankind, where the Fathers of the Church stood and where catechists and homilists stand today, on the level above time that belongs to the Supreme Being, "the same yesterday, today and forever" (Heb. 13:8). "Heaven and earth will pass away, but my words will not pass away" (Luke 21:33). For God is able to speak his Word to man, as the Prophet Amos says (Amos 4:13), and to do so, if he wishes, by choosing Prophets who then both speak his Word to their fellowman and give it an abiding written form for teaching in the literature that marks the historic life of the People chosen to bear that revelation forward in time and out to all the peoples of mankind.

Chapter 3

The Hebrew Prophets and the Bible

"Spiritually we are all Semites," Pope Pius XI stated to the world in 1936 as the anti-Semitic policy of Hitler's National Socialism began to unfold. The Roman Missal calls Abraham, "our father in faith." When catechists of the Catholic Church turn to the Hebrew Fact, standing in history as an objective reality that can be studied empirically, they discover their own roots and enter into their own heritage.

There are two wrong ways to study religion. One is the way of the Cartesian separation, producing both the abstractions of the rationalist natural theology and the antiintellectualist "ways of the heart" and "varieties of religious experience" of the Kantian approach. The other wrong way is that of the Science of Comparative Religion when it is imbued with the philosophical atheism of the modern period. Supercilious, intellectually closed, and proud, the universal fact of mankind's religious life is viewed as a museum piece, a curiosity for modern man to glance at as he goes by, nothing but an interesting relic left behind from an outmoded past.

Then there is a correct way to study religion, quite different in attitude. It is the catechetical approach, open to God the Father Almighty, Creator of heaven and earth, and open to whatever the facts indicate regarding a message from him, a Word of God on human life, purpose, and destiny. This approach transcends the modern period of philosophy and merits the term *postmodern* which will be defined later when the Study of Catechetics turns to its philosophical foundations. When undertaking this way in the study of religion, catechists enter into their own personal heritage, saying in effect: "This is my spiritual inheritance, my human and moral position, the foundation of my personal hope of becoming worthy of the promises of Christ. The attitude of Jesus toward Abraham, Moses, and the Prophets is also my attitude, because I learn it from him, and thus I come to understand better the fact, the nature, and the dynamic historical mode of Divine Revelation.''

Moses and the Prophets

The study of comparative religion has thrown a new light on the Bible and especially upon the Hebrew religion to which the writings of the Old Testament bear witness. It permits the qualitative uniqueness of the Hebrew religion to be seen empirically and to be recognized in a powerful new way. At the same time, this religion is seen to be fully human in its mode: it fits into the universal pattern of mankind's religious life. "There is a vast body of evidence from all ages and cultures," Dawson writes in his Gifford Lectures, "from the lowest to the highest, testifying to a universal belief in prophecy."[1] And: "It is in the Semitic world rather than in the West that the classical type of prophetic religion is to be found, and it is there that the relation between the religious institutions of prophecy and the social order of culture is most fully exemplified."[2]

Putting this another way, the Hebrews will have their "Shamans," indeed, men called apart and set aside for religion. But these religious leaders of the Hebrews will not devote their lives apart for prayer and ascetical practice to the inveterate errors and deeply corrupted religions of the Gentiles. They will have an entirely new religious situation to serve, that new beginning in the order of human relationships to God that originated in the call of Abraham to come out from among the Gentiles and the rank growth of their corrupted religious beliefs and practices.

Thus the Hebrew Prophets raise the most basic questions of Fundamental Catechetics: Is there a Divine Revelation on our planet Earth? What is its nature? How does it reach persons today? Does it take the form of a personal "experience" of all men equally, or is it given to certain men for communication to others by proclamation and teaching? In this case, is it still basically an experience that is described by the Prophet, as well as halting human language permits, to assist others in achieving a like experience of divine things? Or is it something quite different: a Word of God that the chosen human recipient understands, then speaks forth to his fellowmen in the words of human discourse?

In such a case, this Word of God could be handed on among men by teaching. It could constitute a social heritage. There could be a People of God living by this body of teaching as the substance of its culture, analogous to all the other human cultural patterns of the historic peoples and nations of mankind. It will be a fully human way of life, analogous to the pagan ones because partly the same in its humanism but also partly different because free of the religious aberrations of the Gentiles.

The Hebrew Prophets, furthermore, open up still more fundamental perspectives. Men live by the light of reason, the only fundamental difference between the human being and the higher animals. Does this light of reason illuminate comprehensively all that exists? Could it not be that dimensions of reality exist beyond its cognitive power, just as there are wave lengths in the world of matter that bodily eyesight cannot see? If the Supreme Being is an unlimited unique Intelligence, a Person, a Reality who is intelligent in nature, of whom both the material light of eyesight and the intelligible light of natural human understanding are distant reflections, could it not be that the Hebrew Prophets participated in a new and different way in the Divine Light and were given to know aspects of some divine plan that exists regarding human life and destiny on the planet Earth?

In answering such questions and studying the perspectives they raise, the first step is to hear what the Hebrews themselves have had to say about their own Prophets, why they were set apart, and what it was that came to them from on high. One must attempt to see and understand the entire matter from within. To do thus, one must begin with the commanding figure of Moses, whom the Hebrews always have seen as preeminent among all the Prophets of Israel.[3]

The Hebrew People existed prior to Moses and had already that qualitatively distinct character resulting from the call of Abraham that he was careful to bring to their attention and to fix in his writings for coming generations.

At Moses' time the Hebrews were suffering a harsh slavery in Egypt. "And it came to pass in the course of those many days that the king of Egypt died; and the children of Israel sighed by reason of the bondage, and they cried, and their cry came up unto God by reason of the bondage. And God heard their groaning, and God remembered His covenant with Abraham, with Isaac, and with Jacob" (Exod. 2:23–24).[4]

The Call and Mission of Moses

God chose Moses as the instrument for his divine plan of mercy and salvation:

> Now Moses was keeping the flock of Jethro his father-in-law, the priest of Midian; and he led the flock to the farthest end of the wilderness and came to the mountain of God, unto Horeb. And the angel of the Lord appeared unto him in a flame of fire out of the midst of a bush; and he looked, and, behold, the bush burned with fire, and the bush was not consumed. And Moses said: "I will turn aside now, and see this great sight, why the bush is not burnt?" And when the Lord saw that he turned aside to see, God called unto him out of the midst of the bush, and said: "Moses, Moses." And he said: "Here I am." And He said: "Draw not nigh hither; put off thy shoes from off thy feet, for the place whereon thou standest is holy ground." Moreover He said: "I am the God of thy father, the God of Abraham, the God of Isaac, and the God of Jacob." And Moses hid his face; for he was afraid to look upon God. And the Lord said: "I have surely seen the affliction of My people that are in Egypt, and have heard their cry by reason of their taskmasters; for I know their pains; and I am come to deliver them out of the hand of the Egyptians, and to bring them up out of that land unto a good land and large, unto a land flowing with milk and honey. . . . Come now, therefore, and I will send thee unto Pharoah, that thou mayest bring forth My people the children of Israel out of Egypt." And Moses said unto God: "Who am I, that I should go unto Pharoah, and that I should bring forth the children of Israel out of Egypt?" And He said: "Certainly I will be with thee; and this shall be the token unto thee, that I have sent thee: when thou hast brought forth the people out of Egypt, ye shall serve God upon this mountain."[5] And Moses said unto God: "Behold, when I come unto the children of Israel, and shall say unto them: The God of your fathers hath sent me to you; and they shall say to me: What is His name? What shall I say unto them?"
>
> And God said unto Moses: "*I AM THAT I AM;*" and He said "Thus shalt thou say unto the children of Israel: '*I AM* hath sent me unto you'" (Exod. 3:1–14).

This fundamental passage conveys the Hebrew understanding both of the nature of prophecy and of its essential content, the content and word of prophetic revelation. The nature of prophecy is a light from the Supreme Being that illuminates the mind of the Prophet with new insight and understanding. It proceeds as a conversational dialogue between two intelligent beings. And the essential content is a revelation of both the nature of the Supreme Being and the plan he intends to accomplish in human events. It is hardly too much to say that in this revelation of the Name of God the entire Hebrew Revelation is implicitly contained. Hence it will be analyzed in summarizing the doctrine of the Prophets.

After this initial call from God to serve as his Prophet to the suffering Hebrews, Moses lived more and more in intimacy with God, receiving the prophetic light frequently and at the same time exercising the special leadership over the Hebrews that completed their formation as the new people of God, making them to be the bearer of Divine Revelation. Later, when the disasters afflicted upon Egypt by divine power were bearing witness both to the Lordship of Yahweh and to his concern for his People, the prophetic light is described as follows: "And God spoke unto Moses, and said unto him: 'I am the Lord; and I appeared unto Abraham, unto Isaac, and unto Jacob, as God Almighty, but by My name *(Yahweh)* I made Me not known to them' " (Exod. 6:2–3).[6]

Further insight into the nature of the prophetic light and the purpose of Moses' particular call as a prophet is contained in the mighty events when Moses returns to the same mountain in the desert, now at the head of the entire people. Egypt has been left far behind; the Hebrews are on their own way, an austere one but free:

> Israel encamped before the mount. And Moses went up unto God, and the Lord called unto him out of the mountain, saying: "Thus shalt thou say to the house of Jacob and tell the people of Israel: Ye have seen what I did unto the Egyptians, and how I bore you on eagles' wings, and brought you unto Myself. Now therefore, if ye will hearken unto My voice indeed, and keep My covenant, then ye shall be Mine own treasure from among all peoples; for all the earth is Mine; and ye shall be unto Me a kingdom of priests, and a holy nation. These are the words which thou shalt speak unto the children of Israel." And Moses came and called for the elders of the people,

and set before them all these words which the Lord commanded him. And all the people answered together, and said: "All that the Lord hath spoken we will do." And Moses reported the words of the people unto the Lord. (Exod. 19:2–8)

The mode of Divine Revelation is becoming clear from the very text of the Hebrew Scriptures. The Word of God comes in the prophetic light that illuminates the mind of him, the Prophet, whom God has called. He in turn communicates this Word of God to the people. It is supremely important from the viewpoint of modern Catechetics to note that the prophet makes use of the words of the ordinary human discourse of that place and time, which they understand.

Their response is one of divine faith: they accept the words of the Prophet as the very Word of God. It is not the same human thinking elaborated by the Prophet. It is not "science" or "philosophy," as one says today.

The graphic description of the quaking and smoking mountain follows immediately. Here only Moses ascends, to return with the Ten Commandments:

And God spoke all these words, saying: I am the Lord thy God, who brought thee out of the land of Egypt, out of the house of bondage. Thou shalt have no other gods before Me. . . . Thou shalt not take the name of the Lord thy God in vain. . . . Remember the Sabbath day, to keep it holy. . . . Honour thy father and thy mother. . . . Thou shalt not murder. . . . Thou shalt not commit adultery, Thou shalt not steal, Thou shalt not bear false witness against thy neighbor, Thou shalt not covet. . . thy neighbor's wife . . . nor anything that is thy neighbor's. And all the people perceived the thunderings, and the lightnings, and the voice of the horn, and the mountain smoking; and when the people saw it, they trembled, and stood afar off. And they said to Moses: "Speak thou with us, and we will hear; but let not God speak with us, lest we die." And Moses said unto the people: "Fear not; for God is come to prove you, and that His fear may be before you, that ye sin not." And the people stood afar off; but Moses drew near unto the thick darkness where God was. And the Lord said unto Moses: Thus thou shalt say unto the children of Israel: Ye yourselves have seen that I have talked with you from heaven. . . . An altar of each shalt thou make unto Me, and shalt sacrifice thereon thy burnt-offerings, and thy peace-offerings, thy sheep, and thine oxen . . . (Exod. 20:1–21).

There follow the chapters that describe the laws and regulations for the Hebrew worship by prayer and sacrifice centering upon the Tabernacle (meaning "tent") housing the Law, the very substance of the material life. Aaron and his sons become the hereditary priesthood by divine command: "And bring thou near unto thee Aaron thy brother, and his sons with him, from among the children of Israel, that they may minister unto Me in the priest's office . . . " (Exod. 28:12). "According to all that the Lord commanded Moses, so the children of Israel did all the work" (Exod. 39:42). The Hebrew religion is essentially completed with all the arrangements of the Tabernacle. And the result of the Revelation is a closeness of this people to God, present with them in some special way in the tent that was the Tabernacle of the Law: "And he reared up the court round about the tabernacle and the altar, and set up the screen of the gate of the court. So Moses finished the work. Then the cloud covered the tent of meeting, and the glory of the Lord filled the tabernacle. . . . For the cloud of the Lord was upon the tabernacle by day, and there was fire therein by night, in the sight of all the house of Israel, throughout all their journeys" (Exod. 40:33–38).

Part of Moses' prophetic mission was the confirmation of the people in the knowledge of their own physical origin in Abraham, a matter that gives further insight into the prophetic light. In the generations after the Tower of Babel and the dispersion of man in various tongues over the earth, when the moral decline noted in chapter 1 was far advanced, God called Abraham as Prophets were called and made him the progenitor of a new people. Clearly it would be a people of the prophetic light, living in a new and higher level of relationship to the Supreme Being. It is the first of Moses' books in the Bible that records this self-understanding of the Hebrews: "Terah begot Abram . . . in Ur of the Chaldees" (Gen. 11:27–28). "Now the Lord said to Abram: 'Get thee out of thy country, and from thy kindred, and from thy father's house, unto the land that I will show thee. And I will make of thee a great nation, and I will bless thee. . . . ' So Abram went, as the Lord had spoken unto him" (Gen 12:1–4).

The Covenant or Testament gives further insight into the nature of a Prophet's call:

> After these things the word of the Lord came unto Abram in a vision,
> saying: "Fear not, Abram, I am thy shield, thy reward shall be ex-
> ceeding great." And Abram said: "O Lord God, what wilt Thou give
> me, seeing I go hence childless, and he that shall be possessor of my
> house is Eliezer of Damascus?" . . . And behold, the word of the Lord
> came unto him, saying: "This man shall not be thine heir; but he
> that shall come forth out of thine own bowels shall be thine heir."
> And He brought him forth abroad, and said: "Look now toward
> heaven, and count the stars, if thou be able to count them;" and He
> said unto him: "So shall thy seed be." And he believed in the Lord;
> and He counted it to him for righteousness. (Gen. 15:1–6)

By this response of faith in the prophetic light as communicating an understanding that is the Word of God, Abraham became
the father of all who thus believe. As the continuation conveys, this
faith was placed in God as the Creator of the universe and hence
the master of its laws: a personal God who is almighty and for whom
nothing is impossible. For by the laws of nature Abraham's wife
Sarah was already beyond the childbearing age. How then, apart
from a miracle of divine power, could she be the mother of a prog-
eny that would multiply in number as the stars? "And God said:
'Nay, but Sarah thy wife shall bear thee a son, and thou shalt call
his name Isaac; and I will establish My covenant with him for an
everlasting covenant for his seed after him" (Gen. 17:19).

In due time Isaac is indeed born and Abraham's faith is tested
in a way that indicates the centrality of worship by sacrifice among
the Hebrews: it is a figure or symbol or type, furthermore, that
points to the New Testament in the future:

> And it came to pass after these things, that God did prove Abraham,
> and said unto him: "Abraham"; and he said: "Here I am." And He
> said: "Take now thy son, thine only son, whom thou lovest, even
> Isaac, and get thee unto the land of Moriah; and offer him there for
> a burnt-offering upon one of the mountains which I will tell thee
> of." And Abraham rose early in the morning . . . and took Isaac his
> son. . . . . And Isaac spoke unto Abraham his father, and said: "My
> father." And he said: "Here I am, my son." And he said: "Behold

the fire and the wood; but where is the lamb for a burnt-offering?"
And Abraham said: "God will provide Himself the lamb for a burnt-
offering, my son." . . . [At the last moment] "the angel of the Lord
called unto him out of heaven, and said, "Abraham, Abraham." And
he said: "Here am I." And he said: "Lay not thy hand upon the lad,
neither do thou any thing unto him; for now I know that thou art a
God-fearing man, seeing thou hast not withheld thy son, thine only
son, from Me." And Abraham lifted up his eyes, and looked, and
behold behind him a ram caught in the thicket by his horns. And
Abraham went and took the ram, and offered him up for a burnt-
offering in the stead of his son. (Gen. 22:1–13)

Abraham is the man of faith in the Word of God that he understood by the prophetic light. It was faith that responded to the call
to come out from the morally and religiously corrupted Gentile
world of Ur of the Chaldees and faith that sustained him in the
case of Isaac, the son who depended for existence upon the direct
intervention of the Almighty and whom Abraham would have sacrificed in obedience to the word of this same God. From Abraham,
then, Moses' people had come forth, a nation of the prophetic light,
issuing as a people from a Prophet of God. Faith in God was therefore to characterize this people, for faith is the human response to
the Word of God. The entire national life of this People of God
centered upon bearing this revealed word forward in history, practicing its religion. "Men do not believe," Daniélou writes, "if they
think in a general way that God exists, but do not for one moment
think that God takes any part in history."[7]

The mode of the prophetic light that sets these men apart,
making them leaders of the Hebrews and spokesmen of the Word
of God in the words of human discourse, can be studied in each of
the Prophets of Israel. Gideon is a striking example, called to deliver
the Hebrews from the defeats they were suffering on account of
failure to live and practice their religion. "And the angel of the
Lord appeared unto him, and said unto him: 'The Lord is with thee,
thou almighty man of valor' " (Judges 6:12). Gideon left his work
in his field, and led the Hebrews to victory after victory, doing away
with altars of Baal and the pagan customs that Baal's religion introduced among the Israelites: "And it came to pass, as soon as Gideon
was dead, that the children of Israel again went astray after the

Baalim, and made Baal-berith their god. And the children of Israel remembered not the Lord their God . . . " (Judges 8:33–34). This prophetic function, the regeneration of the revealed religion and the renewal of the authentic faith in Yahweh, the One Only God, recurs constantly in the Scriptures.

God's Revelation Given Through His Prophets

Yahweh's call of Samuel to the state and function of the Prophets illustrates graphically the nature of the prophetic light. The boy's mother, Hannah, after obtaining him by prayer to the Creator of Life, dedicated him to the service of the altar with Eli and the priests at the national Tabernacle (1 Samuel 1–2):

> And the child Samuel ministered unto the Lord before Eli. And the word of the Lord was precious in those days: there was no frequent vision. And it came to pass . . . that Samuel was laid down to sleep in the temple of the Lord, where the ark of God was, that the Lord called Samuel; and he said: "Here am I." And he ran unto Eli, and said: "Here am I; for thou didst call me." And he said: "I called not; lie down again." And he went and lay down. And the Lord called yet again to Samuel. And Samuel arose and went to Eli, and said: "Here am I; for thou didst call me." And he answered: "I called not, my son; lie down again." Now Samuel did not yet know the Lord, neither was the word of the Lord yet revealed unto him. And the Lord called Samuel again the third time. And he arose and went to Eli; and said: "Here I am; for thou didst call me." And Eli perceived that the Lord was calling the child. Therefore Eli said unto Samuel: "Go, lie down; and it shall be, if thou be called, that thou shalt say: Speak, Lord; for Thy servant heareth." So Samuel went and lay down in his place. And the Lord came, and stood, and called as at other times: "Samuel, Samuel." Then Samuel said: "Speak; for Thy servant heareth" . . . And Samuel grew, and the Lord was with him, and did let none of his words fall to the ground. And all Israel from Dan even to Beer-sheeba knew that Samuel was established to be a prophet of the Lord. And the Lord appeared again in Shiloh, for the Lord revealed Himself to Samuel in Shiloh by the word of the Lord. And the word of Samuel came to all Israel. (Samuel 3, 1–19 to 4,1)

This is the pattern that recurs in all the Prophets—Elijah, Elisha, Isaiah, Jeremiah, Ezekiel, and all the rest down to Malachi and then on to Mary and Saint Paul.[8] The pattern has certain clear features that constitute Catechetics in its very being as a learned discipline and give it its material and formal objects as a branch of study. The prophetic light begets understandings in the mind of the Prophet, which are the Word of God to him. It is an intelligible light, an understanding of a Word, not an emotional state, and ordinarily not the seeing of a corporeal vision. It is a hearing of a Word from on high. Then this word of God comes to all Israel from the Prophet in the words of human discourse. The Israelites receive it, accept it, believe it as the Word of God. Thus their response is an act of divine faith. By receiving this Word of God in this human way, the people of God likewise come close to God, knowing his mind and his will. But it is a closeness achieved by this faith, and not a direct experience of God, as if each were a prophet unto himself.

It is clear, then, that Divine Revelation on this planet Earth is following the general mode of Providence and its divine government: God carries out his plans by means of specially chosen agents and ministers. The Hebrews are such an agent in their entire being as a people bearing Revelation to and for all mankind. They are to be the minister of this Revelation to the rest of the tribes and peoples, all the Gentile nations, of the planet. And within the Hebrew people the same principle applies: God operates through the ministry of the Prophets, specially called to receive his Word and to communicate it to the rest of the people. This implies that there is a mode of communication and a content that is communicated. Turning to this dimension of the Word of God on the human scene, the Bible as the written Word of God comes immediately into view.

The Bible: From Oral Tradition to the Written Word of God

The Hebrews always believed two things with firm religious and supernatural faith: first, that God had given them his Word through their Prophets, in the form of human words that expressed revealed truth, communicable socially as a doctrine; and second, that God himself had caused this same revealed Word to be consigned to human writing.

The importance of this second fact can hardly be exaggerated, and it is all the more intelligible now that the long period of Prehistory, when men lived on the oral tradition of tribal life, has become known. Writing is the invention that actually created the historic period of human life on earth, and it dates from only about four thousand years before Christ. The system of hieroglyphic writing, still used in the Orient, was supplanted toward the West by the truly marvelous invention of the alphabet. Apparently it was invented only once and has been applied with minor variations to the Semitic and Hebrew tongues, to Greek, and to Latin. Thus it reaches the present day in three forms: the Arabic, the Russian, and the Latin characters used by all the modern Western languages. In the cultural development of mankind toward the fullness of human time, the invention of writing and of the alphabetical form of it in particular stands as perhaps the most important single step. For it provides for the continuity and stability of social heritages and the very flux of change that development implies.

It is to be expected, then, that the People chosen to be the bearers of the Word of God would make use of this invention in its processes of communicating what came from its Prophets.

The Faith of the Hebrews

It was an article of faith among the Hebrews that this was done by the divine command and with the divine assistance: "And the Lord said unto Moses: 'Write this for a memorial in the book, and rehearse it in the ears of Joshua . . . ' " (Exod. 17:14). "The book": already the Bible, from the Greek word *Biblos*, meaning simply "The Book," has come into view in the very text itself, together with the didactic purpose, its practical use as an aid in teaching: "rehearse it in the ears of Joshua." "And . . . He said . . . : 'Moses alone shall come near unto the Lord. . . . ' And Moses came and told the people all the words of the Lord, and all the ordinances; and all the people answered with one voice, and said: 'All the words which the Lord hath spoken we will do.' And Moses wrote all the words of the Lord" (Exod. 24:3–4). Again: "And the Lord said unto Moses: 'Write thou these words, for after the tenor of these words I have made a covenant with thee and with Israel.' And he was there with the Lord forty days and forty nights; he did neither eat nor drink water. And he wrote upon the tables the words of the covenant, the ten words" (Exod. 34:27–28).

Prof. Haag writes:

One must take the tradition seriously, according to which, from the beginning of the Covenant, a text of the Law was fixed in writing. This tradition encounters no serious historical objection. In fact, the contrary is true: in the present state of knowledge concerning juridical custom in the ancient Orient, this type of fixation in writing is positively indicated. The use of writing at this period is no surprise at the present day. It is known now that the syro-palestinian society of the 13th century B.C. knew not only the use of Egyptian hieroglyphic and Babylonian cuneiform writing, but also that of two alphabetical forms, the cuneiform alphabet now uncovered by the excavations at Ugarit, and the inner alphabet of Phoenicia.[9]

The Hebrews themselves always held that the writing of the Prophetic Word of God began under Moses and proceeded after him by his authority, the divine authority exercised by those who sitting on "the chair of Moses" governed this people of Revelation. Moses, seeing his end approaching, prepared Joshua to succeed him.

"Be strong and of good courage," Moses told his successor, "for thou shalt go with this people into the land which the Lord hath sworn unto their fathers to give them. . . . " And Moses commanded them, saying: "At the end of every seven years . . . , in the feast of tabernacles, when all Israel is come to appear before the Lord thy God . . . thou shalt read this law before all Israel in their hearing. Assemble the people, the men and the women and the little ones, and thy stranger that is within thy gates, that they may hear, and that they may learn, and fear the Lord your God, and observe to do all the words of this law. . . . And it came to pass, when Moses had made an end of writing the words of this law in a book, until they were finished, that Moses commanded the Levites, that bore the ark of the convenant of the Lord, saying: "Take this Book of the Law, and put it by the side of the ark of the covenant of the Lord your God, that it may be there for a witness against thee. For I know thy rebellion, and thy stiff neck; behold, while I am yet alive with you this day, ye have been rebellious against the Lord; and how much more after my death? Assemble unto me all the elders of your tribes, and your officers, that I may speak these words in their ears" (Deut. 31:7–28).

The Origin and Nature of the Bible

This "Book of the Law" is the written form of the Word of God to his chosen Prophets that is called universally to this day the Bible, meaning the Book of Books, the book that differs from all other books because it is the written Word of God.

Many other places in the Hebrew Scriptures bear witness to this written form of the Word of God. After warning the people against adopting the ambient idolatry, Joshua heard their renewed promise of fidelity. "And Joshua said unto the people: 'Ye are witnesses against yourselves that ye have chosen you the Lord, to serve Him.' And they said: 'We are witnesses.'—'Now therefore put away the strange gods which are among you, and incline your heart unto the Lord, the God of Israel.' And the people said unto Joshua: 'The Lord our God will we serve, and unto His voice will we hearken.' So Joshua made a covenant with the people that day, and set them a statute and an ordinance in Shechem. And Joshua wrote these words in the book of the Law of God" (Joshua 24:21–26).

It is clear, therefore, that Moses began the writing of the revealed Word of God, that he placed these writings under the authority of the priests, and that prophets coming after him will provide additions to his "Book of the Law of God," which the religious leaders will accept as divine in origin and authorize as belonging to the Hebrew Scriptures.

Thus the prophetic Book of Jeremiah came to be a part of the Hebrew Bible. "And it shall come to pass, when seventy years are accomplished, that I will punish the king of Babylon. . . . And I will bring upon that land all My words which I have pronounced against it, even all that is written in this book, which Jeremiah hath prophesied . . . " (Jer. 25:12–13). Again: "The word that Jeremiah the prophet spoke unto Baruch the son of Neriah, when he wrote these words in a book at the mouth of Jeremiah . . . " (Jer. 45:1). "At the mouth": Jeremiah dictated, it would be said today, to his secretary. Further: "And Jeremiah wrote in one book all the evil that should come upon Babylon . . . " (Jer. 51:60).

Isaiah is explicit regarding the purpose of this written form of the Word of God. It is for the instruction of the people and specifically for the students at his own Prophet's school. "Bind up the testimony," God commands him; "seal the instruction among My disciples'' (Isaiah 8:16). The purpose of stabilizing the people by the divine teaching is explicit. "Now go," Yahweh commands the prophet, "write it before them on a tablet and inscribe it in a book, that it may be for the time to come for ever and ever. For it is a rebellious people, lying children, children that refuse to hear the teaching of the Lord; that say to the seers: 'See not,' and to the prophets: 'Prophesy not unto us right things, speak unto us smooth things, prophesy delusions'. . . . " (Isaiah 30:8–10).

Finally, there is the passage in which Isaiah gives this book its true and substantial name, denoting what the Hebrews believed it to be in reality. "Seek ye out of the book of the Lord," he tells the people, "and read . . . ." (Is. 34:16). This states what the Bible is, according to the Hebrew faith: it is "the Book of Yahweh, the Lord."

Implicit in this Hebrew faith are two doctrinal facts. The first is the fact of the twofold authorship of the Bible, by which it has a long series of prophetic men as its human authors and God himself as its one unique Divine Author. Later on, Christians will call it the collection of letters, messages, sent by the heavenly Father to the human family. The second doctrinal fact is called inspiration, the special assistance that God gave to the human authors so that it be really and truly not merely their human words in the speech and literary genres of the time but at the same time his Word, the Word of God, expressed in the words of their particular human discourse. From the catechetical point of view, the divine authorship is the aspect of the Bible that is of primary interest. This is not to disparage academic learning about the human authorship, a learning that contributes greatly to understanding the meaning of the written word; it simply states that the order of catechesis is distinct and has its own nature and purpose and hence the primary interest as stated.[10]

The Depository of Divine Revelation

The nature and purpose of the Bible are clearly visible in the passages that have been presented. It is the written record of the prophetic light received by these chosen personages of Israel, written for the instruction and spiritual welfare of the children of Israel, themselves descended from Abraham, and existing in their entire

personal, family, tribal, and national being on the level of the prophetic light of Revelation.

Like all peoples of human history, this specially chosen people
will have their literature. But it is a literature that is different, indeed
unique, as anyone who studies it in comparison with the literatures
of the Babylonians, the Egyptians, the Greeks, or the Romans readily
observes. It is exactly as different as the Hebrew Prophets are different from the Shamans, Druids, Dervishes, and Medicine Men of the
Gentile nations. It represents a quantum step upward, to use a term
of contemporary Physics, from the viewpoint of religious and moral
quality. Putting this another way and making it more explicit, the
subject matter and the purpose of the Hebrew literature, collected
by its religious authority into the official "Book of the Lord" kept
by the priests at Jerusalem, are both supernatural. It is the official
set of writings that record the facts about the divine plan for the
salvation and the redemption of Man, God's special creation on the
planet Earth. It is fully and completely human: no other literature
is so absolutely honest in reporting the human condition. At the
same time, the Bible is a completely religious book. It originated
with God as its principal author, who used the human writers as his
instruments. Hence it is called the Holy Bible because it is the written form of the prophetic light, formulated in human discourse
both by direct oral address on the part of the Prophets and by oral
tradition in the life of the Chosen People and in the special form
that the human invention of writing has made possible.

It is clear that the written Word of God, together with oral
discourse, exists and functions in the dimension of human proclamation and teaching.[11] It remains to review the doctrinal content
of the Hebrew Revelation, recorded now in the Bible, before continuing to the communication of it as such, namely, the religious education of the Hebrews.

Chapter 4

Divine Revelation and the Schools of the Prophets

The content of divine revealed truth, a content handed on by teaching, came to the Hebrews from their Prophets. It provides the occasion for biblical Catechetics to note several biblical foundations vitally important for the contemporary catechetical apostolate. One must recall Moses' insistence on the deposit to be guarded faithfully under pain of dire punishment. In this chapter the essentials of this content of the Hebrew Revelation are summarized, together with the process of handing them on by the teaching program of the Hebrews.

This handing on of the Revealed Deposit by teaching constitutes the very essence of Catechetics. Thus this chapter makes manifest the nonbiblical character of the approach of the Modernist Heresy in religious education, where the very idea of a Divine Deposit disappears.[1]

These Hebrew foundations, furthermore, provide the biblical basis for the teaching of the Catholic Church that there are two orders of knowledge, one natural to mankind, the other above the natural order because it comes by divine revelation through the Prophets in their prophetic word.[2]

The content of the divine revelation can be summarized in God's self-revelation, in man's Creation and Fall, and in the choice of the two ways.[3] Then the program for teaching this content is identified: the home, the synagogue, and the *Rabbis* or Teachers of the Torah of Moses.

The Self-Revelation of God as "Yahweh," "God-Our-Creator"

As Saint Augustine says, everything in religion depends on the true concept of God. This is the fundamental importance of God's

Self-Revelation when he revealed his sacred Name to Moses: *Yahweh* in Hebrew, *Ego eimi* in Greek, *Ego sum* in Latin, *I am* in English. This holy Name of God, always sacred to the Hebrews, was revealed to Moses from the mysterious bush that he saw burning but not consumed. This miraculous fact that first caught Moses' attention is the key to the meaning of the Divine Name. This Name expresses the special way in which God exists, a way that is different from that of any other existing reality in the universe. It means that God is the self-existent reality: existence itself. Therefore, he always was and always will be. All other realities come into existence. They have a beginning. This beginning depends upon the creative action of the self-existent Supreme Being. All other realities depend upon him in the very order of their existence. An immensely rich mine of knowledge about God, therefore, is opened to mankind by God's self-revelation to Moses.

The Hebrew faith, in other words, professed belief in God, the Father Almighty, Creator of heaven and earth. This of course is the first Article of the Apostles' Creed, the baptismal faith of every Christian. Hence the absolutely basic biblical foundation of catechetical teaching has been identified.

The word *Yahweh* in the Hebrew Scriptures, as a matter of fact established by linguistic science, does indeed convey this meaning. "The root of *Yahweh*," writes Professor Kuhn, "is hajo, and means 'The One Who calls into being,' 'The life-Creator,' 'the Creator,' in fact. *Yahweh* is the old God of primitive monotheism, the oldest God, the Creator and Sustainer of all things; the same God to whom the [oldest] peoples of the world still pray today."[4] Immense perspectives open to research in this way, for science itself is drawing attention to the world-historical significance of the Hebrew Revelation. This Self-Revelation of God is becoming increasingly visible, in the light of the more recent study of religion sketched in chapter 1, as the beginning of the divine plan, conceived in mercy and love, to come to the aid of mankind's moral and religious degeneracy by renewing the original condition of mankind. Vestiges of this condition, as already noted, have been rediscovered in the recent times of Western outreach to the rest of mankind.

For this religious and moral decline that mankind had suffered, and which had only deepened with the cities and their cultural progress toward the fullness of time, was caused fundamentally by the loss of effective knowledge of God among the Gentile peoples. Polytheism was the reverse side of this picture. With it was the loss of the doctrine of creation. The very concept of creation had disappeared in practice, so much so that it could not be recovered by even the most penetrating of the Greek philosophers, Socrates, Plato, and Aristotle themselves. Everywhere the dimming of the true concept of God the Creator had resulted in popular belief in the eternity of matter. In practice, as a consequence, mankind followed the path of earthly desires and temporal advantage: each individual was becoming his own law unto himself.

Seen from the viewpoint of human need for renewal on the basis of God and his Moral Law clearly known and followed as a practical way of life, the blessings for all mankind promised as the purpose of Abraham's call and the Hebrew Covenant become intelligible and definable. The Hebrew people was called forth into existence from Abraham to be God's instrument in communicating this regenerating and renewing knowledge of God, his nature, his plan, and his Moral Law to all the Gentile nations of the earth.

The meaning of the Divine Name revealed to Moses, then, is immensely significant. The concept of God that it implies can be unfolded into a vast body of teaching about the kind of reality God is. The Teachers of the Torah built up this body of teaching, and it was completed and fulfilled by Jesus of Nazareth.

The Hebrew Scriptures, as a matter of fact, can well be looked upon and used to this day as an elaboration and detailed explanation of the meaning of *Yahweh,* the Divine Name that reveals the essential nature and attributes of the Divine Reality in itself. From his uncreated self-existence, his eternity follows, his unicity, his immateriality. The Hebrew Scriptures may be termed a detailed comparison between his unique divine mode of existing and that proper to any creature at all and specifically to that proper to the human mode and condition as seen and experienced in human life on this planet. Thus one can learn to this day from the pages of the Hebrew Scriptures all the statements of truth on what God is *not.* For in point after point he is known to be not like this, not like that. Thus the Hebrews learned from the prophetic word how to cultivate a sense of the transcendence of God, his Divine Mystery.[5]

Man has no direct experience of God's way of existing. Thinking otherwise is the very sin of the Gentiles and the taproot of their decline and fall into pantheism and polytheism. Beyond man's natural knowledge is faith in the nature of the Divine Reality taught by the prophetic Word and aided by careful and sound thinking on how God differs from all creatures.[6]

Let one passage from Psalm 102 stand here for the entire body of the Hebrew Scriptures in their explanation of the meaning of the Divine Name. "Of old Thou didst lay the foundation of the earth," the Psalmist prays, "and the heavens are the work of Thy hands. They shall perish, but Thou shalt endure. Yea, all of them shall wax old like a garment; as a vesture shalt Thou change them, and they shall pass away. But Thou art the self-same, and Thy years shall have no end."

This is the constantly recurring message of the Prophets: God is *Yahweh,* Being Itself, different in mode from all other realities, and the source of whatever reality other beings have. This is an utterly different intellectual world from that of the Gentile peoples, with their man-made gods and their ideas on the eternity of matter, ideas that generate man-centrism and materialism in practical living. This revealed concept of God given in his Self-Revelation is the principle of that qualitative quantum step upward that the Hebrew Revelation represents and offers potentially to all the Gentile peoples as the blessing of Abraham and his seed.[7]

The Creation and Original Sin of Mankind

This leads to the second heading of doctrine in divine revelation, the concept of man that is implied in this new, and rather renewed, concept of God. It is part and parcel of the doctrine of creation that follows logically when God is recognized as Yahweh, the Father Almighty, Creator of heaven and earth, the source of the very existence of all other realities that make up the universe.

Moses, therefore, was careful to see that the Book of Genesis, teaching the origin of creatures, should stand first among the Hebrew Scriptures.[8] "In the beginning God created heaven and earth" (Gen. 1:1). The human literary forms that express God's prophetic word on the origin and nature of all realities other than God are of course those of Moses' time. And the meaning will be the interpretation given by the supreme religious authority commissioned to teach in the name of God from Moses to the present. Here, seeing the matter from within the Hebrew people, the understanding of this prophetic Word will be summarized that has been professed by Israel through the centuries.

"In Babylon," writes Paul Heinisch, "primal matter existed at the beginning, from which the gods arose."[9] It was so likewise in the pagan thinking, both learned and popular, in Egypt, Greece, and Rome. This is the root of Israel's uniqueness. It held by divine revelation the doctrine of the creation of all things out of nothingness by Yahweh in a free divine act, without the use or shaping of any preexisting stuff or matter. The initial verse of the Bible reveals that God called primeval matter into existence from nonexistence. The rest of the Hebrew Scriptures bear witness to this doctrine of creation on almost every page, where the greatness and power of Yahweh's Lordship over creation, his goodness of purpose in creating, and man's priestly place in his creation are themes that constantly recur.[10]

The Angels

The Hebrews always held, furthermore, that God's creation is not limited to this cosmos visible by human sense organs. There is a higher world of spirits, the angels and the demons. The Hebrew Scriptures bear constant witness to this doctrine: "Bless the Lord, ye angels of His, ye mighty in strength, that fulfil His word, hearkening unto the voice of His word. Bless the Lord, all ye His hosts; ye ministers of His, that do His pleasure" (Ps. 103). The Angels are God's Holy Ones: "So shall the heavens praise Thy wonders, O Lord, Thy faithfulness also in the assembly of the holy ones. For who in the skies can be compared unto the Lord . . . a God dreaded in the great council of the holy ones. . . . O Lord God of hosts, Who is a mighty one, like unto Thee, O Lord?" (Ps. 89). This question is the name of Saint Michael the Archangel: *Who is like unto God?*—expecting the answer *No one is like God.* The invisible world is Yahweh's creation; the angels are his creatures.

The Hebrew Revelation knows further that some of these spiritual creatures, invisible to man by nature, fell by sin and became evil persons. They abused their freedom of will by refusing to serve

God according to their created natures. "I will not serve" was the cry of Lucifer, which Saint Michael countered by demanding, "Who is like unto God?"

This moral universe arising from the decisions made by the free will of intelligent creatures extends downward into the visible cosmos because of the particular nature of man. This is the burden of Moses' prophetic teaching on human origins and his account of the Primitive Revelation given to the first human pair, which stands in the Bible as a part of the Hebrew Revelation. Here the vague indications that the modern anthropological sciences piece together are illuminated by the clear and steady religious teaching that derives from the prophetic light.[11]

Human Creaturehood

Man is a creature of God. He is a creature composed of matter, the visible stuff of this cosmos, united with a spiritual element not unlike the reality of the invisible world of the angels: "Israel at all times firmly believed that the soul, when separated from the body, does not cease to exist."[12] "Like modern primitive peoples and like their neighbors in the ancient Orient, the Israelites always firmly believed that after death man in some way continues to live, that the soul after its departure from the body remains in existence. Death was the end of physical life, but not the end of the human personality. At death the body returned to the dust from which it had been taken, while the non-physical element, the ego or person, went to the netherworld, Sheol."[13]

Primitive revelation, furthermore, reveals the physical unity of the human race by its teaching that there was a first couple. But the heart of the entire teaching is that of mankind's participation in the moral universe of the spirit world, with its power of free decision to obey or disobey the Creator. This participation, furthermore, is taught to mankind by the primitive revelation that Moses knows in the prophetic light and records in the Book of Genesis.

Original Sin

It is the teaching of Moses that the first couple freely participated in the sin of the angels.[14] As a result Adam and Eve fell from the state of original justice in which they had been created. They lost their special gifts and graces, and therefore they could not propagate these blessings to their children. Instead, they propagated a fallen nature forward to all generations of mankind. The human family that descends from them, therefore, populating the earth and forming the object of modern anthropological science, is by nature inclined to lose the original true concept of the living and transcendent God and has a nature bent toward disobedience to his law. The fallen state of human nature is prone to personal sins.[15]

Thus sin is a reality throughout the Hebrew Scriptures. This is one of the most biblical foundations of Catechetics.[16] "Because man is a creature," writes Heinisch in summary, "he is duty-bound to obey God; any disregard of this duty involves sin. As shown in the Paradise account, sin is not an imperfection inherent in nature, but a conscious and considered act against God's authority."[17] Jeremiah spoke for all the Prophets when he warned and admonished even this people descended from the Prophet Abraham and set apart from the corrupted Gentile nations: "Thus saith the Lord: Stand ye in the ways and see, and ask for the old paths, wherein is the good way, and walk therein, and ye shall find rest for your souls. But they said: 'We will not walk therein' " (Jer. 6:16). Sin, infidelity to Yahweh, disobedience even to the Torah, his revealed Law, was a reality, and one of the functions of the later Prophets was to recall the Chosen People to the way of justice and restoration of the holiness of Yahweh. Sin is rebellion against Yahweh, the Prophets cried out in alarm, apostasy from Yahweh, contempt for Yahweh, and infidelity to him: it is the violation of the Covenant.[18]

The teaching of the Prophets, furthermore, was clear on the distinctions between sins. There was the division among sins of thought, word, and deed and between those of omission and of commission:

> More important is the distinction between greater and lesser sins. "Faults" and "hidden sins" (cf. Gen. 17:14; Num 9:13; Ps. 19:13) were such as everyone committed from human weakness, from lack of advertence or from inadequate knowledge of the Law. Over against this class were those sins committed "with a high hand" (Num. 15:30), that is, with full deliberation, with malice, with open revolt against God. . . . Grave sins included worship of idols, . . . magic, divination and use of mediums, blasphemy, violation of the Sabbath, . . . observing pagan practices, omitting circumcision; . . . other

transgressions serious enough to be punished by death included murder, rebelling against parents . . . adultery and other serious sins of
impurity, marrying near relatives, certain forms of harlotry, and un-
natural lust.''[19]

Human Freedom: Choosing Between the Two Ways

God, then, is Yahweh, the Almighty, the Creator, and therefore
the Lord of creation and its Lawgiver. Man is his creature, a moral
being. But in his actual condition he is prone to sinful disregard of
his Creator. This leads to the third heading under which the Hebrew
Revelation can be considered, the distinctive and God-given way of
life that their Prophets taught to the Israelites. It is the Way of Life,
contrasting with the Way of Death. It results from a free personal
decision regarding Almighty God in his Lordship. The Book of
Psalms opens with this choice as its theme; "Happy is the man that
hath not walked in the counsel of the wicked, nor stood in the way
of sinners. . . . But his delight is in the Law of the Lord; and in His
Law doth he meditate day and night. And he shall be like a tree
planted by streams of water, that bringeth forth its fruit in its sea-
son. . . . Not so the wicked; but they are like the chaff which the
wind driveth away. Therefore the wicked shall not stand in the judgment, nor sinners in the congregation of the righteous. For the
Lord regardeth the way of the righteous; but the way of the wicked
shall perish'' (Ps. 1).

The Way of Death

The Prophets teach consistently that the Way of Death is that
of the surrounding Gentile people who no longer know the true
and living God. This was the reason that God called Abraham to
come out from among them. The impotent gods of polytheism are
themselves subject to eternal matter and, according to the pagan
thinking, can only shape it this way or that. In practice, each man
thus becomes a law unto himself and indeed unto his fallen self.
He lives as if there were no God, no moral order, no judgment to
come, and no hereafter. The loss of the original faith in God, the

Father Almighty, Creator of heaven and earth, produces the moral swamp of paganism. Each shapes the stuff, the matter, of his own life as if he were God, determining the law by which life is lived.[20] When the Hebrews took up pagan ideas and practices, disregarding the Covenant and the voices of their Prophets, they sang the Rose Song of the Egyptians, losing faith in the immortality of the human soul as a consequence of losing the true concept of the living God. "By chance we have come into existence," the Rose Song sings, "and afterwards we shall be as if we had not been; for the breath in our nostrils is smoke, and thought is a spark begotten by the beat of our heart; when it is extinguished, the body will disintegrate into ashes and the spirit will vanish as thin air" (Wisd. 2:2–3).

The Way of Life

The Hebrew religion, in stark contrast, is the Way of Life, the life of the soul that knows God the Almighty Father and Creator. Such a soul chooses to move toward him as the happy destiny of the blessed.

The basic article of the Hebrew faith, Moses' Shema, which he received with God's Commandments, binds the Israelites to Yahweh in a personal way of faith that unites the prophetic doctrine with human living. "Hear, O Israel: the Lord our God, the Lord is one. And thou shalt love the Lord thy God with all thy heart, and with all thy soul, and with all thy might. And these words, which I command thee this day, shall be upon thy heart; and thou shalt teach them diligently unto thy children, and shalt talk of them when thou sittest in thy house, and when thou walkest by the way, and when thou liest down, and when thou risest up. And thou shalt bind them for a sign upon thy hand, and they shall be for frontlets between thine eyes. And thou shalt write them upon the door-posts of thy house, and upon thy gates" (Deut. 6:4–9).

Such, then, is the way that leads to life. The first of its duties is faith in Yahweh by means of his Word, which comes through his Prophets. Abraham was a man of firm faith in God, the model for each person of the People of God descended from him.[21] And the first element or article of this faith is to recognize Yahweh as the Father Almighty, the Creator, and therefore to embrace one's own creaturehood, with all its implications of dependence upon the Supreme Being and duty to serve Him by keeping his natural Moral Law. Thus prayer becomes man's first duty, and pleading any earthly excuse for omitting it is the greatest offense to God. The Hebrews, accordingly, have always been a people faithful to the practice of personal prayer unless individuals fall away from their election.

The way of life that recognizes creaturehood willingly accepts the basic laws of life from the Creator, making the Ten Commandments its own and fulfilling by means of them the command of the Shema to love God above all else.

Finally, based on the doctrine on God contained in the meaning of the Divine Name, there was the public worship by the sacrifices, only at the great Temple in Jerusalem, of the Hebrew liturgical calendar. Moses' Book of Leviticus stands in the Scriptures as the detailed prophetical instructions for this continuation of mankind's original mode of worship of God by sacrifice. Sacrifice is a religious ritual by which creatures recognize the rights of the Creator over creaturehood as such.[22] "The major theme of this Book," writes Rabbi Gutstein in his introduction, "is the sanctification of human life. Holiness is a principle regulating every sphere of human life and activity, and governs the body as well as the soul. . . . The concept of holiness in *Leviticus* is unique, inasmuch as it is based on ethical standards, such as purity of life, cleanliness of thought and moral conduct."[23]

Religious Education Among the Hebrews

The fact that this Hebrew people, called into being from the Prophet Abraham, living by the religion given by God through Moses, his Prophet, has endured into the twenty-first century and undertaken its great return to Palestine in the second half of the twentieth century is one of the wonders of universal history. How did it take place? What, from the natural point of view of a people or nation living in history, is its secret? "The survival of the Jews and Judaism," writes Rabbi Julius B. Maller, "is in a large measure due to the continuous emphasis, throughout Jewish history, upon the transmission of ideas and practices from old to young and from one generation to another.''[24] This brings religious education to the center of the stage. The Hebrew people has had a most remarkable system and practice of religious education. Called into being to hear the revealed Word of God, it responded by handing this Divine Revelation forward as the very substance of Jewish national life.

A Teaching of the Prophetic Word

One should be very clear at this point. From the outset, even in the few texts cited earlier, it is evident that the Hebrew Prophets proclaimed and taught a doctrine. It is difficult to find even traces in the Hebrew Scriptures of descriptions of emotional experiencings that the Prophets may or may not have had as they received the prophetic light and heard the prophetic Word of God. They did not give descriptions of emotional states or varieties of religious experience, urging their hearers to evoke similar experiences. The Hebrew Scriptures bear witness to something quite different. The Prophets were men called in a special way to receive a new and higher kind of light into their understanding. It was this insight and understanding, representing an order of knowledge above the ordinary and naturally human one of their fellowmen, that they communicated to them, not in some new language or mode, but in their ordinary human discourse. Thus their fellowmen, by hearing the words of the Prophets and receiving them not as mere human words but really and truly as the Word of God, gained access to this same prophetic light with its higher order of insight and under-standing. As noted earlier, this prophetic message was entirely con-cerned with accurate knowledge about the kind of being Yahweh is, what kind of being man is, and what practical response man ought to make in his way of living so as to choose the Way of Life and achieve happily his final and everlasting destiny.[25] The mode by which the new knowledge is communicated is fully human, indeed specifically human. It makes use of the words of human speech to reach man's intelligence and power of free decision, the very ele-ments that distinguish man as a species among the higher organisms of the planet Earth.

Not Religious Experience but Religious Doctrines

Divine Revelation, then, comes from God to the Hebrews, the people descended from the Prophet Abraham, as a doctrine given them by their Prophets. This doctrine is therefore quite different in origin, content, and mode from the doctrines that the Gentile nations live by and hand on to their young as their respective social heritages. This doctrine is not a human discovery, whether empirical or philosphical, but the Word of God to man from above. It is truth that is revealed. It is fundamentally a participation in God's own knowledge of himself, of the purpose he had in mind when creating man, and of the plan he has for the destiny of mankind. This truth is given to man in the form in which man understands truth, namely, in the judgments of the mind that human speech expresses. Thus the Word of God enters into human social communication, human social life, and can be handed on as a doctrine that is taught, that is learned, that is applied in personal and social living, and that forms the distinctive social heritage of the Hebrew people.[26]

The Hebrews, in other words, can indeed have their own distinctive educational system, like other peoples on the human scene. Its mode will be that of religious education, for the content and the purpose of the teaching will be the communication of this revealed religious doctrine. This is exactly what has taken place. The Hebrew people possesses the original model of a religious education that teaches the revealed Word of God. This religious education is the secret of the survival of the Jewish people into this present century with its drama of the Great Return to Palestine.

Family-Centered Religious Education

The first step in understanding this religious education is to recognize that it is a form of instruction that is fully human in its mode. But it has no mere abstract or speculative purpose, as if it were a Gentile philosophy. Its purpose is one of practical formation, by which each Hebrew takes up Divine Revelation as his personal way of life.

Since it is an instruction that is a formation unto the revealed Way of Life, it is only natural that the Hebrew home was the chief instrument or "method" for teaching the Prophetic Word. The *natural* foundation of human birth and maturation takes place among the Hebrews in the light of this *supernatural* doctrine that God has given them by speaking through his Prophets. In this religious education, from the distant beginnings with Abraham and Moses to the present, the parents are the primary educators and the preschool years of the child are given first importance. "If we do not keep our children to religion when they are young," the Rabbis constantly taught, "we shall certainly not be able to do so in later years."[27] "If anyone should question one of us Jews concerning our laws," Josephus writes, "he would more easily repeat them all than his own name; since we learn them from our first consciousness, we have them as it were engraven on our souls."[28] Philo, writing in Alexandria several centuries before Christ, is equally clear: "Since Jews esteem their laws as divine revelations, and are instructed in the knowledge of them from their earliest youth, they bear the image of the Law in their souls. . . . They are taught, so to speak, from their swaddling clothes by their parents, by their teachers, and by those who bring them up, even before instruction in the Sacred Law and in the unwritten customs, to believe in God, the one Father and Creator of the world."[29] This is of course instruction regarding the Reality of Yahweh, the meaning of the revealed Name of God. It is what Christians call the First Article of the Creed, taken for granted in earlier times but demanding new and special attention in the contemporary problematic.

"It is the duty of the father," writes Rabbi S. Schechter, "to begin to initiate the child into the great truths from his fourth year, for life and religion begin when the child can speak distinctly."[30]

Jewish home life, the interior decorations, and the domestic participation in the great Jewish liturgical festivals form a powerfully effective methodology of formation for the young. Let the Mezuzah illustrate all these instruments of religious education. Each doorpost had to have attached this small cylindrical box of olive wood containing a parchment scroll lettered with twenty-two lines of Deuteronomy, 6:4–9 and 11:13–21. These contain the Shema, the basic article of the Hebrew Faith in the Prophetic Word, and repeat the name of God ten times. A circular opening on the side was prescribed, with the scroll rolled and inserted so that the words "The

Almighty'' were visible through it. Everyone touches it when passing, kisses his finger, and pauses in prayer. "It is clear," Prof. William Barclay writes with the insight of a parent, "how the youngest child would notice this *Mezuzah* and would ask what it meant."[31]

In general, then, the children were formed in the light of revealed doctrine unto the Jewish way of life. Children kept the Sabbath week by week, even though not bound to do so, learning all the time, and memorizing, as soon as they could speak, fundamental statements of the Jewish faith, such as Deuteronomy 6:4 and 33:4. "In no other religion," concluded Epstein, "has the duty of parents to instruct their children been more stressed than in Judaism."[32] Long before he reached school age, the child was learning every day what it is to be a Jew. Each child did so by coming to know the body of truths taught by the Hebrew Revelation.[33]

The Synagogues and Their Schools

What, then, of schooling among the Hebrews? "In the preexilic days of Jewish history," writes Barclay, "there is no trace of schools at all."[34] The homes were the sole instrument of this religious education, and there is no trace of formal schooling for secular purposes. The children are prepared by their parents for moral and religious living, and the instruction is a formation that develops character.[35]

The Schools of the Prophets

Throughout preexilic times, as noted earlier above in the case of Samuel, boys were sent to the Prophets for special religious studies. There were "Schools of Prophets" and divisive conflicts over the truth in religion, visible, for instance, in the account of Elijah's triumph over the prophets of Baal:

> Ahab the King said unto Elijah: "Is it thou, thou troubler of Israel?" And he answered: "I have not troubled Israel, but thou, and thy father's house, in that ye have forsaken the commandments of the Lord, and thou hast followed the Baalim. Now therefore send, and

gather to me all Israel unto Mount Carmel, and the prophets of Baal
four hundred and fifty. . . . . And Ahab sent unto all the children of
Israel, and gathered the prophets together unto Mount Carmel. And
Elijah came near unto all the people, and said: "How long halt ye
between two opinions? If the Lord be God, follow Him; but if Baal,
follow him." And the people answered him not a word. Then said
Elijah unto the people: "I, even I only, am left a prophet of the Lord;
but Baal's prophets are four hundred and fifty men." (1 Kings
18:16–22)

This dramatic incident illustrates the fact that the teaching program of the Hebrews grows directly out of the presence of the
Prophets, who were ministering to the homes. The Hebrew heritage
has never departed from this fundamental approach in religious
education. To the present day the Hebrew school functions as an
auxiliary to the home.[36]

The Synagogues and Synagogue-Schools

The Hebrew school arose after the destruction of the first Temple at Jerusalem by Babylon. As a result of the national need in
the dispersion that resulted, the synagogue was developed as the
institution that became henceforward the hallmark of Jewish national life. Wherever Jewish communities could muster ten men with
the leisure as well as the ability to carry on a program of prayer and
instruction, such a "House of the People" could be founded. All
sacrifices were confined to the Temple at Jerusalem, of course, and
the synagogue never was conceived to be a "temple." Its function
was prayer and instruction in the Torah and the Prophets. "It is safe
to say," writes Rabbi Simon Greenberg, "that element of instruction
played at least as great a part in the founding of the Synagogue as
did prayer. . . . Unique and specifically educational features are an
integral part of it to our own day. . . . The Synagogue building has
always been a center of study for either children or adults . . . and
next to the home the Synagogue has been the most significant educational agency in the life of the Jewish people."[37]

Henri Daniel-Rops states a valid Christian insight into the nature and function of the synagogue. "The importance of the Synagogue," he writes, "and what it stood for in the life of Israel at the

time of Christ cannot be over-estimated. What the town-hall and the church were for the medieval town, the Synagogue was for the Jews. Everybody, without exception, went to the Synagogue, not only for the services, but also for all administrative and judicial business."[38]

The synagogue spread rapidly after the Babylonian Captivity throughout all Judaism, both in Palestine and in the Diaspora. "It is said," Barclay summarizes, "that in Jerusalem there were 480 Synagogues, and that each of them had a school."[39]

Always and everywhere, the synagogue is a holy place consecrated to Yahweh and his Word. At the south end of each synagogue building a movable Ark was placed, containing the sacred books of the Torah and the Prophets, and beside it a holy lamp was kept burning constantly, "in imitation of the undying light in the Temple of Jerusalem."[40] "To the Jew," writes Alfred Edersheim, "the Synagogue was the bond of union throughout the world. There they met to read, from the same Lectionary, the same Scripture lessons which their brethren read throughout the world, and to say, in the words of the same liturgy, their common prayers, catching echoes of the gorgeous Temple-services in Jerusalem. . . . Here the stranger Jew . . . finds himself at home: the same arrangements as in his own land, and the well-known services and prayers."[41]

The Hebrew school has been a part of the synagogue throughout history, functioning either within it or in an adjoining building. After the Babylonian Captivity the role of the Prophet recedes and that of the teacher or scribe increases: "Education was stressed as never before, and its function was entrusted to the scribe."[42] As the word indicates, a "scribe" was simply an educated person, able to command reading and writing. The common form of address for synagogue officials was *Rabbi*, the Hebrew word meaning "teacher."

The Content, Method, and Purpose of the Hebrew School

Biblical Catechetics discovers an important new light as the nature and purpose of the Holy Bible in the fact that it was the chief didactic instrument and the source of doctrinal content in the Hebrew schools on all levels. Perhaps this practical use in forming

the Hebrews into the Chosen People of God was the original motivation of Moses and the Prophets in consigning their revealed teaching to writing. In any case, the fact is clear: whether among children
and youth or on the distinctive and highly specialized level of higher
education, schooling among the Hebrews was entirely devoted to
the written Word of God: "There was only one text-book, and that
was the Scriptures. The very name of the school was *Beth Ha Sepher,*
'The House of the Book.' "[43] At age six or seven every child had to
go to the synagogue school. In the primary years to age ten, the
child learned to read, to write, and to study the text of Scripture
directly. From ten to about fifteen, the youth studied the oral traditions of interpretation of the Sacred Text. The basic minimum that
every Jewish child was expected to master, to understand comprehensively, and then to know by heart were the Shema (Deut. 6:4),
the foundation of the Jewish creed that begins every morning service in the synagogues to this day; the Hallel, the Psalms of Praise
to God (Ps. 113–18) recited in liturgical worship, especially in the
Passover ritual; the account of Creation (Genesis 1–5); and the essence of the Priestly Law (Leviticus 1–8). These are the essentials
of the Hebrew religion.[44] It was a schooling unto familiarity with
Yahweh, what he had done for his people, and how he should be
obeyed in life and worshiped in prayer. Hebrew girls were prepared
for the life of the home, which continued to be the chief instrument
of this religious education and all Jewish boys had to be ready for
their years in the synagogue, for any adult male Jews might be called
upon to read the lessons of Scripture.[45]

What was the method of this religious education? It used what
the culture of the day had developed: oral discourse, explanation,
questioning and the hearing of answers, discussions, examples, ap-
plications to instances, and cases from life. This method was entirely
devoted to the content, the Bible, so that the Word of God might
be understood better and applied more faithfully as a practical way
of life. Doctrine and life among the Hebrews formed one integrated
reality in which the doctrine is the means by which the life is formed
and achieved.

The pattern of the teaching was fourfold. First, there was the
doctrine itself, that our God is Yahweh, our Lord, the Father Almighty, Creator of heaven and earth. The three areas of personal
response and application to life: personal prayer, the Moral Law,

and worship of God by the calendar and ritual that Moses had established, including the sacrifices, culminating in the annual celebration of the Passover.[46]

And the purpose? "The very basis of Judaism is to be found in the conception of holiness. It was the destiny of the Jewish people to be different—and 'Holiness means the difference.' "[47] It is simply education for God, for knowing him as he revealed himself to the Prophets and for living accordingly. "Be holy, for I, Yahweh your God, am holy" (Lev. 19:2). "You must make yourselves holy, for I am Yahweh, your God" (Lev. 20:7). "Be consecrated to me, because I, Yahweh, am holy, and I will set you apart from all these peoples so that you may be mine" (Lev. 20:26)[48]

The Rabbi or Teacher of The Word of God

Every teaching process on the human scene must have teachers, the persons who apply the content and method so as to achieve the purpose. The Hebrews were no different from the other peoples of mankind, except in the fact that the Teacher among them occupied perhaps a higher type of social recognition than that even among the culturally advanced Gentile peoples.

The Teacher in Classical Greece and Rome

Throughout classical antiquity the teacher held the position of greatest respect among all civic and social leaders. The word *didáskalos* among the Greeks "is attested in the sense of 'teacher' from the time . . . of Homer. . . . From the very first it tends to become technical in the sense of 'Master of Instruction.'. . . . The *didśkalos* is not just a teacher in general, but a man who teaches definite skills like reading, fighting or music, developing aptitudes already present."[49] "Didaskein," writes Karl Heinrich Rengstorf, "denotes 'teaching' or 'instructing' in the widest sense, . . . and the word comes increasingly to have technical significance for the Greek-speaking Jews. . . . In the Septuagint, the concern is with the whole man and his education in the deepest sense. Nevertheless, this does not mean that there is any final isolation of the Old Testament from secular *didaskein*. There is always the common link that the object of instruction is everywhere envisaged as in some way the goal."[50]

The object of instruction among the Greeks was the many-branched liberal studies of the *paidéia,* producing the man cultivated in secular learning and worldly pursuits. The *Rabbi* or teacher in Israel had a different object of instruction. Philo of Alexandria was keenly aware of this when he called Moses a *didáskalos aletheías,* a Teacher of the Truth.[51] The object of instruction among the Hebrews is the Word of God communicated to them by the words of the Prophets.

The Rabbi in Israel

It follows that the Rabbi or Teacher in Israel held the highest social position. "The Law was everything," writes Barclay, "and therefore the expounder of the Law was the greatest man in the community."[52] *Rabbi* was the term of address that denoted the greatest respect. The root of the word *Rabbi* means "great," "great one," or "most highly honored person." After the Babylonian Captivity it came to mean simply "teacher" and was regularly translated by the Greek word *didáskalos* in the Hebrew Diaspora.[53] The synagogue officials who instructed the children, on a level of schooling that corresponded to the elementary and the secondary today were commonly addressed as "Rabbi," and the Talmudic traditions indicate what the term signified for the Hebrews: "Respect for a teacher should exceed respect for the father, for both father and son owe respect to a teacher. . . . A man's father only brought him into this world, whereas his teacher, who taught him wisdom, brings him into the life of the world to come. . . . A teacher must be like an angel from heaven, for only then can the Word of God come out of his mouth."[54]

Rabbinical Higher Education

In its most proper and fullest sense, however, the term *Rabbi* was applied in Israel to teachers on the level of higher education. These were men who devoted their entire lives to the study of Moses and the Prophets. A young man who wished to become a Rabbi attached himself to an established Rabbi and became his *mathetēs,* seeking admission to the Rabbi's group of disciples, his full-time students.[55] One of the most familiar sights of postexilic Palestine was this universal phenomenon of Jewish life, the mature Rabbi, going from synagogue to synagogue with his group of disciples constantly in his company. These Rabbis became well known and were in great demand at the synagogues, for the arrival of a Teacher renowned in Israel meant an opportunity for an attractive and beneficial guest lecture. Clearly Jesus will follow this national pattern with his Twelve Apostles, a set of *mathetēs* according to the universal custom of his people.

In its human pattern, higher education among the Hebrews followed the system that was universal in classical antiquity: that of a Master Teacher (the *Didaskalos* or *Magister* in Latin) surrounded by his group of *mathetēs* or *discipuli*: the Rabbi or Teacher with his disciples. One need but think of Plato's "Academy," the group of his disciples who met with him in the grove of Academe near Athens, or of Aristotle's *peripatetics*—the students who walked with him during his teaching. These were but the most famous and best-known instances of the universal pattern, that of the Teacher surrounded by, going about with, his formally recognized group of disciples who were studying to become teachers themselves.

Among the Greeks, *mathetēs,* "disciple," is "the usual word for 'apprentice.' "[56] "The education (of the *mathetēs*) consists in the appropriation or adoption of specific knowledge or conduct, . . . [and] proceeds deliberately and according to a set plan. There is no *mathetēs* without a *didáskalos*. The process involves a corresponding personal relation."[57] All antiquity knew this *didáskalos-mathetēs* relationship, whether in philosophical or in religious culture. When the teachers achieved great fame, when the cause they advocated and the doctrine they presented had continuing personal interest and social significance, abiding "schools" grew classic example, and so, too, the Peripatetics and Stoics and religious traditions such as the "schools" of the Pythagoreans, the Epicureans, and many others in the Classical culture. "The groups which assembled around the great philosophical teachers of antiquity," writes Rengstorf, "were much too solidly established to disintegrate when the teachers died."[58] Rengstorf places the reason for this accurately in what he calls "the principle of tradition." The *mathetēs* or disciple remained "inwardly committed" to his Teacher. "Outward expression of this is to be found in a principle which controlled the whole life and work of the fellowships. This can best be called the principle of tradition. At issue here is that the intentions of a master should be cultivated and his sayings carefully presented and transmitted. The principle is to be found everywhere up to and beyond the time of the New Testament."[59]

It is this common human pattern for higher education in antiquity that the Hebrews followed. Their Teachers, called Rabbis in their own language, functioned according to the universal custom for the time: they gathered about them groups of full-time students (as the twenty-first century would say) who desired to take up the calling of Rabbi themselves and to learn a mastery of the knowledge that was prerequisite.[60] The Hebrew Rabbinate, however, as Rengstorf hastens to point out, had only an exterior or formal likeness to the prevailing cultural pattern:

> The Greek form . . . is not simply taken over as it stands. It is integrated into the central concern of Judaism, that is, concern for the Torah. . . . In Rabbinic teaching, though the individual teacher has an important place, the dominating element is the Torah. In the form controlled by the prominence of tradition this means that Moses is the starting-point and absolute teacher. Rabbinic Judaism is a conscious Mosaism. The authority of the Torah and the tradition contained in it may be seen in the fact that it limits the authority of the individual *Rabbis*. Since the Torah was given to Israel through the mediation of Moses, . . . the decisive point for individual *Rabbis* is to be in agreement with Moses.[61]

The preparation of Rabbis, the very essence of Higher Education, was a Hebrew concern from the time of Moses: "And the Lord commanded me at that time to teach you statutes and ordinances, that ye might do them in the land whither ye go over to possess it" (Deut. 4:14). The formation of a group of future Rabbis by a Master Rabbi was always a preoccupation with the Torah as revealed truth, and the instruction was always the practical one of knowing and doing this revealed Will of God. Thus the younger men were trained to be leaders in the community by virtue of their ability to teach the Torah themselves, forming the entire community into a people versed in divine revelation.

The course of study was lengthy and quite specific. The Rabbis reported in ancient times that the disciples devoted five years to the Divine Scriptures themselves and then upward of fifteen to twenty-five additional years to mastering, always under their own Rabbi, the traditional body of oral explanation and application of the Scriptures called the Mishnah, the Midrash, and the Talmud.[62] "In Rabbinical teaching both teacher and pupil sat. The teacher lectured, with an opportunity for questions . . . [which] opened up a discussion in which others took part. . . . Rabbinical rulings make it plain that the only task of the disciple was to acquire knowledge from his teacher, though not without critical reflection. . . . All Rabbinical listening stands in an ultimate relation to Scripture. But the *Rabbi* is the instrument to make possible for the disciple the right hearing [of the Word of God] which is his concern."[63]

A full-fledged system of higher education, therefore, had developed among the Hebrews, with Master Teachers accredited by public recognition and the use of the formal term *Rabbi*. It was completely human in mode, matching the *paidéia* of the surrounding Gentile world with its *didáskaloi*. But its content and purpose were quite different: it taught a divine wisdom that produced the divinely revealed Way of Life, for its content was the Deposit of Faith, the revealed Word of God that Moses and the Prophets had communicated to the Chosen People descended from Abraham. "Although according to tradition the men of the Great Synagogue [these *Rabbis* of higher education] received the Torah from the Prophets, they themselves were naturally not prophets. . . . The earliest dictum specific to them, namely, 'Be moderate in judgment, raise up many disciples, and make a fence around the Torah,' indicates their concern."[64] It was the concern to hand on this precious Deposit of Divine Truth by their teaching.

Conclusion

Religious Education among the Hebrews is clearly a ministry to elevated and enlightened personal living. It forms persons of God, who combine in life together as the People of God. But does the purpose extend beyond individual persons? In living the life that the Word of God inspires were the Hebrews conscious of contributing to a divine plan for the Hebrew people as a whole? Were they as a People of God oriented toward the future? They were indeed. It remains to consider this further aspect of the Hebrew Revelation.

Chapter 5

The Promises of God, Teacher of Mankind

Biblical Catechetics, the first and fundamental branch of catechetical studies, clarifies here three further basic foundations of Catechetics. The first is the fact that God himself is the Teacher of mankind.
The second is the fact that God taught the Hebrew people to expect
"the Coming One," a prophet like unto Moses, who would be specially anointed by God as the Savior of mankind. The very name of
"Jesus Christ," therefore, upon whom the Christian Revelation will
center, is an integral part of the Hebrew Revelation. Thus the Name
of Jesus Christ is one of the most important and illuminating among
all the biblical foundations of Catechetics. Third, the Prophets
taught the Chosen People to expect this coming Savior to be himself
this Teacher of mankind. These concepts give substance and orientation to every CCD catechism lesson and to every class of Christian
Doctrine in Catholic schools. The purpose of this chapter is to link
these three biblical foundations of Catechetics with the Hebrew Revelation.

The Prophet Isaiah provides this chapter with its theme, the fact
of the Messianic Expectation among the Hebrews, and the strange
further fact that there were two totally opposed interpretations of
the divine teaching in this regard that make it possible to read the
Gospels with understanding and to teach Christian Doctrine with
authenticity and spiritual effectiveness. "Thus saith the Lord, thy
Redeemer, the Holy One of Israel: I am the Lord thy God, who
teacheth thee for thy profit, Who leadeth thee by the way that thou
shouldst go. Oh that thou wouldest hearken to My commandments!
Then would thy peace be as a river, and thy righteousness as the
waves of the sea" (Is. 48:17–18).[1]

The Psalms abound in references to God as the Teacher of his
people. For example: "Ye fools, when will ye understand? He that

planted the ear, shall He not hear? He that formed the eye, shall He not see? He that instructeth nations, shall He not correct, even He that teacheth man knowledge? The Lord knoweth the thoughts of man, that they are vanity. Happy is the man whom Thou instructest, O Lord, and teachest out of Thy Law" (Ps. 94:8–12). This is the context of the divine teaching of the Messianic Expectation: it will not be according to "the thoughts of man." Hence one must be on guard, then and now, in its hermeneutics or interpretation. It is this that Jesus will explain to his followers on the road to Emmaus and in the Upper Room; see Luke 24:13–53.

The idea of "promises" and a "Messianic Expectation" introduce the divine foreknowledge in which his authentic Prophets mysteriously share. Mankind always has sought to know the future. Hence magical practices, cults, divination, and astrology always have abounded in the paganism of antiquity and in the neo-paganism of today. For the Hebrews, all participation in these heathen efforts to know future contingencies in order to plan one's life was forbidden.[2] The Prophets had the true teaching about the future, and this was sufficient.[3]

The Lord of History

God does indeed know the future.[4] His divine knowledge reaches from end to end of His creation, mightily. Yahweh is the Father Almighty. He orders all things, watching over his creation, exercising a universal Providence as the Heavenly Father. It is but a short step in the Hebrew Revelation about God from his Lordship over Creation to him as the Lord of history, the personal histories of individuals, and the great world history of the peoples and nations. The Hebrews learned this almighty power of God over the contingent events of human history during their Passover from their slavery in Egypt. This is the meaning of "The Song of Moses" in chapter 15 of the Book of Exodus: "I will sing unto the Lord, for He is highly exalted. . . . The Lord is my strength . . . and is become my salvation. . . . Who is like Thee, O Lord, among the mighty? Who is like unto Thee, glorious in holiness, fearful in praises, doing wonders? . . . By the greatness of Thine arm they are still as a stone, till Thy people pass over, O Lord."

The Gentile peoples of the whole world and the entire past were religious: they worshiped the Lord of Creation with its sun and moon and stars and the temporal patterns that result from their regular movements. Part of this creation was the seasonal growth of things, the fertility for life, the times for seeding, and the times for harvesting. All this was recognized and acknowledged, dimly and pantheistically, in the nature worship of the pagan religions. The Hebrews purified all this, relating it to Yahweh, God-the-Creator, but added a new dimension, that of God's Lordship over history.

It is fundamental to the Hebrew Revelation that God has a plan in creating, and that this plan operates in the historical unfolding and development of his creation. At the very heart of this plan is the degenerate religious condition of mankind: it is his divine purpose in calling Israel, his Chosen People, into existence upon this planet among all the peoples and nations. God's plan takes place in human history on this earth; he revealed its essential features to his Prophets. Thus there is indeed a knowledge of the future in Israel; it lies at the very heart of the truth that Yahweh, the Divine Teacher, communicated to his People through his Prophets. But it is a different kind of foreknowledge than that which the pagans sought by their magical practices, for it relates to the eternal salvation of persons rather than purposes of temporal life on earth.

God's Plan for the Redemption of Mankind

What was this knowledge of God's plan, embracing past, present, and future on this earth?

As the background for the answer to this question the relationship of the Hebrews to the surrounding Gentile peoples must be considered. In direct comparison with the abject religious and moral condition of the pagan nations, the Hebrew People does indeed represent a qualitative step upward. From Abraham's call they were set apart, and the divine quality of their revealed religion made the difference. At the same time, from the objective point of view, this revealed religion was not given to the Hebrews in a finished and perfected state.[5] From the subjective point of view, furthermore, the sinful tendencies of human nature were operating among the Hebrews just as they were among the Gentiles. Hence the sinfulness that so often surfaces in the pages of the Scriptures, including a way particular to the Hebrews, that of the sin of infidelity to Yahweh in his Covenant. Were the Prophets not constantly striving to recall the Chosen People to penance and fidelity to the Torah?[6]

Thus Jews and Gentiles alike had a deep need for an improvement in their religious situation. They both needed true redemption, namely, liberation from sin and proneness to sin. This is what God planned to effect in the future. In general, his plan goes under the religious term of *the Redemption*, which, with "the Incarnation," will comprise the fundamental teachings of Christian Doctrine. God's plan was concerned with the redemption of mankind from this situation of sinfulness and actual sin. It was in this context that the Hebrew Revelation taught the Chosen People descended from Abraham about the future. Only God could give this teaching, because it involves the future contingencies of human history known to him alone.

This teaching about the divine plan of redemption, which gives the Holy Bible its unity, can be summarized under the following three major headings.

First: The Preparatory Testament of Moses

The Hebrew Revelation taught clearly the nature and purpose of God's call to Abraham and therefore of the entire people that issued from him. Abraham is to be a blessing for all the nations.[7] The Hebrew calling is not for the benefit of their own people alone but for all mankind. Since the root of mankind's misery is in the lack of the true knowledge of God, somehow Israel is to give the revealed concept of Yahweh, God-the-Creator, to the rest of the peoples of the earth: "In God's good Providence Israeli religion was to become the common heirloom of mankind: in time all peoples must turn to the God worshipped on Sion. It was for this mission that Israel was chosen, and for this same reason God raised up Prophets in her midst."[8]

Somehow, then, there was to be in the future a mission of teaching to all the Gentile peoples of the earth, so that they would turn away from their corrupted way of life and moral abominations, by turning to the one true God of the Hebrew Revelation. The

Hebrews understood clearly from the prophetic word that their dispensation of that time, Moses' Covenant, was a temporary and transitory one, preparing for that outreach to the rest of the peoples of the world that would make them that "Light to the Gentiles" of which the Prophet Isaiah spoke: "I will also give thee for a light of the nations, that My salvation may be unto the end of the earth" (Is. 49:6, Masoretic).

Moses' Covenant or Testament, therefore, bound Abraham's people to the God of Revelation to be the bearer of his revealed truth and way of life, to be "the People of the Book," the Holy Bible, until the time came for this teaching mission to the Gentiles. It was a preparatory Covenant. The future extension of God's Self-Revelation and his moral regeneration and renewal to the Gentile peoples will be the work of "the Coming One" and will be predicated upon a new Covenant or Testament sealed with a new Sacrifice to be offered in every place and not in the one place, the national shrine or Temple at Jerusalem. The Hebrews knew this from their Prophet Malachi: "For from the rising of the sun even until the going down of the same My name is great among the nations; and in every place offerings are presented unto My name, even pure oblations; for My name is great among the nations, saith the Lord of hosts" (Mal. 1:11, Masoretic).

How was so far-reaching a transformation of their national life and its worship to be accomplished? The Hebrews could not know. They had to continue their preparatory way quietly and prayerfully, trusting God to make things clear through his Prophets as time went on. The fact is, however, that they knew the temporary character of their preparatory Covenant. This is so essential to the development of the Messianic Expectation among the Hebrews that it well deserves a special study beyond the scope of these pages.[9] One passage from Jeremiah may stand here as an example of the teaching that filled the mind of the Chosen People and contributed toward their mounting Messianic Expectation:

> Behold, the days come, saith the Lord, that I will make a new convenant with the house of Israel and with the house of Judah; not according to the covenant that I made with their fathers in the day that I took them by the hand to bring them out of the land of Egypt; for as much as they broke My covenant, although I was a lord over them,

saith the Lord. But this is the covenant that I will make with the house of Israel. After those days, saith the Lord, I will put my Law in their inward parts, and in their heart will I write it; and I will be their God, and they shall be My people; and they shall teach no more every man his neighbour, and every man his brother, saying: "Know the Lord," for they shall all know Me, from the least of them unto the greatest of them, saith the Lord; for I will forgive their iniquity, and their sin will I remember no more. (Jer. 31:31–34)

Immense perspectives open up in God's promises for the future. Who will explain the precise manner of their fulfillment? The way lies open to merely human hermeneutics or interpretation, a matter that will recur later. Many members of the Chosen People, however, reserved judgment, awaiting the future teaching of an authentic and true Prophet of God to explain it all. They could see, however, and very many did see, that the New Testament to come was to be concerned with the forgiveness of sin and the internal regeneration and renewal of each human person, for this is the teaching that their Prophets gave to them; Jeremiah speaks for them all.

In general, then, the Hebrews understood clearly from the prophetic word that their present dispensation, Moses' Covenant on Mount Sinai, was preparatory. It prepared the way for a Coming One who would teach them all these things when the time came. He would be like unto Moses in that he would be the Lawgiver of this expected new and final Covenant or Testament with mankind. Everything turned about this second component of their Messianic Expectation, the anticipation of this Coming One in future history. This hope sustained the Hebrews in the vicissitudes of their natural life and gave them their unique orientation in thought toward the historical future.

Second: The Coming One, the Expected Messiah

With this second heading in the summary of God's revealed teaching on his plan for the redemption of mankind the Redeemer himself comes before the mind as the very center of the unity of the Holy Bible. "Catechesis must necessarily be Christocentric."[10]

We have here, therefore, perhaps the most important of the biblical foundations of Catechetics. For it is this perception of the Coming One, the Messiah of the Jewish Expectation, the gradual unveiling of his names, functions, and relationship to this future Testament, that pervades the Hebrew Scriptures and unites these writings from beginning to end.

In the first place, it is basic to recognize that the Hebrews were taught by Moses himself to expect an immensely great Prophet to come sometime in their historical future, the One for whom their people are to prepare by means of Moses' Covenant and its renewed moral life. Moses writes:

> When thou art come into the land which the Lord thy God giveth thee, thou shalt not learn to do after the abominations of those nations. There shall not be found among you any one that maketh his son or his daughter to pass through the fire, one that useth divination, a soothsayer, or an enchanter, or a sorcerer, or a charmer, or one that consulteth a ghost or a familiar spirit, or a necromancer. . . . A prophet will the Lord thy God raise up unto thee, from the midst of thee, or thy brethren, like unto me; unto him shall you hearken. . . . And the Lord said unto me: I will raise them up a prophet from among their brethren, like unto thee; and I will put My words into his mouth, and he shall speak unto them all that I shall command him. And it shall come to pass, that whosoever will not hearken to My words which he shall speak in My name, I will require it of him. (Deut. 18:9–19, Masoretic)

With these words Moses, speaking out of the Prophetic Light, gives his people to understand that the Prophet like unto himself is the one to whom they are to listen in learning the nature of his new Testament, of its new sacrificial worship, of the Kingdom of God that it will establish, and of all similar matters. Moses warns, furthermore, that failure in this matter of the Messianic Expectation will draw down the punishment of the Almighty.

In the second place, therefore, there are the questions about the nature of this Messiah or Coming One and of the Kingdom of God that this mighty Prophet, on the level of Moses as the founder of a Covenant or Testament, will accomplish. What did the Hebrews believe about the Coming One, on the basis of indications in the writings of their own Prophets? To begin, they believed that he would be especially anointed by God in order to accomplish the redemption of mankind mentioned earlier. Because of this anointing the Hebrews came to think and to speak of him and indeed to name him as the Messiah, the Anointed One.[11] Since one encounters the name of Jesus Christ, so familiar to Christians, itself an important biblical foundation of Catechetics, at this point, it is well to hear a recognized specialist in these matters. Heinisch writes:

> The Hebrew word *masiah* (*mesiha* in Aramaic and grecized *messias*) signifies *anointed*, even as does the Greek word *Christos*. Through anointing with oil persons and things were consecrated and separated from profane use; and a special efficacy accrued to them. The high priest was anointed (Exod. 29:7; Lev. 8:12), kings were anointed (1 Sam. 2:10; 2:35; 10:1; 12:3). In a figurative sense the prophets were called "anointed," because as organs of the divine will they were equipped in a special manner with God's spirit (3 Kgs. 19:16; Is. 61:1). . . . Now since the spirit of God rests upon the coming Redeemer in all fullness and more than upon any other individual commissioned by God (Is. 11:2), and because God confided to him the three offices of king, prophet and priest, he is called "the anointed one" in an eminent sense. The Messiah expected by the Jews would come at some future day, "at the end of days" as the prophets expressed it. The Targum or Rabbinical commentary on Gen. 3, 15 speaks of Him as *mesihá malká*, King Messiah. . . . It should easily be seen that what oppresses man most is not material or political, but spiritual in nature: the consciousness of sin with all its concomitant evils. Now since a true concept of sin as an offense against God is possible only among monotheists, the hope in a "savior" or a deliverer from the evils of sin can only be found in Old Testament religion. Here sin is present at the very beginning of man's history, but with it a protoevangel of hope in redemption, in forgiveness from an offended God; and the Prophets, pointing to sin and guilt, proclaim redemption and a Redeemer who frees from the guilt of sin. Not only for the preservation of faith in the one true God are we indebted to the Old Testament, but there do we find planted and cultivated hope in a reconciliation with God from whom mankind had wandered away.[12]

From the viewpoint of biblical foundations of Catechetics, it would be difficult to overemphasize this centrality of sin, sinfulness as the human condition, and liberation from sin. Failure to see this is the taproot of the development of the false Messianic Expectation, to be studied later. Without this centrality of sin in the human condition, the New Testament is not intelligible, nor is it intelligible without some understanding of the falsely interpreted Messianic Expectation that arose among the Hebrews and had become quite widespread at the time of Jesus. Furthermore, since it is a question of the purpose of human life and existence, there are visible affinities between the false Messianic Expectation of Gospel times and the so-called Liberation Theology of the late twentieth century. Is the redemption an interior renewal of persons, deep within the self, unto eternal life? Or is it rather what these merely human and worldly deviations teach, a concern to change social and political structures, "out there," as they say, concentrating upon earthly life? The question of the true concept of God, of sin, and of redemption is therefore one of the fundamentals of Catechetics and a prime necessity whenever an ambient atheism affects those catechized.[13]

This dimension, the interior renewal of persons unto eternal life, may well be called the core of the prophetic message and a fundamental theme in the unity of the Bible, which comes from its divine authorship:

> From the very beginning it was God's plan that Israel's religion become matured and deepened through a theology concerning her Messiah, and thus matured, become the religion of mankind. Israel's religion did not begin with Moses. Previously God had spoken with the patriarchs, and already in most primitive times he had planted within the human heart a desire to find its way back to God, freed from sin. That is why we meet prophecies of redemption and of a Redeemer already in the first pages of holy Scripture. In the course of centuries the picture of redemption and of a personal Redeemer from sin became ever more clearly etched. Victory over sin and guilt could not have been realized save through God's love and mercy brought by a unique, personal Mediator whom God willed to send. This is the one central truth that received continual emphasis in the Old Testament prophecies.[14]

The Messianic Prophecies

The divine authorship of the Holy Bible, which is the particular focus of biblical Catechetics, is especially visible in these numerous prophecies that delineate in detail the features and the functions of the coming Messiah. The human authors are like bricklayers working on the walls of some great building. This one sees this feature of the Coming One, another perhaps hundreds of years later sees another feature, and so with the rest. But each and all of the Prophets see him in the prophetic light. Thus a wonderfully unified prophetic anticipation becomes visible in the writings of the Old Testament.

These Messianic Prophecies begin at the very beginning: the Messiah will be the Redeemer from sin promised when the first parents of the human family fell from their special state of grace into Original Sin. "I will put enmity between thee and the woman, and between thy seed and her seed" (Gen. 3:15, Masoretic). The living Tradition of Catholic and Apostolic interpretation always has referred this promise of a future Redeemer to the Messiah, seed or child of a woman, Mary, the mother of Jesus of Nazareth. It is therefore the "Proto-Gospel," the first ray of hope and Good News for fallen mankind.

From this beginning the Messianic Prophecies increase and multiply throughout the pages of the Hebrew Scriptures, presenting now this aspect of the Redeemer and his Redemption, now that. To gather them all here is impossible, for it would take another entire book.[15] The following paragraphs offer only a sampling:

"And Jacob called unto his sons, and said: 'Gather yourselves together, that I may tell you that which shall befall you in the end of days. . . . The sceptre shall not depart from Judah, nor the ruler's staff from between his feet, as long as men come to Shiloh. And unto him shall the obedience of the people be" (Gen. 49:1–12). Jacob was letting them know that the Prophet like unto Moses, for whom they were to prepare and to whom they were to look forward as their national hope, was to be a *descendant of the tribe of Judah*. This prophecy was to be crucially meaningful when Rome conquered Palestine and installed a non-Jewish king. Later the Coming One was called *the Star out of Jacob* (Num. 24:15–19), holding a "sceptre," the sign of kingship. The Prophet Samuel looking into the future by the prophetic light saw that the coming one was to be *the Son of David*, therefore the future king of Israel, but unlike the first King David because his rule will last forever: "Thy throne shall be established for ever" (2 Sam. 7:16). The Psalms, reflecting the common prayer life of the Chosen People, indicate time and again the popular expectation. On the one hand, the Coming One was to be *the Son of God and Ruler of the World* (Ps. 2), simultaneously *a King and a Priest* (Ps. 110). Thus, on the one hand, the Hebrews understood that there was to be a new Priesthood in the future and that their current priesthood by descent from Aaron was to be replaced by a new divine ordinance. But, on the other hand, the Psalms knew that this Coming One would be *the Innocent Sufferer* (Ps. 22) indeed unto death, then freed from the bonds of death (Ps. 16). The Prophet Zachary saw this in the future when he described *the Pierced One* (Zach. 12:9–13:1), yet he also knew that the Messiah would be *the Branch of Yahweh,* a Priest and a King forever (Zach. 3:8–10 and 6:9–15).

The Prophet Isaiah enlarged upon this expectation that the Coming One was to be *the Suffering Servant of Yahweh* in his remarkable prophetic chapters 40–55, which read so much like the Gospels of the New Testament. As Yahweh's special Prophet, the Coming One speaks of his special mission to be Israel's Redeemer and at the same time to extend his redeeming work to the worldwide scene of the Gentile peoples (Is. 49:1–9). He describes his sufferings at the hands of Israel and his rejection by his own Hebrew People (Is. 50:4–11), for he is *the Man of Sorrows,* put to death unjustly in a death that atones for sin, all sin of Jews and Gentiles alike (Is. 52:13–53:12).[16]

The Prophets knew, furthermore, that the Coming One was to be *born of a Virgin,* and they named him Emmanuel, the Hebrew for "God-with-us" (Is. 7:13–14, with Mich. 5:5).[17] Bethlehem, in fact, was actually specified as the place where the Messiah was to be born (Mich. 5:1–3).

The Prophet Isaiah, finally, foresaw some mysterious union of divinity and humanity in the Coming One, for he is to be a light and a blessing to all mankind because of the *Gifts of the Spirit of Yahweh* that were to rest upon him: "And there shall come forth a shoot out of the stock of Jesse, and a twig shall grow forth out of his roots. And the spirit of the Lord shall rest upon him, the spirit of wisdom and understanding, the spirit of counsel and might, the spirit of knowledge and of the fear of the Lord . . . and he shall not judge after the sight of his eyes. . . . And it shall come to pass in that day that the root of Jesse, that standeth for an ensign of the peoples, unto him shall the nations seek; and his resting-place shall be glorious" (Isa. 11:1–10, Masoretic). With this, one comes to the Kingdom of God, so much a part of the Messianic Expectation because it will result from the redeeming work of the Messiah.

Third: The Messianic Kingdom of God

This blessing of all mankind, according to the divine plan of redemption for which the Hebrew nation is called to prepare and to serve God in implementing, introduces the third heading under which the Messianic Prophecies can be summarized. Again the unity of the Holy Bible becomes visible. Hence this is another important biblical foundation of Catechectics, for two reasons: the positive content of this promise and hope in itself and the negative factor of widespread Jewish misinterpretation of the nature of the Kingdom of God that Jesus encounters throughout his life and work.[18]

The Prophets foresaw the nature and properties of the Kingdom that the Messiah was to establish in order to give the revealed concept of God and his plan of redemption to all nations of the earth (Amos. 9:11–15; see Deut. 28:10). Thus the Hebrews could understand that the future Kingdom would be detached somehow from their merely natural nationality, difficult as this was for them, at that time before the event, to conceive. They would need to heed the teaching and follow the leadership of their Messiah when he came. The Prophet Osee knew that this Messianic salvation would be a particular blessing also for Israel, coming after judgment upon its infidelity and then lasting forever (see the entire Prophecy of Hosea). The Prophets, furthermore, seem to have foreseen that the Gentile peoples would enter into the Messianic Kingdom first and the Hebrew People only later (see Is. 11:10–16), as does Saint Paul in Romans 9–11. In any case, this coming new Israel of God will not be limited to the Hebrews but will embrace the Gentile nations of the entire world (Is. 2:2–4).[19]

From the viewpoint of the Hebrews, the most important feature of the coming Universal Kingdom was the fact that it would be a New Covenant or Testament between Yahweh and mankind. Nothing could make them realize better the temporary character of Moses' dispensation and at the same time the greatness of the one to come. The Prophet Jeremiah saw explicitly *a New Covenant* (Jer. 31:31–34, Masoretic), in which all the nations of the earth would profess the Hebrew faith in Yahweh, worshiped now by a new Sacrifice in every place (see Mal. 1:11–12). In fact, the Ark of the first Covenant would disappear, for it would not be needed under the Messiah (see Jer. 3:16). Jerusalem will be the capital of the Messianic Kingdom, indeed (see Is. 2:2), and the Messiah will enter the Holy City as its *Prince of Peace* (Zach. 9:9–110, with Ps. 72). He will be a personal Messiah with all the nations as his Kingdom. But the mode of worship will be quite different, for the Messiah will change both the Aaronic priesthood and the animal sacrifices at the Temple of Moses' dispensation. There will be *a New Sacrifice* in *Bread and Wine* in Messianic times, and it will be offered in every place (Mal. 1:10–11). The readers of the Hebrew Scriptures knew well the Priesthood of the coming Messiah: "The Lord hath sworn, and will not repent: Thou art a priest forever after the manner of Melchizedek" (Ps. 110, Masoretic). And from Genesis 14:18 they knew that "the manner of Melchizedek" meant a priest who offers sacrifice in "bread and wine."

A mysterious double aspect is visible in the prophetic descriptions of the Messianic Kingdom, corresponding to the double aspect of the Coming One as the Suffering Servant and the Glorious King over all the nations. On the one hand, it is a Kingdom associated with the Day of Yahweh, the Judgment of God on both the Hebrew People and the Gentile Nations. The Davidic Kingdom of Moses' dispensation will be destroyed (Ezech. 21:30–32) and there will be a new Shepherd and a new flock, in fact one flock and one Shepherd (Ezech. 37:22–25).

But on the other hand, the judgment is a part of Yahweh's mercy that gives an everlasting salvation to humbled and purified persons and peoples. Judgment and repentance and thus the blessing form the common theme of the Prophets of Israel, as one can see particularly in Osee and Amos. The Messianic times will witness an outpouring of the Spirit of Yahweh upon all peoples (Joel 3:15–5), and this will renew the face of the earth in a religious and moral way. Men everywhere will have new hearts of flesh—there will be a new and higher humanism—replacing the hearts of stone under paganism (Ezech. 36:26–28).

The historical character of the Hebrew religion is of its essence. Yahweh is the Almighty God of special historical events, such as the deliverance of Israel from Egypt. When the Prophets looked forward to the prophetic light, they saw what God sees in his eternal present, events that will take place in the unfolding history of mankind on earth. What Yahweh had done by his almighty mastery over contingent events they believed he would do in the future, and they taught their people so to believe by divine faith. In the Messianic times a personal and hence social renewal will be offered to the Jews and through them to all mankind, which will affect human society and culture, offering it life or judging it with decline and death if it refuses the offer. The Prophets saw coming, on earth, and within history, a City of God where a new kind of peace will dwell. The Psalmist sings, "There is a river, the streams whereof make glad the city of God, the holiest dwelling-place of the Most High. . . . Come, behold the works of the Lord. . . . He maketh wars to cease unto the end of the earth; He breaketh the bow, and cutteth the spear in sunder; He burneth the chariots in the fire. 'Let be, and know that I am God,' " (Ps. 46). Ezechiel, too, saw there regenerating and renewing waters issuing from the house of God: "And by the river upon the bank thereof, on this side and on that side, shall grow every tree for food, whose leaf shall not wither, neither shall the fruit thereof fail; it shall bring forth new fruit every month, because the waters thereof issue out of the sanctuary; and the fruit thereof shall be for food, and the leaf thereof for healing" (Ezech. 47:12).

The Hebrews, taught by God through their Prophets, knew that they lived in a moral universe with the challenge of responsible self-development. Each person must decide daily, over and over again, regarding the Way of Life. They were sustained in their daily moral struggle by their comprehensive historical worldview, their intellectual life of participation in the intentions and plans of Yahweh for the future. This embraced both the future of each person and the future of the Hebrew People preparing for the Messiah and the future of all the peoples of the earth for whom he was to be the blessing of God. For the blessing in Abraham extended to the healing of the cultural life of mankind, the fruits and the leaves of the trees nourished by the waters.

When the Prophets looked into the future by the prophetic light, they were like observers of the stars at night. All are spread across the sky as if equidistant, even though many are millions of light-years farther away. The Prophets usually did not distinguish the chronology of coming events but saw them all at once, participating mysteriously in the divine mode. Thus the woes of the judgment of the nations in the Day of Yahweh are seen intermingled with these blessings of the Messianic times when men and human culture will be regenerated and renewed. But one thing is certain: the Prophets were spokesmen for the historical religion. They foresee and describe in their way the great events that mark the Lordship of Yahweh over human history.

Perhaps it is the Prophet Daniel who summarizes best the teaching of the Prophets on the future of mankind under the impact of the Coming One and his Messianic Kingdom. The Coming One will be *the Son of Man,* a mysterious theandric figure who will bring all the peoples under his eternal rule. In union with him, the Saints of the Most High will receive the Kingdom and its blessings, and, unlike the history of the earthly peoples, kingdoms, and empires, of this Davidic kingdom there will be no end (see Dan: 7).

The Messianic Prophecies as Biblical Foundations of Catechetics

Every page of the Gospels shows Jesus as a Rabbi or Teacher of the Torah presenting to the Jewish People and especially to his Apostles the truth about God's plan of redemption. From his programmatic call at the opening of his public life (see Mark 1:14–15), he is striving to bring his people to know who the Messiah is, how necessary is aversion from sin and love of sinfulness in thinking, how imperative is conversion to the God of holiness, and how important it is to see that the Kingdom is not a social condition or political structure of this world. The Kingdom of God is an everlasting one because its persons have been given a share in the eternal life of God. At one of the decisive climactic moments of Jesus' teaching ministry he tells them, "He who eats my flesh and drinks my blood has eternal life, and I will raise him up at the last day. . . He who eats this bread will live forever. This he said in the synagogue, as he taught at Capernaum" (John 6:54–59). The operating phrase here is "has eternal life," that is, beginning now through the sacraments of Jesus' Church as an entity on earth. It thus begins the everlasting Kingdom of the Messiah.

One may summarize the Messianic Prophecies, first, in the threefold majesty of the Messiah as the Prophet like unto Moses, the King like unto David and from his lineage, and the Priest according to the order of Milchizedek, High Priest of the new worldwide Eucharistic Sacrifice that seals the New and Eternal Testament with all mankind, Jews and Gentiles alike. And secondly, in the fact that the Kingdom of God that is to succeed the Fourth Empire of the Prophet Daniel (see Dan. 7) will indeed be in certain respects a reality of this ongoing human history. It will be in some ways like those four earlier world empires described by the Prophet. But it will not be a kingdom of this world, earthly in aims and purposes and destined to come to its end as do all merely earthly empires. When Jesus is interrogated by Pilate, he will affirm that he is indeed the King of the Jews, and then he immediately adds, "My kingship is not of this world" (John 18:36).

The catechetical bearing of these two points of summary become clear when one ponders the Prophet Daniel on what is to come after that mysterious Fourth Empire in the series of mighty earthly social structures: "The Kingdom and the dominion and the greatness of the kingdoms under the whole heaven shall be given to the people of the saints of the Most High; their kingdom is an everlasting kingdom, and all dominions shall serve and obey them" (Daniel 7:27). Still in the context of a mysterious transition from that earthly Fourth Empire, to the Messiah and his Kingdom, Daniel continues: "I saw in the night visions, and, behold, there came with the clouds of heaven One like unto a son of man, and he came even to the Ancient of days, and he was brought near to him. And there was given him dominion, and glory, and a kingdom, that all the peoples, nations, and languages should serve him. His dominion is an everlasting dominion, which shall not pass away, and his kingdom that which shall not be destroyed" (Dan. 7:13–14; Masoretic).[20]

This is the context of the condemnation of Jesus by the members of the ruling Sanhedrin, who had in mind a different concept of the Messiah, his work, and his kingdom, a condemnation that now the native Jews of Israel are seeing more and more as a mistake.

Asked by the Jewish Council whether he is the Messiah, Jesus answers, "From now on the Son of man will be seated at the right hand of the power of God." "And they all said, 'Are you the Son of God, then?' And he said to them, 'You say that I am.' And they said, 'What further testimony do we need? We have heard it ourselves from his own lips' " (Luke 22:67–71). In Mark's report the reference to the Messianic Prophecy of Daniel is explicit: "Again the high priest asked him, 'Are you the Christ, the Son of the Blessed?' And Jesus said, 'I AM; and you will see the Son of man sitting at the right hand of Power, and coming with the clouds of heaven.' And the high priest tore his mantle, and said, 'Why do we still need witnesses? You have heard his blasphemy. What is your decision?' And they all condemned him as deserving death" (Mark 14:61–64; see Matt. 26:63–66).

There was an immense chasm, then, between the thinking of the Jewish supreme council and what Jesus had been teaching about himself and his mission. Thus the Messianic Prophets are indeed biblical foundations of Catechetics, for they are present in all its Christocentric teaching, whatever the level or circumstance, about Jesus. No one can fulfill the guidelines of the *General Catechetical Directory* (see *GCD* as a whole and especially nos. 40, 44–47, and 52) without taking this drama, immense also in its world-historical perspectives, into consideration. It is time to consider briefly this strangely reduced and deviated concept of the Messianic Prophecies that possessed the minds of the Jewish leaders in this supreme council, for it forms the background of the ministry of Jesus' teaching as reported in the Gospels and thus becomes an integral part of their intelligibility.

The False Messianic Expectation

The thinking of the Jewish Sanhedrin or supreme council of government at Jerusalem noted earlier indicates that the Messianic Prophecies had been subjected to a particular human tradition of interpretation made up of two components: omission of all the references to "the Suffering Servant of Yahweh," as in chapter 53 of the Prophet Isaiah, and concentration on the blessings of the restored and renewed Davidic kingship as if the Prophets taught that they were going to be temporal and earthly blessings. Proceeding from these two faulty approaches in what today is called biblical hermeneutics, a merely human, indeed all-too-human, tradition grew up around the Messianic Expectation. This tradition omitted the idea of redemption from sin that was to generate the spiritual blessings of the Messianic Age and make the Messiah's reign an everlasting one of redeemed persons risen from death and readmitted to the heavenly life forever. In other words, this tradition reduced the Messianic Expectation to the confines of this world and the structures of its political and social life.

Prof. Alfred Edersheim, because of his Jewish background and education, has a helpful chapter in his abiding classic, *The Life and Times of Jesus the Messiah*, titled "What Messiah Did the Jews Expect?" "The general conception which the Rabbis had formed of the Messiah differed totally from what was presented by the Prophet of Nazareth. . . . The most important point here is to keep in mind the organic *unity* of the Old Testament. Its predictions are not isolated, but features of one grand prophetic picture . . . , an organic development tending towards a definite end."[21] Edersheim specifies the problem that Jesus faced: "The purely national elements, which well nigh formed the sum total of Rabbinic expectation, scarcely entered into the teaching of Jesus about the Kingdom of God. . . . Jesus was not the Messiah of Jewish conception, but derived His mission from a source unknown to, or at least ignored by, the leaders of His people."[22] Edersheim exposes accurately the root of this false expectation in the separation of it from God's plan regarding sin, "the one element on which the New Testament most insists. . . . So far as their opinions can be gathered from their writings, the great doctrines of Original Sin, and of the sinfulness of our whole nature, were not held by the ancient Rabbis."[23]

In the absence of felt need of deliverance from sin, we can understand how Rabbinic tradition found no place for the Priestly office of the Messiah and how even his claims to be the Prophet of his people are almost entirely overshadowed by his appearance as their King and Deliverer. This, indeed, was the ever-present want, pressing the more heavily as Israel's national sufferings seemed almost inexplicable, while they contrasted sharply with the glory expected by the Rabbis.[24]

Rome as the Fourth Empire of Daniel

With this development of a merely human Rabbinical tradition of teaching that reduced the Messianic Expectation to the level of earthly life, expecting nothing but the restoration and worldwide expansion of King David's sway by a King Messiah who would be a gloriously victorious military conqueror of this world, the catechist of today becomes better able to understand the context of Jesus' life and teachings. For this deviated expectation began to grow mightily in Jewish national life when Pompey the Great conquered Palestine in 63 B.C. and annexed it to the Roman Empire. From this point the national crises rose in a crescendo across Jesus' lifetime and culminated, as Jesus predicted, in the rebellion of the Jews, the Roman destruction of their Temple in A.D. 70, and the dispersion of the Jews from the Holy Land.

Throughout this period the Jews knew from Jacob's prophecy (Gen. 49:1–12) that the time was at hand for the appearance of their Messiah. For the Romans installed a non-Jew, Herod, as their puppet to rule for them as "King of the Jews." This adroit politician reigned for forty years and was the one under whom Jesus was born and who slaughtered the innocents (see Matt: 2). King Herod sought cleverly to please both the Romans and the Jews. As in the time of King Antiochus and the revolt of the Maccabees under the preceding Greek Empire (see 1 and 2 Maccabees, the concluding books of the Old Testament), Jerusalem took on the appearance of a pagan city with even an amphitheater and gladiatorial shows. Above all, Herod built with and for the Roman legions a great fortress dominating the sacred Temple area. The Jewish People were to understand who had the power and must be obeyed in fear. At the same time he rebuilt, enlarged, and beautified the Second Temple in an immense program of construction that went on for decades. Jesus of Nazareth saw the finishing touches when he came in his youth for the annual pilgrimages.

The Jews, however, were not won over to the Roman program. Gradually the prophetic truth matured in the population: this King Herod is a non-Davidic imposter; "the sceptre has passed from Judah," and hence the Messianic Expectation grew even stronger. The time for King Messiah to appear was at hand.

At this point the false Messianic Expectation began to dominate in the leadership of the Jews. An intense nationalistic desire looked for the Messiah to come suddenly from heaven, from the pinnacle of the Temple as it were, to lead the Jews in a splendid military victory over the hated Romans, a victory to be obtained by the miraculous powers of the Messiah.[25]

Since the revolt of the Maccabees, four chief parties, at once spiritual and political, had formed among the Jews. The Sadducees, the priestly party in the Sanhedrin, were the descendants of the Jews who compromised with paganism and supported both the Greek and the Roman way of life. In their secularization, they had lost the age-old Hebrew and indeed human hope for personal life in the world to come, as one sees in Jesus' encounter with them in Matthew 22:23–33. The Pharisees were the Rabbinical party that refused any cooperation with the pagans, holding themselves and their disciples aloof by strict practices of the Torah and the national customs of Judaism. Third, there were the Essenes, Jews who withdrew altogether from public life.[26] The fourth party was called the League of Freedom or the Zealots and advocated immediate armed revolt against the Romans and conducted guerrilla warfare against them throughout Jesus' lifetime. Two of them were crucified with Jesus.[27] Their idea was that revolt would evoke the Messiah from heaven. The Pharisees held for a more practical approach: the Messiah must come first, for otherwise there is no way for this small people to cope with the worldwide might of Rome.[28]

Apart from the Sadducees, the spirit of violent revolution grew among the population under the Roman conquest, with anticipation that the new leader of whom Moses wrote would emerge any day to overthrow Rome and introduce the Fifth Empire of Daniel, conceived as a glorious kingdom of worldwide Jewish domination in and of this world.

A Special Biblical Foundation of Catechetics

All of this is a biblical foundation of Catechetics because it provides the background for Jesus' teaching as reported in the Gospels. He was totally given to teaching the comprehensive truth about God's plan of redemption, about the Messiah's role, and about the need for personal aversion from sin. Hence his call for personal conversion to the eternal God of holiness and hence his teaching on the nature of the Kingdom of God. It is not to be an empire of this world but rather an everlasting one of persons sharing the eternal life of God in heaven. Jesus was constantly striving to undo the false Messianic Expectation that perverted the divine plan to a merely earthly hope. He was dedicated to the liberation of souls from sin, the kingdom of Satan. For when sin fastens upon human wills and minds, darkness shrouds any higher purpose of life: the human person turns from God to the structures of this world. Liberation then becomes a social process, a political program, and indeed a military action.

Added to this general dimension of catechetical teaching, however, which is valid for all times, places, and peoples, the Rabbinical misconception of the Messiah and his Kingdom of God has a particular revelance today. The reason is the new openness of Jews to the Messiahship of Jesus of Nazareth. After so many centuries of waiting for this earthly King Messiah, after the appearance of no such this-worldly savior even in the horrors of the Holocaust in the twentieth century, more and more Jews are reconsidering Jesus of Nazareth. This is especially true of the population of native Jews in the new state of Israel. But it is also true of Jews everywhere in the world. Catechists, therefore, in the present time, are frequently called upon to help such seekers of their Messiah and to assist them with authentic evangelization and catechesis. This introduces the heart of the matter for biblical Catechetics, the way of teaching the Catholic faith to all persons of whatever age and background, but in particular where Jews are concerned.

The True Messianic Expectation

The Hebrew Revelation, taught by its prophetic Word of God, was entirely concerned with the fact of sin, Original Sin, and the resulting personal sins of mankind generally in all its peoples and nations. Let one Psalm illustrate the fact of this teaching: "The fool hath said in his heart: 'There is no God.' They have dealt corruptly and have abominable iniquity: there is none that doeth good. God looked forth from heaven upon the children of men, to see if there were any man of understanding, that did seek after God. Every one of them is unclean, they are together become impure; there is none that doeth good, no, not one" (Ps. 53, Masoretic).

This is the authentic teaching of all the Prophets: All men and women have sinned as a result of the sinful nature, its proneness to sin, which the entire human family has inherited from the first parents. This condition affects all human beings alike, Jew and Gentile. Catholic priests and the catechists who assist them in the apostolate of teaching the Catholic Faith need to keep certain basic principles and attitudes in mind in this helping of Jews who are seeking their Messiah and are reconsidering the person, teaching, and redemption worked by Jesus of Nazareth. A brief summary of them is given here as a set of biblical foundations of Catechetics especially relevant and practical today.

First, one must reflect on the fact that the Covenant and election-factor, as it is called, did not and does not exempt Jews from sin and sinfulness. This human condition does, however, tend to express itself in a certain special way in the case of the Jews, namely in the form of infidelity to the Covenant. One need only read their Prophets. This infidelity becomes visible in the form of the false Messianic Expectation, the substitution of a merely human interpretation for the full meaning of the Messianic Prophecies taken as a whole. The judgment of the Jewish leaders against Jesus of Nazareth, accordingly, becomes understandable. It resulted from sinful thinking, averted from God and converted to this world alone. Hence the initial programmatic call of Jesus (see Mark 1:14–15) for personal *metanoia* or change in fundamental thinking about the purpose of human life. It was because of deception that the Sanhedrin rejected Jesus. The result has been a psychological tendency of Jews to turn their minds away from the very possibility that Jesus was Emmanuel, Yahweh visiting his people as their Redeemer in the person of the eternal Son of God. The very thought becomes something too horrible to entertain. Hence biblical Catechetics must proceed carefully with twenty-first-century seekers from among this Chosen People, always in terms of the full truth of Christian Doctrine.[29]

The second principle of biblical Catechetics for Jews and Gentiles alike is contained in *The Roman Catechism,* the most official catechetical guide of the Catholic Church for pastors and the catechetical teachers who assist the priests. When explaining the Article of the Apostles' Creed, that "Jesus suffered under Pontius Pilate, was crucified, died and was buried," this *Catechism* teaches that "we are not to be surprised that the Prophets, before the coming of Christ, and the Apostles after his death and resurrection, labored so zealously to convince mankind that he is the Redeemer of the world, seeking to bring all men under the power and obedience of him who was crucified."[30] "The reasons why the Savior suffered are also to be explained," this *Catechism* continues, 'that thus the greatness and intensity of the divine love towards us may the more fully appear. . . . We shall find the principal causes in the hereditary contagion which comes from the Fall of our first parents [and] in the sins and vices which have been committed by human persons from the beginning of the world to the present day; and in those which shall be committed to the end of the world."[31] Thus a true biblical foundation comes into view: all sinners, and not just "the Jews," are guilty of the crucifixion of Jesus. In fact, *The Roman Catechism* goes further: "The guilt of us sinful Christians takes on a deeper hue of enormity when contrasted with that of the Jews: according to the testimony of the Apostle, if they had known the hidden wisdom of God, 'they would not have crucified the Lord of glory' (1 Cor. 2:8). But we, on the contrary, both profess to know him and yet we deny him by our actions. Hence we too seem, so to speak, to lay violent hands on him" (see Tit. 1:16).[32]

The third principle is given by Vatican II within the times of the "After Christians," the times of the apostasy of the once-Christian nations, when the new dialogue between the remnants of both Jews and Catholic Christians began to take place. "Since Christians and Jews have such a common spiritual heritage, this sacred Council wishes to encourage and further mutual understanding and appreciation. . . . Even though the Jewish authorities and those who followed their lead pressed for the death of Christ (see John 19:6), neither all Jews indiscriminately at that time, nor Jews today, can be charged with the crimes committed during his passion. . . . . The Church always held and continues to hold that Christ out of infinite love freely underwent suffering and death because of the sins of all men, so that all might attain salvation."[33]

With this we approach the end of the Hebrew Bible and the opening of the time of fulfillment in the Christian Revelation. The

Gospels report the conflict between Jesus and the Rabbinical tradition sketched earlier as the false Messianic Expectation. They report something in addition, furthermore, the fact that the Jewish people listened to Jesus and supported him massively. In fact, the leaders at Jerusalem dared not lay hands on him, it is stated more than once, because they feared this popular support. They were able to arrest him in the darkness of night only because one of his own Twelve had betrayed him to them. The study of the Christian Revelation, then, will confirm the principles of biblical Catechetics summarized earlier.

Conclusion

This point, the future popular support for Jesus of Nazareth, may serve to conclude this overview of the Hebrew Revelation. There is indeed the negative side, the resistance of the human factor so that the divine plan is not carried out with the uninhibited success that full cooperation apparently would have given. But that plan is nevertheless carried out: it stands as a fact in salvation history, the ongoing history of mankind. The fullness of time has come.

The times of the Prophets who followed Moses climax in the sixth century B.C., in the Fall of Jerusalem, the destruction of the First Temple, the captivity in Babylon, and the return from exile to build the Second Temple, which the Hebrews expected to stand until the Messiah came (see Hagg. 2:6–9). After this the voice of prophecy becomes still. The Rabbis or Teachers of the Torah carry the life of the Chosen People forward by their teaching, a teaching of the Prophetic Word of God, which is simultaneously a formation unto the Hebrew way of life. Thus it is the forerunner and the prototype of that catechetical teaching program that the Messiah will develop and mandate for all nations.

The teaching program of the Prophets in the Old Testament will find in the teaching program of Jesus both its fulfillment and its continuation out among all the Gentile peoples of the world. A large segment of the Jewish population, furthermore, prepared quietly in a spiritual manner, as one will see in the case of a particular Holy Family at Nazareth. They were sustained by their hope for the Coming One of whom Moses wrote and by their expectation of the spiritual blessings of the Messianic Age.

Part II
The Christian Revelation

Fulfillment and Teaching Mission to All Nations

Christ is the power and wisdom of God, as St. Paul teaches. Hence he who does not know the Scriptures knows neither the power nor the wisdom of God. Ignorance of the Scriptures is ignorance of Christ.

—Saint Jerome

Chapter 6

Jesus Christ and His Revealed Religion

Let us hear the Holy Spirit state the object of this study:

> In many and various ways God spoke of old to our fathers by the prophets; but in these last days he has spoken to us by a Son, whom he appointed the heir of all things, through whom also he created the world. He reflects the glory of God and bears the very stamp of his nature, upholding the universe by his word of power. When he had made purification for sins, he sat down at the right hand of the Majesty on high, having become as much superior to angels as the name he has obtained is more excellent than theirs (Heb. 1:1–4).
>
> In the beginning was the Word, and the Word was with God, and the Word was God. He was in the beginning with God; all things were made through him. . . . He came to his own home, and his own people received him not. But to all who received him, who believed in his name, he gave power to become children of God. . . . And the Word became flesh and dwelt among us, full of grace and truth; we have beheld his glory, glory as of the only Son from the Father. . . . For the law was given through Moses; grace and truth came through Jesus Christ. No one has ever seen God; the only Son, who is in the bosom of the Father, he has made him known. (John 1:1–18)
>
> That which was from the beginning, which we have heard, which we have seen with our eyes, which we have looked upon and touched with our hands, concerning the word of life—the life was made manifest, and we saw it, and testify to it, and proclaim to you the eternal life which was with the Father and was made manifest to us—that which we have seen and heard we proclaim also to you, so that you may have fellowship with us; and our fellowship is with the Father and with his Son Jesus Christ. And we are writing this that our joy may be complete. (1 John 1:1–4)

The New Testament

These texts written for our information by Jesus' Apostles, read across the centuries in the Masses for Christmas, present the majestic Person, true God and true man, to whom the New Testament bears witness. Biblical Catechetics becomes now the catechetical study of the New Testament and turns to Jesus Christ. He has been indeed the object of study in the earlier chapters on Moses and the Prophets, for they had him in view, as Saint Augustine teaches, when they looked forward in hope to the Messiah and his Messianic Age.[1] This was especially true in chapter 5. Its topics, the Messianic Prophecies as biblical foundations of Catechetics, "The False Messianic Expectation," and "The True Messianic Expectation," actually discuss the context of Jesus' life on earth.

It is time, then, to take the Bible once again in hand. It is readily apparent that the New Testament is a relatively short conclusion to "the Book of the Lord," the Hebrew Scriptures. It consists of the four Gospels, the Acts of the Apostles, the Epistles written by the Apostles, and the Book of Revelation. This last book of the Bible corresponds wonderfully with Genesis, the first book: wonderfully because the entire Bible, thus begun, thus fulfilled by the life and work of Jesus the Messiah, and thus ended, is a wonderful work of God, the divine Author who is the cause of the unity of the whole.

The New Testament is entirely governed by the principle of fulfillment: "Do not think," Jesus stresses, "that I have come to abolish the Law and the Prophets. I have not come to abolish but to fulfill them" (Matt. 5:17). It is this fulfillment that testifies to and implements the divine authorship of the Bible as a whole. It is this that gives it its unity, the unity of the Prophets foretelling and preparing for the Messiah and the Messiah coming in person and arranging to abide with us on earth all days until the end of the world (see Matt. 28:16–20).

Gospel Catechetics

In the study of this New Testament from the catechetical point of view, it is correct to say that biblical Catechetics becomes "Gospel

Catechetics." The Gospel, the "Good News" of Jesus' initial pro-grammatic call as he entered his public life (see Mark 1:14–15), governs this study from this point forward, because the Gospel is simply Jesus' program of evangelization and of teaching, the Acts of the Apostles show the continuation of Jesus' program by the men he taught and sent forth to teach that same program to all nations, the Epistles provide a set of insights into the initial progress of this work, and the Book of Revelation sustains the hope of all the teach-ers of Jesus' program until he comes again. For the Original Sin in the Book of Genesis will be overcome in Jesus' final victory over sin and death and hell.

The nature of Catechetics and the purpose of catechists is to do the same teaching that Jesus did and which he entrusted to his Apostles and their successors to carry out after him. Biblical Catechetics is the study of what divine Revelation is in itself and how it is handed on by teaching. This now receives a new and sharp focus: it is the study of what the Gospel is in itself and how it is handed on by teaching. It is that specific ecclesiastical science that helps catechists today to do this teaching with secure footing in this conclusion of the Bible, studying at first hand in the Gospels the content and method of Jesus the divine Teacher.

One can approach this as a person of the contemporary Church by keeping in mind the guidelines of the *General Catechetical Direc-tory* (GCD) and *Catechesi tradendae*.[2] These directions for doing the work of catechetical teaching find their biblical foundations in this study of "biblical, or Gospel, Catechetics." In brief review, the fol-lowing are some of the most important of these guidelines.

GCD, no. 10: "Revelation: God's Gift." Citing *Dei Verbum* no. 2, of
   Vatican II, the *GCD* points out: "Catechesis ought to take its
   beginning from this gift of divine love. . . . Revelation [is] the
   act by which God communicates himself in a personal way." The
   study of Jesus' teaching, culminating in his Eucharistic Sacrifice,
   will provide the biblical foundations of this initial and fundamental position.
GCD, no. 11: "This plan of salvation is realized by deeds and words
   having an inner unity: the deeds wrought by God in the history
   of salvation manifest and confirm the teaching and realities signified by the words, while the words proclaim the deeds and

clarify the mystery contained in them," quoting *Dei Verbum,* no
2. This divine plan was "brought to perfection in Christ." Again,
this calls for the catechetical study of the life and work of Jesus
Christ in the Gospels.

GCD, no. 12: "Christ is the Mediator and at the same time the
fullness of all revelation," again quoted from *Dei Verbum,* no. 2.
"Christ is not only the greatest of prophets who by his teaching
fulfilled those things which had been said and done by God
in earlier times." The phrase "by his teaching" governs these
directives and will receive its biblical foundation in the study of
Jesus as a *Rabbi* or Teacher of his people in the fullness of time,
according to the Gospels. It calls, furthermore, for relating the
teaching of Jesus to "the Deposit of Faith and Morals," which
his Apostles guarded and handed on in their own teaching. Jesus
himself, *GCD,* no 12, continues, "is the eternal Son of God,
made man, and thus the last event to which all events in the
history of salvation look, and which fulfills and manifests the
final plans of God." The paragraph then quotes *Dei Verbum,* no.
4: "Jesus thus perfected Revelation by fulfilling it," cited *Lumen
Gentium,* no. 9.

GCD, no. 13: "The Ministry of the Word . . . is an Act of Living
Tradition." *Dei Verbum* is quoted again, no. 8: "What was handed
on by the Apostles includes the plan of salvation which contributes to the holiness of life and the increase in faith of the
People of God." This is already the concept of the Deposit of
Faith and Morals, for it is this Deposit that is "handed on" by
living teachers. This is the very idea of a "Living Tradition."[3]
"The Church's shepherds proclaim . . . and explain . . . the Deposit of Faith which has been committed to them . . . [and] set
forth the divine Revelation such as it is taught by the Magisterium."

GCD, no. 52: "Jesus Christ, the Center of the Entire Economy of
Salvation: The history of Salvation is being accomplished in the
midst of the history of the world."

GCD, no. 53: "Jesus Christ, True Man and True God in the Unity
of the Divine Person." One can say that this states the purpose of
catechetical teaching, for everything else in Christian doctrine
follows from the accurate explanation of this answer to the question "Who, then, can this be?" "Jesus Christ," the *GCD* continues, "as man worked with his hands, thought with a human

mind, acted with a human will, loved with a human heart, [and] is truly the Word and the Son of God. . . . Catechesis must proclaim Jesus in his concrete existence, that is, it must open the way for men to the wonderful perfection of his humanity in such a way that they will be able to acknowledge the mystery of his divinity. . . . Catechesis ought daily to defend and strengthen belief in the divinity of Jesus Christ."

GCD, no. 40: "Christocentrism of Catechesis." With this the *Directory* gives its summary of catechetical content and its basic principle of catechetical method: "Christ Jesus, the incarnate Word of God . . . is the center of the Gospel message within salvation history. . . . Hence catechesis must necessarily be Christocentric."[4]

This set of directions given by the *GCD* in these times after the Second Vatican Council need their biblical roots and foundations. Providing them is the purpose of this study of biblical Catechetics: it identifies them in the Gospels and shows them in the teaching program of the Apostles.

It is difficult to see how a contemporary catechetical teacher can carry out these directives of the contemporary Catholic Church without the study of these biblical roots and foundations. Without them these directives become a dead letter and the catechist takes up some other form of religious education.

When the biblical roots and foundations are identified and studied, however, the catechist perceives a wonderful identity and continuity from Jesus' teaching program in the New Testament, the program of Jesus' newly founded Church of the Apostles, and that of the Roman Catholic Church of the Vicar of Christ today. The perception of this identity and continuity, established by objective scholarly analysis of the text of the New Testament, ministers greatly to the self-image and effectiveness of the catechist.

The Deposit of Faith and Morals

The GCD in no. 13, cited earlier, introduces this concept of a "Deposit of Faith" that pastoral care "proclaims and explains," a phrase that provides the concept and the content of Evangelization

and Catechesis. The idea of a definite "Deposit of Faith" is therefore central in the handing on of the Faith. This is the task of
catechists. It is accomplished by a process of teaching and learning.

Since 1835, the contemporary Catholic Church has been repeatedly concerned with the purity and integrity of this Deposit.
Again, therefore, persons of the contemporary Catholic Church
need to keep in mind what the Supreme Magisterium has been
teaching in regard to it. The following paragraph summarizes the
solemnly defined doctrine of the First Vatican Council.

Revealed religion possesses a teaching of faith that is not given
to mankind as a philosophical doctrine subject to progressive elaboration by human ingenuity. For the constant consensus of the Catholic Church holds that there is a twofold order of knowledge, distinct
not only in origin but also in subject. These orders are distinct in
origin because in one order we know by natural reason, in the other
by divine faith. They are distinct in object because in addition to
what natural reason can attain, there are proposed for our belief
mysteries hidden in God, which cannot be known unless divinely
revealed. Hence this teaching of faith has been given to mankind
as a Divine Deposit entrusted to the Church to be guarded faithfully.
This guarding of the Deposit takes place by an ongoing infallible
teaching that preserves the same meaning for Christians today as
that teaching had for the Apostles. Hence it belongs to the very
idea of revealed religion that the original meaning of the Articles
and Dogmas of the Faith must be perpetually retained. The persons
of revealed religion, therefore, are bound to exercise care in this
basic matter, never changing the meaning of the Articles and Dogmas under the pretext of a new comprehension under the light of
advances in merely natural science and merely human philosophy.
In a word, it is never licit to say that one can give these teachings
of revealed religion a meaning different from the one that the
Church has understood and still understands.[5]

Clearly this is a comprehensive and penetrating statement of
position. It is the very character of catechetical teaching solemnly
affirmed by the Magisterium of the contemporary Catholic Church.
But without the study of the biblical foundations and roots of this
position it, too, is likely to become a dead letter: the catechist for
lack of comprehension will take up some substitute form of religious education.

From the directives of the GCD and from this solemn definition of the deposit by the First Vatican Council it is clear that this Deposit has a very special character. It is a treasure that Jesus entrusted to his Apostles and to all teachers in the Church who in any way succeed into the mission of the Apostles. When they hand on this Deposit by their teaching, those who learn it from them receive it as the very Word of God. This was true in the times of the Apostles, across the centuries, and today. This is why Saint Paul praises the Thessalonians. "We thank God constantly for this," he writes, "that when you received the Word of God which you heard from us, you accepted it not as the word of men but as what it really is, the Word of God, which is at work in you believers" (1 Thess. 2:13).

It is the further and primary task of biblical Catechetics to uncover the biblical foundations of all these truths about the Deposit of Faith and Morals. This it does by studying Jesus the Divine Teacher, together with the content of his teaching and its nature as a teaching out of the prophetic light, that second and higher order of knowledge as defined by Vatican I and discussed in chapter 2.

One of the most fundamental reasons for guarding this Deposit, in addition to its sacred origin and character, is the fact that it is the witness of the Apostles, a witnessing continued in the Catholic Church, to Jesus in his Lordship. This makes it a body of truth and doctrine that abides yesterday, today, and forever (see Heb. 13:8).

The Ravages of the "Purely Rational Exegesis"

Here, looking forward to the catechetical study of the New Testament, everything that was discussed in chapters 1 and 2 should be reviewed, especially the topic of atheistic hermeneutics. For the problems regarding the Bible as a whole and the principles for their solution come into a new and sharper focus regarding the New Testament because the Person and the work of Jesus Christ are concerned. The outcome of the exegetes who use the wrong approach to Sacred Scripture was stated forthrightly by Saint Pius X in his Encyclical *Pascendi*: they reduce the Holy Redeemer to the status of "an ordinary and mere man."

"In the interpretation of Scripture," writes Pope Pius XII, "they will not take into account the analogy of faith and the Tradition of the Church. Thus the teachings of the Fathers and the Magisterium would have to be judged by Holy Scripture as interpreted by a purely rational exegesis, whereas Holy Scripture is to be explained according to the mind of the Church which Christ our Lord has appointed guardian and interpreter of the whole deposit of revealed truth."[6] This becomes doubly urgent and significant where the Gospels are concerned because of their apostolic witness to Jesus.

The fundamental error, therefore, is an exclusive emphasis on the human authors and details of their human authorship. These details are studied and researched exclusively by the tools of the human sciences: history, archaeology, and the biblical languages. The error lies in the belief that true and full understanding will result, whether the object studied is one verse or one book of the Bible or the Bible as a whole.

There is no intention here to disparage this human scholarship and expertise in these natural disciplines. There are always scholars who do this study of the human authorship without prescinding from or excluding the analogy of faith and the Tradition of the Church. Indeed, many such scholars work in close cooperation with the Holy See as consultants in the preparation of the many documents, noted in Chapter 1 and 2, since the *Providentissimus Deus* of Leo XIII. The problem is with those who put their faith in that other approach, the "purely rational exegesis."

Cardinal Baum, addressing the Extraordinary Synod of Bishops (1985), presents an analysis that complements that of Cardinal Ratzinger cited in chapter 2. Cardinal Baum writes:

> Exegetes are no longer disposed to interpret Scripture in the light of faith, and hence they end up calling in question essential truths of faith, such as the divinity of Christ, the Virginal conception, the salvific and redeeming value of Christ's death, the reality of the Resurrection, and the institution of the Church by Christ.
>
> The results of this so-called scientific exegesis are being diffused in seminaries, theological faculties and universities. They are reaching the ordinary faithful now, by means of catechisms and even at times in preaching. *Dei Verbum* (of Vatican II) has recommended a

scientific exegesis, but within the limits of our faith: in this field the mere application of the historical-critical method is not enough. For that very reason the Council insisted on the unity between Scripture and Tradition in *Dei Verbum*, nos. 9–10, requiring that Scripture be read and explained *in the same Spirit in which it was written* (no. 12). Insisting on the unity of the whole of Scripture, in the light of the Church's living tradition and the analogy of faith, the Constitution *Dei Verbum* laid down norms for theological and ecclesial exegesis which should assist in deepening our faith.[7]

At the same Synod of Bishops (1985) Cardinal Kim of Seoul, Korea, noted modern biblical exegesis as one of the areas in which dissent from the Magisterium is leading to chaos amongst the faithful. "The so-called pluralism of the last twenty years," he writes, "manifesting itself everywhere in exegesis, dogmatic and moral theology, cannot be reconciled with the doctrine of Vatican II and with the constant teaching of the Magisterium."[8]

There are, then, ravages in the life of the contemporary Church recognized by leaders at the highest level. One may say in summary that two chief ones are the direct concern of biblical Catechetics in its catechetical reading and study of the New Testament.

The first is the withholding of the Bible from Catholics generally, spreading doubt and discouragement among those who do not have the benefit of specialized studies in the sciences that bear upon the human authorship of the Bible. The notion spreads that the Bible is the exclusive domain of professors of this "purely rational exegesis" and their followers in the pulpits and on the committees that produce textbooks for religious education.

The second is the fact that this novel phenomenon in the Church lays hands on Jesus himself, in his Person and in his work as the divine Redeemer of mankind. This is that reduction of him, as Saint Pius X says in the passage of *Pascendi* noted earlier, to the status of "an ordinary and mere man." Written in the first decade of the twentieth century, it now seems prophetic in the light of current use of the movies and the media to disseminate this unhappy reduction not only to the status of an ordinary man but even to that of an unfortunate and fallen man.[9]

The Divine Authorship and Unity of the Bible

What can be done to parry the ravaging effects of this "purely rational exegesis?" How preserve the true nature of Catechetics from its confusions and chaos? What is needed is the recovery of the approach to the Bible that characterized the Fathers of the Church, applied now specifically to the Gospels. Here one must review the principles given in chapter 2 and bring them into the sharp focus that results from the presence and teaching of Jesus the Messiah. For he is the fulfillment of Moses and the Prophets. As Jesus himself says, speaking to the Jews, "If you believed Moses, you would believe me, for he wrote of me" (John 5:46). It is clear that this, and from the many instances of Jesus' use of the Old Testament in his teaching, that Jesus himself manifests the divine authorship of the Bible. This aspect of his presence and his teaching will be studied in its proper place in later chapters.

When biblical Catechetics turns to the study of the New Testament, therefore, becoming Gospel Catechetics, it will contribute greatly to the solution to the problems and ravages noted earlier. For it will put this recovery of the Patristic approach to the Bible into a new and more concrete focus. It will become a concrete demonstration of the way to recognize the divine authorship of the Bible and thus to adopt a new and different approach, one that solves the problems and avoids the mistakes of the "purely rational exegesis." In chapter 2 it was noted that the Fathers of the Church gave primacy to the divine authorship of the Bible and only a secondary and instrumental role to its various human authors. How they did this is a large subject. Here one can only summarize two fundamental points, each of which calls for much study and research.

The first point concerns the Patristic concept of God. The Fathers of the Church were the founders of Christian philosophy, with its own kind of metaphysics and the natural theology that results from it. As Saint Augustine teaches, everything in religion depends upon the correct and true concept of God.[10] This true concept is given to mankind in God's own biblical Self-Revelation. Taking up the aspirations and tentative efforts of the greatest Greek philosophers, to teach a natural theology as the seventh of their seven Liberal Arts, the Fathers of the Church developed this discipline into a fully articulated natural foundation for this revealed teaching. In this metaphysics the mind becomes able to see the intelligible truths and then to ascend from them to recognize the real existence of the Supreme Being of the universe. The mind reaches the sublime truth that this Being is transcendent, meaning that his mode of existing is unique, different from that of all other existing things. His act of existing is unlimited, whereas all other realities have acts of existing specified and limited by their essences, which make them to be their particular kind of thing. God's essence is his existence, the actual existence of all perfections without defect and without limit. Then the mind recognizes that God gives their actual existence, thus limited, to all other realities outside himself. They are his creatures. God, furthermore, in the teaching that Saint Augustine elaborated most fully, is the administrator of their succession in time. He is Almighty in his power first to create and then to supervise. He himself does this from a position outside space, in the sharp point of eternity, and outside time, in the eternal now, closer to each creature than it is to itself. This bears directly upon the witness of the Gospels to the miracles of Jesus.

How does this metaphysics relate to the divine authorship of the Bible? It provides the natural foundation for recognizing the unity of the Bible because it has this almighty and omnipresent personal Supreme Being as its primary Author. He is able to supervise the vicissitudes of the human authorship, bringing each human author to serve the unity of the Bible.

This natural theology, built up by the metaphysics that recognizes God's "invisible nature, namely his eternal power and deity" (Rom. 1:20), is the natural prerequisite in education for study of the divine authorship of the Bible, just as the natural sciences of history, archaeology, and biblical languages are prerequisite for specialized study of the human authorship.

Thus there is an intrinsic relationship between the contemporary renewal of Christian philosophy in Catholic higher education and the solution to the problem of the "purely rational exegesis." For when this exegesis is analyzed, it is found to rest upon a different kind of philosophy with an alien metaphysics that produces an inadequate concept of God. When the Patristic approach to the Bible is recovered, their natural metaphysical science, their seventh Art that culminates Christian education must necessarily be contained in the recovery.

With this the Bible is restored to Catholics generally. The problem of its limitation to the sciences of the human authorship is solved.

But, one may ask, what of the Catholics who have not had the opportunity to study this natural foundation for the divine authorship, the Catholics of the parishes and especially the parents of the Catholic children? The answer is in the nature of this metaphysics of the Fathers of the Church. It is the academic development of the natural metaphysics of mankind, reflected in natural right reason as used in human living, and visible in the structure of all the human languages on earth. Ordinary Catholics, therefore, thinking about God with natural soundness and receiving his biblical Self-Revelation, are able to recognize the unity of the Bible that witnesses to its divine authorship.

Thus the Bible is restored to all Catholics and especially to the catechetists who hand on Jesus' doctrine by their own teaching. They see the divine authorship and concentrate on it. They recognize the role of the human authors as the instruments of God's authorship. They trust the Church, which has guarded the text, along with the Jews, bringing it across the centuries, and publishing it today with due regard for the ongoing research on the human authorship.

The second fundamental point is the way the Fathers recognized the divine authorship. The way is the fulfillment of the Hebrew prophecies in the Person and work of Jesus Christ. They do this by discerning the fact that Moses and the Prophets in the Old Testament announced in manifold detail the future Messiah and his Messianic Age. Then they explain that these prophecies are fulfilled in Jesus of Nazareth and the mission of his Church to teach and baptize all the nations of the world (see Matt. 28:16–20). Thus they teach their people how to offer the Eucharistic Sacrifice of the New Testament, making it each one's own personal Passover from sin to grace and thus from this earthly life to the eternal life of heaven.

For a classic example of this Patristic approach one can study the *Contra Faustum* of Saint Augustine. For Faustus represented the Manichean variation of the Gnostic Heresy that so troubled and threatened the Early Church. Faustus refused to accept the Old Testament, separating the New Testament from it and interpreting it in the light of the human knowledge and mythologies of that time. Augustine demonstrates analytically that Moses and the Prophets did indeed write of Jesus and his Messianic Age, the time of the worldwide Eucharistic apostolate of his Church.[11]

From this it follows readily that biblical Catechetics actually has a significant role to play in the recovery of the Patristic approach to the Bible. This will become clearer during the catechetical study of the New Testament in the later chapters and when Jesus' own use of the Hebrew Scriptures is considered.

The Catechetical Approach in the Gospels

In this ecclesiastical science of Catechetics one does not approach the Gospels as a doubter or an unbeliever. The professor and the students in Catholic higher education, the catechist and the catechumens in the parishes, are baptized Catholic Christians. Hence they have as their guiding star the Faith that they professed in their baptism. This study exemplifies "faith seeking understanding," as Saint Anselm puts it in his definition of theology.

Now when the New Testament is the object of catechetical study, biblical Catechetics concentrates upon the Person and the work of Jesus Christ. It seeks to understand Who he is and how he solves the problems of the religious situation of mankind. It studies him as the last and greatest of the Prophets of Israel. Like all the Prophets, he emerged from his hidden life in Nazareth as a publicly recognized Teacher of the revealed Word of God. Catechetics comes into focus as the study of Jesus as a Teacher. It learns what his teaching program was: its content, mode, method, and purpose. Thus the biblical foundations of authentic catechetical teaching today become specific and concrete.

"Ignorance of the Scriptures," Saint Jerome writes, "is ignorance of Jesus Christ." One gets to know Jesus and his revealed religion by this kind of catechetical study of the Gospels and the Epistles. One knows him as he really was, a Teacher who founded a Teaching Church.

The New Testament can be studied, and rightly, from other points of view, that of dogmatic theology, for example, or spiritual theology, or of prayer and meditation, or of the history of the Apostolic Church. These are all good and have their place. But the catechetical point of view is something different and is often overlooked. Perhaps this is a root cause of current confusion and even chaos in religion and religious education.

Biblical Catechetics, finally, helps to answer practical questions: How does one organize catechetical programs and do catechetical teaching today? What is the original Deposit of Faith and Morals? Has the Church published it, making it available for catechists today? The chief practical principle that derives from the New Testament is the Christocentrism that the GCD defines in paragraph 40, cited earlier. Saint Augustine places this Christocentrism in its full biblical context in his classic definition of catechetical method: "Catechesis is complete when the beginner is instructed from the text, 'In the beginning God created heaven and earth,' down to the present period of Church History."[12]

Augustine follows with his golden rule for the catechetical study and practical use of the Bible. "This does not mean that we must repeat verbatim the whole Pentateuch, all the books of Judges, Kings or Ezras, the entire Gospels and all the Acts of the Apostles. . . . Neither time serves for this nor does any need call for it. . . . We ought to present all the matter in a general and comprehensive summary, choosing certain of the more remarkable facts . . . , spreading them out to view and offering them to the minds of our hearers to examine. But the remaining details we should weave into our narrative in a rapid summary."[13]

Augustine then concludes his golden rule for catechetical teaching with Christocentrism with a passage that states again the Patristic approach to the Bible: "In truth for no other reason were the things we read about in the Holy Scriptures written before Our Lord's coming than to announce and prefigure the Church which was to be, that is to say, the People of God throughout all the nations, which is the Body of Christ."[14]

Chapter 7

Jesus Christ, Teacher and Prophet in Israel

Jesus Christ culminates and completes the unfolding plan of God's Revelation to mankind. The catechetical study of the Bible reflects this progression. These final chapters on Jesus our Divine Teacher and on Jesus our Divine Savior take up the fullness and the mediation of Divine Revelation to mankind.

Over five centuries had passed since the period of the great Prophets of the Old Testament. Under their leadership, the suffering of the destruction of Solomon's Temple and of the captivity in Babylon had been endured. Then came the return of the remnant to Palestine, the building of the Second Temple at Jerusalem, and the reconstitution of the Hebrew way of life according to the Torah. The voice of prophecy stilled. The role of the prophet recedes and that of the Rabbi, the teacher, increases. These Rabbis were "scholars . . . who steeped themselves in the study of Sacred Wisdom and imparted their knowledge to disciples. This institution—teacher and his circle of students—became the characteristic mark of Jewish life for centuries. . . . They were regarded as the elite of the nation, men who considered the learning of the Law as the very purpose of Life."[1]

As these five centuries proceeded, the Hebrews lived quietly, accepting their humbled condition as a small eastern Mediterranean people under foreign domination. Empire succeeded empire. Persia toppled Babylon from power and authorized the return of the Jews from exile. Then came Alexander and the universal ascendancy of the pagan Greek culture. It was the time of the heroic resistance of the Maccabees. And by Jesus' time the Greek power had fallen to the Roman Empire, the powerful military might from the West. The Hebrews had been annexed to the Roman Empire by Pompey the Great. A Roman garrison was quartered at the Temple. Roman policy permitted subjugated peoples to retain their local heritage of culture, custom, and government. So, too, Palestine. But the Roman power was stark, it reached everywhere, it had its imperial laws, and it exacted heavy taxation.

The Jews continued living quietly, teaching and practicing their Revealed Religion. There was much restlessness, however, movements of resistance to the Roman power, currents of thought on liberation, and guerrillalike groups of young zealots who wanted action now. For there was a general expectation of the Coming One. The time was considered to be quite near at hand. The Second Temple was still standing and functioning, indeed, but under the Roman shadow. The Expected One was to come while it still stood. But what of the royal dynasty of David? Had it not been terminated by the Romans? This King Herod, was he genuine? Or did he not indicate that the time for the Messiah was exactly three years? Life went on quietly, with much thought and conversation. Underneath, there was a social phenomenon peculiar to the Hebrews because of the Prophets: a strong undercurrent of expectation and of readiness to hear.[2] It was at this point after Pompey, under the rule of the Roman Empire and its puppet king in Jerusalem, that Jesus appears in public as a Rabbi with a characteristic circle of students. He came upon the Jewish scene with electrifying social force, a powerful figure who was to have a lasting historical impact upon both the Jews and the Gentiles.[3]

Jesus' Human Social Presence As a Teacher

It is instructive for catechists to reread the New Testament from the catechetical point of view.[4] As a first step in this process and to illustrate its benefits one can ask the Gospels how Jesus presented himself among men of his own time. What was his *Sitz im Leben,* as the Germans say, his concrete social presence and function? How did he appear among men of his day? How did people see him? What did he do? What was his self-identity, to use a current phrase, socially? The answers emerge from the way people addressed him, not only his circle of followers but people generally, reflecting concrete social recognition.[5]

Jesus As a Teacher in Saint Mark's Gospel

Unlike Matthew, Mark gives a report on the content of Jesus' teaching in only one passage, 4:1–34: "And he began to teach beside the sea. And a very large crowd gathered about him, so that he got into a boat and sat in it on the sea; and the whole crowd was beside the sea on the land. And he taught them many things in parables, and in his teaching he said to them, 'Listen! A sower went out to sow. . . .' And when he was alone, those who were with him with the Twelve asked him concerning the parables" (Mark 4:1–10).

The verbs in his passage denoting Jesus' activity are in *didask-*, the root of a cluster of Greek words that denote the work of the professional teacher, the *Didáskalos*.[6] "And in his *didachê*, he said to them, 'A sower went out to sow.' . . ." Immediately after this classic scene at the shore, Mark reports the anxiety of his followers in the storm at sea: "*Didáskale*," they say to him, "[Teacher,] do you not care if we perish?" Who then were these followers? Students? What other category of persons would use *Didáskalos* as their way of addressing him in this circumstance?[7] Mark himself soon gives the answer: "And leaving that place, he went into his own country, and his disciples [*mathetai*] followed him" (Mark 6:1).

This Greek word *mathetai*, translated "disciples," has a special significance in the current context, for it is the correlative of *Didáskalos* in the world of the Greek *paidéia* or education. It means a group of students gathered around their teacher or Rabbi and denotes an ordinary and accepted social phenomenon universal among the peoples of classical antiquity, whether the Jews in Palestine or the various Gentile peoples federated into the Roman Empire. We shall return to this word *mathetēs* later when discussing the training that this Teacher gave his followers.

This public and social recognition is witnessed in Mark's report on Jesus' instructions for preparing "the first day of Unleavened Bread, when they sacrificed the passover lamb." "Go into the city," he told them, "and a man carrying a jar of water will meet you; follow him, and wherever he enters, say to the householder, 'The Teacher [*ho Didáskalos,*] says, Where is my guest room, where I am to eat the passover with my disciples?' " (Mark 14:14). This manifests the way people at large saw Jesus and named him: he is a Teacher who has a group with him studying and learning the Torah, preparing on the level of Jewish higher education to become teachers themselves.

At times the Greek of Mark's Gospel retains the Hebrew word for "Teacher." At the Transfiguration, "Peter spoke to Jesus: 'Rabbi,' he said, 'it is wonderful for us to be here; so let us make three tents . . . ' " (Mark 9:5).[8] Descending from the mountain, Jesus saw his disciples involved with a great crowd. "What are you discussing with them?" "And one of the crowd answered him, 'Teacher [*Didáskale* in the Greek], I brought my son to you, for he has a dumb spirit . . . and I asked your disciples to cast it out, and they were not able.' . . . " (Mark 9:17). Later the disciples, his *mathetai*, asked him why. He explained briefly, accurately, clearly, to the point, as a teacher would.

After this he took his disciples on a private trip through Galilee. The purpose was didactic, educational, "for he was teaching his *mathetēs*" (Mark 9:31), where the root translated "teaching" is in *didask*—the Greek verb that denotes the professional activity of teaching. The mode of address used by this inner circle of disciples is clear. "John said to him, Teacher [*Didáskale,*], we saw a man casting out demons in your name, and we forbade him, because he was not following us" (Mark 9:38).[9] So James and John together when they approached him said, "Teacher, [*Didáskale,*] we want you to do for us whatever we ask of you . . . to sit one at your right hand and one at your left, in your glory . . . " (Mark 10:35).[10] And Peter: seeing the fig tree, "Peter remembered and said to him, 'Look, Rabbi . . . ' " (Mark 11:21), another passage of Mark's Greek that retains the ordinary Jewish word for "teacher."[11]

The human mode of addressing Jesus was the ordinary one in the teacher–student relationship, the socially accepted term in the educational process of that day.

Perhaps Jesus' opponents bear the best witness to the fact that his human social presence was simply that of an officially and commonly recognized Teacher in Israel. The chief priests and scribes "sent to him some of the Pharisees and some of the Herodians, to entrap him in his talk. And they came and said to him, 'Teacher (*Didáskale* in the Greek), we know that you are true, and care for no man; for you do not regard the position of men, but truly teach the way of God. Is it lawful to pay taxes to Caesar, or not'?" (Mark

12:13–14). The Sadducees, who say there is no resurrection, came up with the same intention: "Teacher *[Didáskale]*, Moses wrote for us . . . , there were seven brothers . . . " (Mark 12:19)[12].

Judas was a disguised opponent within the inner circle of students. His mode of addressing Jesus will conclude these instances in Mark's Gospel: "Now the betrayer had given them a sign, saying, 'The one I shall kiss is the man, seize him and lead him away safely. . . .' So when the traitor came, he went straight up to Jesus and said, 'Rabbi!' and kissed him" (Mark 14:44–45). Here again the Greek original of Mark's Gospel preserves the Hebrew word for "teacher."[13]

Exegetes generally agree on the fact that Saint Mark's Gospel stands nearest to the origins, for it reflects Peter's first hand view of Jesus' human life. In Mark, the human presence of Jesus as a Rabbi or Teacher in Israel and his social acceptance as such "stands clearly in the foreground."[14]

Jesus As a Teacher in Saint Matthew's Gospel

Here the same fact is witnessed but in a characteristically different way. In Matthew, the disciples do not address Jesus as *Didáskale* but as *Kyrie*, "Lord." So in the storm at sea: "They went and woke him, saying, 'Save us, Lord [*Kyrie* in the original Greek text], we are perishing.' And he said to them, 'Why are you afraid, O men of little faith?' Then he rose and rebuked the winds and the sea; and there was a great calm" (Mark 8:23–27). Likewise at the Transfiguration: "And Peter said to Jesus, 'Lord [*Kyrie*], it is well that we are here . . . ' " (Mark 17:4). *Rabbi* is used in Matthew's Gospel as the term of address only by Judas within the inner circle of disciples. Scholars surmise that Teacher as Jesus' title was felt to be not quite adequate any longer for the Eleven at the time when the current Greek text of Matthew was finalized in the Apostolic Church: "One must assume that the term *Kyrie* connoted for Matthew such a high appreciation that it was not a fitting word in the mouth of the traitor."[15]

In Matthew, however, people in society at large and also his opponents address Jesus as "Teacher" exactly as in Mark. Many instances of direct address bear witness: "And a scribe came up and said to him, 'Teacher [*Didáskale,* in the Greek], I will follow you wherever you go' " (Matt. 8:19). The rich young man asked him, "Teacher [*Didáskale*], what good deed must I do, to have eternal life?" (Matt. 19:16). Another Rabbi questioned him as an equal: "Teacher [*Didáskale*], which is the great commandment in the Law?" (Matt 22:36). Both the Pharisees and the Sadducees recognize his social position in their effort to entrap him, exactly as in Mark, by addressing him deferentially as *Didáskale* (cf. Mark 22:15–16 and 22:24). Society at large sees him according to Matthew simply as a teacher in Israel. The tax collectors questioned Peter, "Does not your Teacher [*ho Didáskalos*] pay the tax?" (Matt. 17:24). The Pharisees bear the same witness: "Why does your Teacher [*ho Didáskalos*] eat with tax collectors and sinners?" (Matt. 9:11).

Jesus himself states his position to his disciples: "But you are not to be called *Rabbi* [the Hebrew word is preserved in the Greek text], for you have one teacher, and you are all brethren . . . , neither be called masters, for you have one master, the Christ" (Matt. 23:8–10). This was a favorite text of the Early Church catechumenate, cited over and over in developing the theme "Jesus Christ, the Divine Teacher."[16]

The full force of Matthew's witness to Jesus' social position as a Rabbi in Israel, however, is in his summaries of the content, the *Didachē,* of Jesus' teaching, which will be discussed here.

Jesus As a Teacher in Saint Luke's Gospel

Here where a Gentile associate of Saint Paul is doing a "Gospel for the Greeks," the Hebrew word *Rabbi* disappears entirely from the original text. *Didáskalos* is used throughout as the term of address for Jesus and in the manner of Matthew, not by his inner circle of disciples but by people at large and by his opponents: "Simon, I have something to say to you. . . . 'What is it, Teacher, *Didáskale?*' " (Luke 7:40). Listening to Jesus' forthright discourse, a lawyer said, "Teacher [*Didáskale*], in saying this, you reproach us also" (Luke 11:45). One of the multitude, a ruler and the Pharisees observing his Palm Sunday entrance into Jerusalem all address Jesus as *Didáskale,* Teacher (cf. Luke 12:13, 18:18, 19:39).[17]

In Luke there is somewhat less emphasis on *Teacher* as the standing term of address for Jesus in his public life. "Luke remains true to the tradition, however, and allows his readers to see Jesus consistently as a Teacher in Israel."[18] Luke's Gospel has its own characteristic way of doing this by the frequent use of the Greek verbs in the root *didask-* to denote Jesus' activity. He was *teaching*.[19] "He stirs up the people, *teaching [didáskon]* throughout all Judea, from Galilee even to this place" (Luke 23:5). When he teaches in the synagogue at Nazareth, where he studied and prayed as a boy and youth, in an atmosphere filled with expectancy and tense with crosscurrents, Luke gives the fine details that describe a Rabbi of his day: he stands, unrolls the Scroll, reads the passage, then sits to teach. "And the eyes of all in the Synagogue were fixed on him . . . " (Luke 4:16–21).

Jesus As a Teacher in Saint John's Gospel

Does Saint John bear the same witness? At variance with a certain style in biblical scholarship in these last two hundred years, it is now increasingly recognized that Saint John presents Jesus with the eyewitness immediacy of Mark and with more of the wording and flavor of the Palestinian tradition than Luke and even Matthew. John gives independent support to the Synoptics, furthermore, in their presentation of Jesus as a Rabbi, a Teacher in the accepted form of his place and time.[20] In fact, John's Gospel can be seen best from this didactic point of view: Chapters 2–12 describe Jesus' public activity as a Rabbi, and chapters 13–17 reveal the way he taught his inner circle of the twelve full-time disciples, unique passages that correlate with the trips in the Synoptics when he took the Twelve aside for specialized instruction and formation.

The particular instances in the Greek text of Saint John's Gospel are illuminating. When John the Baptist pointed Jesus out with the singular phrase "Behold the Lamb of God!" there was a stir among the younger men: "The two disciples heard him say this, and they followed Jesus. Jesus turned, and saw them following, and said to them, 'What do you seek?' And they said to him, 'Rabbi (which means Teacher), where are you staying?' " (John 1:37–38). John's Greek text actually uses the word *Rabbi* and gives its Greek equivalent, *Didáskalos*.[21] The two young men stay overnight with the prospective new Rabbi and report back the next day: "We have found the Messiah (which means Christ) . . . " (John 1:41). Forthwith they began to enlist candidates for a Talmudim, a group of student-followers for this Rabbi, and on the basis of this particular understanding. For already they were animated in some degree by the hope for the Messiah that the Prophets had instilled into Israel.

Nathaniel addresses Jesus from the beginning with the Hebrew term: "Rabbi, you are the Son of God! You are the King of Israel!" (John 1:49). The disciples generally throughout John's Gospel address Jesus as Rabbi: see John 4:32, 9:2, and 11:8. But John can report their using *Kyrie* as well, indeed in one and the same passage: "Rabbi [so in the Greek], the Jews were but now seeking to stone you, and are you going there again? . . . Lord *[Kyrie* in the Greek], if he has fallen asleep, he will recover" (John 11:8 and 12).[22] So, too, Peter, answering the pointed question "Will you also go away?": "Simon Peter answered him, 'Lord [*Kyrie* in the Greek], to whom shall we go? You have the words of eternal life . . . ' " (John 6:68). And: "Lord [*Kyrie*], do you wash my feet?" (John 13:7).

Unlike the Synoptics, those outside the inner circle of disciples also regularly use the word Rabbi, which is retained in the Greek text of John. So Nicodemus: "Rabbi, we know you are a teacher come from God" (John 3:2).[23]

Jesus himself formally declares that he is a Teacher and that he has been doing nothing but teaching: "You call me Teacher [*ho didáskalos*] and Lord *[kai ho Kyrios]*; and you are right, for so I am" (John 13:12). This is what he declares his activity throughout his life to have been, officially when under questioning, as reported in Mark: "Day by day I was with you in the temple teaching, and you did not seize me. But let the Scriptures be fulfilled. And they all forsook him and fled" (Mark 14:19).

Conclusion

In summary, then, the evidence in the original text of all four Gospels is perfectly clear: in his humanity, in his human social presence among men of his time, Jesus was a formally recognized and certified Teacher in Israel. It was his customary activity, pursued perseveringly despite obstacles and political interference: "And he left there and went to the region beyond the Jordan, and crowds gathered to him again; and again, as his custom was, he taught them" (Mark 10:1).[24]

Today a particular apparatus, state boards, diocesan religious education offices, and the like govern the socially recognized and professionally accepted position of a teacher. At that time, the teacher was likewise a professional person, recognized socially, but the apparatus was that of the classical culture. "To be a *didáskalos*," writes Rengstorf, "there was needed the further fact of the presence of disciples. . . . The fact that in the case of both Jesus and John (John 1:35 ff.), certain men had been so gripped by their words that they set themselves in the position of pupils and disciples meant that in the eyes of their contemporaries the final presupposition had been externally fulfilled for granting them the title of *Didásaklos,* for addressing them as *Didáskale,* and for reckoning them among the teachers of the people."[25] This is the way Jesus' humanity was perceived and accepted by the Jewish people of his day: "That Jesus is addressed as *Didáskale* presupposes the fact that he outwardly conforms to the Jewish picture of the *Didáskalos.* This is indeed the case."[26]

Jesus, then, functioned as a Rabbi of his place and time, a matter of special significance and importance in the present time when there is such widespread interest in his humanity.[27] Jesus Christ was a Teacher in Israel.[28]

Didachē: Jesus Had a Definite Content in His Teaching

Our purpose here is not to do the systematic and comprehensive study of doctrinal content furnished by the treatises on New Testament Theology.[29] In keeping with the nature of catechetical study, our intention is simply to document the fact of content in Jesus' teaching at a time when content has all but disappeared in many areas from religious education. Then we shall see that the Bible itself was the general content that Jesus taught. This will be followed by a study of the prophetic mode in which Jesus did his teaching. Finally, we shall reflect from the pedagogical point of view on the dimension of personal formation of his Apostles to which his teaching ministered.

The Gospel Fact That Jesus Taught a Content

The original Greek texts of the four Gospels are literally sprinkled with action verbs in the root *didask-*, and the derivative noun *didachē* recurs constantly.[30] This massive fact in the documents answers the question regarding content, both in Jesus' teaching then and in catechesis today. For these are the standard words of the Greek language to denote the teaching profession and its activity. All teachers "teach Johnny," as the phrase goes; at the same time, the common sense of mankind in all cultures and ways of life has always recognized that the teaching of Johnny is accomplished by giving him a doctrine, a content of truth that the teacher possesses and the learner needs.[31]

First, then, the witness of the original Greek of the Gospels: "And he went into Capernaum; and immediately on the Sabbath he entered the Synagogue and began to teach [verb in *didask-*]; and they were astonished at his teaching (*didachē*) (Mark 1:21). "They were all amazed," Mark continues, "and said, What is this?—A new teaching [*didachē*]?" (Mark 1:27). Describing what Jesus was doing in the boat at the seashore, Mark states explicitly: " . . . he taught [*didáskei*] the people" (Mark 2:13). "He taught [verb in *didask-*] them many things in parables, and in the course of his teaching [*didachē*] he said to them . . . " (Mark 4:3). When the authorities made it unsafe for him in Judea, he transferred his activity to Perea on the other side of the Jordan. "And again crowds gathered round him, and again he taught [verb in *didask-*] them, as his custom was" (Mark 10:1).

It is the same in the other Gospels, for instance John: "When the festival was half over, Jesus went up to the temple and began to teach [in *didask-*] (John 7:14). The Jews were astonished at his ability and doctrine, and asked who had given him this learning. "My teaching [*didachē*] is not from myself," he replied; "it comes from the one who sent me. And if anyone is prepared to do his will, he will know whether my teaching [*didachē*] is from God, or whether my doctrine [*didachē*] is my own" (John 7:14–15).[32] His disciples accepted him initially as that culminating Prophet of whom Moses wrote. This is the same question—not whether it is a teaching but whether the teaching is a content elaborated by human science and philosophy or whether it is Divine Revelation, the word of God spoken by Jesus as God's Prophet. The Jews had a certain readiness to accept his teaching in this dimension because it was familiar from their historic past. It was the *content* of his teaching that was questioned formally after his betrayal and arrest: "The high priest questioned Jesus about his disciples [*Mathetai*] and his teaching [*didachē*]. Jesus answered, 'I have spoken openly for all the world to hear; I have always taught [verb in *didask-*] in the synagogue and in the Temple where all the Jews meet together: I have said nothing in secret. But why ask me? Ask my hearers what I taught [verb in *didask-*]: they know what I said' " (John 18:19–20).[33]

The Special Witness of Saint Matthew's Gospel

Saint Matthew's Gospel is distinguished by its seven lengthy reports on the content of Jesus' teaching.[34] These doctrinal passages deserve close attention from the catechetical point of view for two reasons. First, they reflect Jesus' activity as a teacher in Israel, basing his teaching upon the Hebrew Torah as the Word of God and expounding its true and authentic meaning. "These blocks of doctrine in Matthew," writes Normann, "represent a teaching of the Torah."[35] Second, they reflect at the same time the catechetical teaching program of the earliest Church, the Church of the Apostles, and illustrate the way Jesus' teaching was continued by the Church that he sent to teach and for which he had prepared his Apostles as teachers. "The *Sitz im Leben* of Matthew's Gospel," Normann concludes, "was the needs of catechesis in the Christian communities."[36] But it would be wrong, an unscholarly type of philosophical slant read back from modern times into those times, to assume that the Church of the Apostles simply invented this teaching, imagining things, as it were, by itself. When the stylistic features of these seven blocks of didactic material systematically presented in Saint Matthew's Gospel are analyzed closely, as Scripture scholars who specialize in the areas concerned are able to do, it becomes clear that they have a characteristic pattern, that of a particular teacher using in his own way the genre of teachers in Israel generally: "Behind these doctrinal passages one comes to realize anew that there stands the figure of Jesus as a Teacher."[37]

The Sermon on the Mount is justly regarded as the gem among the reports on the content of Jesus' teaching that Matthew recorded on behalf of the Church of the Apostles. Its very length, Matthew 5:1–7:27, with its solemn didactic introduction and conclusion, indicates its importance in the particular purpose and plan of this Gospel.[38] Jesus sits exactly as the Rabbis were accustomed to sit when they taught. The setting on a "mountain" maintains the ancient traditions of mankind regarding the High Places of God and reminds the Jews in particular of Moses and Mount Sinai: this is a *divine* teaching. The central position of the teaching is continuity and fulfillment, not abrogation and revolt: "Do not think that I have come to destroy the Law or the Prophets. I have not come to destroy but to fulfill. For amen I say to you, till heaven and earth pass away, not one jot or one tittle shall be lost from the Law till all things have been accomplished" (Matt. 5:17–18).

It would be difficult to overemphasize the importance of this concept of fulfillment. It will become the guiding light for both content and method in the catechetical teaching program that Jesus sent his disciples to carry out to all nations. It means that the entire heritage of the Hebrew religious education will pass fulfilled into the religious education of the Teaching Church. Matthew bears witness to the grand sweep of Jesus' teaching: "Jesus as a Teacher represents in Matthew's presentation of his basic content and approach the continuity of the economy of salvation, for he continues the Torah in force."[39] Jesus leaves the Hebrew Torah untouched in its substance of revealed truth when he fulfills it by teaching a higher level of the spiritual life and a more perfect concept of justice.

Jesus Teaches the Divine Authorship of the Bible

The content of Jesus' teaching was the Bible. In his day, of course, it was the Hebrew Bible, replete with predictions and promises of the coming Messiah and his Messianic Age. Jesus taught out of what we today call the Old Testament. He taught that he himself in person is the fulfillment of these predictions and types. Thus he made use of the Bible constantly in his teaching. The record of this teaching is contained in the writings of his Apostolic men, which have been gathered by the authority of the Church into the New Testament.

Jesus' use of the Old Testament in his teaching is an important biblical foundation for catechetical teaching today, and for two chief reasons.

First, Jesus teaches the Bible comprehensively, that is, in its complete fullness just as written by God himself through the instrumentality of Moses, the Prophets, and all the other human authors under the authority of Moses. This places Jesus' teaching into diametrical opposition with the prevailing Jewish interpretation of their Scriptures, which arose by selectivity instead of comprehensiveness. The Jewish leaders and Rabbinical teachers had come to overlook and suppress passages such as chapter 53 of the Prophet Isaiah on the Suffering Servant of Jahweh and those bearing on sin, the internal affliction of persons, and redemption from it. Thus there arose that false Messianic Expectation described in chapter 5. One could not become a follower of Jesus without turning away from that secularized and worldly expectation of a Messiah as a powerful military and political leader, in and of this world and its structure, who would lead the Jews to victory over the Roman Empire. Jesus taught a quite different concept of the Messiah and of his Messianic Age—and he did so by his use of the Bible.

Why is this a biblical foundation of catechetical teaching today? Because it teaches the true purpose of human life, which is not to be found in earthly life and its structures. The Messiah is a divine messenger who calls individual persons to turn away from sin and to be converted to God in order to share his divine life forever in heaven. Then the Messiah introduces the Messianic Age, full of glories and splendors of the redeemed persons and their interior lives, which will become visible in holy lives, especially those of the Saints. From beginning to end Jesus teaches this conversion of persons unto life everlasting. This is a basic foundation for catechetical teaching today, for the catechist is called to teach this same inner conversion from sinful addiction to this world to God and his eternal life in the world to come.

Second, Jesus' use of the Bible is a biblical foundation for catechesis today because he demonstrates and exhibits graphically the divine authorship and hence the unity of the Scriptures. In this way Jesus himself helps the catechist to perceive the divine authorship of the Bible. This assists greatly in overcoming the ravages of the merely human approach to the Bible that has been noted.

How does Jesus accomplish this immense benefit for the teaching of the Catholic faith today? He does so by pointing to the prophetic predictions in the Old Testament that are fulfilled in his own person as the Messiah and in the spiritual blessings of the redeemed souls that will flow forth from his Eucharistic Sacrifice of the New and Eternal Testament. By his teaching program Jesus will cause this Sacrifice to be offered in every place among the Gentiles, fulfilling the Prophet Malachi. Persons who turn from sin and to God by communion with this new sacrificial worship will be taking part in the blessings of the Messianic Age. Thus the divine authorship and unity of the Bible become visible as a fact.

This inestimable benefit of Jesus' teaching restores the Bible to the hands of catechetical teachers today as the *Holy* Bible. Jesus simply accepts the Sacred Scriptures as the authority of the Chair of Moses that has handed them on in the life of the Jewish people. Jesus, furthermore, does not allow questions of detail on the human authorship to become the center of interest. Jesus' primary focus is on the divine authorship that binds the various books of the Bible into the unity of fulfillment in himself and his redemptive work.

It would demand a separate book to study in detail Jesus' use of the Holy Bible.[40] Here we can illustrate with a few samples and invite each catechist to further study of this biblical fundamental of Catechetics, for it is, one may say, the heart and soul of all catechetical teaching, "which must necessarily be Christocentric," as the GCD, no. 40, summarizes the matter.

At the head of our samples and examples there must certainly stand Jesus' programmatic call with which he opened his public life: "Now after John was arrested, Jesus came into Galilee, preaching the Gospel of God, and saying 'The time is fulfilled, and the Kingdom of God is at hand; repent, and believe the Gospel' " (Mark 1:14–15). This is a sweepingly comprehensive use of the Bible, for it proclaims that the fulfillment of the entire body of Old Testament predictions and promises is at hand in Jesus' own coming. The Messianic Age is beginning in his person. The entire Jewish nation was electrified by Jesus' call and flocked to hear him.

At his own boyhood synagogue in Nazareth, Jesus reads Isaiah 61:1–2 and says, "Today this Scripture has been fulfilled in your hearing" (Luke 4:16–30). In an encounter with Jews of the false Expectation who were resisting his teaching Jesus says explicitly, "The Scriptures . . . bear witness to me" (John 5:39).

When Jesus fasted in the desert for forty days in preparation for his public ministry as the Messiah of the Jewish nation, Satan tempted him with visions that embodied the false expectation of earthly triumph and glory. Jesus cast them aside with masterful countercitation of the Bible. One can turn to chapter 6 of Saint John's Gospel for the sequel in Jesus' Eucharistic teaching on the resurrection of the body and life everlasting: "After this many of his disciples drew back and no longer went about with him" (John 6:66).

John the Baptist, suffering in prison, sent word to ask, " 'Are you he who is to come, or shall we look for another?' And Jesus answered, 'Go and tell John what you hear and see' " (Matt. 11:2–6, also Luke 7:18–23). Forthwith and in detail Jesus cited chapter 61 of Isaiah: he himself is fulfilling the prediction by doing the deeds that open the Messianic Age.

Jesus stresses that Psalm 110 calls him "David's Lord" (see Mark 12:36, with the parallels in Matthew and Luke). Jesus is the Messiah, David's son, humanly speaking, but at the same time he is more than a merely human descendant. Jesus uses the same Scripture in his solemn declaration before the Sanhedrin (see Mark 14:62) and combines it with Daniel's prophecy on the Son of man (Daniel 7). Always in his teaching Jesus corrects the false interpretation of such texts. His Kingdom of God belongs to an order higher than earthly kingships and empires. It is ruled from the right hand of God; it is a priestly and redemptive kingship; it is not of this world but will last forever. Jesus cites the Prophet Zachary (Mark 14:37) to teach that he is the Shepherd-King who is to be smitten and put to death; he is the Suffering Servant of Isaiah 53 (see Luke 22:37 and Mark 10:45). In fact, Jesus teaches that the Prophet Jonah is the type of his own coming resurrection (see Matt. 12:38–42).

This sampling may perhaps suffice to show the pervasive presence of the Old Testament in Jesus' teaching and its fulfillment in himself, his redemption from sin, and his opening of eternal life to all persons who turn to him.[41]

Jesus taught *from the Bible* that in his person the Messiah of the Prophets has come and that the glories of the Messianic Age, the spiritual glories of redeemed souls, have begun. He did his teaching by explaining the meaning of the Bible as a whole, a meaning that gives it its transcendent divine unity. Jesus, true God and true man, is uniquely in a position to teach this true meaning and interpretation. Everything becomes clear when the omnipotence of God is considered and his lordship over the succession in time of the human authors of his Holy Bible. It was this that Jesus had in mind when he reminded his mother that he must be about his heavenly Father's work, that of teaching the fullness of divine revelation and mediating it out to all nations by the program of teaching by which he trained his Apostles.

Jesus Reveals the Trinity of Divine Persons

With this we continue to consider the way Jesus used the Holy Bible in his teaching, a particular way that provides a fundamentally important Biblical foundation for catechetical teaching today when the Mysteries of the Trinity and the Incarnation have suffered eclipse by the mounting crisis of faith in the late twentieth and earlier twenty-first centuries. Jesus revealed the Trinity of Divine Persons, first, by identifying himself, God the Son, with Yahweh, the One God of the Hebrew Revelation, and, second, by teaching the reality of God the Holy Spirit, a point to which we shall return in the next chapter.

For the present, we shall consider a set of texts in the Gospels that indicate how Jesus taught his followers in such a way that they gradually became able to make Peter's profession: "You are the Christ, the Son of the living God" (Matt. 16:16). In doing his teaching, using the Old Testament, Jesus referred to himself what the Hebrew Scriptures said of Yahweh. The cumulative effect of these Gospel passages is that of "a striking and daring claim."[42] Jesus identifies himself with Yahweh in a way that his Jewish hearers, formed in the Hebrew Scriptures from their birth, would immediately perceive. We Gentiles have become accustomed to saying that Jesus taught "the divinity of Christ," making use of the Hebrew Scriptures to do so.

"Heaven and earth will pass away," Jesus teaches, "but my words will not pass away" (Mark 13:31). It is a common teaching of the Old Testament that the Word of God abides permanently, in contrast with the cosmic order, as his hearers would recognize immediately.[43] But now it is the word of Jesus for which the identical claim is made.

"And the blind and the lame came to him in the temple, and he healed them. But when the chief priests and the scribes saw the wonderful things that he did, and the children crying out in the temple, 'Hosanna to the Son of David,' they were indignant" (Matt. 21:14–15). They reproached Jesus, expecting him to disown this Messianic acclamation. Jesus refused to do so but positively confirmed it by citing the Hebrew Scriptures: "O Lord, our Lord . . . whose glory above the heavens is chanted by the mouth of babes and infants. . . ."[44]

"Behold, I have given you authority to tread upon serpents and scorpions," Jesus tells his disciples, "and over all the power of the enemy; and nothing shall hurt you" (Luke 10:19). Here Jesus is alluding to Yahweh's gift of immunity for his faithful followers that had become proverbial in the Old Testament. Jesus' followers understand the connection: they begin to think that Jesus actually is Yahweh visiting his people.

In Luke 20:19, Jesus' hostile Jewish hearers understand quite clearly that he himself is the cornerstone that they are rejecting: it will fall upon them and crush them. This is a clear allusion to Isaiah 8:14–15, where the "Lord of hosts . . . will become a rock of stumbling to both houses of Israel."[45]

Jesus makes use of three Messianic texts that taken together point to an identity of the Messiah and Yahweh. He himself of course is this Messiah. He is the pierced one of Zechariah 12:10, for whom one day Jerusalem will mourn; he is the smitten shepherd of Zechariah 13:7–8, and he is the Coming One of Daniel 7:13–14, the king coming on the clouds of glory as Yahweh himself.

Finally, there are the many places of the Hebrew Scriptures on the coming of Yahweh on the Day of the Lord for judgment. Jesus refers them to himself as the Son of Man.[46] The coming of Jesus *is* the coming of Yahweh for judgment. This "Day of the Lord" begins with Jesus' public life; it will be finished with his Second Coming. Jesus in his teaching pictures himself, announces himself, as Yahweh is pictured in the Old Testament coming out with an angelic retinue. It is Jesus, the Son of man, who sits on Yahweh's throne of judgment.

"Jesus seems to have suggested," writes Professor France, "not only that he had come to do the work of God (as the Messiah and Suffering Servant), but that he and his Father are one."[47] This, in fact, is exactly Jesus' teaching. When Philip asked him to show them the Father, Jesus answered, "Have I been with you so long, and yet you do not know me, Philip? He who has seen me has seen the Father. . . . Do you not believe that I am in the Father and the Father in me? The words that I say to you I do not speak on my own authority; but the Father who dwells in me does his works" (John 14:8–10).

This may serve to illustrate Jesus' use of the Hebrew Scriptures in his teaching. This teaching of his own divine Sonship provides the foundation in the Bible for the doctrine of the Divine Trinity, to which we shall return later when considering the training Jesus gave his Apostles for continuing his own teaching program and in the next chapter on the specific content of that teaching.

Conclusion

Jesus teaches the divine authorship of the Bible by pointing out its unity through its fulfillment in himself. This is the great fact of facts about the Bible that bears witness that God is its Author.

The witness of the Apostles to the content and character of the teaching they received from their Rabbi is consistent and striking. Matthew concludes the Sermon on the Mount with the note that Mark uses to introduce his single summary of the content of Jesus' doctrine (Mark 1:21 ff.). "And when Jesus finished these sayings, the crowds were astonished at his teaching, for he taught them as one who had authority, and not as their scribes" (Matt. 7:28–29).

Jesus is a Rabbi, a Teacher, in Israel, indeed, but one who teaches with a new kind of power and authority.[48] His disciples continue to feel confirmed in their original insight and decision in his regard: "We have found him of whom Moses in the Law and the Prophets write, Jesus the son of Joseph of Nazareth" (John 1:45).

This is a dimension of Jesus' teaching that demands special consideration, for it is the scriptural foundation of authenticity and therefore power in catechetical teaching to this day.

Kērygma: The Prophetic Quality of Jesus' Teaching

If Jesus in his concrete humanity was a Rabbi of his time and place and the Gospels as historical documents make this ever more clear as their historicity is better understood by historical science, there was this other fact that he was a Rabbi with a difference. His disciples, the group of students gathered about him, could not and did not miss this fact. The next step in the study of Jesus as a Teacher is to analyze from the original Greek text itself what the precise nature of this "new teaching" was, this teaching "with power and authority" that made him appear different from all the other Rabbis of the day, the entire order of the Scribes, whether Pharisees or Sadducees. This has practical value in contemporary catechetics, for Jesus trained his disciples to teach as he did, in such a way that not only the positive content but also the difference in mode would transfer to them and be for all time one of their distinguishing marks.[49]

This analysis has to do with another verb denoting Jesus' activity, quite different from those in *didask-*. It is the verb that has its root in the Greek noun *Keryx*. It can begin with a second reading of the Gospel according to Saint Mark. But first, what was a *Keryx*? What did the Greek word *Keryx* mean in the human world of Graeco-Roman culture? What is a *kērygma*?[50]

Used upward of ninety times in Homer, *Keryx* was an important word in Greek life and literature, as were indeed its counterparts in the other languages of antiquity—the Hebrew and the Latin included. For it denoted an important official in public life, the "herald" in the service of a king or representing officially the governing body of a city-state.[51]

Two qualities were required for appointment to the position of a herald. First, as Aristotle noted in his *Politics*, was a penetrating, stentorian voice. In the times before printing, radio, and television, before electronic amplification, the herald or town crier was the accepted way for rulers to make contact with their peoples. Needless to say, the role of the herald was essential in the armies of antiquity. The second quality was far more important, formal rather than the merely material one of a suitable voice. It was the loyal disposition of the candidate for appointment to this office never to tamper with the message. The herald must communicate the message, Plato and Aeschylus agree, exactly as handed to him by the authority whom he serves and represents, for the essential point about a herald is the fact that nothing in the content of the message comes from himself. It is a word from a higher power that stands behind the herald. The herald neither adds to it nor substracts from it. A herald never gives his own opinion: his function is simply to serve as the speaking tube, as it were, for the ruler he represents. Heralds were not diplomats: they did not discuss or negotiate. They simply delivered the message with the most complete accuracy and in a way no one would mistake or fail to hear. The herald is simply the executive organ of the authority who appointed him and who delegated him to act in each instance.

Throughout classical antiquity and among all peoples the herald had religious status. Among his duties was the preparation of the official sacrificial worship of each person or each city-state and the supervision of the ceremonies. His person was considered sacred and immune from enemy attack, much like a Red Cross worker in recent times. Wars were known to break out in antiquity when a city presumed to violate the safe-conduct of a herald. For this official shared in the religious concept of kingship in antiquity: the ruler of the city governed on behalf of the city's gods. So, too, the herald: he spoke on behalf of the gods whom civic life served and worshiped.

A herald is an official delegated to call, to wake, to proclaim a piece of news, to communicate a message on behalf of a supreme authority. It was so also among the Hebrews, as both the Bible and writers like Philo and Josephus bear witness.[52]

Keryx in the Gospels

Turning to Saint Mark's Gospel, the words in *keryx-* meet the reader from the beginning, hammering home a concept. First, the nature of Saint Mark's short writing ''the beginning of the Good

News about Jesus Christ, the Son of God" (Mark 1:1).[53] Then the arousing impact of John the Baptist, with the use of *keryx*- to denote the precise nature of his activity: "John did baptize in the wilderness, and preach [with root in *keryx*-] the baptism of repentance (*metanoías*), for the remission of sins" (Mark 1:4). "And [he] preached [with root in *keryx*-], saying: There cometh one mightier than I after me . . . " (Mark 1:7).

Immediately Mark introduces this Mightier One: "Now after John was arrested, Jesus came into Galilee, preaching [verb rooted in *keryx*-], the Gospel of God, and saying, 'The time is fulfilled, and the Kingdom of God is at hand; Repent [verb rooted in *metanóia*], and believe [verb rooted in *pistis*, faith] in the Gospel' " (Mark 1:14–15). This is an immensely compressed passage, masterful in evoking what actually happened. It has all the fresh immediacy of direct eyewitness testimony. Christian literature since the beginning has evaluated Mark's Gospel as a reporting of Peter's manner of describing the simple truth about the way it all began and took place. This evaluation continues to ring true, and the more so as the "Modern" climate in Christian intellectual life gives way to a "Postmodern" one.

The opening chapters of Saint Mark's Gospel must be read with an eye upon the verbs in *keryx*- in order to grasp today the sense of immediacy with which the disciples report their experience and the stirring impact upon all Palestine that moved the Chosen People to their depths. The coming of Jesus was more than that of simply another Teacher of the Torah in the customary pattern. His coming was an event, for it was an announcing or proclaiming of a piece of news in the mode of a herald.[54] It moved this People of Israel to their heart and soul because they had been schooled by the Prophetic Word to expect just such news. How it would come they did not know. But its basic content they could recognize, and they even had some idea when it would come. The time could well seem at hand for the average Jew.[55] Only this general background of a populace schooled in the great expectation of "him of whom Moses in the Law and the Prophets wrote . . . " (John 1:45), coupled with the nature of Jesus' message, enables the reader of Mark in the twenty-first century to grasp what was taking place.

He taught in the synagogue at Capernaum as any of the teachers would. But the teaching was different. The difference was in the mode of a herald as well as in the content: "They were astonished at his teaching; for he was teaching them as one having authority, and not as the Scribes" (Mark 1:21–22). And he cured a demoniac before them all in this same synagogue. "And they were all amazed, so that they inquired among themselves, saying, 'What is this? What new doctrine is this? For with authority he commands even the unclean spirits, and they obey him' " (Mark 1:27).

Mark's report describes the impact upon the population laconically yet sweepingly, as only an eyewitness could do. "And at once his fame spread everywhere throughout all the surrounding region of Galilee" (Mark 1:28). There were no telephones, radios, television, or newspapers. The reader today must put himself into a sudden word-of-mouth situation in which everyone was talking, reporting, communicating to his neighbor: "Have you heard . . . ?" And it was like lightning: "at once" . . . "everywhere" . . . "throughout all Galilee."

A little later Jesus was at Simon's residence in Capernaum, which he was using as his personal base. "And the whole city was gathered together about the door" (Mark 1:32). This is no ordinary teacher. The whole population is involved, and pressure mounted. "He went on to a lonely place and there he prayed" (Mark 1:35). Simon and the disciples followed Jesus, knowing already his habits and where he was to be found. "And they found him and said to him, 'Everyone is searching for you' " (Mark 1:36). *Everyone.* But the populace in general does not find him. Only the inner circle of the Teacher's students knows where to go. Curing a leper by a word, "I will; be thou made clean" (Mark 1:41), Jesus charged the man not to talk but to report quietly to the priests of the Hebrew religion. The man did not listen: "He went out, and began to publish and spread abroad the fact, so that Jesus could no longer openly enter a town, but he was out in the country; and people came to him from every quarter" (Mark 1:45).

Returning to Capernaum, Jesus was reported to again be "at home." Again the populace gathered, "so there was no longer any room for them, even about the door. And he was preaching the word of God to them" (Mark 2:1–2). Shortly after, Jesus went out to the edge of the town beside the Sea of Galilee. "And all the crowd gathered about him, and he taught [verb in *didask-*] them" (Mark 2:13).

The Prophetic Word of Jesus

Verbs denote activity. Jesus was active as a *Didàskalos* as the verbs in *didask-* bear witness, but the Greek text is sprinkled also with the verbs in *keryx-*, denoting this special quality of his teaching. "Let us go on to the next towns," he said to his disciples, "that I may preach [rooted in *keryx-*] there also; for that is why I came out" (Mark 1:38). When Jesus' training of the inner circle had reached a certain point, he sent them to do what he had been doing. "He summoned the Twelve and began to send them forth two by two . . . and he instructed them. . . . And going forth, they preached [root in *keryx-*] that men should repent [root in *metánoia*] . . ." (Mark 6:7–12). Already Jesus was talking to them in worldwide terms, instructing them for this same mission in universalized form. When the disciples asked him to explain his teaching on the end of the world, he linked it explicitly with his program: "The gospel must first be preached [root in *keryx-*] to all nations" (Mark 13:10). The matter had to be a common theme of Jesus' teaching given to the inner circle, for he simply takes it for granted in his defense of Magdalen when the disciples argue over an action of hers: "Wherever the gospel is preached [root in *keryx-*] in the whole world, what she has done will be told in memory of her" (Mark 14:9).

When the verb *keryssein*, rooted in the office and function of a *keryx* throughout antiquity, is translated by the English word "*preach*," a vital element of meaning fails to be communicated today.[56] It would be difficult to find a better illustration for the use of a human word with its human meaning to convey the very Word of God. For the supreme Authority whom the Herald represents is in this case God the Father Almighty, Creator and therefore Supreme Lord of heaven and earth. The universal kingship or rule of God over all creation stands at the very heart of Revelation, and it is the essential message or *kerygma* of the New Testament.[57] Jesus came as the Herald of the fulfillment of the Word that the Prophets had taught the Hebrews: the transfer to a new and different testament, the announcement that the times are now fulfilled, that the Kingdom of God, promised by all the Prophets, is now at hand. Jesus came to announce this Word from God—and to bring it into reality. The consummation of human history is already present in his person and his work. The ending of human history has begun to take place. One thing with this news is the call for *metánoia* on the part of each person hearing it. God has come near! His time is at hand! Turn to him, therefore, and rethink the purpose of human life! This is the essence in Christianity and in the catechetical teaching of the Christian message. It is a *didachē*, a *doctrina*, a teaching, indeed, but the content is different from any of the other bodies of knowledge and contents of learning on the human scene. It is a content from God, a *kērygma* that involves the personal decision and personal life of the learner in the dimension of his relationship to the Lord of God of the universe and hence of his everlasting destiny.[58] As Jesus is a Teacher in Israel but different, so the teaching program he organized, exemplified, and sent his students to continue is a teaching on the human scene but different. It has a different quality and nature and frame of reference because it is "kerygmatic" in the correct sense: the authoritative message or Word of God on human destiny.[59]

Jesus' human presence as a Rabbi or *Didáskalos* is not changed or suddenly somehow denied when it is recognized that he was a Herald who announced that new turn of events that the Jews were expecting, the transition and fulfillment of which Moses and all the Prophets wrote. This means rather that the content of Jesus' teaching is a *kērygma*, divine in origin, nature, and authority. This dimension qualifies the nature of the content of his teaching, and is supposed to do so whenever and wherever teachers in his name do his teaching, to the end of the world. It is a teaching that takes place in the world-historical perspective of Yahweh's plan in human history, his plan of revelation, redemption, and salvation for mankind. This is perfectly normal. For a herald proclaims a message that is true and can therefore be analyzed and explained by teaching. In itself it is a content of truth of an especially important, solemn, and officially authoritative character. It is a *kērygma* from God that places a call to each who hears it. When it is explained and handed on by a teaching that helps each to respond to the call, that teaching shares in the mode of the *kērygma* and becomes a teaching that is different and indeed unique on the human scene.

As the heralds of classical antiquity went before their kings proclaiming their message, so Christianity hurries through this world, calling with a herald's authority and voice: the end is coming, the kingdom of God is near, indeed at hand. Christianity brings into historical reality what Moses and the Prophets prepared and foretold. The hallmark of Christianity is fulfillment. This is what Jesus the Rabbi taught the inner circle of his disciples, as he prepared them gradually to understand better and brought them step by step to the point where he could send them as he himself had been sent. How he did this is a large subject, one that reveals Jesus from a new direction as the master Teacher in Israel.

Discipleship and Apostolicity: Jesus' Special Teaching of His Twelve Apostles

The course of events turning about the masterful figure of this new Teacher in Israel forced the rulers of the Jewish nation in Jerusalem to come to a decision regarding both John the Baptist and Jesus of Nazareth. For John the Baptist was presenting himself to the people as an authentic Prophet of God, fully in the line of the Prophets of earlier centuries. The people, furthermore, were accepting him as such. And now John was drawing attention to Jesus as the Coming One, the One of whom Moses and the Prophets wrote. Jesus was the purpose of John's preaching. John was his forerunner, sent to prepare the way for him.

This Jesus of Nazareth, as a matter of fact, was growing rapidly and mightily as a Teacher among the Jewish people. Disciples, in the formal sense of the classical *mathetēs* were gathering to him in significant number. He was an attractive leader. He had health and strength and a royal bearing.[60] He was an absolute standout as a speaker. The Gospels themselves bear witness, for a group of police officers sent by the Jerusalem government to arrest Jesus came back empty-handed. "No one laid hands on him. The officers then went back to the chief priests and the Pharisees, who said to them, 'Why did you not bring him?' The officers answered, 'No man ever spoke like this man' " (John 7:44–46).

Hence crowds gathered to hear him, and those who declared themselves his disciples, followers in the precise sense of *mathetēs*, learners associated with a *Rabbi*, Teacher, came themselves to be a crowd.[61] "And coming down with them (the Twelve), he took his stand on a level stretch, with a crowd of his disciples [Greek *mathetai*], and a great multitude of people from all Judea and Jerusalem, and the sea coast of Tyre and Sidon. . . . " (Luke 6:17).

The concern of the authorities at Jerusalem to analyze and evaluate the phenomenon is clear in the Gospels. Emissaries were sent repeatedly both to John and to Jesus, questioning, observing, reporting back. No records have survived to inform regarding the sessions of the Sanhedrin at Jerusalem. But sessions there had to be agitated, tense, even stormy, as Nicodemus gives to understand. The question had to be faced. Was John truly and really a Prophet, the spokesman of Yahweh? If so, he had to be heeded. When John pointed Jesus out as the expected One, the duty became clear: the Government of Israel was obliged to go to this Teacher, as the people were beginning to do, and to learn from him what to do, how to reorganize things in the light of the fulfillment of the Prophets, how to help him to implement the Messianic Age with its long-expected outreach to all the Gentile nations. Would the weight of the official structures of the Jewish nation be thrown behind this Teacher? Or would this entire phenomenon be written off as something merely human, another of the misguided movements of those hot-headed young Zealots who wanted action now in liberation from subjection to Imperial Rome?

This agonizing question continued to paralyze the Jewish leadership long after it had come to its official decision and position. For Jesus' popular support was a hard reality.[62]

Sessions, therefore, there had to be, with constant interplay between the Sanhedrin and Herod, Rome's puppet King of the Jews. The decision was made, and those like Nicodemus who wished it had been different felt obliged to contact Jesus secretly, by night.

The nature of the official decision became public knowledge in the arrest of John. Jesus takes with perfect calm the loss of official support by the rulers of his people. He does not stall, does not wring his hands, does not seek a political compromise of some kind with the holders of Moses' authority. He simply transfers the scene of his activity to Galilee, less directly under the control of Jerusalem, and proceeds with his calling as a Rabbi, a Teacher, in Israel: "Now when he heard that John had been delivered up, he withdrew into Galilee" (Matt. 4:12). "And after John had been delivered up, Jesus came into Galilee, preaching the gospel of the kingdom of God, and saying, 'The time is fulfilled, and the kingdom of God is at hand. Repent, and believe the Gospel' " (Mark 1:14–15).

Jesus Calls and Institutionalizes His Twelve Apostles

The issue is joined. Jesus proceeds with his Father's work of business, that of fulfilling divine Revelation and of organizing its mediation to all mankind by teaching. He accepts realistically the fact of the official negative position of the Jewish government regarding John the Baptist and himself. He calmly sets about to found and build that new institution that he himself calls "my Church" (see Matt. 16:18).

Jesus does so by calling twelve of his disciples to become his full-time Rabbinical Talmudim, a set of men whom he will teach and train to carry his program of teaching out to all the Gentile peoples of the earth (see Matt. 28:16–20). In Saint Mark's Gospel they are called simply "the Twelve" (see Mark 4:10, 9:35, 10:32, 11:11, 14:10, 17, 20, and 43). "He appointed twelve to be with him, and to be sent out to preach" (Mark 3:14). In the parallel passages of Saint Matthew they are called "the Twelve Disciples," while St. Luke, writing for the Gentiles, characteristically calls them "the Twelve Apostles." It would be excessive to give all these references here. But whoever pursues and ponders them will see that it is Jesus himself who accomplishes this immensely important institution of his Twelve Apostles. For the catechetical study of the Bible, this move on Jesus' part is fundamental, for it solves the modern pseudo problem of the so-called Jesus of history and the Christ of faith. The vital point is to see this move as a personal decision and accomplishment of Jesus—indeed, the Jesus of history.

For there are two perspectives upon the work of Jesus the divine Teacher. One is to see it from his living teaching of his Twelve prior to his crucifixion, looking forward into the coming Christian era. The other is to take one's stand in the Christian era, see the tradition of catechetical teaching, and trace it back to the powerful Teacher who stands at the head of the Apostolic Tradition. The first is proper to this study of biblical Catechetics; the second will be a major theme of the second volume of this manual.

In each perspective a pattern of teaching emerges: a teaching of faith in the Three Persons and of the triple response to it as one's Way of Life: prayer to God our Father and creator, love of God the Incarnate Son by keeping his commandments; and fidelity to God the Holy Spirit by Eucharistic living. Thus Jesus the Divine Teacher becomes clearly visible as the originator of the Apostolic Tradition and of the Apostolicity that constitutes his Church. This Apostolicity, furthermore, is defined precisely in terms of Jesus' doctrine, which he placed on deposit with his Twelve Apostles. The Gospels bear massive witness to Jesus' teaching of the Trinitarian faith and the response of the catechumen to each divine Person. The future catechumenate will bear the same witness.

It is basic to stress that Apostolicity is constituted and defined in terms of Jesus' doctrine. It is his choice of his Twelve to receive a special teaching that reveals him fully as a Teacher in Israel. For these Twelve *mathetai* are disciples in the sense of higher education as it was organized and conducted throughout classical antiquity, as already noted, both among the Gentile peoples and in the Rabbinate of Israel.[63]

With one mind and his whole heart Jesus proceeds to perform his mission in life. His enterprise is a hazardous one due to the official refusal at Jerusalem. He cannot promise himself the kind of success with the Jewish people that official support would have given him.[64] But hazardous or not, sweepingly successful or not, he must be faithful to his mission, that of organizing the Messianic Kingdom.

Jesus' plan is to set up a new Israel of God, a new people baptized with the spiritual fire of the Holy Spirit. He must constitute this people and open it up to all the Gentile nations. He must launch it into human history with all the elements essential to its mission. This mission is nothing else than the unification of all mankind in a new supernatural unity of one faith in the fullness of Divine Revelation and one Baptism into the new and higher life that all the Prophets had foreseen. All of this is signified by the precise number twelve, as in the twelve tribes of the Old Law.

In his choice of the twelve special *mathetai* and by the special teaching he gave them Jesus is personally, from the human point of view, fully revealed as a Rabbi, a Teacher, of his time and place both in general content, the Torah, and in all his methods of teaching. At the same time, he continues to be a Rabbi with a difference, for world-historical perspectives are present from the outset and the outlines of the entity that he called "My Church" are already coming into view.

Teaching is always and on all levels the communication of some content of truth by means of the method suitable and proper to this particular truth that is given to others. How did Jesus form the Twelve for the purpose he had in mind? It was by the fully human process of teaching, on the level of "higher education" as it was carried on at that time. Jesus continues to be a Master Teacher in Israel, with the human side of his calling completed now with this select group of full-time learners. He is a Rabbi with his Talmudim, exactly like the rest, from the human point of view. The difference that marked him as a Teacher, the difference that the crowds noted, will only appear when the method and the content of his teaching are analyzed in close detail, together with the fact that he chose them, not vice versa, for the purpose he had in mind, that of preparing them to be sent as he himself had been sent by his Father in heaven.[65]

Jesus' Formation of the Apostles

How, then, did Jesus teach them? First, and chiefly, by his example, by the way he lived. It was part of "higher education" at that time that the group of students actually lived full-time with the teacher, so that they came to know his approach completely and comprehensively from within. This highly personalized and formative aspect of method lives on in the graduate seminar of the modern university, especially in the German universities, or in the tutorial method that John Henry Newman exemplified as a professor at Oxford.[66] In the case of Jesus, the Twelve were now constant companions who witnessed the way he taught the general body of his followers, his *mathetai*, all of them, but not in this intimate, full-time, special sense that was their own unique privilege. They learned not only the content he was giving but also the mode, so different from that of the other Rabbis. For he was always teaching in the mode of the formal object of Revelation. *But I say to you . . .* Above all, they came to love him, for he attached them to his person. This will be discussed in the next chapter.

It grew upon them that he was constantly finalizing the Revelation made to Moses and doing so with authority. Always they faced the question: Who then can this be? (Mark 4:41). The answer came home to them gradually. They observed him in all this teaching he was doing and learned how to be sent to teach the same content and to present it in that same mode, namely, on the authority of God revealing.

But their call to this special discipleship enabled them to study him from the viewpoint of the example of his personal private life. The Gospels bear witness to what they saw: he exemplified the celibate life, and he spent time, much time, systematic daily time, in prayer.[67]

But Jesus also taught the Twelve by constant purposive doctrinal discussion, much as professors today take their advanced degree candidates informally into their confidence in the university seminars. Frequently these discussions resulted from teaching that Jesus gave to the broader group of his disciples at large or from the occasion of encounters with representatives of the now-hostile authorities at Jerusalem. It is difficult to exaggerate this privilege enjoyed by the Twelve. Since they were with him constantly, these sessions of teaching-and-learning went on ceaselessly. Indeed, there were times, as the Gospels bear witness, that he took them apart for extended periods for the express purpose of teaching and forming them in the light of developments in his public life in Palestine.[68] "I will not now call you servants," he tells them in a passage that reveals the inner nature of this school that formed the Twelve, "for the servant knoweth not what his Lord doth. But I have called you friends: because all things whatsoever I have heard of my Father, I have made known to you" (John 15:15). It is in this attractive context that the content of Jesus' doctrine was given to them, a content that was the luminous fulfillment of the Divine Revelation that had been given to Abraham's people by the Prophets. Jesus himself stated the principle that guided all his teaching and his entire formation of his Twelve Apostles: "Do not think that I have come to destroy the Law of the Prophets. I have not come to destroy, but to fulfill" (Matt. 5:17).

The Pattern or Method of Jesus' Teaching Program

Jesus not only gave his Apostles the content of his teaching; he also showed them how to be faithful teachers of it themselves, guarding the purity and integrity of the doctrine that he placed on deposit with them.

Jesus did this by giving the Apostles a pattern or type or method or standard procedure in handing on the essentials of his doctrine. Saint Paul bears witness to the fact that the Church at that earliest time possessed and used that pattern in all its catechetical instruction and formation of converts. "You who were once the slaves of sin," he writes to the Romans, "have become obedient from the heart to the standard of teaching to which you were committed" (Rom 6:17). This key phrase, *typos didachēs* in the Greek, is rendered variously in the English translations as the "form" or "patterns" or "standard" of the teaching. The Jerusalem Bible uses a noteworthy translation: "the Creed you were taught." At first sight it may seem somewhat bold to render *typos* as "the Creed." Yet when one ponders the role that the Apostles' Creed will have when the teaching in the catechumenate comes into full view in the writings of the Fathers of the Church, it appears to be exactly correct. The Fathers make it massively clear that this pattern or syllabus for the teaching is the faith in the three Divine Persons together with the response, already noted earlier, of personal prayer, Gospel morality, and Eucharistic living. This triple response is related respectively to the Father, the Son, and the Holy Spirit. This is the *typos didachēs*, the pattern of Jesus' teaching, from that time to the present. The catechumenate and the printed catechisms exist already in germ, or as the acorn that will grow into the mighty tree of the Christian era.

Was this *typos didachēs* the invention of the later Christian community, as Bultmann and his followers imagine? This question will be taken up later when the actions and writings of the Apostles, now out on the mission that Jesus gave them, are studied. For the present, one can ponder the commentary of a renowned exegete on Romans 6:17. "Three conclusions result from this text," he writes. "First, the *typos didachēs* means an 'exemplar' or 'model'. . . . ; secondly, it is authoritative, containing God's Will for a new way of life . . . ; thirdly, it is a rule which binds all the Churches, the preachers and teachers being obliged to conform to it in their work."[69]

Already the four marks of the Church are visible here in their original nucleus. This *typos* of the Apostolic teaching constitutes the Apostolicity of the Church. The Church is Holy, because this teaching produces the new way of life. And it results that the Church is

One and Catholic, for this credal *typos* guides and protects a teaching that is one and the same always and everywhere. It is One, Holy, Catholic, and Apostolic, as the Creed will profess.

Thus it becomes clear that this Trinitarian pattern is not a later invention of the "community." It is the masterstroke, humanly speaking, of Jesus the Teacher of his Apostles. The Trinity of Divine Persons forms the very heart of the content of Jesus' teaching of Divine Revelation.[70] The fact that he not only gives his content to the Apostles but also arranges that it be the *typos* or *pattern* or "Creed" that guides the teaching intact when it is handed on to others constitutes this masterstroke. It moves Jesus' program forward in time, the same in every place, always and everywhere raising up disciples who follow Jesus in the new Way of Life.

In retrospect, humanly speaking, one must say that Jesus Christ is the greatest and most lastingly effective teacher who ever has appeared on the human scene.[71]

C.H. Dodd, the Anglican professor at Cambridge University and a leading exegete of the twentieth century, writes as follows about Jesus' work with the Bible and its interpretation:

> It must be conceded that we have before us a considerable intellectual feat. The various Scriptures are acutely interpreted. . . . Very diverse Scriptures are brought together so that they interpret one another in hitherto unsuspected ways. . . . This is a piece of genuinely creative thinking. Who was responsible for it? The early Church, we are accustomed to say. . . . But creative thinking is rarely done by committees. It is individual minds that originate. Whose was the originating mind here? . . . The New Testament itself avers that it was Jesus Christ Himself who first directed the minds of His followers to certain parts of the Scriptures as those in which they might find illumination upon the meaning of His mission and destiny. . . . To account for the beginning of this most original and fruitful process of rethinking the Old Testament we found need to postulate a creative mind. The Gospels offer us one. Are we compelled to reject the offer?[72]

Catechists, basing themselves on biblical Catechetics, feel no such compulsion. On the contrary, the catechetical study of the Bible places Jesus in true perspective as the great and powerful Teacher in his public life who continues his same program in the catechesis of his Body, which is the Church.

Chapter 8

The Credal Summary of Jesus' Teaching

"My teaching is not mine," Jesus told the Jews at the Temple, "but his who sent me" (John 7:16). This is the summary of chapter 7. Jesus' teaching in its mode of divine authority is given to mankind out of the prophetic light, that of Moses and the Prophets, but now perfected, completed, and final.

Hence the Catholic Church solemnly defines the concept of the Deposit of Faith: "The teaching of faith, which God has revealed, has not been proposed as a philosophical discovery to be perfected by human ingenuity, but as a divine deposit handed over to the Spouse of Christ to be guarded faithfully and explained infallibly. . . . [Therefore,] if anyone should say that with the progress of knowledge it is sometimes possible that dogmas proposed by the Church can be given a meaning different from the one that the Church has understood and still understands, let him be anathema."[1]

The content of Jesus' teaching, therefore, does not come from the human empirical sciences or the human philosphies. It stands changelessly above the level of human reason, for it comes out of the prophetic light, the very Word of God spoken now by the lips of God Incarnate.[2]

When John Henry Newman, the future cardinal, was a youth of fifteen, he was reading David Hume, suffering his solicitation to the atheistic way of thinking. Among Newman's papers was found a project of his from that same time: he undertook to gather passages from Scripture, especially the Gospels, that provide the foundation for the Articles of Faith summarized in the Apostles' Creed. No doubt this was a part of his victory over Hume.

Something similar is offered in this chapter. The twelve headings of the Creed of the People of God are taken as the basis for a

169

synthetic summary of Jesus' teaching. For as the Apostles' Creed of the earliest Church was its official summary of Jesus' teaching for baptismal profession, personal prayer, and catechesis, so the Creed of the People of God is the developed form of the Apostles' and Nicene Creeds given by the Holy See to the Church today as a secure guide in the doctrinal chaos after Vatican II.[3] Thus by reflecting on the unity of the Creed of the People of God and the Gospel reports on Jesus' teaching, biblical Catechetics makes another contribution toward the authenticity of catechesis today. This unity results from the fact that it is the same Jesus who taught his Apostles in his public life and who teaches through his Apostles in his Body, which is the Church. This will be a major theme in volume 2 of this manual.

1. The Reality of God, the Father Almighty, Creator of Heaven and Earth[4]

In one of his final teaching encounters Jesus answered a group of the Sadducees, who say there is no resurrection: "Is not this why you err—because you know neither the Scriptures nor the power of God?" (Mark 12:24). So far had the doctrinal decline gone among the Jews, and so great was the need for renewal of the Prophetic Religion, for the Sadducees were the priestly party, one of the two parties ruling from Jerusalem. A Scribe, noting that Jesus had answered them well, asked him further which was the first commandment of all. "But Jesus answered him, 'The first commandment of all is, Hear, O Israel! The Lord our God is one God; and thou shalt love the Lord thy God with thy whole heart, and with thy whole soul, and with thy whole mind, and with thy whole strength. This is the first commandment. And the second is like it: Thou shalt love thy neighbor as thyself. There is no commandment greater than these' " (Mark 12:20–31); Jesus is quoting Deuteronomy 6, the Hebrew Shema).

> This reply of Jesus enables us to touch the rock on which the whole Christian religion rests—faith in God alone. To formulate this faith, Jesus revived the daily prayer of every Israelite, the Shema. . . . . It is the faith of Israel, then, that gives to Christian faith the basic formula on which the huge edifice will be erected. The Mosaic and prophetic

revelation is not effaced, but fulfilled, by the Gospel. The affirmation of the one God, only Lord, loved above all things, will be sacred to the Christians as much as and even more than it was to the Jews; this is what the martyrs will confess unto death. To this intransigence of faith will be united, more ardent than ever before, the jealousy of love. The Son of God will have Christians understand, as no man had ever yet understood, what it is to love God above all things.[5]

Jesus' teaching represented the renewal of the Hebrew listings of prophetic religion as well as its crown and fulfillment. It was impossible to brand him objectively as teaching a deviation from the authentic Hebrew religion. "No one after that ventured to ask him questions" (Mark 12:34).

Thus Jesus taught the Twelve. Gradually they learned what he meant by his constant use of "My Father," expressing his own relationship to Yahweh, as distinct from "your Father,": "Your Father, who sees in secret, will reward you" (Matt. 6:4). Always in Jesus' teaching the first principle and foundation is the transcendent personal reality of the God of Revelation, the Lord God of the Hebrew Testament and of the Jewish people to the present. There is no sign of pantheism, the natural experiencing of the divine in and through the natural life and phenomenon of the cosmos.

Jesus' teaching by his words and by his example of prayer was entirely in the context of the Hebrew faith in Yahweh, the personal and intelligent Supreme Being, the transcendent Creator of the cosmos and of everything in it, including especially man, body and soul. It emphasized the almighty power of the Heavenly Father to exercise his divine Providence over all that exists and happens, above all over the whole of human history, and over the smallest events in the myriad personal histories of his individual human creatures:

> Therefore I say to you, do not be anxious for your life, what you shall eat. . . . Look at the birds in the air: they do not sow, or reap, or gather into barns; yet your heavenly Father feeds them. Are not you of much more value than they? But which of you by being anxious about it can add to his stature a single cubit? . . . Therefore do not be anxious, saying, "What shall we eat?" or "What shall we drink?" or, "What shall we put on?" (for after all these things the Gentiles seek); for your Father knows that you need all these things. But seek

first the kingdom of God and his justice, and all these things shall be given to you besides. (Matt. 6:25–34)

This is theism in its full sense, at the opposite pole from atheism whether explicit or in its disguise as pantheism. Thus Jesus' teaching is a wonderfully logical unfolding of the meaning of that synthetic call of the herald from God in Mark 1:14–15: "And after John had been delivered up, Jesus came into Galilee, preaching the gospel of the Kingdom of God, and saying, 'The time is fulfilled, and the kingdom of God is at hand. Repent and believe in the gospel.' "

When this meaning is fully unfolded, the remaining eleven chief headings of Jesus' teaching will have been imparted comprehensively to the Twelve. The entire program is masterfully summarized in his two points that bear upon the doctrinal deficiency of the Sadducees. He is teaching the almightiness of God's power, with the basic attitude that ought to follow among men; and he is teaching the correct interpretation, the right understanding, of all the Scriptures in terms of the fulfillment he is giving to them by opening up the final times of human history. For this is the meaning of the Kingdom of God that he is announcing and which he will begin to build upon these twelve special disciples whom he is teaching and training and forming with this purpose in view.[6]

2. The Holy Trinity: Jesus Reveals the Inner Life of Yahweh

There are indications in the Old Testament, indeed, that in God there is more than one Divine Person.[7] But these are only indications, hardly recognizable as such before the Revelation made by Jesus Christ. For in the preparatory stages of Revelation the unique and absolute Oneness of the Divine Nature had to be established by the Prophets in the face of the ambient polytheism.

The teaching of Jesus Christ, as noted in the previous chapter, was a sustained revelation of the inner life of the Supreme Being. The Gospels bear witness to this teaching on every page. Each Gospel can be read from the viewpoint of its witness to God the Father, then of its witness to God the Son, and finally from the viewpoint of its witness to God the Holy Spirit. The Acts of the Apostles, furthermore, bear a special witness to the personal reality of the Holy

Spirit, sent now, as Jesus promises so explicitly in the Gospels, upon the Church of these same Twelve special students who will be called the Apostles. When the Gospels are given these three readings, it will be observed that the Three Divine Persons are present rather equally in the pages of the New Testament: the Christian Revelation is fundamentally the disclosure to mankind of this personal inner life of Yahweh, the living God of the Hebrews.

Jesus' teaching, then, became gradually quite clear to the Twelve. This One Only God, Yahweh of the Hebrews, the Creator of Life and the Lord of History, *is* the Father, *is* the Son, *is* the Holy Spirit. The Twelve learned the double aspect of the Divine Mystery, the fact that God is simultaneously One and Three.[8]

The Names of the Three Divine Persons are central to Jesus' teaching program. These Names denote the divine Reality that the Twelve will learn to profess as the very heart of the new faith, the Gospel, that Jesus is teaching. They will be teachers of this same doctrine in their turn, for this is the purpose of the training they are receiving. In fact, as has been noted in the last chapter, the Three Divine Persons will give not only the *structure* of the emerging Christian profession of faith in God but also the *standard* or *pattern* or *syllabus* of the teaching that their Teacher will send them to do in his name, continuing his teaching program.

3. Jesus Teaches the Twelve the Mystery of the Incarnation

The basic question and even theme of each written Gospel is simply, "Who, then, is this?" (Mark 4:40). Who is this Teacher? The Twelve learned gradually to know the full answer, to make it part of their teaching, and thus it has entered into the Catholic profession of the Apostolic Faith. In teaching and forming them unto the new and final faith in Yahweh One and Three, Jesus was revealing to them what he knew from within the Trinity: he himself is one of the Three Divine Persons. Yahweh *is* himself, the Divine Son; Yahweh *is* his Eternal Father; Yahweh *is* the Holy Spirit whom they will learn how to give as the supreme Gift to men in the religion their Teacher is establishing.

All beings or substantial realities reveal their natures by their activities. The Twelve were able to see readily, self-evidently, that their Teacher is fully and truly a man, with the same human nature and human activities as they themselves possessed. At the same time, gradually, and indeed in a most human way from the pedagogical point of view, they came to realize that they were witnesses to a true and factual theophany, a visible manifestation of God to man. The four written Gospels are actually a sustained witnessing to this theophany as a fact.[9] In a most human way; for any other way would have left them frightened, not to say overwhelmed. They were living with what Christians will term *the mystery of Christ;* they needed to come to know it by a careful progressive teaching that unfolded it as a mystery of *faith.*[10] Thus Jesus taught them.

One chief instance of theophany among the many that can be studied to which the Gospels bear witness regarding this program of the Teacher for his Twelve was his baptism in the Jordan by John the Baptist: "And behold, the heavens were opened and he saw the Spirit of God descending like a dove, and alighting on him; and lo, a voice from heaven, saying, 'This is my beloved Son, with whom I am well pleased' " (Matt. 3:16–17).

The two titles Son of Man and Son of God are frequent in the New Testament writings. Both together are keys to understanding how Jesus taught the Mystery of the Incarnation to the Twelve. In teaching the reality of the Three Divine Persons, Jesus lays the foundation for recognizing who he himself is. The Gospels reflect the process by which the Twelve (or better perhaps the Eleven, for one through his own fault never came to this knowledge) came to know that Jesus *is* Yahweh, *is* the Second of the Divine Persons. He *is* this One Only God, the Emmanuel, the God-with-us whom the Prophets saw coming, Yahweh visiting his people in the human nature he assumed by being born in time of the Virgin Mary. There were indications throughout Jesus' teaching presence to the Twelve by which they came to know his eternal preexistence and to recognize that their Teacher is the subject of a double generation, one in eternity, utterly beyond and prior to this temporal and visible cosmos, the other in time by birth from his mother. Thus there are in Christ, the Twelve came gradually to know, two distinct natures, each generation terminating in one and the same Person. And since the Person is the Eternal Son, it is Yahweh who has come, visiting his people and accomplishing this final teaching program that fulfills all the Hebrew Prophets. This is Yahweh in the Person of the Eternal

Son. The *Person* is not the Father, not the Holy Spirit, but the Son of God. But he and the Father and the Holy Spirit are One. "Philip, who sees me, sees the Father"; "I and the Father are one" (see John 14:8–11); "Before Abraham was, I am" (John 8:58). The Hebrew Revelation with its Shema is being fulfilled, not altered or destroyed: the unique Oneness of the Deity continues in the doctrine of the Trinity that the Son Incarnate is revealing.

"Who then is this?" the Twelve asked themselves more than once. They came to know. They will pass the answer forward in their own catechetical teaching program: Jesus Christ is true God and true man, which the official catechisms of the Church state as an Article of the Faith.[11]

Thus Jesus established by his teaching the two chief doctrinal facts of his religion, each a mystery of faith: the Trinity and the Incarnation. It remains to see how Jesus elaborated them in his teaching of the Twelve and how he provided for the handing on of these doctrines into the future by teaching.

4. The Following of Christ

It was the manifest intention of Jesus as a Teacher, which he stated explicitly more than once, to offer himself to the Twelve as a paradigm or model to imitate and to follow.[12] In his life among us, to which these privileged Twelve are the abiding witnesses, he was manifestly full of grace and truth. He taught and exemplified a wonderfully attractive new way of life, the Gospel way, the way of the Beatitudes. At the heart of this way of living was his new Commandment of love, fulfilling the moral law of Moses. It was new not in its content (the Ten Commandments abide: "If you love me, keep my Commandments" [John 15:14]) but in its motivating point of reference: "as I have loved you" (John 13:34). Each follower of Christ is to love his fellowmen *as Jesus did*, namely, in complete unselfishness, for the sake of love of the Heavenly Father of all men.

Jesus gave an example, first of all, of a human life lived entirely for the Heavenly Father, oriented toward the transcendent God. Jesus' was a life, in other words, not this-worldly and merely horizontal, but directed to a purpose beyond this world. This is theism in life and action. It came home to the Twelve as much or more from Jesus' example of celibacy and the practice of prayer than from his doctrinal teaching, clear and explicit as it was.

Since it was clearly Jesus' intention as the Apostles' Teacher to give them a formation unto union with God, unto the living of the interior life, a carrying of each one's cross for the love of God, it had to be a humanly satisfying day for him when they came with that special request "Lord, teach us to pray" (Luke 11:1). Forthwith he gave them the Our Father. From that moment it has been the characteristic prayer of Christianity and the abiding pattern for catechetical instruction in prayer.[13]

In giving the Twelve the formative example of his own way of life, Jesus was never in any doubt as to his own self-identity. He knew from the outset of his teaching that he is true God and true man, able therefore to offer a divinely perfect pattern of human behavior.[14] This is clear from Jesus' baptism with its theophany, the beginning of the Public Revelation that Jesus is teaching. Jesus himself knew who he was, and his task was to bring his Twelve gradually, by skillful teaching, toward Peter's Confession made on behalf of all (see Matt. 16:16 and John 6:68–69).

Thus the full Catholic Profession of Faith emerges from Jesus' teaching and formation of his Twelve. The human side of his life and activity was obviously visible to them, in both its humanity and the sustained perfection of its humanness. The divine side was revealed in the works he did that only God can do and in many of his words of doctrinal teaching. Not least among these are the awe-inspiring *I AM* passages, in which Jews recognized immediately that he was applying the divine name, Yahweh, to himself.[15]

When the witness of the Gospels is studied from this point of view, that of Jesus' didactic purpose in his handling and teaching of his Twelve, it becomes clear that he has two chief things in mind. The first is to prepare them to be sent by him as he was sent, to be teachers of the revealed Word of God that they learned from him; the second is to bring them to the point where they profess the Apostolic Faith, the Faith that begins in Peter's profession. Thus in being sent to teach they will have what they are to teach, namely, this same Profession of Faith, together with the *metanoia*, the human response of conversion to God that accepts this Word of God as a new Way of Life.

5. The Holy Spirit

Our knowledge of Jesus' teaching comes from the witness of these same Twelve in the writings they either did themselves or supervised later when continuing his teaching program. This witness makes it quite clear that Jesus gave them to know of a Third Divine Person in the inner life of Yahweh, the Living God. As Jewish men, brought up and schooled in the religion of Moses and the Prophets, the Twelve believed already in God the Father, in his almightiness and in his goodness, which assured Providential care over his people. Jesus could presuppose this Hebrew faith. It has been noted earlier that he was constantly building their faith in a second article of revealed truth: in himself as the Second Divine Person.

At the same time, his teaching was leading them to faith in a Third Divine Person, to whom he refers continually and whom he promises to send to them in two particular ways. Thus all three Divine Persons are equally present in the Gospels *as Persons* distinct from one another and at the same time each equally Yahweh, the one unique divinity of the Hebrew Revelation. This Third Divine Person has his own name, the Holy Spirit.[16] He is present in the Gospels as One who is promised, and in the other Apostolic writings of the New Testament, especially in the Acts of the Apostles, he is manifestly present as One poured out upon the followers of Christ.

What were the particular ways in which Jesus promises to send this Holy Spirit upon the Twelve? Chiefly two. First, he promises to send the Holy Spirit as the Spirit of Truth, to illuminate, protect, and govern them in their own teaching that they will be sent to do. Second, he promises to send the Holy Spirit as the Spirit of prayer and holiness, the Lord and Giver of Life, the very supernatural life that Jesus is teaching. One need but review what he stressed so pointedly to Nicodemus (see John 3:1–21). This interior life is the Way of Life of the Hebrew Prophets, contrasting with heathenism in all its forms, the Way of Death away from which Abraham was called. It is the Way of Holiness: "Be you perfect as your Heavenly Father is perfect" (Matt. 5:48). To be able to accept so high a standard, men need help. Jesus taught the Twelve to have confidence. He will provide this help by sending the Holy Spirit upon human persons to make them holy. Thus the purpose of the Law of Moses, to serve God with joy, will be fulfilled (see Ps. 95:94).

The witness of the Twelve in their future writings makes it manifest that Jesus reveals the reality of One God in three Divine Persons. When he calls upon men to "believe the Gospel" (Mark 1:15), Jesus is demanding this Trinitarian faith, "the central fact of Christianity".[17] With the Revelation of the Holy Spirit, Jesus is already turning the minds of the Twelve to the new Israel of God, the Church that he is preparing by his very teaching, for the Twelve are to be its foundations. The Holy Spirit will animate this coming Church: the Lord and Giver of life, he will be sent to illuminate, vivify, protect, and govern the Church. But even more, Jesus was teaching them the structure of the faith he is asking as their personal response to his teaching. When their Profession of Faith emerges into full view, it will be threefold, a religious profession in the name of the Father and of the Son and of the Holy Spirit.

To put this another way, the Profession of the Apostolic Faith, the Faith Jesus taught his Twelve, will contain three basic Articles of Faith, relating to each of the Three Divine Persons. These three articles emerge from his teaching. When at last Jesus sends the Twelve to baptize in terms of this Trinitarian Profession, they will understand well what they are to do. They will have in hand the pattern for their own teaching, that baptismal pattern or standard, the *typos didachēs* that we have seen in the previous chapter. Later on in the life of the Church it will be called the Apostles' Creed. The foundation is laid in this way for seeing accurately the nature of the Church for which Jesus is preparing foundations in this teaching of his Twelve. It will be a Church animated by the Holy Spirit. And it will be a Teaching Church, continuing his own teaching of the Trinitarian faith in the pattern he himself is giving.[18]

6. The Blessed Virgin Mary

As a part of the gradual process of their learning, the Twelve came to realize that Mary, the mother of Jesus, remained ever a virgin.

Jesus let them know at the outset, at Cana of Galilee, her position with him, namely the power of her intercession (cf. John 2:1–12). He praised her in a most public way not for the physical fact that she was his mother but for the kind of person she was, one who "hears and keeps the word of God." She was a woman of the faith and its practice as her way of life. She was already what he was teaching the Twelve to be.

Jesus allowed the Twelve to know her with the closeness of friends in daily association. From the writings that came later from this same group of special disciples it is clear that a large group of women, who could be naturally under the leadership and tutelage of Jesus' mother, followed him in their own special way with a ministry of their own. As Jesus and the Twelve were "journeying through towns and villages, preaching and proclaiming the Good News of the kingdom of God," Luke notes that women were "with him [and] the Twelve": he names three and adds that there were "many others." These "used to provide for them out of their means" (Luke 8:1–3). When the end came, "many women were there, looking on from a distance, who had followed Jesus from Galilee" (Matt. 27:55–56). Meditative reflection on such passages has enabled Christians to realize that Mary was at least the inspiration, if not the one who actually organized and supervised this irreplaceable woman's ministry for her Son and his work as a Teacher.[19]

The presence of the mother of Jesus in the documents that have been carried forward in history from the Twelve is a veiled one. But the presence is real, and only shallow minds with superficial approaches can miss it. When the teaching that Jesus was giving to his Twelve is pondered, it is clear that his mother grew in their minds as they learned gradually who he is and became able to profess the Faith in God for which he was calling. They came to realize that this is the Mother of God. This made clear the reason for her power of intercession. At last they became able to recognize her as their own mother and hence the Mother of the Church they were being prepared to found: "Woman, behold thy son," Jesus said to John: "then he said to the disciple, 'Behold thy Mother' " (John 19:26–27). When his teaching program will have been interrupted and terminated, then wondrously reconstituted, it will be noted that the Eleven "were continuing steadfastly in prayer with the women and Mary, the mother of Jesus" (Acts 1:14).

This closeness of the Twelve to the mother of Jesus that began during his teaching of them, indeed as a deliberately planned part of that teaching, brought them to know and understand, with a fullness proper to their own closeness to him as his special disciples the privileges of Mary as the New Eve. These privileges result from her altogether unique closeness to Jesus her Son. For she was far closer to Jesus than were the Twelve. Those who are feminine, or who appreciate femininity and motherhood, rightly understand this matter.[20]

It becomes possible in this way to recognize Mary as the basic source of the information of Jesus' infancy that the Twelve incorporated into the Gospels. The matter is treated in a beautifully reserved and veiled way, which one would expect. When Jesus' teaching and self-revelation had been completed and the outcome had transpired, the Twelve knew her privileges well, the fact that she was "full of grace," the fact of her perpetual virginity, and the fact that Joseph was Jesus' fosterfather, not his father. She was able to tell them many things when they were ready at last to hear her speak about them. For as they came to know by faith the preexistence of the Eternal Son and to recognize him as the Person actually present with them, Jesus their Teacher, they turned to her with a new reverence and devotion and with a new openness to her own particular and unique witness about her Son. It was basically her witness that was incorporated by them when they came to supervise the writings of those chapters in Matthew and Luke that are familiar to everyone today as the Infancy Gospel.[21]

7. Original Sin

Doubtless the Twelve penetrated best and most effectively into the Mystery of Christ as the completion and fulfillment of the Hebrew Revelation by coming to know the privileges of Mary. Since they were Jewish men, raised and schooled in the religion of Moses and the Prophets, the concept of Mary as the New Eve, "full of grace" and "blessed among women" (Luke 1:28) had a richness of meaning. For they knew well the sin of the first parents of all mankind and its consequences for each human person.

The four Gospels and indeed the entire New Testament can be reread from the viewpoint of each of these main headings of Jesus' teaching of his Twelve. Such a reading is nowhere more closely related to the Mystery of Christ and hence more beneficial to the catechetical teacher than in this instance of sin. For the human condition of sin and sinfulness and of suffering from the effects of sin is at the heart of catechetical teaching. There is no way to understand Jesus as mankind's Redeemer except the reality of sin be recognized and accurately understood. For the reality of sin was at the heart of Jesus' teaching of his disciples generally and particularly in his formation of the Twelve.

To begin with, Jesus accepted and confirmed the teaching of the Hebrew Prophets on the Way of Life as contrasted with the Way of Death. This was in fact basic in his fulfillment of the Prophets (see Matt. 5:17–20). The Way of Death is the Way of Sin, of disregard for Yahweh, of heathenism in practice. Abraham was called to come out from the heathens to the new Way of Life in holiness with the light and help given by the God of the Hebrew Revelation. This is what Jesus is renewing and fulfilling in final form: "I am the way, the truth and the life" (John 14:6).

Integral with his attitude toward the Prophets was Jesus' respect for the Hebrew Scriptures and the tradition of religious teaching to which they bear witness. This religious teaching begins with the Primitive Revelation of the Creation and the Fall of Adam and Eve, namely, the First Man and the First Woman, the original pair whence all mankind has descended. It is a religious teaching that proceeds in the context both of the consequences of this Original Sin and of the divine plan to forgive, heal, and save men and women from the misery and the despair of the human condition. Jesus made this entire heritage of religious teaching his own. Again: "Do not think that I have come to destroy the Law of the Prophets. I have not come to destroy, but to fulfill" (Matt. 5:17).

"In the beginning," Jesus teaches with regard to Moses' concession of divorce, "it was not so" (Matt. 19:8). Jesus leads his disciples to see sin and sinfulness in the largest perspectives of human history, to recognize sin as a catastrophe that entered history after Creation and as a progressively growing misery. They came to understand the real nature of the Kingdom of God that he was proclaiming: he is ushering in the completion of God's plan to do away in mercy with sin among men and its effects upon men. When one stops to realize that the Twelve were schooled in this Hebrew expectation, the electrifying impact of his teaching upon them and upon the Palestinian public becomes clearer to catechetical teachers far removed in space and time. In their constant discussions among themselves and in the questions they put to him, always at the center is this program, long anticipated, of Yahweh's religious renewal of mankind that he is teaching them to help him accomplish.

Sin and sinfulness are present constantly in Jesus' teaching and in its circumstances. There is the blindness of the Jews and a hardness of heart toward his message. The Twelve observed it constantly and experienced it with him many times (see Mark 9:18, Matt. 17:16, and Luke 9:41). Pensively, silently, they saw that he had to curse the impenitent cities (see Matt. 11:21 and Luke 10:13), and unable to help but only learning and noting the awesome fact, they saw him weep over Jerusalem, this capital city of the Hebrew Revelation (see Luke 19:41).

The cause of this blindness that makes the progress of Jesus' teaching program among the people so uncertain and so halting is sin. He came as light, but men have loved the darkness rather than the light, for their works were evil (see John 1:1–18, 3:16–21). All the Twelve, or at least Eleven, marked this situation, but especially John. How often this must have been discussed in the sessions when they were alone with Jesus! God alone is good, Jesus would explain (see Mark 10:18, Matt. 19:17, and Luke 18:19). So he taught them (see Matt. 7:11, 12:34, Luke 23:31, Matt. 6:12, 18:25–27, and Luke 7:42). Always he is quiet and calm about the human situation, never upset, never scornful, never bitter. The Twelve come to realize that he has a plan that dominates the situation and copes with it.

Later on, that Apostle who was called by the Risen Christ to join this Twelve will specify the root cause of this universal condition of sin, sinfulness, and the effects of sin. It was the Original Sin of Adam and Eve, the first parents of all mankind: "Through one man sin entered into the world and through sin death, and thus death passed unto all men because all have sinned" (Rom. 5:12).

As the work of their Teacher proceeded, the Twelve came to understand better than any of the earlier Prophets the true reality and nature of sin and the fundamental need of all men for the mercy of God. For they were taught by Jesus that it is human nature *as fallen* that is transmitted to all men. It is a human nature stripped of the original grace and beauty that had clothed it at Creation: it is a human nature injured in its own natural powers and subjected to the dominion of death.

Together with this understanding of the human condition, they came to see their Teacher ever more clearly as related to the fact of sin. For he was constantly exercising power to free men from all the unfortunate effects of the sin-induced human condition, including death. At the same time, he was in direct conflict with Satan, who holds mankind in bondage precisely through this sin and sinfulness. That Christianity is in conflict with demons is witnessed throughout the New Testament. Unless this fact is seen and evaluated properly, the fundamental nature of Jesus' teaching program cannot be correctly understood:

> Parables, stories, prophecies of the last days—all repeat to us the same lesson: the great sin of which humanity is guilty, and which God chastises so severely, is to be concerned only with the goods and joys of earth and to forget God. . . . . Throughout the course of Our Lord's life the conflict is continued, especially in the exorcisms which from beginning to end mark Jesus' ministry (see Matt. 8:29, Mark 3:11, 5:7; Luke 4:41). These deliverances of possessed persons are works of mercy, performed to relieve men, but they are also a battle against Satan, and it is thus that Jesus presents them . . . (see Matt. 12:28–29)[22]

So Jesus taught all his disciples but his Twelve in particular. Always he shows realistic candor regarding sin as the universal cause of human unhappiness and misery. And always the positive hope, the parable of the Prodigal Son, the mercy of God to do away with the guilt of sin, and the power of God to do away with the effects of sin, even to death itself. This positive side of Jesus' teaching accordingly comes next for summary survey.

8. Jesus Himself As the Redeemer of Mankind

The Twelve had come to Jesus originally as the Messiah, the long-awaited Redeemer. John the Baptist announced him as such: "Behold the lamb of God, who takes away the sin of the world!" (John 1:29). "Again the next day John was standing there, and two of his disciples. And looking upon Jesus as he walked by, he said, 'Behold the lamb of God!' And the two disciples heard him speak, and they followed Jesus" (John 1:35–37). John himself was one of the two, with Andrew, brother of Simon, who will be given a new name, Peter. After spending time with Jesus, they were convinced:

"We have found him of whom Moses in the Law and the Prophets wrote, Jesus the son of Joseph of Nazareth" (John 1:45). But they had much indeed to learn about the nature of the Redemption, understanding hardly at all the Baptist's word that he is God's lamb of sacrifice—who is somehow connected with the removal from mankind of sin and its consequences.

The Twelve began to learn about Jesus as the Redeemer by observing his almighty power over these consequences. "They brought to him all who were ill and who were possessed," writes Saint Mark. "And the whole town had gathered at the door. And he cured many who were afflicted with various diseases, and cast out many devils" (Mark 1:33–34). Matthew puts it in sweeping summary: "And Jesus was going about all Galilee, teaching in their synagogues, and preaching the gospel of the kingdom, and healing every disease and every sickness among the people. And his fame spread into all Syria; and they brought to him all the sick suffering from various diseases and torments, those possessed, and lunatics, and paralytics; and he cured them. And there followed him large crowds from Galilee and Decapolis and Jerusalem and Judea, and from beyond the Jordan" (Matt. 4:23–25).

The Gospels need to be accepted as they are and read as they were written, as a witness from within the learning experience of the Twelve. They saw a truly vast movement of the people to their Teacher because of this mighty power to heal and to cure. For all men everywhere desire to be liberated from these various bodily ills.

Jesus, however, had much more to teach than the mere fact of his power in the matter. His teaching was a constant correction of fallen thinking about the nature of human freedom and liberation. He had to do this even with the Twelve, perhaps more in their case than with his disciples at large. For they tended to be touched, some more, some less, with Satan's concept of freedom: to desire it simply as personal self-assertion, apart from the truth, apart from any law that Subsisting Truth builds into the reality that it creates. This is the very idea of sin. It can manifest itself in the order of human sexuality. It can be simply an attitude of self-seeking and self-indulgence in various forms and in different kinds of human relationships. Above all, it can express itself in the political and social order, seeing evil only out there in its structures and not within human persons. At the moment of Jesus' choosing of the Twelve for this special teaching program, there was a strong current to define human liberty simply as freedom from Roman rule. The Messiah would be this kind of political liberator, one not unwilling to grasp military power to restore a temporal sway great and glorious as David's had been. It was common among the Jews, and especially among the Galileans, to see liberation in this merely earthly, political, and temporal way, wanting nothing but its kind of action now. The Twelve were more than a little touched by this common aberration about the Messiah and the nature of the Kingdom of God that the Prophets had taught them to expect.[23]

Jesus' teaching was consistently designed to raise his followers to an interior and personal concept of human freedom and liberation. There are interior spiritual illnesses and deformities of the human spirit that the bodily sufferings of man, the blind eyes, the deaf ears, and the crippled limbs, only reflect and make manifest.

Hence there was a positive side to Jesus' teaching that brought his hearers gradually to see him correctly as the Redeemer and to recognize that true Redemption is liberation from sin. Thus he taught all his followers, but especially the Twelve, his doctrine of the Cross: "Whoever does not bear his own cross and come after me, cannot be my disciple" (Luke 14:27).

And Jesus insisted that each and all must be washed clean, indeed by himself. Each and all must start new, being born again and accepting his teaching as little children trust their parents: "Amen I say to you, whoever does not accept the kingdom of God as a little child will not enter into it" (Mark 10:15).

All during Jesus' arduous task of teaching the often slow, dull, and recalcitrant Twelve, one needs but think of his "Get thee behind me, Satan" to Peter: he was letting them see models that illustrated for them what redeemed human persons are like. One was his Virgin Mother. For they came to venerate her for her spiritual qualities, recognizing a fullness of grace in her that their written Gospel will record. The other was himself. Redemption restores the right order to God the Creator, just as sin violates it. The orientation of Jesus' humanity to his heavenly Father set this right order constantly before the eyes of the Twelve. It was the very meaning of that life of prayer that they finally asked him to teach them and help them imitate. Living with him as his intimate companions they learned to know this human Son of Mary with the phrases of the

Prophets: as *Emmanuel*, the Son of the Living God, the Father of the Coming Age, the Prince of Peace, patient, obedient, innocent, meek, and humble of heart. What he meant by human liberation, freedom, and redemption came home to them from the models he offered perhaps even more than from the words of his teaching.

It was difficult for the Twelve, ordinary Jews as they were, to accept the fact that this Teacher with his truly Messianic power in word and deed was at the same time Yahweh's Suffering Servant (see Isa. 53). Yet Jesus held to it in all his teaching and public action with a purposiveness that led across his years with them toward the cross. It was a lengthening shadow of rejection by the rulers at Jerusalem and hence by many of the confused people. His mother saw this shadow and suffered it as a mother would. The Twelve likewise saw it, but not with her acceptance in humble faith in God. The doctrine on Jesus as the Redeemer is the very substance of the New Testament and is written into all its pages. It is a Redemption from sin and all its consequences, including death above all. "For this is the will of my Father who sent me, that whoever beholds the Son, and believes in him, shall have everlasting life, and I will raise him up on the last day" (John 6:40).

Such are the promises of Christ, and such was his formation of the Twelve. They did not fully understand in the beginning, as their own witness in the Gospels makes clear. But it was indeed the teaching they received: Jesus' program is a comprehensive, final, otherworldly liberating victory for human persons over sin and all its effects: "The words and teaching of Jesus, then, are of infinite and critical importance for those who hear them. Yet they lead on inevitably to the supremely important event—his death. This event, which in the narrative has been foreshadowed throughout the ministry, is solemnly shown to be its completion by the words 'It is finished' (John 19:30)."[24]

One thing is certain: it was in this context of the Redemption that Jesus himself was teaching and preparing, that he established the entity he called "My Church" (Matt. 16:18).

9. The Catholic Church

It has been noted already that Jesus' call of the Twelve to this special School was a deliberate action toward establishing, constituting, and founding the new Israel of God. For the former Israel of

God that ruled at Jerusalem from the Chair of Moses, through some tragic spiritual blindness was refusing to hear the announcement of John the Baptist, refusing therefore to come to the teaching of Jesus in obedience and faith.

The word *catholic* is the Greek term meaning "universal." Jesus and his Twelve ordinarily spoke the Aramaic dialect of Hebrew commonly used in Palestine at the time.[25] But the Gospels bear witness that Jesus prepared the Twelve for a *universal* mission, exactly as the Greek word used later to name his Church signifies. For this question of universality was one of the most fundamental points of conflict with the Rabbinate under the authorities at Jerusalem. Jesus' task was to prepare his Twelve, as Moses and the Prophets wrote, for a New and Universal Testament. He had to prepare them to break out of the isolation and restrictions of the all-too-human Jewish nationalism, with its set of minute national usage and custom. Much of this was a merely human cultural growth, "the traditions of your fathers," not needed, at least not any longer, for the Divine Tradition of the Word of Yahweh. Jesus schooled the Twelve in this universal perspective: he was constantly teaching and training them to be founders of his Church who would continue his program of teaching the completion and fulfillment of Divine Revelation. His Church was to be One, with one Supreme Head to effect that unity. Hence Simon's new name denoting his unique function in the Constitution of Jesus' Church, which will be discussed briefly later. Jesus' Church was to be Holy, a School of Holiness, of redemption from sin and of victory over its effects. It was to be Catholic, namely, sent to all the Gentile nations of the whole world. And it was to be perpetually what he taught and prepared his Twelve to found. Since they were the ones he "sent," the "Apostles," his Church is to be "Apostolic," abidingly resting on these men who were the foundations because of the teaching and formation he gave them.

The authorities at Jerusalem were well aware that Jesus was founding a new religious organization, a challenge to their position because it was shaping up as the new "Israel of God." The people at large, while confused by the lack of support for Jesus on the part of Jerusalem, were moving to Jesus in numbers that posed for them a definite problem. Hence there were numerous conflicts with officials representing the ruling Pharisees and Sadducees, the Scribes and Rabbis who were so distinctive and universal a part of Jewish life in Palestine. Always the break with the Rabbinate takes place on the question of Jewish national exclusiveness, hedged about with the tangled growth of human custom about the original nucleus of the divinely revealed Torah. This national exclusiveness had grown to the proportions of a pride that blocked the nature of the Hebrew religion and foiled the Divine purpose of choosing the Hebrew People. These conflicts were occasions for Jesus to teach the truth on the matter to his Twelve. The Word of God is now to be open to all the Gentile nations and peoples. Indeed the Twelve are being prepared to be teachers of all nations, teachers of his own program. For he himself had been sent to the Jewish people, to win it, if possible, for this universal mission and, if not possible, then to launch the mission despite the lack of their powerful assistance from the human point of view.

Jesus' calling of the Twelve for special teaching and formation, as noted in the previous chapter, was therefore an absolutely decisive event, one with world-historical significance and potential. It was the free choice of Jesus, in loyalty to his heavenly Father who sent him, a decision made after long prayer to God (see Luke 6:13–16, Mark 13:13, Matt. 10:4, and Mark 3:19). Hence the special importance of Jesus' training of them by doing, when he sent them out to teach his message (see John 20:21). Matthew records comprehensively how he instructed them and gave them power before sending them out to the towns and villages of Palestine (see Matt. 9:35–10:42). This is the Master Teacher in action: he is training them for their later mission to reach all the Gentile nations.

In this "Catholic" or universal character of his mission, implemented by founding his Church upon the Twelve as the new Israel of God, Jesus again was not destroying the Prophets but fulfilling them. Like the Israel of God descending from Moses, with its High Priest on Moses' Chair at Jerusalem, and now so strangely and tragically blind to its fulfillment in the coming of him "of whom Moses and the Prophets wrote" (John 1:45), this new Israel was to be a structured, hierarchical, and priestly organization. Jesus himself will be its High Priest. He will constitute the basic unifying structure by his appointment of Simon, brother of Andrew and son of John, naming him Peter, "the Rock," the great stone, the Profession of Faith, in the foundation of his Church. The New Israel of God will carry out to the Gentile peoples the basic pattern of the Hebrew religious organization, not destroying but fulfilling it, with a priest-hood organized hierarchically with a sacrifice now to be offered in every place, as the Prophets foretold (Mal. 1:11), and with Sacraments that give the new birth unto a new and higher life for which Jesus' doctrine calls.

10. The Sacraments and the Eucharistic Sacrifice

When the Gospels are read from their reality as witnesses from within the Twelve to the teaching Jesus gave them, and when the rest of the writings of the New Testament are studied as documents that show their practice when he sent them out, Jesus Christ emerges clearly as the Founder of the Sacraments and the Sacrifice of the New Law.

As their faith grew by which they recognized who he was, incarnate with them in his human nature, they came to know the sacramental principle with a new finality and completeness. His human nature was itself the supreme Sacrament by which Yahweh had come uniquely close to his people, fulfilling Moses and the Prophets also in this way.

Jesus' constant call for faith finds its concrete goal and purpose in his placing of "Sacraments" in his Church. He calls for faith not only in God's being, his existing reality, but also in God's Almighty power in activity and operation. This is the very idea of divine Providence: it makes faith in God, the Father Almighty, qualitatively different from knowledge about God achieved by human reason and philosophy. Jesus calls for faith in the divine intention to apply the fruits of Redemption by means of sacraments, fulfilling the common religious aspiration and practice of mankind across the ages. Jesus' Sacraments will be Sacraments of faith that call for faith, that give faith, that result from faith. His Sacraments will be more than symbols, for they will cause what they signify, actually giving the Holy Spirit and his grace.

The Twelve knew at the outset that John the Baptist presented Jesus to them as the one who would institute this kind of new and final Sacrament of Baptism: "He who sent me to baptize with water had said to me, 'The man on whom you see the Spirit come down and rest is the one who is going to baptise with the Holy Spirit. Yes,

I have seen and I am the witness that he is the Chosen One of God"
(John 1:33–34). Jesus himself stressed with Nicodemus that his religion calls for this spiritual rebirth into the state of redemption from
sin. "I tell you most solemnly," he told Nicodemus, "unless a man
is born through water and the Spirit, he cannot enter the kingdom
of God" (John 3:5).

At the same time, the Twelve knew from the beginning that
Jesus somehow was the new Lamb of God, for again John the Baptist
had presented him as such: "John said, 'Behold, the Lamb of God,
who takes away the sin of the world!' " (John 1:29). Jesus prepared
all his disciples, but the Twelve in particular, for the institution of
a completely new Sacrament for his continuing personal presence
and activity in washing his followers clean and sustaining the new
life given in the baptismal rebirth. Here, of course, catechetical
teachers must ponder chapter 6 of Saint John's Gospel carefully. It
ends with the failure of many of the disciples at large to rise to this
faith in the Almightiness of the divine power and with the direct
challenge to the Twelve. "What about you, do you want to go away
too? Simon Peter answered, 'Lord, who shall we go to? You have
the message of eternal life, and we believe; we know you are the
Holy one of God.' Jesus replied, 'Have I not chosen you, you Twelve?
Yet one of you is a devil.' He meant Judas, son of Simon Iscariot,
since this was the man, one of the Twelve, who was going to betray
him" (John 6:67–71).

This was without doubt a high point in Jesus' teaching and
formation of his Twelve. It not only promises the culmination of
the sacramental principle in what will be known as the Sacrament
of the Holy Eucharist. It also begins to show Jesus revealing how
this Sacrament will be at the same time the Sacrifices of the New
Law, of the new Israel of God, replacing the sacrifices of the Old
Law offered at the Temple in Jerusalem. The betrayal, first noted
here, makes him the victim of this Sacrifice. Thus his Church will
be the Temple of the New Law, and its sacrifice will be offered in
every place, as the Prophet Malachi foretold, instead of the one
place at Jerusalem. Again fulfillment: "For from the rising of the
sun even unto the going down of the same my name is great among
the nations; and in every place offerings are presented unto my
name, even pure oblations; for my name is great among the nations,

saith the Lord of hosts'' (Mal. 1:11, official Jewish translation of the Masoretic text).

Jesus instituted all the Seven Sacraments of the New Law, himself personally, as a part of his teaching and formation of the Twelve. "For the sacraments are the instruments of grace, and the Author of grace alone has the final power to institute them. . . . Christ not only kept the institution of the Sacraments in his own hands, but himself promulgated those of them that presented the chief difficulties for faith: Baptism, the Eucharist, Holy Orders, Penance. He even announced them in advance, insisting for example with Nicodemus that Baptism would be a new birth, and with the Jews of Capernaum that his Flesh would be true meat and his Blood true drink."[26]

From the teaching that Jesus gave to the Twelve two basic Articles of Faith come into being and profession. First, the doctrine that there is one Baptism instituted by Christ, for the remission of sins. And the second is faith in the Sacrifice of the Cross, by which Jesus Christ redeemed all men from Original Sin and from all personal sins committed by each of us members of the human family.

Thus did Jesus proceed logically and consistently in teaching and forming the Twelve to be with him the founders and themselves teachers of the new Israel of God, the fulfillment of all that Moses and the Prophets wrote. It remains to consider the purpose of this universal Church and then Jesus' teaching on the Last Things, which lie in the future before all mankind.

11. The Church in the World

The Twelve, helped by the forceful public announcements of John the Baptist, recognized that Jesus was the long-awaited Holy One of Israel of whom Moses and the Prophets wrote. Raised and taught as Jewish men, the Twelve understood readily that the Messiah is a royal figure, a King of kings who will rule over the Gentile nations for their welfare and peace. Familiar with the Prophets, they knew that the Messiah would be made manifest to all the Gentile nations of the world. He was to be their Ruler, the King of their kings. A true world empire is in prospect. Let a few short samples of the prophetic word in the Masoretic text suffice to show the general mentality of the Twelve and to indicate the perspectives that opened before them as their Teacher brought them more and more deeply inside his program: "Behold, I sent my messenger . . . the Lord, whom ye seek, will suddenly come to His temple" (Mal. 3:1). "Yea, all kings shall prostrate themselves before him; all nations shall serve him. May his name endure forever; may men also bless themselves by him; may all nations call him happy" (Ps. 72). Then there are those final chapters of the Prophet Isaiah, which the Twelve heard Jesus apply explicitly to himself in the Synagogue at Nazareth (see Luke 4:16–30): "Arise, shine," the Prophet calls to Jerusalem, "for thy light is come, and the glory of the Lord is risen upon thee. . . . Lift up thine eyes round about and see: they all are gathered together and come to thee. . . . The wealth of the nations shall come to thee . . . and their kings in procession . . . And they shall call thee The City of the Lord, the Zion of the Holy One of Israel. . . . The Lord shall be unto thee an everlasting light and thy God thy glory. Thy sun shall no more go down. . . . For the Lord shall be thine everlasting light" (Isa. 60). It is the Suffering Servant of Yahweh who will thus benefit and bless the Gentile nations, as the mysterious chapter 42 of Isaiah foresees: "Behold My servant, whom I uphold, mine elect, in whom My soul delighteth; I have put My spirit upon him, he shall make the right go forth to the nations. . . . Thus saith God the Lord, he that created the heavens and stretched them forth. . . . I the Lord have called thee in righteousness . . . and set thee . . . for a light to the nations" (Isa. 42:1–6). And again: "And now saith the Lord that formed me from the womb to be His servant . . . To raise up the tribes of Jacob, and to restore the offspring of Israel; I will also give thee for a light of the nations, that my salvation may be unto the end of the earth" (Isa. 49:5–6).

The whole world, Isaiah proclaims, is going to call Jerusalem the City of God, for it will be the religious capital of all the Gentile peoples, the Holy City of the New Testament from which the Messiah, the Suffering Servant of Yahweh, the Holy One of Israel, will rule them all.[27]

How will this be? When will it be? The Twelve, men of Moses and the Prophets, were full of questions. Jesus taught them patiently, persistently, consistently. All of this will indeed be accomplished. Moses and the Prophets will be fulfilled. But not in the military and political way that most men tend to expect. Not by armed revolt against Rome. It will be fulfilled by his own teaching program, which he is preparing them to continue, the teaching program that is linked with Redemption from sin and rebirth to the new and higher life of internal personal renewal. His rule over the Gentile peoples will result from this teaching mission and program. Thus he taught them. And so they acted, as the Acts of the Apostles will bear witness. The new Israel of God will be a phenomenon in this world, within the concrete facts of unfolding human history, and at the same time it will transcend history, where all human things begin and flourish and die. This rulership over the world, this new kind of world empire, will be an everlasting one. So the Prophets foresaw. So Jesus taught his Twelve.

Thus they understood that their Teacher was to be the Teacher of all the nations, founding upon them and their own continuation of his program a kingdom that should endure forever. The Kingdom of God is indeed at hand, already in its beginnings. They understood the power of this teaching. If the Gentile nations accepted it, men's purposes in life would be lifted up, their personal characters changed, and the tenor of their lives renewed. The ancient errors of paganism would disappear (see Isa. 26:3). Religious ignorance with its attendant vices would be healed. A wonderful transformation would take place, one that will utterly change the face of the earth. All this is concrete and immediate. For the Messiah, teaching and applying the Redemption from sin to individual persons will constitute the way, the truth, and the life for the Gentile nations. And this will constitute him as the Ruler of human society in the world at large, outside of Palestine. For the redeemed persons will have a healing and humanizing effect first upon domestic society, then upon the institutions and structures of civil society, including even the political order and its rulers. Thus the Messiah will indeed be the King of kings and the Prince of peace by means of his saving doctrine of Redemption and of spiritual rebirth by means of his Sacraments. He will hold sway in human society as the Teacher and Ruler of public no less than private life.

The immensity of the prospect must indeed have been the subject of many discussions, both among themselves and in the questionings they put to Jesus their Teacher.

Gradually he brought them, most of them, to see more clearly. The new Israel of God cannot remain within the isolating merely human traditions that the Jerusalem authorities wish to maintain by accommodation with the pagan Roman Empire. But at the same time, the new Israel of God is not to be an earthly and secular world empire established by military uprising against Rome. It is to be "My Church," the religious organization for teaching the new doctrine of the Messiah, a saving doctrine because it will apply the fruits of the Redemption. This will indeed be a "world empire." It will be in this world, ruling over the Gentile nations as the Prophets foresaw, but it will not be of this world. It will be a new and higher kind of sway over men's minds and hearts. It will be the peaceful result of this teaching program that he is preparing the Twelve to carry forth to all the Gentile nations, and it will be destined to last forever: "Of his kingdom there will be no end" (Nicene Creed).

A great Epiphany or manifestation of Yahweh to the pagan world is being actively prepared by Jesus the Teacher.[28] What will be the outcome of his effort to bring his Twelve to the knowledge of Yahweh's plan for mankind as a whole? Before I summarize the outcome with these Twelve privileged companions and students, it remains to consider Jesus' answers to their many questions on the modes and the times of it all.

12. The Last Things

Jesus' teaching was oriented beyond this earthly life. He lifted the minds and hearts of all who heard him beyond this cosmos to the higher purpose of everlasting life. For him it is simply a matter of faith in the almighty power of God coupled with the intention of God revealed in the Scriptures: he reduced the Sadducees to utter silence by making these two points (see Matt. 22:23–33). Martha, one of the women who had been following his teaching closely, was well catechized on the matter. Jesus came to her after the death of her brother Lazarus. " 'Your brother,' said Jesus to her, 'will rise again.' Martha said, 'I know he will rise again at the resurrection on the last day.' Jesus said: 'I am the resurrection. If anyone believes in me, even though he dies he will live, and whoever lives and believes in me will never die. Do you believe this?' 'Yes, Lord,' she said, 'I believe that you are the Christ, the Son of God, the one who was to come into this world.' When she had said this, she went and called her sister Mary, saying in a low voice, 'The Master [the *Didáskalos* in the Greek text of John] is here and wants to see you' " (John 11:23–29). Martha is a witness to both Jesus as a Teacher in Israel and the basic orientation of his teaching. He taught men to look forward to the eternity beyond death, which will be finally conquered on the Day of the Resurrection, "when human souls will be reunited with their own bodies."[29] In a certain valid sense, all of Jesus' teaching, summarized under these previous eleven headings, bears upon the call of each human person to the resurrection of the body and life everlasting. This doctrine on the Last Things is the corollary and culmination of them all.

Man has a natural desire to know the future, as all the religions of history make manifest. The Prophets in Israel always were in touch with this human desire. In fact, "to prophesy" often came to have the specialized meaning of foretelling future contingent events. The Twelve knew well that their Teacher was a prophet, and they knew their work with him bore upon the future events that were the ardent interest and expectation of the entire Jewish people. In fact, Mark 1:14–15, Jesus' initial heralding of the times of the Kingdom of God, is for Jews already not only Messianic but also apocalyptic: it is a proclamation from God in the context of the Last Things.

Hence the Twelve were naturally full of questions. The relationship between the Teacher and his Twelve special full-time students is nowhere exhibited better than in these questions. They were obviously perfectly at ease with him, humanly at ease, man to man:

> As he was leaving the Temple, one of his disciples [one of *the mathetai*, in the Greek, i.e., one of the Twelve] said to him, "Look at the size of those stones, Master *[Didaskale* in the original Greek text]! Look at the size of those buildings!" And Jesus said to him, "You see these great buildings? Not a single stone will be left on another: everything shall be destroyed.[11] And while he was sitting facing the Temple, on the Mount of Olives, Peter, James, John and Andrew questioned him privately, "Tell us, when is this going to happen, and what sign will there be that all this is about to be fulfilled?" Then Jesus began to tell them, "Take care that no one deceives you. Many will come using my name and saying, 'I am he,' and they will deceive many" (Mark 13:1–6).

The compact summary of Jesus' teaching, clearly designed to answer the Twelve and to prevent them from falling victim to future deceptions, continues in chapter 13. It has its parallel in the great eschatological discourse of Matthew 14 and its brief summary in Luke 21:5–36.

Jesus, too, is perfectly at ease with his Twelve and wonderfully candid. He tells them what they need to know in view of the mission for which he is preparing them, revealing to them that part of his own knowledge that his own mission from his Father makes relevant to them. "If the Son declares to the Apostles," writes Journet, "that he knows not the day or the hour of the end of the world (Mark 13:32), it means that he has no mission to reveal it to them (Acts 1:17). The text of the Acts throws light on that of the Gospel."[30]

Catechists reading and using the Gospels in their teaching do not need to be specialized Scripture scholars to recognize two distinct things in Jesus' teaching. The first concerns a period of teaching extending out to all the nations of the earth, a teaching that witnesses to him as the Creator, Redeemer, and Savior of mankind. How long will this period be? The second will be Jesus' return at the end of the world to judge the living and the dead. When will this be? These two points with their questions are not the same thing. Both are in Jesus' teaching as witnessed in the Gospels. Somehow, the time of the end seems not yet to be fixed. It is a future contingency known to God alone and to Jesus as a Divine Person. Jesus seemed to indicate to the Twelve that it would correlate in a mysterious way with the teaching mission for which he was preparing them, depending on the fidelity with which the teaching of all nations would be carried out and the obedience in Divine Faith with which the teaching would be received.[31]

Jesus taught a specific doctrine on the Last Things: that he himself is coming to judge the living and the dead, that human persons live in a moral universe, choosing either the Way of Life or the Way of Death, and that God wishes each human person to be saved. Jesus' teaching calls each person to come to a glorious resurrection of his own body, triumphant with Jesus over death, and looking forward with hope in the divine power to the happiness of life everlasting. The teaching program for which Jesus is preparing his Twelve will continue the heralding of his own message, that original Messianic and Apocalyptic call of Mark 1:14–15: "The Kingdom of God is at hand: Repent, therefore, and believe the Good News!" In the words of a noted theologian of the period late in the twentieth century after Vatican II: "The Church [is] a herald ever calling through the desert of this world and preparing the path to the Lord (see John 1:23, from Isaiah 40:3) and as 'a standard set up unto the nations (Isaiah 11:12) . . . inviting to itself those who have not yet believed.' Thus the Church is of its nature pilgrim and missionary, and consequently lives and works eschatologically."[32]

Conclusion

Jesus has been forming his Twelve by a sustained program of teaching on the level of higher education as it was carried on in Palestine at that time. Higher education forms the leaders upon whom society depends. His program, with this wonderfully complete and synthetically articulated body of doctrine, was the fulfillment of Prophetic Revelation, the fullness of the Word of God to mankind. The new Israel of God had its doctrine together with its leaders who were to teach that doctrine.

It is time to look briefly at the degree of success Jesus had with his Twelve and what the sudden turn of events was that terminated Jesus' School as a Rabbi or *Didáskalos* or Teacher in Israel. These events introduced an entirely new perspective into his program for teaching the prophetic Word of God to all mankind.

Chapter 9

The Redemption: Jesus Our Divine Savior

The hallmark of Christians ever since the Apostles has been love for their holy Redeemer and thanksgiving for his Redemption. One need but think of the Stations of the Cross in the churches, of the place of the Crucifix, of the Sign of the Cross, and indeed of the Eucharistic Sacrifice itself, for the Greek word *eucharist* means "Thanksgiving."

In recent times, however, under the social influence of secularism and atheism, the sense of sin has declined among men, even among the young, with a corresponding indifference to the very idea of the Redeemer and his Redemption. "There is a special circumstance today," writes Pope Saint Pius X. "An atmosphere of unbelief has been created which is most harmful to the interior and spiritual life. This atmosphere wages war upon any idea of a higher authority, any idea of God, or revelation, of the life to come, and of mortification in this life."[1]

The renewal of love for the Holy Redeemer, therefore, and of thanksgiving for his Redemption is a primary task and challenge for catechists today. The Redemption is the climax of biblical Catechetics and the completion of the work of Jesus the Divine Teacher. For Jesus himself did all of his teaching in the full light of his divine knowledge of the series of events that would put an end to his public life as a Teacher in Israel. This can be seen perhaps best in his teaching on the Holy Eucharist (John 6), but it is also visible in each of the credal headings of the previous chapter, especially those on sin and redemption. Although he predicted these events to his Twelve, they largely missed the point. For him himself, however, his program of teaching is one unified body of doctrine with these events of the Redemption. The Apostles came to realize this after Pentecost when they or their younger assistants wrote the four Gospels: in each one the account of the redeeming events occupies the chief space and gives the culmination and significance of all the earlier doctrine of their Teacher.

The Doctrine of the Redemption

In order to renew the Christian love and thanksgiving, the catechist today needs to stay firmly on the bedrock of the true doctrine of the Redemption.

The Redemption of mankind was accomplished in the series of events that conclude each of the four Gospels. Four events took place at that time, one is going on at present, and one is still to come. They are the passion, death, resurrection, and ascension of Jesus into heaven, his present session at the right hand of the Father, constantly interceding for us, and his second coming on the last day when he will raise up all human persons in their own bodies. Death will have been overcome in this, his complete victory over sin. The banishment from heaven will end: the gates will reopen for us humans to enter the lost Paradise and to live forever in the presence of the Three Divine Persons, all the Saints, and all the loved ones.

The secret of all catechetical renewal is a teaching that brings the catechumen to understand these events from within. Each must be helped to see that Jesus permitted these events voluntarily, making of them his redeeming sacrifice. Then each one must see that in his divine knowledge and consciousness Jesus had each one of us, each catechumen personally, in his mind. "The life I now live in the flesh," writes Saint Paul. "I live by faith in the Son of God, who loved me and gave himself for me" (Gal. 2:20). In this remarkable statement, true for himself and true for each Christian person, Saint Paul establishes the motive for catechetical teaching: if Jesus so loved me in these redeeming events, should I not respond with love for him? "We love," Saint John says, "because he first loved us" (1 John 4:19). Jesus loved us with mercy when we were still in the state of sin. Thus catechumens can be brought to love their Holy Redeemer and to be thankful for his Redemption.[2]

This doctrine of the Redemption is summarized by the Church herself in the *GCD*, paragraph 54:

God so loved sinners that he gave his Son, reconciling the world to himself (see 2 Cor. 5:19). Jesus therefore as the Firstborn among many brethren (see Rom. 8:29), holy, innocent, undefiled (see Heb. 7:26), being obedient to his Father freely and out of filial love (see Phil. 218), on behalf of his brethren, sinners that they were, and as their Mediator, accepted the death which is for them the wages of sin (see Rom. 6:23; GS 18). By this his most holy death he redeemed mankind from the slavery of sin and of the devil, and he poured out on it the spirit of adoption, thus creating in himself a new humanity.[3]

Keeping this doctrine of the Redemption in mind, we can turn to consider the Gospel account of the passion, death, resurrection, and ascension of Jesus from the viewpoint of the way God made use of these sorrowful human contingencies to culminate the work of the Divine Teacher.

The Sudden End of Jesus' Teaching

The deed of Judas Iscariot, who betrayed Jesus into the hands of the Jewish Government, caught the other disciples by complete surprise. The popular support for Jesus was so strong that the authorities dared not move in on him by day for fear of a riot on his behalf. Hence they welcomed this betrayal from within the Twelve. The redemptive passion of Jesus began, therefore, when Judas left their Passover meal to tell the Jews where to go and to lead them in the night to arrest him.

The Outcome of Jesus' Teaching of the Twelve

The Twelve special students were ordinary Jewish men, honest and simple men of the out-of-doors, mostly fishermen on the Sea of Galilee. They had the basic synagogue education common to all Jews, but only that. Jesus called ordinary men, not educated in the Rabbinate. It is fair to think that this was deliberate on Jesus' part. They were men of natural common sense in thought and language. Jesus appreciated and recommended these qualities: he wanted forthright men of "yes" and "no."

Furthermore, Jesus, obedient to his mission from his Heavenly Father, put himself consistently on their level. He was infinitely patient with their inadequacies and blindnesses, their unthinking reflection of the popular attitudes of the day, their proneness, for example, to go with the Galilean *lestes* or "freedom fighters." Always he was in good humor with them, correcting them, pointing out the reasons for his teaching, and explaining the truth of it to them. The relationship of the Twelve to their Teacher, one can see in the lines and between the lines of the four Gospels, was free, easy, pleasant. Above all they admired him, loved him in a manly way. Later he will question Peter on this point. He was their Teacher. They were glad and proud to be his *mathetai*. No other disciples in Israel had a Teacher so commanding in word and in work. Their own importance grew as the crowds flocked to him and his program became a veritable movement beginning to engage the populace of Palestine as a whole.

Jesus' work as a Teacher in Israel was well and carefully done. His choice of the Twelve and the way he formed them was aptly designed to achieve its purpose, the teaching of his own doctrine, the revealed Word of God now completed and fulfilled. It is important for catechetical teachers to grasp the foundation of what the Gospels tell us. This means to "give diligent attention to the three stages which mark the teaching and the life of Jesus before they (the written Gospels) came down to us. First, Christ the Lord chose disciples (see Mark 3:14; Luke 6:13). Secondly, they followed him right from the beginning, saw his work and heard his words. Thus thirdly, they were in a position to become the witnesses of his life and of his teaching (see Luke 1:2; Acts 1:21–22; Luke 24:48; John 15:27; Acts 1:8; 10:39; 13:31)."[4] This direct witness is fundamental for their writings in the New Testament.

At the same time, Jesus did not enjoy unmixed success in his work as a Teacher. The honesty and truthfulness of the Gospels as witnesses from within this special School are supported by the manner in which they describe what actually happened. It was an otherworldly teaching. Fallen nature prefers a this-worldly teaching. Furthermore, it was morally demanding, a School of Holiness: "Be you perfect, as your Heavenly Father is perfect" (Matt. 5:48), words that were spoken not only to Jesus' disciples but also to all his followers in general. But it was a much more concerted demand upon the

Twelve.[5] There was both a slowness to understand and an unwilling-
ness to accept his teaching, even among the Twelve.

In addition, they were all men of their time and place, with its
particular qualities of human culture, social aspirations, and political movements. This will always be the case with Jesus' teaching, of
course, until the end of time. Jesus' teaching, however, is from
above. It relates to each and all cultural, social, and political situations but identifies with none of them. In the case of the Twelve, all
were more than a little touched by the false Messianic Expectation
current among the Jews of that day, which watered down its religious
character, its relationship to the redemption from sin, and perverted it to political purposes in and of this world. And it seems
clear that some of the Twelve were attracted to the Galilean *lestes*,
the freedom fighters, who, thinking the Messianic day at hand,
sought to prepare and perhaps hasten it by armed resistance to
Rome. Satan's ideology, described so graphically in the account of
Jesus' temptations suffered when he was in the desert preparing for
his mission, was an accurate summary of the kind of thinking behind
the false Messianic expectation. From the human point of view,
Jesus had no easy task as the Teacher of this specially chosen group
of Jewish men. Let us reflect on three instances.

Saint John, the Beloved Disciple and Best Student

The young John, unmarried, keen of mind, open to the teaching, was at the same time an energetic "Son of Thunder," in sympa-
thy to some degree with the Galilean underground against the
Roman imperial rule. Every class has its star pupil. Jesus' teaching
was fully human also in this regard. John was his brightest pupil,
the one who understood him best and took his teaching more fully
to heart. John learned fully the lesson that the Kingdom of God is
in this world but not of it, that it results from the redemption from
sin, that it is within persons first and only through their new life
does it radiate upon temporal structures, political activity, and cultural works. To get some insight into the measure of Jesus' heart-
warming success in teaching this young man, one has only to read
the treasures that the Church has carried down the centuries from
him, the Gospel according to Saint John and his Epistles.[6]

Saint Peter, the Vicar of Christ

Simon, to whom Jesus gave the new name Peter was a quite different character. But there is a far more important consideration that must be related to the ninth general area of Jesus' teaching touched upon in the previous chapter, "The Catholic Church." For Jesus gave this particular man among his Twelve an office and a function absolutely basic in the constitution of his Church, to which the new name corresponds. It will be Peter's function, based on his Profession of Faith, to provide the foundation-rock upon which the unity and stability of the edifice will be built: " . . . You, Simon, are *Peter*, the Rock: and upon this Rock I will build My Church" (Matt. 16:15–20). Peter will have the office and function of confirming his brethren in the program for teaching this faith, which they will be sent to carry to all the Gentile nations of the world: "Go, teach all nations . . . " (Matt. 28:19). This teaching program, furthermore, will be a pastoral care of those who are taught by it, for it brings them into the world of redemption from sin: "Jesus said to him, 'Feed my sheep' " (John 21:17).

It is obvious that this view of Simon Peter's office and function, as it came from Jesus' teaching, will be interpreted differently by Christian churches, which in the vicissitudes of history are no longer in union with Peter's successor in the Catholic Church. Yet the Acts of the Apostles are there to document the fact that Peter behaved after Jesus' time exactly as the Gospels bear witness to his office and function. Furthermore, the easiest way to evade the matter, namely, to claim that this same man, Simon Peter, never went to Rome to found the Church there and to function as its first bishop, has become scientifically untenable in the twenty-first century due to the archaeological excavations at Rome that have corroborated the scattered bits of literary evidence that have survived from Christian origins on Peter's apostolate in Rome.

Hence under Providence a new openness toward Simon Peter's office and function, by Jesus' own arrangement and appointment as a part of his teaching and formation of his Twelve, has been developing among the Christian churches separated from the See of Saint Peter by unfortunate historical vicissitudes. This is fundamental for catechetical teaching to bear in mind in the twenty-first century when the ecumenical movement toward the recovery of unity among all who profess the Name of Jesus Christ is a common interest and a growing reality.

Judas Iscariot, the Betrayer

Judas Iscariot, somber and unhappy figure, is the third instance. For he was the one of the Twelve who betrayed Jesus into the hands of the authorities at Jerusalem who were seeking some way to apprehend him and put him to death. In his case Jesus suffered as all teachers suffer, especially in the humanities and above all in religious education, when a student refuses the ideas and values of the doctrine and fails to apply them in personal life.

There is a significant body of research on Judas Iscariot.[7] For present purposes Judas's betrayal can be summarized briefly as the factor that brought the public life of this Rabbi or Teacher in Israel to an abrupt and humanly unforeseen end.

Judas Iscariot came gradually to be possessed more and more by the ideas that Satan put to Jesus in that triple temptation to make the false Messianic expectation his own approach, going along with the popular aspiration to political, social, and even military action on behalf of "redemption" conceived as a change in structures out in society instead of within the hearts and souls of individual persons.[8] It is reasonable to suppose that Jesus discussed that triple temptation more than once with his Twelve, for it is basic to the nature of the Kingdom of God and the purpose of his teaching. Always Jesus was teaching them to see the nature of Yahweh's plan for interior redemption and life everlasting. Not action now, as if evil were simplistically out there in social structures. But Judas Iscariot would have none of it. Alienation set in. Jesus came more and more to appear to Judas as an impractical dreamer, a mere man who spoke well and attracted people but all the more dangerous because of it. Jesus was actually a danger to what needed to be done. Always Judas has his own ideas, and he came finally to subscribe to a different doctrine: the ideology of the triple temptation, the ideology of the authorities at Jerusalem. The apostasy of Judas was in the realm of doctrine, the "hermeneutics" or interpretation of Moses and the Prophets. Yet the unhappy man feigned friendship, systematically protecting his position as a member of the preferred circle, the Twelve. Judas Iscariot did not believe Jesus' teaching on the Bread of Life (see John 6:26–29), yet the rest of the Twelve did not suspect it until after the betrayal actually took place: "Judas did not believe in Jesus as the true Messiah in the spiritual sense. The confession of Simon Peter is an express declaration of faith in the divinity of Christ (see John 6:69). Judas rejects this faith internally, according to the meaning of John, 6:70."[9] Then Judas Iscariot dissimulates. He stays within the Twelve when so many of Jesus' general disciples walked no more with him. He stays within, even in the face of the pointed question to the Twelve that evoked Peter's confession (see John 6:67). A year later Judas Iscariot has "matured," so to speak: he is hardened for the betrayal, "utterly disappointed in the non-political and unworldly character of Christ the Messiah."[10]

The Eucharist and the Cross: Jesus' Redeeming Sacrifice

Saint Augustine, commenting on Saint John's Gospel, speaks for Christian meditation upon this dark side of Jesus' life as a Teacher in Israel when he simply notes that Jesus turned the unfathomable wickedness into the occasion of a greater good, the redemption of mankind. God does not give human freedom, then prevent its exercise. Quietly Jesus accepted the situation, recognizing the eternal will of his Heavenly Father that he should do so. "Learn of me," Jesus had told his Twelve, "for I am meek and humble of heart" (Matt. 11:29). John the Baptist, speaking as an authentic Prophet in Israel, had announced Jesus when his public life began as the Victim for sin: "Behold the Lamb of God, who takes away the sin of the world" (John 1:29). He stressed this with his own disciples, "Behold, the Lamb of God" (John 1:36), and two of them forthwith followed Jesus. It was the beginning of Jesus' disciples.

Now the time had come: the betrayer had gone forth from the Passover with Jesus and was in his negotiation with the Jewish authorities. The Passion of Jesus was commencing. Jesus of course had seen these events in his divine mind's eye throughout all his teaching, and he saw Judas now. The Eleven, however, had no inkling of what was to transpire. They knew in a general way as Jews raised in Moses and the Prophets that the Messiah was to be "a priest according to the order of Melchisedek" (Ps. 109), that he would found the new and final Testament (see Jer. 31:31–34), and that he would seal this New Testament with a sacrifice to be offered everywhere among the Gentiles (see Mal. 1:10–11). But they had no idea that the moment had come this very evening and that the place was this very Upper Room where Jesus had ordered them to prepare the Passover. They did not have Jesus' foreknowledge: they had to learn, indeed with shock, as the events of this Thursday and the following Friday unfolded.

The Central Teaching of Biblical Catechetics

With this, biblical Catechetics reaches a culminating point. For it is the work of catechists to teach all of this in a formative way, so that the catechumens know and love this new Sacrifice offered everywhere, making their communion with it their way of return to the Father in heaven. It is a catechetical teaching that explains the series of events and their meaning. Out of these events comes the very heart of the Catholic faith: the Eucharistic Real Presence, the identity of the Sacrifice of the Mass and the Sacrifice of the Cross,[11] and the ordination of the Apostles and their successors as priests of Jesus Christ.[12] It assists catechists greatly in this teaching to visualize what took place that evening in the Cenacle. It helps all, furthermore, who want to know better the roots of the Catholic faith in the Scriptures.

The sequence of events in the Cenacle runs from Jesus' very special preparation for the Passover, to his institution of the Holy Eucharist recorded in the Synoptic Gospels, to the chapters in Saint John's Gospel that inform us about Jesus' elevated discourse to his Eleven and concludes with the departure from the Cenacle to the Garden of Olives.

The Distinction Between the Passover and the Eucharist

What, then, actually took place? How are the Jewish Passover and Jesus' new Sacrifice in bread and wine, "according to the Order of Melchisedek" (Ps. 109, with Gen. 14:17–20), related? In answering this question there is a basic point of the internal order of the events. Chapters 13 and 14 of Saint John record the conversation at the traditional Passover meal with the lamb sacrificed at the Temple; the conversation is lively; the Apostles freely intervene; they ask various questions. The crucial verse is John 14:31, when Jesus says to them, "Rise, let us go hence." Many exegetes have interpreted this to mean that the group at that point left the Cenacle out into the darkness and the single-file path descending to cross the Kidron and on to the Garden of Olives. In such a case chapters 15–17, perhaps the most spiritually elevated passage in the entire Bible, would have been spoken by Jesus on the way—somewhat implausible because of the nature of the pathway.

It seems preferable, therefore to follow the lead of Father Lagrange, the foremost Catholic exegete of the twentieth century and founder of the famed École Biblique in Jerusalem. He notes the implausibility and points to John 18:1: "When Jesus had spoken these words (namely John Chapters 15–16–17) he went forth with his disciples across the Kidron Valley, where there was a garden, which he and his disciples entered."[13]

This opens the way to understand "Rise, let us go hence" (John 14:31) as a simple movement of the group to another location within the Cenacle, for it was "a large upper room, furnished" (Luke 22:12).[14] It was not a departure from the Cenacle; this comes at John 18:1. It becomes therefore highly probable that Jesus had instructed Peter and John to prepare a second location at the other end of the Cenacle, not a place to recline at the table as in the Passover but perhaps a long table about forty-two inches high, about which the group could stand. On it Jesus would have requested Peter and John simply to place some bread and a chalice of wine.[15]

The Doctrine of Faith in the Holy Eucharist

This reconstruction of the setting in the Cenacle, based on indications in the Gospel itself, helps in catechetical teaching of the truths that are certainly contained in the Gospels and in the doctrine of the faith. These are, first, the institution of the Eucharistic Sacrifice as distinct from the Jewish Passover and, second, the fact that Jesus ordained his Apostles as the priests of this sacrifice, which seals the New and Eternal Testament of God with mankind.[16]

We come, then, to the solemn moment when Jesus institutes this Eucharistic Sacrifice (see Matt. 26:26–29, Mark 14:22–25, Luke 22:14–21, and 1 Cor. 22:23–26). When teaching the doctrine that rests on these accounts in the New Testament, the catechist must keep in mind with the catechumens who it is who speaks and acts. It is the Almighty Supreme Being of the universe, who has but to speak in order to effect what his words say. Thus the doctrines of the Incarnation and the Redemption are intrinsically related: "What is astonishing to us, with our feeble intelligences, our ineffectual wills, is that things so great should be said and done so briefly, so simply: 'This is my Body,' and behold the Eucharist. 'Do this in commemoration of me,' and behold, the Priesthood. But that is the way, the divine way of Jesus. 'Take up thy bed and walk'; the paralytic gets up. 'Thy son is cured,' and he is cured. 'Damsel, come'; 'Young man, arise'; 'Lazarus, come forth from the tomb.' "[17]

It is also fundamental to note the sacrificial expression in Jesus' Eucharistic words. His Body is "given"; his Blood is "poured out for you." These words can only refer to Jesus' immolation on the cross the next day. He knew his coming immolation in his divine mind. He institutes this Sacrament and Sacrifice conscious that his Passion had already begun in Judas' decision to betray him. Thus the separate consecration of the bread and wine, effecting the Real Presence of Jesus under their appearances, is the offering of his Redeeming death on the cross, when his body and blood will be physically separated. Thus the Mass and the cross are one and the same Sacrifice of the New Testament. When he tells his priests to "do this in memory of me," they will repeat the Eucharistic oblation of the Victim of the Cross in every place and at all times to come.[18]

It is noteworthy that Jesus' meditation (John 15–17), after ordaining his Apostles into his Priesthood and giving them Holy Communion, is not interrupted. There is no sign of the convivial conversation at the previous Passover meal. A holy calm and reverence fills the Cenacle as the Apostles listen to this supreme discourse in the religious history of mankind.

Biblical Catechetics is now in a position to summarize the world-historical greatness of the Eucharistic Sacrifice. Mankind always and everywhere has worshiped God by sacrifice, from the simple offering of the first fruits of their food-gathering by the primitives through the elaborate official sacrifices of the great empires, Babylon, Persia,

Greece, and Rome. This worship of the God of Creation was based on the agricultural seasons. Moses refounded this ancient sacrifice, making it a worship of the Lord God of history whose mastery of contingent events saved the Chosen People from slavery in Egypt and brought Israel across the desert to the promised land. Now, in the Cenacle, Jesus refounded the ancient worship once again, taking the Jewish Passover sacrifice and elevating it to the level of his Sacrifice on the cross. He himself is now the Victim offered, and he himself is the High Priest offering the Victim, either himself personally as at the Last Supper or by his priests who accomplish the same offering in his Person and by his power. The Holy Sacrifice of the Mass is the fulfillment of the religious history of mankind.[19]

Catechists by their teaching bring their catechumens to love their holy Redeemer and to be thankful for the Redemption, helping them to deepen their conversion by their personal Holy Communion in this Eucharistic Sacrifice. For now it is a Passover indeed, but elevated to the passing over of each communicant from the slavery of sin to the coming resurrection of the body and eternal life in heaven. In all this Eucharistic teaching the Holy See itself offers the basic attitude and theme there in the words of the Saint Pius X Catechism: "Why do you believe that Jesus Christ is truly present in the Eucharist? I believe that Jesus Christ is truly present in the Eucharist because he himself said that the consecrated bread and wine are his body and blood, and because the Church teaches this; but it is a mystery, a great mystery."[20]

After instituting the Eucharistic oblation by which the Sacrifice of Redemption will be offered in every place under the New Testament, Jesus and his Eleven went according to their custom to the Garden of Olives for prayer and meditation. "Now Judas, who betrayed him, also knew the place; for Jesus often met there with his disciples" (John 18:1–2).

The ensuing events of Jesus' Passion and death on the cross are described in great detail in the written Gospels. Cathechists should use these Gospels in all teaching of the Redemption, noting how preponderant this account is in each Gospel. It is clear that the Apostles attached a supreme value to Jesus' death on the cross when they wrote or supervised the writing of the Gospels. With the Apostles, catechists today should do all their teaching out of consciousness of who it was who died, for this gives Jesus' death on the cross its infinite power to win the forgiveness of the sins of mankind. This is the Redemption. It reopens the gates of Paradise, the Resurrection of the body and life everlasting for each human person.[21]

" 'It is finished','" Jesus said from his cross, "and he bowed his head and gave up his spirit" (John 19:30). He had fulfilled his mission. He voluntarily accepted his Passion, turning the unjust atrocity of it into his immolation, completing the Sacrifice that he began to offer by the Eucharistic oblation the evening before. Thus he prepared his victory over death in his coming Resurrection, which makes the general Resurrection known to all mankind.

It is Good Friday night. Laying him shrouded in the tomb, all withdrew, his mother, now with the Apostle John, and all the rest.

The Resurrection: Jesus Christ, Son of God, Our Lord

It is Easter morning, the third day later: "Mary Magdalene came to the tomb early, while it was still dark, and saw that the stone had been taken away from the tomb. So she ran and went to Simon Peter. . . . 'They have taken the Lord out of the tomb, and we do not know where they have laid him' " (John 20:1–2). This is the fact of the empty tomb. Then all four Gospels witness to the appearances of the risen Jesus.

Immediately this Easter fact becomes the very center of the Catholic faith, which is handed on by catechetical teaching. Saint Paul is explicit on this vital point for biblical Catechetics: "I delivered to you as of first importance what I also received, that Christ died for our sins in accordance with the scriptures, that he was buried, that he was raised on the third day in accordance with the scriptures, and that he appeared to Cephas, then to the Twelve. Then he appeared to more than five hundred brethren at one time, most of whom are still alive" (1 Cor. 15:3–6).

Is the Resurrection of Jesus a historical fact? Indeed it is! It is subject to documentation like other historical facts. All of our knowledge of facts that took place in the past rests upon documents that are worthy of our faith. This is true of our knowledge of Socrates, of Cicero, of Francis of Assisi, of Napoléon. It is likewise true of Jesus, the Rabbi or Teacher of Israel, who was betrayed and suffered under Pontius Pilate, died, and was buried. On the other hand there were reports from persons who bore witness that they saw him alive, touched him, talked with him, and all this not once but many times throughout these unique forty days. These reports were recorded in writing many times in the Early Church and accumulate to a massive documentation.[22]

To be reasonable regarding Jesus, at least as reasonable as men consent to be about Socrates, Cicero, and the rest, one must accept the documents as they are, in the way they have survived, with openness to what they witness. It is not reasonable to complain about them, to subject them to quibbles, to protest that they ought to be something other than what they are. It is an evasion to assert that no one saw the Resurrection of Jesus as it actually took place. Why? Because the soldiers guarding the tomb saw it actually taking place. It is impacted upon them as a reasonable person would expect. And it took a great deal of money to purchase their silence (Matt. 28:4 and 11–15). One takes records as they are.

Let the words of the great German exegete Heinrich Schlier, once a student under Bultmann, suffice. Commenting on the richly varied documentation in the New Testament, Schlier notes that the fact of the Resurrection of Jesus was "the nucleus and central theme" of all the original sermons recorded in the Acts of the Apostles. From the outset this central theme was "cast into a didactic form, becoming thus the point of departure of catechesis."[23] "The event of the Resurrection," Schlier continues, "is reported by narratives placed side by side (in the Gospels of the New Testament) without any editorial harmonization. . . . The confusion of the whole is neither disordering nor upsetting. One feels no need to construct any one correct pattern in the unfolding of the facts surrounding and following the central fact. For that fact in itself is certain."[24]

Catechetical teaching possesses in this central fact of the Resurrection of Jesus its point of departure, as Schlier says correctly, but also as its own central inspiration, its essential content and the motivation for handing its content on as the revealed Word of God. For this event, witnessed as a precise and public historical fact by the entire New Testament, is presented throughout as an action of God. It culminates and completes the wonderful works of God that have planted Revealed Religion into human history since the choice of Abraham and the writings of Moses and the Prophets. The New

Testament simply continues the literary genre of the historical writings of the Jewish People. If God exists and is the Creator and Lord of history, then such a planned series of interventions on his part is possible. Christianity, in fulfillment of the Hebrew Revelation, documents the fact that the possibility was realized in the life, Passion, death, and Resurrection of Jesus the Rabbi or Teacher in Israel. Thus he becomes Jesus Christ the Divine Teacher of mankind in and through his Resurrection. This establishes Catechetics as a teaching of the Word of God. And the basic Easter joy of Christianity is the joy of the catechist in the work of the catechetical apostolate.[25]

It remains to touch upon the aspects of Jesus' activity during the forty days after Easter that complete and confirm all his previous teaching during his public life.

The Forty Days: Jesus Restores His Apostles and His Teaching Program

During these unique forty days Jesus revives and resurrects his work as a Teacher, interrupted and apparently ended once and for all by the betrayal. In doing so he established Catechetics as the teaching of the Word of God and projects it forward to the end of time.

The first step was his kindly and forgiving recovery and rehabilitation of his demoralized Eleven. Jesus finds them now at last truly humble, open to his teaching and able deeply to profess the Catholic faith that he is true God and true Man (see John 20:26–29). He prepares them for confirmation by the Holy Spirit. At the end of the forty days he sends them to continue his own teaching mission to all nations.

Jesus begins with Peter, his appointed vicar and leader. The other ten will be recovered and restored in and through Peter. With Peter, they are all filled with shame and remorse. Jesus sees in them a new openness to his teaching. Their merely Jewish national aspirations for a temporal world empire on the model of the Davidic Kingdom are now crushed. They are ready to understand what Jesus had been teaching from the beginning.

In a most humanly and divinely kind way Jesus forgave his Eleven. He helped them recover confidence, rehabilitating them personally, psychologically, and spiritually. All of this restores to them the universal pastoral mission in the New Israel of God for which he had been preparing them all along. "Peter was grieved because he said to him the third time, 'Do you love me?' And he said to him, 'Lord, you know everything; you know that I love you.' Jesus said to him, 'Feed my sheep' " (John 21:17). From that moment Peter and his successors will exercise the supreme pastoral authority in Jesus' Church.

Furthermore, thanks to the offering Jesus made of himself on the occasion of the wretched act of Judas, doing him in to the death, his disciples now had the Eucharistic Sacrifice of the New Testament. In it Jesus is both Priest and Victim. This gives the work of the Apostles a dimension of divine power and efficacy. At last they understood what John the Baptist had said at the beginning: "Behold the Lamb of God, who takes away the sins of the world" (John 1:29).

Jesus Finalizes His Program of Catechetical Teaching

In the forty days Jesus reaffirmed to his Apostles the basic pattern, content, and method of catechetical teaching that we saw in chapters 7 and 8. He began to do this on Easter Sunday itself with the two disconsolate disciples on the road to Emmaus. Saint Luke's Gospel reports:

> Peter . . . went running to the tomb. He bent down and saw the binding clothes but nothing else; he then went back home, amazed at what had happened. That very same day, two of them were on their way to a village called Emmaus, seven miles from Jerusalem, and they were talking together about all that had happened. Now as they talked this over, Jesus himself came up and walked by their side; but something prevented them from recognizing him. He said to them, "What matters are you discussing as you walk along?" They stopped short, their faces downcast. . . . "You must be the one person staying in Jerusalem who does not know the things that have been happening there these last few days." "What things?" he asked. [The Risen Jesus is a Teacher, as always. This is an instance of the catechetical question-and-answer method at its best. He takes them where they are, beginning his lesson there]. "All about Jesus of Nazareth," they answered,

"who proved he was a great prophet by the things he said and did in the sight of God and of the whole people; and how our chief priests and our leaders handed him over to be sentenced to death, and had him crucified. Our own hope had been that he would be the one to set Israel free." [Clearly they were still thinking in terms of the false Messianic expectation with its merely external and political concept of freedom] . . . . Then he said to them, "You foolish men! So slow to believe the full message of the prophets! Was it not ordained that the Christ should suffer and so enter into his glory?" Then, starting with Moses and going through all the prophets, he explained to them the passages throughout the scriptures that were about himself (Luke 24:12–35).

This is the heart of catechetical method. It explains the historical facts about Jesus as the fulfillment of the Hebrew Revelation. Catechetics will call this fundamental principle of method Christocentrism in teaching.[26]

. . . [At the village] he went in to stay with them. Now while he was with them at table, he took bread and said the blessing: then he broke it and handed it to them. And their eyes were opened and they recognized him; but he had vanished from their sight. Then they said to each other, "Did not our hearts burn within us as he talked to us on the road and explained the scriptures to us?" They set out that instant and returned to Jerusalem. There they found the Eleven assembled together with their companions, who said to them, "Yes, it is true. The Lord has risen and has appeared to Simon. Then they told their story of what had happened on the road and how they had recognized him at the breaking of the bread (Luke 24:12–35).

This shows Jesus himself as the first catechetical Teacher, establishing the fact that Catechesis is a practical teaching closely linked with the Liturgy and indeed specifically with the presence of the Risen Jesus in the Holy Eucharist.

The writings of the New Testament bear abundant witness that Jesus' Apostles looked upon themselves as teachers who continue Jesus' mission of teaching.[27] It is only reasonable to suppose that Jesus gave the Eleven this same kind of detailed explanation of the pattern of teaching that emerges from the fact of his Passion, death, and Resurrection. "He had shown himself alive to the Apostles he had chosen through the Holy Spirit . . . ," Saint Luke writes in his synthetic way, "after his Passion by many demonstrations: for forty days he had continued to appear to them and tell them about the kingdom of God" (Acts 1:2–3). Since this Kingdom of God was to be established among men by the apostolate of his Church sent to teach all the nations, the process of this teaching everywhere according to that one and the same *typos* or pattern of syllabus followed by all her teachers, the reasonable mind is forced back to its original source. This source has to be Jesus himself, the Teacher who forms this new Israel of God by his teaching.

Thus the first Easter morning and the forty days do indeed bear witness to the origin and nature of catechetical teaching. From this Resurrection morning forward to the end of human history, catechetical teaching will always be a human teaching, a union of content and method, with all the dynamism of interpersonal discourse and communication. Generically it will not differ from the educational process of the arts, sciences, and disciplines of human culture as such. But it will be a teaching that has its own specific nature. The content will be the Mystery of Christ. The method will be the principle of fulfillment: the explanation of the fact that everything concerning Jesus of Nazareth took place according to the Scriptures of Moses and the Prophets. This process of catechetical teaching, furthermore, will always and everywhere follow one and the same basic and characteristic pattern of syllabus [*typos* in Saint Paul's Greek, Rom. 6:17). This pattern has two fundamental parts. First, an explanation of the work of the Three Divine Persons in the creation, the redemption, and the sanctification of human persons, calling each to prepare for the coming judgment by seeking to be holy as the Heavenly Father is holy. Second, by explaining the *metanoia* or conversion to the Way of Life that is the human response to this divine call. This Way of Life is constituted by three sets of personal actions, which the teaching explains to each person: personal prayer, the sacramental life, and Gospel morality. Thus from beginning to end it is a teaching that continues Jesus' own work as the culminating Teacher in Israel, a practical teaching that enables souls really to hear God calling each one to the new life of his Kingdom and that helps each one deepen this personal response of conversion to the God of Revelation.[28]

It is quite clear that this teaching continues flexibly in relationship to all manner of human situations, the substance of the twelve general headings under which Jesus' teaching was summarized in chapter 8. The difference now is his own actual immolated state as the continuing Lamb of God, the Victim of the Sacrifice of the New and now final and everlasting Testament. Jesus' work during these forty days is the full illumination of the understanding of the Eleven with regard to the nature and meaning of the teaching he had been giving them throughout his public life ever since John the Baptist had pointed him out to them: "Behold, the Lamb of God, who takes away the sin of the world!" (John 1:29).

In this rehabilitation of his Eleven, Jesus concludes his work of forming them to be themselves the founding teachers of the New Israel of God. Thus Jesus completes the Christian Revelation by arranging for its mediation to all nations. New light and understanding flood their souls. Now they see. Above all, the reality and the mission of the Three Divine Persons who share equally the one Divine Nature of Yahweh, the God of the Hebrew Revelation, become luminously clear to the Apostles. The Divine Trinity will always be the hallmark of the Christian Revelation. And the reality and meaning of the Incarnation come home to them with finality: they realize fully now that their beloved Teacher has been Yahweh himself visiting this planet in the Person of the Eternal Son.

Many things he said now become fully understood realities to them: "He who sees me sees him who sent me. I have come as light into the world" (John 12:44–46); "Believe the works, that you may know and understand that the Father is in me and I am in the Father" (John 10:38); "Jesus said to them, 'Truly, truly, I say to you, before Abraham was, I am' " (John 8:58); and so much else, so much that "if all were written down, the world itself, I suppose, would not hold all the books that would have to be written" (John 21:25). All of Jesus' teaching flooded in upon the Apostles. Now they saw it all, understood it all, with the luminous synthetic comprehensiveness of the Prophetic Light. And in addition Jesus was comforting them and giving them confidence by promising the Holy Spirit to them precisely to help them in their role of teachers continuing to teach this Christian Revelation in his Name.

The reality and the missions of the Three Divine Persons has now taken shape in their minds as the most fundamental truth of the Christian Revelation. The Trinitarian outline of the profession of their Apostolic faith is already present in their minds, ready for the Sacrament of Baptism they will administer, and ready for use as the pattern or standard or *typos* in the preparatory teaching they will do when they give and explain this Christian Revelation, this Christian faith, to those whom they prepare for the living of the sacramental and Eucharistic life.

Revelation, given to them by Jesus their Teacher as a light from beyond this world, is not and never will be a doctrine elaborated by their own thinking or research. Furthermore, it closes with these men who were Jesus' own specially chosen students and received his teaching in the closest, most direct, most personal manner possible. This doctrine on the closing of public Revelation with the Eleven has been constant in the Church. It follows from their closeness to Jesus the Teacher and is a corollary of his Self-Revelation as the Son of God. They understood the finality of the Christian Revelation: they had been taught the Word of God by God himself teaching them in the human words of his human discourse as their Teacher. To expect some other teacher or to anticipate some other teaching in the future that will supplant Jesus' teaching or to lift it to a higher level of wisdom is incompatible with the Person they now knew him to be and with the principle of fulfillment that he taught. For the Apostolic faith now recognizes him as Jesus the Messiah, the final and definitive Divine Teacher of all mankind.[29]

This brings into view the heart of the matter, the next synthetic consideration of Jesus the Divine Teacher.

Kyrios: The Transfer of the Divine Name to Jesus

The nature of human language and its role in Divine Revelation are fundamental in Catechetics. Human persons must use human words to express divine things and to teach them to others, including human children. Perforce: because language is the specifically human mode of communication.[30] By the same token, God uses human words when revealing his own Word to mankind. Naturally, for he himself created human nature to be linguistic in its specific mode of communication. Thus the Eternal Word, incarnate and using human discourse in his teaching, is the culmination also in this sense of the Prophetic Revelation.

A case in point, perhaps the most important illustration for catechetical use, is offered by *Marana*, the Semitic (Aramaic) word meaning "Lord," with its Greek equivalent *Kyrios*. These two words were in common use throughout the Hellenistic world as the title of rulers of the city-states and commanders of military forces. There is nothing more human than this word and its meaning.[31]

When the Hebrew Bible was translated into Greek, producing the standard Septuagint version used throughout antiquity by Greek-speaking Jews of the Diaspora, the sacred name Yahweh was translated regularly as *Kyrios* in the Greek.[32] Thus this particular human word acquired a unique religious meaning: it now denotes he who is the Creator of heaven and earth and the Supreme Lord of human history: Yahweh himself. Linguistic scholars hold that the Greek *Kyrios* has roots in the Sanscrit, denoting one who has strength and power. For the Hebrew scholars who produced the Septuagint, it was simply natural to choose Kyrios as the Name in Greek for he who is the Almighty, the creative source of all being, reality, and goodness.

It was his Divine Name, *Marana* or *Kyrios* that the Apostles transferred to Jesus when he rose from the dead and began his forty days of familiar conversation with them, visibly present to many among his followers but to the Eleven in a special way. That the transfer of the Divine Name began immediately is the meaning of the dramatic episode of the doubting Thomas: "Eight days later the disciples were in the house again and Thomas was with them. The doors were closed, but Jesus came in and stood among them. 'Peace be with you,' he said. Then he spoke to Thomas, 'Put your finger here, look, here are my hands. Give me your hand; put it into my side. Doubt no longer but believe.' Thomas replied, 'My Lord and my God' " (John 20:26–28).

The confession of faith in Jesus as "the Lord" begins thus in the forty days and becomes the central point of the heralding of the Gospel and the teaching of its facts and truths that the Eleven now begin to do.

The Lordship of Jesus, the foundation of all Christocentrism in Catechetics, is central to the profession of the Apostolic faith from its beginnings in Jerusalem. It is significant that vestiges of the original Aramaic spoken in Jerusalem remain to this day in the Greek manuscripts of the New Testament. Saint Paul in his Epistles frequently wrote a final word of greeting in his own hand. So in First Corinthians 16:20–24: "This greeting is in my own hand—Paul. If anyone does not love the Lord [*Kyrios*], a curse on him. *Maran atha*. The grace of the Lord [*Kyrios*] Jesus be with you."[33] The entire New Testament can be considered as a witness of the transfer of this Divine Name to Jesus, from Saint Stephen's confession (Acts 7:56–59) through all the Epistles of Saint Paul, especially in the opening salutations.

Let us hear one of the foremost exegetes of the twentieth century as a conclusion on this consideration of the Lordship of Jesus that establishes the Scriptural basis of the Divinity of Christ and of Christocentrism in Catechetics: "The Messiah in Christianity is no ordinary king or national hero, such as the Jews expected. He is the heavenly Messiah of the Apocalyptic writings, Daniel's Son of Man. He is a supernatural being who leads a divine life on earth in a human form. This is how Jesus conceived his mission, and the first Christians understood it in the same way. . . . The name of *Kyrios* which Christ bears was given to him by God. . . . *Kyrios* as applied to Christ is the same name which belonged to God in the Old Testament."[34]

This title, *Kyrios*, which denotes the profession of faith in Jesus made definitively by the Eleven because they were witnesses of his Resurrection, embodies the essential doctrine of Christianity: "That the Risen Jesus is *Kyrios* is stated throughout the New Testament."[35] "The title 'Lord' represents a basic intuition of Christianity, and one of its most essential doctrines."[36]

Apostolicity: From Disciples to Apostles, Jesus Sends His Church

Here again the New Testament witnesses to a final instance of the wonderfully kind work of rehabilitation of his Eleven special students that the Risen Jesus was accomplishing during the forty days. He completes and concludes the founding of his Church, which had been his essential purpose in giving them his program of teaching and formation prior to the betrayal.[37]

Jesus completes his work of constituting his Church in its essential structure by two actions, both witnessed in the New Testament as a whole and particularly in the Gospels and the Acts of the Apostles. By this first action Jesus gave these Eleven men, whom he had chosen and whom he has been teaching, a twofold spiritual power to act in his name as his instruments. By this second action he sent them forth to all the nations of the world. Jesus is thus literally himself personally the source of the term *Apostles*, from the Greek word meaning to "send forth," by which his inner circle of students are known to this day.[38] By endowing them with this twofold spiritual power that they carried forth with them, Jesus constituted his Church, himself personally. This unique Church will be always to the end of time recognizable on earth by this fundamental and constitutive note of "Apostolicity."

This consideration of Jesus' work during the forty days confirms the reality of his ongoing presence to mankind as the Divine Teacher. For this Church is constituted to be his Teaching Church. It is sent to be himself continuing his own teaching mission by its Apostles and their Successors. Clearly nothing illuminates more fundamentally the nature of catechesis and the self-image of catechetical teachers.[39]

The twofold spiritual power comes first into view, for it constitutes the Church that Jesus then sent forth. These two powers, while intrinsically related and always located in Jesus' Apostles and their successors to the end of time, are nevertheless distinct.[40] It is only by considering them separately that the fundamental nature of catechesis comes correctly into view.

The Sacramental Power

The first power is the *Sacramental Power*. Jesus conferred it upon his Eleven when he ordained them to a participation in his own Priesthood. By virtue of this power they are the priests of the New Testament. "It is a power to offer the sacrifice and to confer the sacraments of the New Law, a power coming from Christ, transmitted by the Apostles and their Successors, not to be given a second time to the same person, but to be 'stirred up' (St. Paul's phrase) since it resides permanently in the soul, and setting up a difference of rank, a Hierarchy—there we have the power of orders as it appears in the Scriptures."[41]

The heart of this priestly power, the center around which the other Sacraments turn like planets around the sun, is the Mystery of Faith, the Real Presence of Jesus Christ in the Holy Eucharist. For this Real Presence makes the Sacrifice of the New Testament *real*; namely, it has a Victim, which it offers: Jesus Christ crucified in redemption of mankind. And it makes Holy Communion different from ordinary meals, in that it is the Bread of Angels that is received, Jesus Christ who made this so clear and explicit in his teaching, as chapter 6 of Saint John bears witness. Thus in this Sacrifice the followers of Jesus participate as the Jews participated in the Passover Sacrifice by the sacrificial banquet with a lamb made victim in the Temple.

The Eucharist continues the presence of Jesus Christ the Divine Teacher in his Church by virtue of the ministry of his Eleven exercising this priestly power. The Eucharistic Presence will be the fountainhead of teaching in his Church. It will ensure that the concept of God is correct in the thinking of his disciples across the coming centuries. For the Eucharist teaches the Almighty power of God. God is the Creator of all that is and exercises Almighty power over his creation. This fulfills and completes the Hebrew faith in the Almighty. When the thinking of Christians proceeds within this Eucharistic faith as its guiding star, furthermore, it will acquire a new lucidity about substantial reality, as distinct from the phenomena or appearances of things. This will help ensure that the concept of man is correct in the thinking of his disciples across the centuries. For this substance of things, a deeper and more profound aspect of their reality, cannot be known by the sense of the organism but only by a qualitatively distinct power of insight and understanding given by the spiritual power of intelligence. Thus the Eucharistic Presence stabilizes human thinking, so prone to lose itself in phenomena and to become blind to intelligible reality. It assists it to rise from the two kinds of knowledge in man to recognize the two kinds of being, matter and spirit, united in the human person.

Jesus Christ the Divine Teacher, through the endowment of teaching he is giving to his special students, is thus at the fountainhead of a potential renewal of philosophy, enabling it to see better the reality of God and of the human soul. Such a renewal of philosophy, furthermore, will by the very nature of things radiate out to renew all the teaching of the other human arts, sciences, and disciplines, so that the historic reality of Christian culture can come into being.[42]

The Teaching Power

The second spiritual power that Jesus conferred upon his *mathetai* is his own *Teaching Power.*

As the Master Teacher in Israel, Jesus was of course preparing his Twelve to teach his own doctrine, which was the fulfillment of the Revelation of God to Moses and the Prophets. Jesus clearly intended that they should be themselves teachers in his Name. In fact, he began to send them as heralds and teachers in those months prior to the betrayal. In these forty days he completes and confirms them as the teachers of the Christian Revelation. This is their final rehabilitation as persons. And it expresses his mastery over contingent events, even over the betrayal that led to his own crucifixion. Only God enjoys such mastery. The Eleven realize by a full interior illumination that their Teacher is the Lord of history: they are now able to apply his principle of method in their teaching with a personal mastery of their own, the fact that everything about Jesus took place "according to the Scriptures." And they are in full possession of their teaching, received from Jesus Christ the Divine Teacher. This content has his herald's message, which they will proclaim as witnesses to him, and it contains his call for faith and *metanoia.* Even the pattern or syllabus of this content, it has been noted already, has been given to them in the revelation that there are Three equal Divine Persons in the one unique Nature of Yahweh, the God of Revelation. Thus their teaching will relate in a unique, constantly recurring way to the Three Divine Persons and their work for the creation, redemption, and sanctification of human persons. Jesus himself has given the substance of catechetical teaching to his Eleven, "the explicit content of faith amounting to two points which, in the supernatural mystery of their riches, contain all the Articles of the Creed: namely, that 'God is, and rewards those who seek after Him' (Hebrews 11:6)."[43]

The work of Jesus, the Rabbi or Teacher in Israel, is finished. The forty days are near their end. As Jesus Christ the Divine Teacher, he is ready to send his students out as his Apostles, on their worldwide and perhaps centuries-long mission.

This introduces the second of Jesus' two actions in constituting his Church. For, as mentioned earlier, Jesus gave his Church its essential structure first by endowing the Apostles with the twofold Pastoral Power and second by sending them forth to all nations, exercising that Pastoral Power by his authority. This sending of the men whom he personally has been teaching and forming to continue his teaching mission from his Father will give them their new name, the Apostles. The mission to all the Gentile nations, a mission that is to last until the end of human history in the Second Coming of this same Jesus, will always be "Apostolic." Both the government and the teaching of his Church will be "Apostolic." This note of Apostolicity constitutes his Teaching Church for all time.[44] Whenever it is present in the centuries and wherever among the peoples of the planet Earth, it will always be heralding and teaching this one and same message as its doctrine: the message and doctrine to all mankind taught by the Son of God Incarnate in his public life on earth.

It is this great fact, truly world-historical in prospect and intention, and this participation in the heralding of the Good News and the teaching of the *metanoia* of personal response to it that gives purpose, content, and method to Catechetics and self-identity to the catechist.[45]

It is fitting to conclude this section with Jesus' own final words to them that are the charter of the Kingdom of God on earth. "Now the eleven disciples went to Galilee, to the mountain to which Jesus had directed them. And when they saw him they worshiped him; but some doubted. And Jesus came and said to them, 'All authority in heaven and on earth has been given to me. Go therefore and make disciples of all nations, baptizing them in the name of the Father and of the Son and of the Holy Spirit, teaching them to observe all that I have commanded you; And lo, I am with you always; yes, to the close of the age' " (Matt. 28:16–20). And he ascended into heaven. After the Ascension, "they returned to Jerusalem . . . to the Upper Room . . . and with one accord devoted themselves to prayer, together with the women and Mary the mother of Jesus'' (Acts 1:12–14).

Conclusion: Fullness and Mediator of Biblical Revelation

Jesus the Divine Teacher has concluded the mission he received from his heavenly Father, being made flesh and dwelling among us to conclude Divine Revelation to mankind. He himself in Person and in the doctrine he placed on deposit with his Apostles is the fullness and fulfillment of this Divine Revelation.

Jesus is likewise the mediator of this revealed truth by the instrumentality of the teaching of it. This is why he prepared his Apostles to be its teachers. This is why he sent them to teach it to all the peoples and nations of the earth. This is how they came to have the *typos didachēs* (Rom 6:17), the pattern or standard or credal syllabus by which he taught them to do his teaching.

His doctrine from beginning to end is a truth that the mind sees, and at the same time it is a practical teaching that calls for conversion to God away from sin. It is a teaching that forms to the new Way of Life, the eternal life of the world to come. Thus again Jesus is the last and greatest of the Prophets.

When he sent his Apostles forth on their mission to all the nations of mankind, he launched the Messianic Age in universal history, constituted by the spiritual regeneration and renewal of persons directly and of earthly structures indirectly, depending upon the response of the individual persons to his call and his teaching. This Messianic Age is Eucharistic in its nature: it will depend upon the personal response to sacramental living, Gospel morality, and prayer out among the nations that will be taught.

All of this constitutes catechetical teaching in its very essence and Eucharistic center.

When the scene is surveyed in retrospect, it is clear that Jesus Christ is the most powerful and influential Teacher who ever has appeared among men. This is the final conclusion of biblical Catechetics on Jesus the Divine Teacher, the one that illuminates the greatness of the calling and the importance of the function of all catechists who teach the Deposit of Faith and Morals in the line of succession from the Apostles.

Chapter 10
The Word of God

The *Word of God* is a constantly recurring phrase in the New Testament. It is the first step in knowing the minds of the Apostles and their close associates who produced the Acts of the Apostles and the Epistles. What did they mean by this "Word of God"? How did they see themselves in relation to it? Were they convinced that the "Word of God" is uttered on the human scene in human words and indeed by themselves? Was it the mind of the Apostles that they uttered this Word of God by the mandate of Jesus, who sent them to "teach all nations, baptizing them" (Matt. 28:19)? Does this link catechetical teaching directly with the Word of God and the handing on of it to other persons?[1]

If all this is the case, then the nature and the importance of the mission of the catechist receive a fundamental illumination. Bearing these questions in mind, we proceed to the use of *the Word of God* by the Apostles.

The Word of God As Used in the New Testament[2]

The definite article *The* is significant in *The Word of God*. It indicates that the Word of God is something definite, concrete, structured, an individually recognizable truth given by teaching.[3] A parallel in Jesus' question, "When the Son of Man comes will he find *the* faith on earth?" (Luke 18:8), where the inspired Greek original uses the definite article. It means therefore the particular, structured, and definite faith that Jesus entrusted to his Apostles as a precious Deposit.

The *word* means the spoken expression of the inner truth of a mind. In this case, *The Word of God* means a truth in the mind

225

of God that is expressed audibly on the human scene. It is used interchangeably with *The Gospel* or *The Gospel of Jesus*: for the Apostles and their writings these are one and the same thing.[4]

Clearly the concept of God that each one has in mind, catechists and catechumens, is crucial to the very idea of a Word of God.[5] One must believe that God is a really-existing, intelligent Person. "For lo, he who forms the mountains and creates the wind, declares to man what is his thought" (Amos 4:13). Moses and all the Prophets have this realization about God. Jesus teaches constantly on the basis of it. His Apostles have the same concept: it is present in each instance of their use of *The Word of God.*

"For we are not," says Saint Paul, speaking for all the Apostles, "peddlers of God's Word; but as men of sincerity, as commissioned by God, in the sight of God we speak in Christ" (2 Cor. 2:17). The Apostle is commissioned, mandated, by God not to speak his own merely human word but the very Word of God himself. "Having this ministry by the mercy of God." Saint Paul says elsewhere, ". . . we have renounced disgraceful, underhanded ways; we refuse to practice cunning or to tamper with God's Word, but by the open statement of the truth we would commend ourselves to every man's conscience in the sight of God" (2 Cor. 4:1–2).

"For the Word of God is living and active, sharper than any two-edged sword, piercing to the division of soul and spirit, of joints and marrow, and discerning the thoughts and intentions of the heart. And before him no creature is hidden, but all are open and laid bare to the eyes of him with whom we have to do" (Heb. 4:12–13). Here the Epistle to the Hebrews brings the concept of the Almighty, all-knowing personal God explicitly before us: the Word of God is linked directly to him who is everywhere, knows everything, and sees everything. Hence Saint Pius X urges catechists to inspire in the children the Christian concept of life and the sense of responsibility in each human act toward the Supreme Judge.

Saint Paul is full of the fact that the Word of God comes to men by the words of his Apostles and their Successors. "How are men to call upon him in whom they have not believed? And how are they to believe in him of whom they have never heard? And how are they to hear without a preacher? And how can men preach unless they have been sent?" (Rom. 12:14–15). This is essential to the very idea of evangelization and catechetical teaching. Saint Paul relates the Word of God to the practical living of life by Christians: "The older women . . . are to train the younger women to be . . . submissive to their husbands, that the Word of God be not discredited" (Tit. 2:5).

Let Saint Peter, the Vicar of Christ and leader of the Apostles, conclude this sampling. He speaks for them and for the entire Early Church: "You have been born anew, not of perishable seed, but of imperishable, through the living and abiding Word of God" (1 Pet. 1:23). Saint Peter and all the Apostles heard these words that Jesus addressed to his heavenly Father at the Last Supper: "I have given them the words which thou gavest me, and they have received them and know in truth that I came from thee; and they have believed that thou didst send me" (John 17:8). This is the why *The Word of God* meant what it did to the Apostles, as their use of the phrase bears witness.

Frequently in the New Testament *The Word* is used absolutely, without further qualification; but the context makes it clear that the Apostles had the Word of God in mind when doing so. They also used simply *The Gospel* and *The Word of Christ* to mean "The Word of God." This will be essential when we come to analyze the Deposit of Faith. In exploring the mind of the Apostles regarding this basic reality, the fact that there is a really existing Word of God on earth among us, one must remember constantly their absolute conviction that Jesus is the Lord God visiting his people: when he speaks, it is the Word of God that is being spoken. Here one need but give a few samples of the many places in Acts and the epistles. "Our Gospel," Saint Paul writes to his Thessalonians, "came to you not only in word, but also in power and in the Holy Spirit, and with full conviction" (1 Thess. 1:5). Here he means the human word that they heard with their human ears and understood with their human minds. There is more to the word they heard than the merely human: they were hearing the very Word of God. "You received the Word," he continues, "in much affliction, with joy inspired by the Holy Spirit" (1 Thess. 1:6). He means the Word of God.

"Our Gospel," Saint Paul writes to the Thessalonians, "came to you not only in word, but also in Power and in the Holy Spirit and with full conviction" (1 Thess. 1:5). The word *Gospel* here, as generally in the apostolic writings, means "The Word of God," not a mere human word. Speaking of the Day of Judgment, he writes to the Romans: "On that day when, according to my Gospel, God judges the secrets of men by Christ Jesus" (Rom. 2:16). Frequently Saint Paul uses *my Gospel* (see Rom. 2:16, 2 Cor. 4:2–4, 2 Thess. 2:13–14, and 2 Tim. 2:8). "The Gospel which was preached by me is not man's gospel. For I did not receive it from man . . . but it came through a revelation of Jesus Christ" (Gal. 1:11). When he went to Jerusalem to see Peter and the other original Apostles, Saint Paul "laid before them . . . the Gospel which I preach [verb in *keryx*] among the Gentiles" (Gal. 2:2).

These examples bear witness to the mind of the Apostles: the Word of God is the Gospel, and the Gospel is the Word of Jesus, the Word that Jesus speaks, the word that he deposited with his Apostles in his program for teaching them and preparing them to be teachers in his name.

The Meaning of the Genitive in The Word of God[6]

The preposition *of* as a part of speech in the English language, as in languages generally, has two meanings. Determining the one that the Apostles had in their use of *The Word of God* is essential for the study of the Deposit of Faith later and for catechetical teaching in apostolic times and in the present day.

According to the *Oxford Dictionary,* the genitive *of* denotes either the *source* of a thing or its possessor. One may say John's book or the book of John, meaning that he bought it at a bookstore and is its possessor. In this sense God is the possessor of his Word, his Bible, as he is the possessor of all things by right of creation. But one may also say "the Book of John," meaning that he wrote the book. He is its author and its source. This is the subjective genitive of the grammarians, and this is the sense it has for the Apostles when they say "the Word of God." God is the one who speaks this Word: he is its source and origin. It comes from him to those who hear it and indeed with his authority. The Word of God is given to men on the authority of God speaking and revealing his mind.

"We are not, like so many, peddlers of God's Word; but as men of sincerity, as commissioned by God, in the sight of God we speak in Christ" (2 Cor. 1:17). "The Word of God is living and active, sharper than any two-edged sword . . . and discerning the thoughts and intentions of the heart. And before him no creature is hidden, but all are open and laid bare to the eyes of him with whom we have to do" (Heb. 4:12–13). Such passages reveal clearly the minds of the Apostles and the Early Church. "The Word of God," writes the exegete Heinrich Schlier, "had become something of a technical term in the Apostolic Church. . . . The generative 'of God' does not signify the content about which the discourse speaks, and also not primarily merely a quality of this word. It means, rather, God as the Person from whom it comes and by whom it is spoken. . . . God as the one from whom it comes means that God is the source of this Word."[7]

Thus one comes to the subjective genitive, a term also used by grammarians in defining this part of speech. It denotes the living subject who does the action, such as an author who writes a book. Here it means the living god speaking and revealing his mind to men.[8] "The phrase 'of God' in these passages," Schlier continues, "refers to the subject who does the speaking."[9] We shall return to this at the end of this chapter when considering again who it is that speaks this Word. It is essential to the concept of a priceless Deposit of Faith and Morals and thus to the very nature of evangelization and catechetical teaching.

The Word of the Apostles Is Simultaneously the Word of God

The greatness and almighty power of God make it possible for him to use human creatures and their human speech to express to mankind his own very Word of God. This is the idea of all prophetic religion.[10] It is central to Jesus' fulfillment of prophetic religion that he not only himself personally spoke the Word of God to mankind as the Divine Teacher but that he gave this same power to the Apostles whom he prepared to continue his teaching program. For him and for his Apostles, the Word of God is simultaneously the human words spoken by the Apostles, proclaimed by them, and taught by them: "He who receives you receives me, and he who receives me receives him who sent me."[11]

All the Apostles were filled with the conviction that the Word of God is at one and the same time their own human words spoken out to the hearing of men. Saint Paul expresses this conviction in many instances. He calls the Word of God or the Gospel of Christ *"my* word" and *"my* Gospel." Hence the exegete Schlier concludes: "The Word which God speaks is simultaneously the word which the Apostle speaks."[12] Some examples will show this.

"Our Gospel," Saint Paul writes, "came to you not only in word but also in Power and in the Holy Spirit and with full conviction" (1 Thess. 1:5). On the basis of his proclamation and teaching, he tells them: "You turned to God from idols, to serve a living and true God, and to wait for his Son from heaven, whom he raised from the dead, Jesus who delivers from the wrath to come" (1 Thess. 1:9–10).

Saint Paul's conviction in this matter is clear when he tells the Corinthians that "my speech and my message were not plausible words of wisdom [i.e., human philosophy], but in demonstration of the Spirit and power, that your faith might not rest in the wisdom of men but in the power of God" (1 Cor. 2:4).

"On that day," he writes to the Romans, "according to my Gospel, God judges the secrets of men by Christ Jesus" (Rom. 2:16). Saint Paul returns to this conviction, stressing it: "Now to him who is able to strengthen you according to my Gospel and the preaching of Jesus Christ, according to the revelation of the mystery which was kept secret for long ages but is now disclosed and through the prophetic writings is made known to all nations" (Rom. 16:25–26). Through Saint Paul's proclamation of the Word of God the substance of the Hebrew Revelation is being given to the Gentiles as the very Word of God.

"We refuse to tamper with God's Word," Saint Paul tells the Corinthians, " . . . and even if our Gospel is veiled, it is veiled only for those who are perishing" (2 Cor. 4:2, 4). Again: "To this God called you through our Gospel, so that you may obtain the glory of our Lord Jesus Christ" (2 Thes. 2:14). And again: "Remember Jesus Christ, risen from the dead, descended from David, as preached in my Gospel, for which I am suffering and wearing fetters like a criminal" (2 Tim. 2:8). "For I would have you know, brethren, that the Gospel which was preached by me is not man's gospel. For I did not receive it from man . . . but through a Revelation of Jesus Christ" (Gal. 1:11). After fourteen years Paul went to Jerusalem to see Peter and the Apostles. "I laid before them . . . the Gospel which I preach [verb in *keryx]* among the Gentiles" (Gal. 2:2).

From these and similar passages it is clear that the Gospel proclaimed in human words by the Apostles is the very Word of God.
"St. Paul's apostolic Gospel," concludes Schlier, "*is* the Word which
Jesus speaks. . . . The human speaker speaks the Word of God. . . .
God's Word and the word of the Apostle are obviously one, or are
at least so intertwined that when one receives the apostolic word he
hears the Word of God, of Christ."[13] Saint Paul summarizes it himself: "So we are ambassadors for Christ, God making his appeal
through us" (2 Cor. 5:20). "The word of the one sent, the apostle,
is therefore the Word of God, the Word of Christ."[14] "Remember
your leaders, those who spoke to you the Word of God. . . . Imitate
their faith. Jesus Christ is the same yesterday and today and forever.
Do not be led away by diverse and strange teachings" (Heb. 13:7–9).

All of this is given sweeping summation by Saint Paul: "We
thank God constantly for this, that when you received the Word of
God which you heard from us, you accepted it not as the word of
me, but as what it really is, the Word of God, which is at work in
you believers" (1 Thess. 2:13). "That the Word of God lies hidden
in the words of man is a fact. Only Faith perceives this."[15] For this
is what the Faith is.

How can God's Word, one may ask, be also the word of men,
of the Apostles? The general answer given by the Holy Spirit in the
New Testament is the fact that Jesus gave his Apostles the power
through his Holy Spirit to be witnesses to him by their preaching
(kerygma) and their teaching: for he sent them to teach all nations
what he had taught them and in the same authority by which he
had taught them (see Matt. 28:16–20). Note again the passage from
Hebrews 13:7–9 given earlier and likewise Galatians 1:11.[16] The
Apostles have the power of the Holy Spirit to proclaim Jesus as
Savior and to call for conversion to him. The Apostles have received
this mandate and power from Jesus as witnesses to his Resurrection.
They have the power to be ministers of the Word. When Peter took
the lead in forming the Order of Deacons, he made the principle
clear: "It is not right that we give up preaching the Word of God to
serve tables. . . . We will devote ourselves to prayer and the Ministry
[Greek: *diakonía*] of the Word."

The more general reason that God's Word is able to come to
us in the words of men lies in the very nature of prophetic religion.
God's greatness, power, and omnipresence, closer to us creatures

than we are to ourselves, make it not only possible but also easy for him to choose certain persons to be his spokesmen, whether Moses and the Prophets or Jesus and his Apostles.[17]

The Ministry of the Word

In the light of the foregoing, it is proper to take up another basic concept of the New Testament, that of ministry, *diakonía.* But before doing so it is well to consider the *GCD,* for it relates the concept to catechetical teaching today. One should bear this in mind through the coming study of the Deposit of Faith and the Apostolic catechesis.

The Ministry of the Word in the GCD

The key to this entire relationship between catechetics today and the concept of *the Ministry of the Word* in the New Testament is contained in the title of part 2 of the *GCD,* nos. 10–35: "The Ministry of the Word." The *GCD* begins with Vatican II: "What was handed on by the Apostles includes everything which contributes to the holiness of life and the increase in faith of the People of God; and so the Church, in her teaching, life, and worship, perpetuates and hands on to all generations all that she herself is, all that she believes."[18] This is a key passage to bear in mind as the Deposit of Faith and the catechesis of the Apostles are explored in the coming chapters, together with "The Ordinary and Universal Magisterium" in the solemn definition of Vatican I.[19] All the activities of the Church mentioned earlier communicate Jesus' fulfillment and summary of divine revelation, but only "teaching" does so in the formal and specific sense of a "magisterium," which means the activity of conducting a teaching office. All of this indeed is the basic theme of this present manual, for all centers on the nature and purpose of "The Deposit of Faith and Morals."

"This is why the Ministry of the Word," the *GCD* continues, "can be considered as that which gives voice to this living tradition, within the totality of tradition."[20] From the study and analysis of catechetical teaching it will become clear that the voices of the men of Holy Orders, together with the voices of their catechists, are the ones that bring all of this into clear and immediate focus.

Continuing, the *GCD* introduces explicitly the idea of the Deposit. "The Church's shepherds not only proclaim and explain directly to the People of God the Deposit of Faith that has been committed to them but, moreover, make authentic judgments regarding expressions of that Deposit and the explanations that the faithful seek and offer. They do this in such a way that "in holding to, practicing, and professing the heritage of the Faith, there results on the part of the bishops and faithful a remarkable common effort." From this it follows that it is necessary for the Ministry of the Word to set forth the Divine Revelation such as it is taught by the Magisterium."[21]

In this luminous passage the *GCD*, published after Vatican II in 1971, links the Deposit of Faith and Morals coming from Jesus and his Apostles with the catechetical order of teaching, the teaching of the Magisterium in its ordinary form. Much religious knowledge is presupposed here that will be made explicit in the coming chapters.

Continuing, the *GCD* points out that Faith is the response to the Word of God.: "By faith man accepts revelation, and through it he consciously becomes a sharer in the gift of God."[22] "The Ministry of the Word takes many forms, including catechesis. . . . There is the form called evangelization. . . . Then there is the catechetical form . . . and the liturgical form. . . . Finally, there is the theological form, that is, the systematic treatment and the scientific investigation of the truths of Faith."[23] Which of these forms is the more fundamental, underlying the others? The study and analysis to come will clarify that Catechetics occupies this position, as Apostolicity the other three marks of the Church, because its object of study is the Articles of Faith in themselves and in their transmission by the other three forms.

The high purpose and function of the Ministry of the Word is clarified by the *GCD:* "Faith is a gift of God which calls men to conversion. . . . Catechesis performs the function of disposing men to receive the action of the Holy Spirit and to deepen their conversion. It does this through the word, to which are joined the witness of life and prayer."[24] This is fundamental for catechetical teaching today, for it opens the way to the perception that through the human words of present-day catechists it communicates the very Word of God as the Apostles understood it. In fact, it links Catechetics today with Jesus the Divine Teacher, who opened his public life of teaching by his call to conversion (see Mark 1:14–15).

Finally, the *GCD* rejects the contemporary aberration of the experience approach in religious education: "It is not sufficient for catechesis merely to stimulate a religious experience, even if it is a true one; rather, catechesis should contribute to the gradual grasping of the whole truth about the divine plan by preparing the faithful for the reading of Sacred Scripture and the learning of tradition."[25] In the lapidary mode of the Supreme Magisterium the immense effect of the Heresy of Modernism upon catechetics is rejected. It will remain to analyze in detail the nature of this heresy and the process of its experience approach in religious education in a later part of this manual.

Bearing in mind this remarkable contemporary statement, it is time to turn to the Ministry of the Word in the mind of the Apostles. For the complete correspondence between the two will become evident.

Apostleship As Ministry of the Word in the Acts and Epistles

Here catechetical teaching begins to come into view as a part of the original office, function, and mandate given by Jesus to his Apostles. In the days of the Earliest Church, still headquartered in the Cenacle at Jerusalem, the Twelve appointed the Order of Deacons for service of the tables, saying, "We will devote ourselves to prayer and the Ministry of the Word" (Acts 6:4). This comes from Jesus himself, for in the same act by which he taught and empowered his Apostles to teach the Word of God he created the *Diakonía* or Ministry of the Word. For their heralding and teaching were completely subordinated to this Word of God. It was a service of this Word. The Apostles understood their function in this way, as a few examples will show.

Saint Paul speaks of "our authority which the Lord gave for building you up" (2 Cor. 10:8). Chapters 1 and 2 of Galatians are entirely devoted to this service of the Word of God in terms of maintaining its purity and integrity when it is taught.[26] "I am aston-ished," Saint Paul tells his Galatian converts, "that you are so quickly deserting him who called you to the grace of Christ and turning to a different Gospel. . . . There are some who want to pervert the Gospel of Christ. But even if we, or an angel from heaven, should preach to you a gospel contrary to that which we preached to you, let him be accursed. . . . For I would have you know, brethren, that the Gospel which was preached by me is not man's gospel. For I did not receive it from man, nor was I taught it, but it came through a revelation of Jesus Christ" (Gal. 1:6–12). This contains the entire substance of this chapter on the Word of God and sets the stage for understanding the Deposit of Faith and Morals. The Ministry of this revealed Word is the official result of the mandate, the sending to teach the Word of God among men in the words of the Teaching Church, building up the Church of God.

Again: "Through Jesus Christ our Lord . . . we have received grace and apostleship to bring about the obedience of Faith for the sake of his Name among all nations" (Rom. 1:5). "The sending mandates two inseparable things," comments Schlier, "to proclaim the Gospel, and its fulfillment in the *Diakonía* or Ministry of the Word."[27] Again this brings the catechumenate and Catechetics into view already in the New Testament: "Paul, called to be an Apostle, set apart for the Gospel of God" (Rom. 1:1). "I serve . . . in the Gospel of God's Son" (Rom. 1:9). "How are they to believe in him of whom they have never heard? And how are they to hear without a preacher? And how can men preach unless they are sent?" (Rom. 10:14–15). "For Christ did not send me to baptize but to preach the Gospel, and not with eloquent wisdom, lest the cross of Christ be emptied of its power" (1 Cor. 1:17). "When I came to Troas to preach the Gospel of Christ, a door was opened for me in the Lord . . . to spread the fragrance of the knowledge of him everywhere" (2 Cor 2:12–14). "Our sufficiency is from God, who has qualified us to be ministers of a new covenant" (2 Cor. 3:6). "Continue in the Faith, stable and steadfast, not shifting from the hope of the Gospel which you heard, which has been preached to every creature under heaven, and of which I, Paul, became a minister" (Col. 1:23). "The Gentiles are fellow heirs, members of the same body. . . . Of this Gospel I was made a minister according to the gift of God's grace" (Eph. 3:6–7). And again the central passage regarding the deacons: "We will devote ourselves to prayer and to the Ministry of the Word" (Acts 6:4). "If only I may accomplish my course," Saint Paul says at the end of his life, "and the ministry I received from the Lord Jesus, to testify to the Gospel of the grace of God" (Acts 20:24). Saint Paul was always careful to report to Saint Peter at Jerusalem, where the Holy See of Jesus' religion was still located: "When we had come to Jerusalem, the brethren received us gladly. . . . After greeting them, Paul related one by one the things God had done among the Gentiles through his ministry" (Acts 21:17–19).

The Word of Jesus Is the Word of God

The passages given here make it luminously clear that Saint Paul and the other Apostles for whom he speaks were thinking of a very definite form of the Word of God. They were not thinking primarily of the Word of God spoken by Moses and the Prophets and written down in the books of the Hebrew Scriptures, our Old Testament, although this was of course the general background of their mind.

They were thinking primarily of the Word of Jesus, deposited with them in teachable form as the synthesis and summary of biblical revelation. This Word of Jesus is the Gospel that the Apostles preached and taught to their converts. The Word of Jesus is the Word of God placed in their hands as a divine Deposit, a teaching of faith to be guarded by them, indeed infallibly, in their own evangelization and teaching.[28]

This aspect of the mind of the Apostles is central to the very idea and nature of Catechetics. It will be the direct object of study in the two following chapters on the Deposit of Faith and on the catechetical teaching of the Apostles. It is basic to carry this aspect of the Ministry of the Word forward into these chapters, and indeed throughout this manual, for it is central to the very idea of the Deposit of Faith and Morals that is handed on by teaching.

Thus the stage is set to move from the Ministry of the Word to "The Ordinary and Universal Magisterium" of the Teaching Church. This ordinary form of the Magisterium is chiefly and fundamentally catechetical, as already noted. This dimension of Catechetics will be analyzed in detail in the coming chapters. The teaching office of the Apostles and the Gospel to which they minister have a common origin in Jesus the Divine Teacher. The official apostolic word is the Ministry of the Word of God: never one without the other.

Guarding the Purity and Integrity of the Word of God

The Ministry of the Word is subordinate to the Word of God itself: the Word of God is Lord over the Apostle. "In many and various ways God spoke of old to our fathers by the prophets; but in these last days he has spoken to us by a Son, whom he appointed the heir of all things, through whom also he created the world. He reflects the glory of God and hears the very stamp of his nature, upholding the universe by his word of power" (Heb. 1:1–3). The Apostles were filled with this conviction and hence had the greatest reverence for the Word of Jesus, their Divine Teacher.[29]

Hence Saint Paul's admonition to Timothy, his successor as a bishop: "O Timothy, guard the deposit!" (1 Tim. 6:20). This is done by giving the Word of God a service and ministry in subordination to it. The Apostle, Saint Paul stresses, must place no obstacle to it when he proclaims and teaches it. It stands above and is independent of those who minister to it. It is the Word of Christ, who is God; hence it must be kept *official* in the Church of God, of Christ. The Apostle must leave the Word of God to be what it is. This is what it means to be a Minister who serves the Word of God.[30]

Saint Paul emphasizes this in many places, as already seen in the passages cited earlier. "Continue in the Faith," he admonishes the Colossians, "stable and steadfast, not shifting from the hope of the Gospel which you have heard" (Col. 1:23).

It is important to note that for Saint Paul the worst obstacle to the guarding of the Deposit comes from merely human philosophies of all places and times. The reason of course is the fact that the Deposit of Faith and Morals comes from Jesus and the higher order of the prophetic light, while human science and philosophy exist on the lower and merely human level.[31] Saint Paul confronts the entire edifice of this merely human science and philosophy in the classic passage of 1 Corinthians 1:17–2:17: "For since, in the wisdom of God, the world did not know God through wisdom, it pleased

God through the folly of what we preach to save those who believe"
(1 Cor. 1:21). "Wisdom" here refers to the Greek philosophy that
the Gentiles loved so much. "When I came to you, brethren," Saint
Paul continues, "I did not come proclaiming to you the testimony
of God in lofty words or wisdom. For I decided to know nothing
among you except Jesus Christ and him crucified. . . . My speech
and very message were not in plausible words of wisdom, but in
demonstration of the Spirit and power, that your Faith might not
rest in the wisdom of men but in the power of God" (1 Cor. 2:1–5).

The worst obstacle, then, to authentic Ministry of the Word is
the false philosophy of this world that reduces the Word from the
higher order of heaven to the order of sociology, psychology, and
other merely earthly ideologies. The Apostle is charged to add nothing to the Word of God and to omit nothing: he speaks and teaches
only what is there in it, given from on high by Jesus the Divine
Teacher.[32] And the entire teaching centers upon the words of consecration at the Eucharistic Sacrifice, for here the Word of God to
mankind reached its culmination at the Last Supper.

The Work of Jesus the Divine Teacher

It was mentioned earlier that the Apostles were thinking of the
Word of God primarily as the teaching that Jesus had deposited with
them and not the Word of God as diffused in the many books of
Moses and the Prophets. Here the greatness of Jesus in his humanity
as the final Teacher of the Word of God comes into view. In those
times before the invention of printing, when the oral method of
teaching was in common human use, Jesus could hardly send his
Apostles and their successors loaded with the scrolls of the Hebrew
Scriptures to carry on his mission. He did something quite different,
which establishes his greatness as a teacher. He summarized the
Word of God in a short synthesis upon the pattern or standard of
the profession of faith in the Three Divine Persons and the human
response of the baptized to it: sacramental living, Gospel morality,
and personal prayer. Thus Jesus presents the Word of God, diffused
in the Hebrew Bible, our Old Testament, in a new teachable form,
easily carried in memory by his Apostles and all who succeeded
them in their teaching: the bishops, priests, deacons, and catechists

who helped them. With this, catechetical teaching appears as Jesus' own program continued. It continues as the Word of God given to the catechumens who are taught. The coming chapter will analyze in detail this great fact about Jesus' work as the Divine Teacher of mankind.[33]

The Word of the Church Is the Word of God

Saint Paul and the other Apostles bring us in this way to the step from the earthly life of Jesus to the life of the Church, the Body of Christ. This life of the Church takes place to the Apostolic Succession to which the Epistles to Timothy and Titus bear witness in the New Testament. The Apostles ordained men like Timothy and Titus to be bishops over the churches they had founded. This is the Apostolic Succession: the bishops are the successors of the Apostles:

> When the Church in her creeds calls herself apostolic, she expresses, besides the doctrinal identity of her teaching with that of the Apostles, the reality of the continuation of the work of the Apostles by means of the structure of succession in virtue of which the apostolic mission is to endure until the end of time. . . . The Catholic Church, which has developed through the ages and continues to grow by the life given to her by the Lord through the outpouring of the Holy Spirit, has always maintained her apostolic structure, faithful to the tradition of the Apostles which lives and endures in her. When she imposes hands on those to be ordained and invokes upon them the Holy Spirit, she is conscious of handing on the power of the Lord who makes the bishops, as successors of the Apostles, partakers in a special way of his threefold priestly, prophetic and royal mission. In turn, the bishops impart, in varying degrees, the office of their ministry to various persons in the Church.[34]

This is a basic statement of the Supreme Magisterium, for when it speaks of "the doctrinal identity of her teaching with that of the Apostles" it illuminates the Ordinary and Universal Magisterium, chiefly catechetical, as a teaching of the Word of God. It remains to see this fundamental of biblical Catechetics in the mind and word of the Apostles.

The Church Teaches the Word of God

We have come, then, to the essential question for Catechetics and catechists today. Does the Word of God pass forward into the times of the Church after the death of the last Apostle? Does the Apostolic Succession mean this as well as the succession of government and the worship of God by the Eucharistic Sacrifice? Does the word of the Apostles, speaking and teaching the very Word of God, continue in the Church? Since the Word of God that the Apostles proclaimed and taught to their first churches is the Gospel of Jesus, witnessing to him and giving him as the Holy Redeemer and Divine Savior to souls in the sacraments and especially the Holy Eucharist, it becomes fundamentally important to analyze the passage from the Apostolic churches to the Church after their time.

The answer is given, both directly and indirectly, by the Apostles themselves in many texts.

"When Timothy comes," Saint Paul writes to the Corinthians, "see that you put him at ease among you, for he is doing the work of the Lord, as I am. So let no one despise him" (1 Cor. 16:10–11). But Timothy is a bishop appointed by Saint Paul to succeed himself in one of the churches he founded. "The work of the Lord" is of course chiefly the proclaiming and the teaching of the Word of the Lord. Again: "We sent Timothy, our brother and God's servant in the Gospel of Christ, to establish you in your faith and to exhort you" (1 Thess. 3:2). But their faith is in the Word of God. Saint Paul's Epistles to Timothy and Titus are literally filled, of course, with admonitions to teach the sound doctrine. "A bishop must be an apt teacher" (1 Tim. 3:2). "Follow the pattern of the sound words which you have heard from me, in the faith and the love which are in Christ Jesus; guard the truth that has been entrusted to you by the Holy Spirit who dwells within us" (2 Tim. 1:13–14). Again Saint Paul clearly expects Timothy to guard the Word of God by his own teaching. "But as for you," Saint Paul tells Titus, the bishop who is his successor, "teach what befits sound doctrine" (Tit. 2:1). "Declare these things, exhort and reprove with all authority" (Tit. 2:15).

Not only Timothy and Titus but also the first Deacons take up the teaching of the Word of God (see Acts 6:8–15). And Philip "proclaimed to them (in Samaria) the Christ. . . . Now when the

Apostles at Jerusalem heard that Samaria had received the Word of God, they sent to them Peter and John" (Acts 8:4, 14).

Saint Paul addresses the elders of the church at Ephesus: "Take heed to yourselves and to all the flock, in which the Holy Spirit has made you guardians, to feed the Church of the Lord" (Acts 20:28). These elders are successors to the Apostles who proclaim and teach the Word of God, feeding the flock. Saint Paul makes the Apostolic Succession visible in his description of the Church: "And his gifts were that some should be apostles, some prophets, some evangelists, some pastors and teachers . . . for the work of the ministry, for building up the body of Christ" (Eph. 4:11–12). "This is why I left you in Crete," Saint Paul tells Titus, "that you might . . . appoint elders in every town. . . . For a bishop, as God's steward, . . . must hold firm to the sure Word as taught, so that he may be able to give instruction in sound doctrine and also to confute those who contradict it" (Tit. 1:5–9). The reality of the Apostolic Succession in the teaching of the Word of God could hardly be stated more explicitly: "Let the elders (i.e., bishops) who rule well be considered worthy of double honor, especially those who labor in preaching and teaching" (1 Tim. 5:17). "We beseech you, brethren," Saint Paul urges the Thessalonians, "to respect those who labor among you and are over you in the Lord and admonish you" (1 Thess. 5:12). The principle of the Apostolic Succession is already at work while Saint Paul is still alive.

The Acts and Epistles bear witness to the presence of "teachers" in the earliest Church of the Apostles: "And his gifts were that some should be apostles, . . . some pastors and teachers . . . , for the work of the ministry" (Eph. 4:11). "You have become dull of hearing. For though by this time you ought to be teachers, you need someone to teach you again the first principles of God's Word" (Heb. 5:11–12). There were teachers, much like CCD teachers in the Church today. What did they teach, if not the Word of God? Saint Paul names some of these teachers. "You learned . . . the Gospel . . . from Epaphras our beloved fellow servant. He is a faithful minister of Christ on our behalf" (Col. 1:17). Again the Apostolic Succession is explicit, and it exists in those teachers of the Word of God. "Epaphras, who is one of yourselves, a servant of Jesus Christ, . . . has worked hard for you" (Col. 4:12–13). And Archippus: "Say to Archippus, 'See that you fulfill the ministry which you have received in the Lord' " (Col. 4:17). Also Stephanas: "Brethren, you know that the household of Stephanas were the first converts in Achaia, and they have devoted themselves to the service of the saints; I urge you to be subject to such men and to every fellow worker and laborer" (1 Cor. 16:15–16). Again the Apostolic Succession into the times of the Church is clear: these are teachers of the Word of God. Then there was that remarkably great teacher Apollos, whom Saint Paul mentions more than once: "Now a Jew named Apollos, a native of Alexandria, came to Ephesus. He was an eloquent man, well versed in the Scriptures. . . . He taught accurately the things concerning Jesus" (Acts 18:24–25). "What then is Apollos? . . . A servant through whom you believed" (1 Cor. 3:5, and see 1 Cor. 16:12). Since faith resulted from his ministry, it had to be a teaching of the Word of God.

The Origin of Divine Tradition

All of this brings into view the handing on of the Word of God, which is the Gospel of Jesus, to the Church after the death of the last Apostle. Here the Latin verb *tradere* becomes essential. It means "to hand something to someone else." In classical Greece and Rome it became a technical term in formal education: to hand on a body of doctrine to others by teaching them. The Apostles adopted it for the process of handing on the Word of God. The ministry of the Word of God thus originates and continues a *traditio,* the noun from *tradere:* "the immortal Tradition of the Holy Church of God."[35] This introduces the very idea of a "Deposit," the catechetical teaching of it, and "The Ordinary and Universal Magisterium," which the Church came to define in solemn manner at the First Vatican Council.[36]

Saint Paul was very conscious of this aspect of the Apostolic Succession in the life of the Church, as a few instances will show: "Now I would remind you, brethren, in what terms I preached to you the Gospel, which you received, in which you stand. . . . For I delivered to you as of first importance what I also received, that Christ died for our sins in accordance with the Scriptures, that he was buried, that he was raised on the third day in accordance with the Scriptures" (1 Cor. 15:1–4). He himself stood at the very beginning of this handing on of the Gospel. He writes similarly to the

Colossians: "As therefore you received Christ Jesus the Lord, so live in him, rooted and built up in him and established in the Faith, just as you were taught" (Col. 2:6–7). And to the Philippians: "What you have learned and received and heard and seen in me, do" (Phil. 4:9). Then his sweeping basic statement: "When you received the Word of God which you heard from us, you accepted it not as the word of men but as what it really is, the Word of God which is at work in you believers" (1 Thess. 2:13). As Saint Paul saw the end of his own life approaching, this thought of the Tradition comes strongly to him: "Follow the pattern of the sound words which you have heard from me, in the faith and love which are in Christ Jesus; guard the truth that has been entrusted to you by the Holy Spirit who dwells within us" (2 Tim. 1:13–14). Again the Deposit of Faith and Morals becomes visible. This truth entrusted to Timothy came by hearing: it is the oral Tradition at its origin. "What you have heard from me," Saint Paul admonishes Timothy before, "entrust to faithful men who will be able to teach others also" (2 Tim. 2:2). Saint Paul is telling Timothy how to hand on this Deposit himself to others who will teach it faithfully. (See also 1 Tim. 1:3–7; 4:6–7; 6:2–5; 2 Tim. 3:10–17; and Tit. 1:9).

From such passages catechetical teaching is already visible: it is the most fundamental component of this immortal Tradition of the Holy Church of God because it teaches and explains the Word of God, the faith as such in itself and in its elements. It teaches what it received from Jesus and his Apostles and only that, without adulteration, addition, or omission. All this results from the passages given earlier. The Gospel of Jesus, which is the Word of God, is thus handed on as a doctrine full of the presence of Jesus and the power of the Holy Spirit, Eucharistic at its very center. It is the Word of God that is being formulated into an abiding teaching, the Tradition of the Church. Catechetics is visibly the fundamental component and process in this Tradition, this handing on of the Word of God.[37]

By this catechetical teaching in his Church Jesus will conquer space and convert the pagan Roman Empire. This great fact, deeply significant for catechists today, will become the object of study in one of the later chapters. It is a teaching that centers upon Jesus' presence in the Holy Eucharist. The Eucharistic Sacrifice is the culmination of the teaching, for it brings ever more numerous persons into the new Way of Life. All catechetical teaching is preparation for the Eucharistic presence and communion, and this is the Ministry of the Word at its highest point.

With this we have come to the conclusion of this chapter on the Word of God. It remains to recall briefly the foundation that makes the Word of God the uniquely precious and valuable thing that it is on earth among mankind.

The Living God

Everything in religion, Saint Augustine stresses, depends on having in mind the right idea of God. This phrase *The Word of God* can mean anything or nothing if God is not rightly conceived and understood.

"The way of the good and blessed life," Saint Augustine writes, "is to be found entirely in the true religion wherein one God is worshipped and acknowledged with purest piety to be the beginning of all existing things, originating, perfecting and containing the universe. Thus it becomes easy to detect the error of the peoples who have preferred to worship many gods rather than the true God and Lord of all things."[38] "Therefore the mind has to be healed," he continues, "so that it may behold the immutable form of things which remains ever the same, preserving its beauty unchanged and unchangeable, knowing no spatial distance or temporal variation, abiding absolutely one and the same. Men do not believe in its existence, though it alone truly and supremely exists. Other things are born, die, are dissolved or broken up. But so far as they exist they have existence from the eternal God, being created by his truth."[39]

The Word of God is uniquely the reality and the treasure it is because it has been spoken to mankind by this Supreme Being, the Creator of mankind. It comes as the Gospel of Jesus, a message of mercy, hope, and salvation to his human creatures in the darkness of their exile from him. Only when God is kept in mind as a personal reality, all-knowing, all-good, and loving, can the phrase *The Word of God* take on its true and full meaning. This concept of God is the essence of the Hebrew Revelation. The Apostles were Jewish men whose minds were deeply formed by the scriptures of the Old Testament. The elevated concept of God in the Psalms came to them in their daily prayer. They were imbued with the teaching of Moses and the Prophets: "Who is like to thee, O Lord, among the gods? Who is like to thee, majestic in holiness, terrible in glorious deeds, doing wonders?" (Exod. 15:11). The Prophet Amos speaks for all the Prophets and the Apostles: "For, lo, he who forms the mountains and creates the wind . . . declares to man what is his thought" (Amos 4:13).

The Epistle to the Hebrews puts the entire substance of the mind of the Apostles on the Word of God in its opening passage: "In many and various ways God spoke of old to our fathers by the Prophets; but in these last days he has spoken to us by a Son, whom he appointed the heir of all things, through whom also he created the world" (Heb. 1:1–2).

With this, one is prepared to take up the same reality of God's Revelation by his Word from a different point of view, in an analysis of the Deposit of Faith and Morals.

Chapter 11

The Evangelization and Catechetical Teaching of the Apostles

This chapter concludes this study of biblical Catechetics. We have seen Jesus the Divine Teacher at work as the fullness and mediator of biblical Revelation, entrusting his teaching to his Apostles as a Divine Deposit handed over to them and their Church to be guarded faithfully and explained infallibly.[1] In chapter 10, the Word of God is seen to be the Word of Jesus given to the Apostles. Hence it is a Deposit of supreme value handed to mankind from them by teaching. Jesus gave them the teachable content and structure for their own teaching of it to all nations. This chapter has the pleasant and interesting task of studying what Jesus' Apostles said and did in launching their mission, as witnessed by the Acts of the Apostles and their Epistles.

The Apostles are unique figures in the religious history of mankind. The bishops, priests, and deacons, the men of Holy Orders who succeeded them, are not "Apostles" in the same sense as they were. For they were called by the Lord God himself, incarnate and speaking to them in his human words. They saw the Risen Jesus. They were taught and formed by him, God himself, and sent forth by him. "Paul an Apostle—not from men nor through man, but through Jesus Christ and God the Father" (Gal. 1:1): so Saint Paul expresses this uniqueness of the Twelve. "You are . . . members of the household of God," he writes to the Ephesians, "built upon the foundation of the Apostles and Prophets, Christ Jesus himself being the cornerstone" (Eph. 2:19–20). Saint John records the way the early Christians perceived the Church: "The wall of the city had twelve foundations, and on them the twelve names of the Apostles of the Lamb" (Rev. 21:14). The Apostles are indeed unique figures in the Catholic Church: "For all time the Church abides bound to the initial Word of the Apostles and their witness. Hence the lifetime of the Apostles, the Apostolic Age of the Church, has unique significance for the coming life of the Church. All of this constitutes the dignity and the meaning of the Apostles. In so far their office and function does not pass on to their Successors."[2]

We turn, then, to these Apostles in their words and actions after the crucifixion of their Lord, who had taught and formed them for their mission. They had in hand from Jesus their Deposit of Faith and Morals. What did they do about it? How did their mandate to teach it to all nations unfold under their direct action? What did they do with this Divine Deposit? Why? To what purpose? We seek the answers directly from them.[3]

Saint Peter and the Jerusalem Kērygma

St. Peter's initial heralding of the message about Jesus is reported in the first ten chapters of the Acts of the Apostles, called therefore "The Jerusalem Kērygma" by scholars.[4] Jesus' activity in his public life is denoted in the Gospels chiefly by the two Greek verbs, one rooted in *didask-*, his teaching, the other rooted in *keryx,* the "herald" or official spokesman for the Supreme Being of the universe.

The herald, known historically in the English language as the town crier, official spokesman for the town council, is a constantly recurring figure in the life of mankind. Stentor is the herald in Homer's poems: from him comes the first qualification of this official, that he have a great "stentorian" voice. The second qualification is his absolute fidelity to the message from the ruler: he simply delivers it, without addition or subtraction, without any negotiation. The herald's attitude is loyal fidelity to the authority for whom he is the official spokesman. This word, then, *keryx,* or herald, was adopted by the Sacred Writers to denote Jesus' activity and now for that of Saint Peter.[5] After the crucifixion, Saint Peter stands forth in these chapters of Acts exactly as an official herald proclaiming a message. This message is the essential content of Christianity. It contains the substance of the Apostles' Creed and the outline of what will become the four Gospels. The herald's voice of Saint Peter as the Vicar of Christ deserves careful study, for it grounds the correlation of evangelization and catechetical teaching to the present day.[6]

Peter *stands*, exactly as a herald does. Jesus, "seeing the crowds, went up on the mountain, and when he sat down, his disciples came to him . . . , and he taught them" (Matt. 5:1–2). Teachers sit; heralds stand, raising their voices:

> But Peter, standing with the Eleven, lifted up his voice and addressed them saying, "Men of Judea . . . this is what was spoken of by the Prophet Joel: and in the last days it shall be, God declares, that I will pour out my Spirit upon all flesh, . . . before the day of the Lord comes, the great and manifest Day. And it shall be that whoever calls on the name of the Lord shall be saved." Men of Israel, hear these words: Jesus of Nazareth, a man attested to you by God with mighty works and wonders. . . . As you yourselves know—this Jesus, delivered up according to the definite plan and foreknowledge of God, you crucified and killed by the hands of lawless men. . . . This Jesus God raised up, and of that we are all witnesses. Being therefore exalted at the right hand of God, and having received from the Father the promise of the Holy Spirit, he has poured out this which you see and hear. . . . Let all the house of Israel therefore know assuredly that. . . . God has made him both Lord and Christ, this Jesus whom you crucified" (Acts 2:14–36).

This is the basic content and pattern of the Apostolic kērygma. Saint Peter, always the spokesman for the Apostles because of his primacy, gives on other occasions the same substance in other words. "What God foretold by the mouth of all the Prophets," Peter tells the crowd at the Temple, "that his Christ should suffer, he thus fulfilled. Repent, therefore, and turn again, that your sins may be blotted out, that the times of refreshing may come from the presence of the Lord, and that he may send the Christ appointed for you, Jesus, whom heaven must receive until the time for establishing all that God spoke by the mouth of his holy Prophets from of old" (Saint Peter's second sermon, Acts 3:12–26).

While this discourse was taking place, the Jewish authorities at the Temple seized the Apostles and put them in custody overnight, "being grieved because they were teaching [verb in *didask-*] the people and proclaiming in the case of Jesus the resurrection from the dead" (Acts 4:1–7). The next day the Apostles are placed on trial before the Jewish Sanhedrin. Again Peter proclaims the *kērygma* to the assembled authorities:

> Then Peter, filled with the Holy Spirit, said to them, "Rulers of the people and elders, if we are being examined today concerning a good deed done to a cripple, by what means this man has been healed, be it known to you all, and to all the people of Israel, that by the name of Jesus Christ of Nazareth, whom you crucified, whom God raised from the dead, by him this man is standing before you well. This is the stone which was rejected by you builders, but which has become the head of the corner. And there is salvation in no one else, for there is no other name under heaven given among men by which we must be saved" (Acts 4:8–12).

The authorities felt helpless. They released the Apostles, therefore, "charging them not to speak or teach at all in the name of Jesus. But Peter and John answered them, 'Whether it is right in the sight of God to listen to you rather than to God, you must judge; for we cannot but speak of what we have seen and heard' " (Acts 4:18–20).

Peter and the Apostles, accordingly, continued to herald the truth about Jesus; again they were to be arrested and brought before the Sanhedrin. "We severely charged you"; the Jewish high priest charged them, "not to teach [verb in *didask-*] in this name, and behold you have filled Jerusalem with your teaching [didachē], and want to bring this man's blood upon us" (Acts 5:27–28). "But Peter and the Apostles answered, and said, 'We must obey God rather than men. The God of our fathers raised Jesus, whom you put to death, hanging him on a tree. God exalted him to his right hand as Leader and Savior, to grant repentance *[metanoia* in the Greek] to Israel, and forgiveness of sins. And we are witnesses of these things' " (Acts 5:29–32). Thus Peter courageously turns the occasion into another proclamation of the Jerusalem Kērygma.

Finally, there is Saint Peter's discourse, significant for the world mission, to Cornelius, the officer of the Roman legion in occupation of Palestine, and his household:

> Truly I perceive that God shows no partiality, but in every nation anyone who fears him and does what is right is acceptable to him. You know the word which he sent to Israel, preaching good news of

peace by Jesus Christ, the Lord of all, the word which was proclaimed [Greek verb in *keryx*] throughout all Judea, beginning from Galilee after the baptism which John had preached: how God anointed Jesus of Nazareth with the Holy Spirit and with power; how he went about doing good and healing all that were oppressed by the devil, for God was with him. And we are witnesses to all that he did both in the country of the Jews and in Jerusalem. They put him to death by hanging him on a tree; but God raised him up on the third day and made him manifest; not to all the people but to us who were chosen by God as witnesses, who ate and drank with him after he rose from the dead. And he commanded us to preach [Greek verb in *keryx*] to the people, and to testify that he is the one ordained by God to be judge of the living and the dead. To him all the Prophets bear witness that every one who believes in him receives forgiveness of sins through his name. (Acts 10:34–43)

Such, then, is the Jerusalem Kērygma heralded by Peter on behalf of all the Apostles in the name of God. It is a powerful witness to the facts about Jesus and the faith of the Apostles. When one ponders these heraldings of Peter, so varied in wording and so identical in substance, it becomes clear that we are actually hearing the Apostles' Creed. All the phrases of the Apostles' Creed as it is known, professed, and prayed today can be constructed from these discourses of Peter. All of this has been summarized well by Badcock, the Protestant scholar in credal research. "The earliest apostolic preaching," he writes, "of which we have record had as its nucleus the Messiahship and Lordship of Jesus, one or both. Correspondingly, the earliest confession of faith demanded was faith in the Messiahship or Lordship of Jesus, and this would run, 'I believe that Jesus is the Christ, or the Lord'; or 'I believe in Jesus Christ the Lord.' "[7] It stands to reason that Peter proclaims only what he was taught by Jesus: everything presupposes the Trinitarian pattern of the faith and the personal response to it, the *metanoia* of sacramental living, Gospel morality, and personal prayer.

The Apostolic Kērygma in Saint Paul

"Now I would remind you, brethren," Saint Paul writes to the Corinthians, "in what terms I preached to you the Gospel. . . . For

I delivered to you as of first importance what I also received, that Christ died for our sins according to the Scriptures, that he was buried, that he was raised on the third day in accordance with the Scriptures, and that he appeared to Cephas, then to the Twelve; then to more than five hundred brethren at one time. . . . Last of all, as to one untimely born, he appeared also to me" (1 Cor. 15:1–8). In this fundamental passage Saint Paul bears witness to the Deposit of Faith and Morals in itself and to the fact that it was being handed on by teaching. He himself received it from the teaching and not by the revelation given to him personally regarding the person of Jesus.[8] Always the teaching was showing the connection of the *kērygma* about Jesus with the Hebrew Scriptures and their fulfillment. And always the teaching, now already a tradition, a *tradere* by the teaching, sees the passion of Jesus in the light of its redeeming power. The revelation came from God; the facts about Jesus came to Saint Paul by the tradition of catechetical teaching.

And thus we come to the way the Jerusalem Kērygma was taken out to the Gentiles by Saint Paul:

> Paul and his company set sail . . . and came to Antioch of Pisidia. And on the sabbath day they went into the synagogue and sat down. . . . So Paul stood up, and motioning with his hand said: "Men of Israel, and you that fear God, listen: . . . of this posterity [he had recounted the history of Israel] God has brought to Israel a Savior, Jesus, as he promised. . . . Those who live in Jerusalem and their rulers, because they did not recognize him nor understand the utterances of the Prophets which are read every sabbath, fulfilled those by condemning him. Though they could charge him with nothing deserving of death, yet they asked Pilate to have him killed. And when they had fulfilled all that was written of him, they took him down from the tree, and laid him in a tomb. But God raised him from the dead; and for many days he appeared to those who came up with him from Galilee to Jerusalem, who are now his witnesses to the people. And we bring you the good news that what God promised to the fathers, this he has fulfilled to us their children by raising Jesus. . . . Let it be known to you therefore, brethren, that through this man forgiveness of sins is proclaimed to you, and by him everyone that believes is freed from everything from which you could not be freed by the law of Moses." (Acts 13:13–39)

A stormy week ensued, a clash of belief and refusal to believe among the Jews and increasing interest among the Gentiles: "The next sabbath almost the whole city gathered together to hear the Word of God. . . . And Paul and Barnabas spoke out boldly, saying, 'It was necessary that the Word of God should be spoken first to you [Jews]. Since you thrust it from you, and judge yourselves unworthy of eternal life, behold, we turn to the Gentiles' " (Acts 13:44–46).

So begins the amazing career of the Apostle to the Gentiles. The "times of the Gentiles" are beginning, to be fulfilled in some distant future when Jerusalem will no longer be "trodden down by the Gentiles" (Luke 21:24). These "times of the Gentiles" will be filled with the proclamation of the Jerusalem Kērygma and the explanation of it by the teaching of the Ordinary and Universal Magisterium, the tradition of catechetical teaching and Eucharistic worship.[9] This is the "Rule of Faith" in actual exercise, visible and already operating in the New Testament.[10]

Saint Paul's Epistles are written to Gentile Christian communities, to persons already evangelized and well instructed in the content of the Christian message. These two processes of initial proclamation and subsequent systematic teaching in the elements of Christian doctrine are always presupposed. How else could they understand these Epistles when they were read in their churches? All his Epistles bear witness to the taking of Saint Peter's original Jerusalem Kērygma out to the Gentiles. The substance of Jesus' teaching is being given to them, free of the practices and merely human traditions of the Jewish nation and its earlier preparatory testament. It is now given as the New Testament of the new Israel of God.

Saint Paul's self-identity as a minister of Jesus' Word of God structured for teaching is now readily understandable. "Our Savior," he tells Timothy, " . . . abolished death and brought life and immortality to light through the Gospel. For this Gospel I was appointed a preacher and apostle and teacher" (2 Tim. 1:10–11): in the Greek, *ego keryx kai apostolos kai didaskalos*, "a herald, apostle and teacher" of the Deposit of Faith and Morals.[11] He says the same thing more than once: "I was appointed a preacher *[keryx]* and apostle . . . and a teacher of the Gentiles in Faith and truth" (1 Tim. 2:7).

What does this ringing declaration mean? It gives us an insight into the greatness of Saint Paul's understanding of his mission. The

Gospel is the *kērygma,* the Good News announced as a message of supreme importance. It is the Word of God coming from Yahweh, the One True God of the Hebrew Revelation, the Father Almighty who is the Creator of the world and the Lord of its history. It announces the opening of the final epoch of universal history, the Christian era of the time remaining until the Second Coming of Jesus in glory. It proclaims that the Kingdom of God is at hand and the general judgment approaching. This is the climax of Divine Revelation and salvation history, the divine plan manifested in the three great historical stages. Primitive Revelation and the Hebrew Revelation are being fulfilled and completed now in the Christian Revelation. It is a message that is delivered by Jesus, God the Son Incarnate, to his Apostles as a Deposit of Faith and Morals to be handed on as a teaching to all the peoples and nations of the earth.[12] The content of this *kērygma* or message is a set of formulated truths that come from above. And thus catechetical teaching is present from the time of Jesus and his Apostles. It is important for the field of catechetical teaching to note Saint Paul's emphasis that he is not only a herald but also a *didaskalos,* a teacher of these truths.

Saint Paul alludes in many places to his role in handing on the original apostolic *kērygma.* After fourteen years on his mission to the Gentiles, he went to see Saint Peter and the Apostles at Jerusalem: "I laid before them (but privately before those who were of repute) the Gospel I preach [verb in *keryx*] among the Gentiles, lest somehow I should be running or had run in vain" (Gal. 2:2). Again Saint Paul witnesses to the authority of Saint Peter over the Catholic Church in its earliest stage. "We have this ministry . . . ," Saint Paul tells the Corinthians, "the light of the Gospel of the glory of Christ, who is the likeness of God. For what we preach [verb in *keryx*] is not ourselves, but Jesus Christ our Lord, with ourselves as your servants for Jesus' sake" (2 Cor. 4:1–5).[13] "My Gospel," he concludes to the Romans, " . . . is the preaching [Greek *kērygma*] of Jesus Christ" (Rom. 16:25); he had introduced this Epistle solemnly, saying: "I, Paul, a servant of Jesus Christ, called to be an Apostle, set apart for the Gospel of God . . . the Gospel concerning his Son . . . according to the spirit of holiness by his resurrection from the dead, Jesus Christ our Lord" (Rom. 1:1–4). We shall conclude this sampling of these places in Saint Paul with his praise of his beloved community (we would say parish today) at Thessalonia. "You turned to God from idols," he tells them, "to serve a loving and true God, and to wait for his Son from heaven, whom he raised from the dead, Jesus who delivers us from the wrath to come" (1 Thess. 1:9–10). This *metanoia* or conversion to God is exactly that called for by Jesus in his public life (see Mark 1:14–15 and indeed the Gospels as a whole). "We thank God constantly for this, that when you received the Word of God which you heard from us, you accepted it not as the word of men but as what it really is, the Word of God" (1 Thess. 2:13).

In these words to the Thessalonians "we have the summary of the discourse of instruction which Paul preached to the pagans."[14] Generalizing on these formulations in Saint Paul, Lucien Cerfaux concludes: "They bring us back to the vocabulary of the primitive community (at Jerusalem). Nearly always the two formulas 'The Lord Jesus' and 'Our Lord Jesus' are connected with the essential data of the Faith: the parousia, the death, the Resurrection and the teaching handed down by the Apostles."[15] "From this teaching there springs a confession of Faith in Christ as Lord."[16]

It is clear, then, that the original *kērygma* of Saint Peter at Jerusalem continues in the apostolic *kērygma* of Saint Paul on his missions to the Gentiles. It is the substance of catechetical teaching to this day. Its content is the Deposit of Faith and Morals; it begets the profession of faith that the converts make in their baptism; it gives them the new Eucharistic Way of Life that they take up. With Saint Paul this Word of God, of Jesus, structured by him for teaching, begins to make its way to us Gentiles by the Ordinary and Universal Magisterium of the Church. Everything in this tradition of teaching goes back to Jesus and depends upon him. Jesus gave this teaching its basic structure when he revealed the Three Divine Persons, Father, Son, and Holy Spirit. Jesus is the Second Person: everything in this *kērygma*, proclaimed and taught, is divine, the very Word of God.

The Apostolic Kērygma or Apostles' Creed

It is now possible to understand the conclusion reached by the credal research of the *Symbolforschung*. The substance and even the basic Trinitarian structure of the Apostles' Creed are already present in the New Testament.[17] The earliest Church, the Church in that wonderful period of twenty years after the crucifixion when no writing of the New Testament yet existed, when all was oral tradition and teaching, manifests a pattern or form in which the apostolic *kērygma* is accurately, briefly, comprehensively, and, above all, *officially* summarized. It is the Apostles' *kērygma*. We of the Latin West call it the Apostles' Creed, the profession of our baptismal faith and the syllabus of the teaching that explains that faith and its Eucharistic Way of Life.

At this point biblical Catechetics is in a position to see the absolute unity between Jesus teaching his Apostles in his public life and his Apostles teaching the People of God in the time after the crucifixion.[18] The heart of Jesus' Christian Revelation is the fact of the Triune God. Yahweh, the God of the Hebrew Revelation, is One God. There is only one God. But Three Divine Persons, each equally divine, exist and subsist in this one unique transcendent divine nature. Jesus therefore existed in his divine nature prior to his Incarnation. He is the preexistent *Logos:* "The Word became flesh and dwelt among us, full of grace and truth" (John 1:14).

The Jerusalem Kērygma of Saint Peter is the heralding to the Jews of this Christian Revelation. Saint Paul heralds the identical Christian Revelation. The Apostolic *kērygma* is based upon this Christian Revelation given and taught by Jesus, summarizing it, proclaiming it, and teaching it in view of Baptism into the new Way of Life.

It is readily apparent that this is the substance of what we call the Apostles' Creed, called the Symbol of Faith in the Early Church. He gives the Creed its very form or pattern or structure in the three basic Articles of Faith in the Three Divine Persons. It is a heralding that evokes the personal response of conversion, expressed in sacramental living, Gospel morality, and personal prayer. Thus it is the taproot of that form or pattern or structure of catechetical teaching that will emerge into clear view in the coming life of the Church. It will develop into the Nicene Creed, the Creeds of the great medieval Councils, the Creed of Vatican I, and the Creed of the People of God after Vatican II. Always the substance is the same, while the various wordings express the growing understanding in the life of the Church: a wording that always preserves the original Trinitarian pattern that comes from Jesus and his teaching.

This is the basic fact that underlies the catechetical teaching of the Apostles after the crucifixion. Always they continue Jesus' teaching in the *typos didachēs* (Rom. 6:17), the pattern that he gave them. Neither they nor much less the "community" had any idea but that of Jesus, their Divine Teacher. With this, we can turn to consider the catechetical teaching of the Apostles in greater detail.

Catechetics: The Teaching Program of the Apostles

The Word of God, which for us is the Word of Jesus (chapter 1), has been deposited with the Apostles and the Priesthood of Jesus under the successors of Saint Peter (chapter 2). Jesus' Deposit of Faith and Morals is basic and central. So far the Deposit has been considered in itself. Now we analyze it dynamically in the process by which it is handed on by teaching. We do so, still in biblical Cathechetics, by seeing the fact and the procedure of the Apostles themselves. In the Acts and the Epistles the Apostles of course do not give *ex professo* descriptions of their work: their writings have a different occasion and were written for their own specific purposes. They did not do treatises on their teaching. The fact of the teaching and their procedure must be seen by indirect lighting, so to speak, for the Acts and the Epistles everywhere presuppose recipients who had been well instructed in the content of the Deposit of Faith and Morals. There had to be in operation a very effective teaching program by which they became Christians practicing the new life of Eucharistic worship. The Apostles, furthermore, frequently allude to the teaching that was being done in the apostolic churches.

This is to do a catechetical reading and study of the writings of the Apostles. The first objective is to gather the places that show the apostolic teaching program as an actual fact; then one can proceed to an analysis of its content and method.[19]

This fact is already visible in Saint Peter's first proclamation of the *kērygma*. After the account of his discourse, already given, his hearers came to him asking what to do. "And Peter said to them, 'Repent, and be baptized every one of you in the name of Jesus Christ for the forgiveness of your sins; and you shall receive the gift of the Holy Spirit . . . ' So those who received his word were baptized, and there were added that day about three thousand souls.

And they devoted themselves to the Apostles' teaching [*didachē* in the Greek] and fellowship, to the breaking of bread and the prayers" (Acts 2:37–42). This passage is illuminating: the Apostles were conducting a *didachē,* just as Jesus their Divine Teacher had done and taught them. It related to Baptism, prayer, and the new Eucharistic Way of Life. Since it was a *didachē,* that Greek word for a definite process of teaching a particular content, it was a systematic instruction according to the needs of the recipients. Always it would proceed on Jesus' Trinitarian pattern, with the components of the new life of prayer, the Eucharist Sacrifice and Gospel morality, and the Ten Commandments of Moses now kept with Jesus' new motive of the love of God. Always it was an instruction in the Trinitarian faith and on taking up the new Way of Life for which the faith calls.

From its very beginning, therefore, the Church is a *teaching* Church. It is reasonable to think that this "Apostles' teaching" was taking place in the Cenacle, their headquarters after the crucifixion. They were simply continuing the program that Jesus their Teacher had headquartered at the house in Caphernaum.[20] As the Scandinavian research indicates, the apostles continued to conduct this *didachē,* this formal program of instruction, at the Cenacle until their dispersion after A.D. 42. In it the groundwork was laid for the writing of the four Gospels. After their dispersion, similar bases for the instruction were organized at Rome, at Antioch with Saints Paul and Barnabas, and at Ephesus under the supervision of Saint John. Thus the discourses of Saint Peter's Jerusalem Kērygma contains in germ the very life of the Teaching Church that will grow out of the Cenacle.

Many places in the Acts of the Apostles and their Epistles allude to the *fact* of the teaching program that was the very life of the apostolic Church.[21] "God has appointed in the Church first apostles, second prophets, third teachers" (1 Cor. 12:27). Saint Paul himself was one of these teachers: "Now in the church at Antioch there were prophets and teachers, Barnabas, Symeon . . . and Saul" (Acts 13:1). St. Paul's consciousness that he was a herald and a *teacher* of the Gospel has been noted earlier. These teachers play a vital role in the unity of the apostolic Church, as we see in chapter 4 of Ephesians, Saint Paul's call for unity and its protection from the winds of doctrinal error; "There is one body and one Spirit . . . , one Lord, one faith, one baptism. . . . And Christ's gifts were that some should be apostles, some prophets, some evangelists, some pastors and teachers . . . so that we no longer be children, tossed to and fro and carried about with every wind of doctrine" (Ephes. 4:4–14).[22]

Again Saint Paul bears important witness: "Let him who is taught the Word share all good things with him who teaches" (Gal. 6:6). In this vital passage, both "taught" and "him who teaches" are in the Greek *katechein:* it is a clear witness to the fact of a catechetical teaching that already has its own name. "It results clearly from our text that there were catechists who were charged by a competent authority with the task of instructing the new converts. . . . And also that there were catechumens to whom the Word was taught, namely, the Gospel of Christ; and that therefore there was a system of catechetical teaching, without which there could be neither catechists nor catechumens."[23] Saint Paul gives a similar powerful ray of indirect lighting when he says to the Thessalonians: "Brethren, we beseech and exhort you in the Lord Jesus, that as you learned from us how you ought to live and to please God, just as you are now doing, you do so more and more. For you know what instructions we gave you through the Lord Jesus" (1 Thess. 4:1 2). Clearly it was a Deposit of *Morals* as well as Faith that was being taught in this systematic instruction the Apostles gave to their converts in view of their Baptism.

We may conclude the witness of Saint Paul to the fact of systematic catechetical instruction with a glance at his Epistle to the Romans. "We, though many," he writes, "are one body in Christ. . . . Having gifts that differ according to the grace given to us, let us use them: if prophecy, in proportion to our faith; if service, in our serving; he who teaches, in his teaching; he who exhorts, in his exhortation" (Rom. 12:5–8). At the center of Romans and as the fulcrum of this challenging and carefully wrought Epistle on sin and grace stands one of the most important witnesses to the fact of the apostolic teaching program. "Thanks be to God," he writes, "that you who were once slaves of sin have become obedient from the heart to the standard of teaching to which you were committed, and, having been set free from sin, have become slaves of righteousness" (Rom. 6:17).[24] This "standard of teaching," this *typos didachēs* in the Greek, is absolutely practical in terms of the Way of Life, contrasting with the Way of Death. We shall return to it later in connection with the method of the apostolic teaching. Here one can simply note that it teaches the truth of our redemption in Jesus Christ and gives the power of the Holy Spirit to renew and regenerate persons from within, who therefore live "in the new life of the Spirit" (Rom. 7:6).

The Church of the Apostles was a *Teaching* Church: this fact emerges from all these places in the new Testament. Reading between their lines, one becomes aware of the massive presence of the apostolic teaching program, already called catechetical: an oral instruction in view of initiation into the sacramental and Eucharistic life of the Church.[25]

"The Greek word *catechein* (with its derivatives) is found several times in the New Testament. It means to make a teaching 'sound back' and hence to instruct in a content of doctrine."[26] Apparently it was Saint Paul who wished the simple oral teaching of the Word of God to adopt this rather rare Greek word for an oral instruction that echoes back from the hearers. "Echo" is contained in the very word. It means, writes Prof. Hermann Wolfgang Beyer,

> To instruct someone, to teach, especially in respect of the rudiments of a subject or skill. . . . Paul himself uses *catechéo* exclusively in the sense of "to give instruction" concerning the content of the Faith. . . . This is the high value he attaches to the significance of *katechein,* for he teaches that faith comes through hearing. In Gal. 6:6 he draws a contrast between the catechist *(katechon)* who gives instruction in Christian doctrine and the catechumens *(katechoumenos)* who receive this instruction. It thus establishes the claim of the teacher to support, and therewith confirms the validity and necessity of a professional teaching ministry in the congregation. The *katechountes* of Gal. 6:6 are to be equated with the *didaskaloi* (teachers) of 1 Cor. 12:28 and Eph. 4:11. Hence Paul uses not only the common *didaskein* (to teach) but also the much rarer word, hardly known at all in the religious vocabulary of Judaism, as a technical term for Christian instruction. He desires thereby to emphasize the particular nature of instruction on the basis of the Gospel.[27]

With this strong corroboration of the fact that the Apostles had an organized and systematic teaching program, witnessed in the New Testament itself, one can give attention in greater detail to its content, method, and purpose.

The Content of the Apostolic Teaching

Teaching on the human scene always has been a dynamic process of communication that unites a definite content of doctrine with the particular method proper to it. Content and method do not occur separately: the components of the process cannot be separated in reality. For the purpose of analysis and study, however, they can be considered separately. So, too, with Jesus' teaching program, continued now in the work of his Apostles.

It is absolutely essential to recognize that Jesus the Divine Teacher stands at the origin of the content of the apostolic teaching. The Apostles' content was taught to them by Jesus in person. And he himself states solemnly to the Jews, "My teaching [didachē in the Greek] is not mine, but his who sent me" (John 7:16). Jesus' teaching *is* the Word of God.

The content of the Apostles' teaching, therefore, has been discussed in chapter 10 on the Word of God. It will be analyzed in detail in chapter 1 of volume 2 on the Deposit of Faith and Morals that is the Word of God entrusted by Jesus to his Apostles. In particular, everything that was said about the Deposit as teachable is relevant here. We need but bear it in mind as we look more closely at the apostolic witness to the teaching of a definite and precise content of doctrine.

Fernand Prat quotes Reuss, a German exegete of the last century: "The Epistles of Paul are addressed without exception to persons already familiar with the ideas of the Gospel; they are by no means intended to give either elementary or complete instruction to their readers. Dogma is mentioned fragmentarily and as occasion calls for it; often it is simply alluded to, as to something already known. The real Christian instruction had been given orally, and no doubt in sequence and entirety."[28] "Nothing is more certain. . . . St. Luke addresses his Gospel to a catechumen, not so much to initiate him into a knowledge of Christianity, as to make known to him 'the truth of those words in which he had been instructed' orally" (see Luke 1:1–4).[29]

This is precisely the indirect lighting from the Acts and the Epistles that illuminates the previous systematic catechetical instruction the converts had received in preparation for their Baptism and

their new Way of Eucharistic Life. As Prat points out, this instruction, all oral, was historical (about the life, redeeming death, Resurrection, ascension, and Second Coming of Jesus to judge the living
and the dead), dogmatic (the Christian doctrines that result), liturgical (on participation in the Eucharistic Sacrifice), and moral (that
is, the Gospel morality that continues the Prophet's teaching on the
two ways, the Way of Life, the keeping of the Ten Commandments,
contrasted with the Way of Death, sin in all its forms): "The new
converts had to persevere in the doctrine of the Apostles (Acts 2:42),
to 'obey from the heart unto that form of doctrine into which they
had been delivered' (Rom. 6:17), and to 'avoid things contrary to
the doctrine which they had learned' (Rom. 16:17). All this presupposes a fixed and precise oral teaching."[30]

Can scholarship today identify the wording of this initial teaching that the converts received? The effort to do so has been made
by A. Seeberg as a part of the German *Symbolforschung,* the research
on the origin and earliest form of the Apostles' Creed.[31] "We grant
Seeberg that his embryonic *Credo* did really form part of the apostolic system of instruction, but we do not think that this *Credo* was
presented everywhere under an almost invariable form, and especially that it was limited to that form. . . . But without stopping to
deal with criticisms in detail, the primitive formulary of Faith was
certainly founded upon the dogma of the Trinity."[32] This is to say
that the three-article framework and the substance of the Apostles'
Creed were already present from the very beginning. It has been
noted already that this substance is the essential and not this or that
particular: it is the substance of the Apostles' Creed that was being
explained in the teaching and professed at Baptism. The wording
would vary slightly from place to place and in coming times, just as
the discourse of explanatory teaching would vary with each individual teacher. It would take several centuries before the set pattern
of words in our present Apostles' Creed became fixed for common
use throughout the Latin Rite of the Roman West. The fact is, however, that it existed in its substantial meaning, its Trinitarian frame,
and its Christocentric facts from its origin with Jesus and its continuation as the content of the apostolic teaching. One must bear in
mind constantly that it was an oral teaching using a fixed plan or
syllabus, which the teachers carried in their memory. Always it was
an explanatory teaching of the interrogatory Creed of the baptismal

profession, together with the syllabi for teaching the components of the new Way of Life.

This brings us to the structure of this catechetical content as a whole. Can one see already that definite structure that will emerge into view in the writings of the Fathers of the Church and which the *Roman Catechism* will reflect after the invention of printing? It seems so, when one reflects on Jesus' own teaching. For he certainly taught his Apostles the following four areas or components of his content. First, he taught them to profess the faith in the Divine Trinity: in God the Father, Creator of heaven, earth, and each human person; in God the Son, the Redeemer who died and rose again; and in God the Holy Spirit, Lord and giver of the new Eucharistic Way of Life. The Gospels, furthermore, contain clearly his teaching of the three components of human response to this faith: sacramental living, Gospel morality, and personal prayer. As noted in chapter 2 on the Deposit, each of these four areas had its own syllabus or points for oral teaching. It was this concrete program that Jesus gave to his Apostles, mandating them to teach it to all the nations of the world (see Matt. 28:16–20). This they proceeded to do, as the New Testament witnesses, and this the Church that they founded continues to do to this day. This is the essence of the catechetical tradition of the Catholic Church.[33] "Thus was born from the earliest time a catechetical structure, the kernel of which goes back to the origins of the Church. . . . [It is] not an artificial system, but simply the synthesis of the mnemonic material indispensable to the Faith, which reflects at the same time elements vitally indispensable to the Church: the Apostles' Creed (also known as the Symbol of the Apostles), the Sacraments, the Ten Commandments, and the Lord's Prayer. These four classical and master components of catechesis have served for centuries as the depositary and resumé of Catholic teaching."[34]

There is yet another New Testament witness to the content of the catechetical teaching of the Apostles, illuminating it from a new direction. It declares that the content was taught on two levels, elementary and higher: "Therefore let us leave the elementary doctrines of Christ and go on to maturity, not laying again a foundation of repentance from dead works and of faith toward God, with instruction about ablutions, the laying on of hands, the resurrection of the dead, and eternal judgment" (Heb. 6:1–2). This phrase, "the elementary doctrines of Christ," is actually the definition of catechetical teaching given by the Holy Spirit in the Bible.

"What are the principal articles of this primitive catechism?" asks Prat. "The Epistle to the Hebrews (6:1–2) gives us a concise idea of it."[35] These Articles of Faith on the elementary level are always those of the baptismal profession, the interrogatory Creed. The converts are exhorted by the Apostle to rise to a level of higher teaching or education in the faith. Many Epistles, Romans, Galatians, and Hebrews, to cite a few examples, minister to this higher level when they are explained by teachers in the communities.

To conclude, one cannot improve upon the Oxford scholar J. N. D. Kelly's statement: "The early Church was from the start a believing, confessing, preaching Church. . . . The Christians of the Apostolic Age conceived of themselves as possessing a body of distinctive, consciously held beliefs. . . . The references to an inherited corpus of teaching are clear enough. . . . The documents themselves testify to the existence of a distinctively Christian teaching. In this sense at any rate it is legitimate to speak of the Creed of the primitive Church."[36]

The Church of the Apostles was a *Teaching* Church with a definite content of doctrine, the Trinitarian baptismal profession with the three components of *metanoia* or conversion in personal response to it. In no sense was it giving "experiences" or using an "experience approach." It was giving doctrine by teaching. This doctrine is the Word of God; it is the Deposit of Faith and Morals; it is the original *kērygma* of Saint Peter in Jerusalem. Catechetical teaching was in no sense an "invention" of the "community" or of the Church later on. At its origin stands Jesus the Divine Teacher, to whom the teaching bears witness.[37] Hence it was the same in substance and pattern always and everywhere: "This system of instruction was not left to individual inspiration, but was identical in its import and uniform in its presentation."[38]

What was the cause of this factor that gave unity to the universal Church and gives it today? It was that method, that *typos didachēs* (Rom. 6:17), humanly speaking, that Jesus gave to his Apostles, to which we now turn.

The Method of the Apostolic Teaching

There certainly is a supernatural dimension of the method from the very beginning, namely, the assistance of the Holy Spirit, which Jesus promised to the Apostles and their Church: "I will pray the Father, and he will give you another Counselor, to be with you forever, even the Spirit of truth" (John 14:16–17. "These things I have spoken to you, while I am still with you. But the Counselor, the Holy Spirit, whom the Father will send in my name, he will teach you all things, and bring to your remembrance all that I have said to you" (John 14:25–26). Clearly the work of the Holy Spirit is to sustain in its purity and integrity the handing on of Jesus' teaching to his Apostles and their successors.

Is there a human factor, a secondary cause, cooperating with the Holy Spirit in this process of transmission by teaching? There was indeed. It is implied by Jesus himself in the passages just quoted. It is that *typos didachēs* (Rom. 6:17), that "pattern of the teaching" that all the teachers followed. Here one should recall all that has been said on the standard oral methods of mankind that Jesus, his Apostles, and indeed all their successors in this teaching used for fifteen centuries, until the invention of printing. We have noted the four simple sets of points that constituted the syllabi or guides for explaining the faith in itself and the triple response of the *metanoia,* the conversion. Always catechesis began with the great fact of creation, explaining our belief in God the Father Almighty, Creator of heaven and earth. After the explanations, the teacher would ask, "Who created us?" The answer came back singly or in chorus, "God created us." "Who is God?" "God is the all-perfect Being, Creator and Lord of heaven and earth." "What does *all-perfect* mean? What does 'Creator' mean? What does 'Lord' mean?"[39] And so for all the points of the four syllabi, in a lively exchange that consolidated in memory the essentials of the explanations given by the catechist.[40] This kind of procedure is simply taken for granted in the writings of the Apostles, for it was universally in practice on the elementary level of teaching.

The method of the catechetical teaching of the Apostles, however, had two characteristics proper to itself. The first was its Christocentrism. The Lord Jesus is the object of all the heralding and teaching: "To me . . . this grace was given, to preach to the Gentiles the unsearchable riches of Christ" (Ephes. 3:8). "Christ is preached [verb in *keryx*] as risen from the dead" (1 Cor. 15:12). "What we preach [verb in *keryx*] is not ourselves, but Jesus Christ as Lord" (2 Cor. 4:5).[41]

The second characteristic was its use of the Hebrew Scriptures, our Old Testament. The use of a short set of excerpts from the prophecies called the "Testimonies" has been noted in chapter 2. Scholars have reconstructed these guides for the apostolic teaching.[42] The Apostles' Creed states the principle that guided this teaching when it says that Jesus died "according to the Scriptures" and rose again "according to the Scriptures." The method at work in all the teaching was to show that Jesus fulfilled the prophecies of the Hebrew Scriptures: this consolidated the divine faith of the catechumens and illumined their minds with the greatness of the divine plan for human salvation.

From this it is but a step to what was and is the methodological principle of all catechetical teaching: it gives its doctrine as the very Word of God, on the authority of God revealing. The parents and the catechists are channels, spokespersons, for God. This principle of method was given explicitly by Jesus himself on the first day of his Resurrection to the two disconsolate disciples on the road to Emmaus. " 'O foolish men,' he said to them, 'and slow of heart to believe all that the Prophets have spoken! Was it not necessary that the Christ should suffer these things and thus enter into his glory?' And beginning with Moses and the Prophets, he interpreted to them in all the Scriptures the things concerning himself" (Luke 24:25–27). Later the same day Jesus came to his Apostles in the Cenacle at Jerusalem with the same guiding principle or method: "He opened their minds to understand the scriptures, and said to them, 'Thus it is written, that the Christ should suffer and on the third day rise from the dead, and that repentance and forgiveness of sins should be preached [verb in *keryx*] in his name to all nations, beginning from Jerusalem. You are witnesses of these things" (Luke 24:45–47). When Jesus, his Apostles, and their successors in catechetical teaching do this kind of explaining, they give the Word of God in the teachable form given it by Jesus.

Finally, the Apostles imitated Jesus their Divine Teacher in never discouraging their catechumens. They never taught the high demands of Gospel morality first, before the sacramental life, as if this law were thrust upon human nature to keep by its own strength. This would be indeed discouraging. Jesus always taught, with an encouraging smile, the sacramental life first, which gives the new strength, and then the demands of Gospel morality as the following of Christ.[43]

Content and method, then, both existed in the catechesis of the Apostles, for it was a genuine human teaching. Central to it was its insistence on the traditional doctrine, to be handed on in a way which guards its purity and integrity as a divine deposit entrusted to the bishops, priests and catechists of the Church. This brings us to its purpose, for it witnesses to Jesus and the Holy Spirit who give the grace of the new Way of Life.

The Purpose of the Apostolic Teaching

Saint Peter in his first Jerusalem *kērygma* on Pentecost gives the purpose of Jesus' redemption, the outpouring of the Holy Spirit upon the redeemed. "This is what was spoken by the Prophet Joel," Saint Peter tells the Jews: "In the last days. . . . I will pour out my Spirit upon all flesh" (Acts 2:16–17). "Repent and be baptized every one of you in the name of Jesus Christ for the forgiveness of your sins; and you shall receive the gift of the Holy Spirit" (Acts 2:38).

This is the purpose of the apostolic proclamation and teaching. It is a warfare upon sin, a preaching of conversion from sin to God, and a teaching that "deepens this conversion."[44] This illuminates the numerous conflicts of Jesus with Satan and his possession of souls. The Kingdom of God is built by conquering the kingdom of Satan. When the Apostles and the Church continue this teaching they launch an immense campaign to overcome the rule of Satan over mankind by sin. In fact, this will bring the structure of the Christian era until Jesus' Second Coming into existence.

Instances abound in the writings of the Apostles, which show that freedom from sin, newness of life, and the new creation of the redeemed person were constantly in their minds as their purposes.

Saint Paul's Epistle to the Romans as a whole is a treatise on conversion to God from sin unto the new life of grace: "We were buried with him by baptism into death, so that as Christ was raised from the dead by the glory of the Father, we too might walk in newness of life" (Rom. 6:4). Saint Paul insists on the point and stresses it in detail: "For if we have been united with him in a death like his, we shall certainly be united with him in a resurrection like his. We know that our old self was crucified with him so that the sinful body might be destroyed, and we might no longer be enslaved to sin. For he who has died is freed from sin. . . . You must consider yourselves dead to sin and alive to God in Christ Jesus" (Rom. 6:5–11).

The Deposit is Jesus' truth on faith and also on *morals.* Saint Paul teaches the Deposit of Morals in the second half of each of his Epistles, and always it is a warning against sinful acts.[45] Let Romans stand for all the apostolic teaching on this aspect of the Deposit. "Let not sin therefore reign in your mortal bodies," Saint Paul continues, "to make you obey their passions. Do not yield your members to sin as instruments of wickedness, but yield yourselves to God as men who have been brought from death to life, and your members to God as instruments of righteousness" (Rom. 6:12–13).

The catechetical teaching of the Apostles in handing on the Deposit of Morals is reflected in the two final chapters of Colossians. "Set your minds on things that are above. . . . Put to death therefore what is earthly in you: immorality, impurity, passion, evil desire, and covetousness, which is idolatry. On account of these the wrath of God is coming. In these you once walked, when you lived in them. But now put them all away: anger, wrath, malice, slander and foul talk from your mouth. Do not lie to one another, seeing that you have put off the old nature with its practices, and have put on the new nature, which is being renewed in knowledge after the image of its Creator" (Col. 3:2–10).

Chapter 4 of Ephesians relates the unity of the teaching "One Lord, one Faith, one Baptism" (Ephes. 4:5) to the *metanoia*, the conversion to God from the sinful actions of the old nature (see Ephes. 4:15–32). Again the teaching finds its purpose in the call to turn away from sinful actions: "Let the thief no longer steal. . . . Let no evil talk come out of your mouths. . . . Do not grieve the Holy Spirit of God. . . . Immorality and all impurity or covetousness must not even be named among you, as is fitting among saints" (Ephes. 5:3).

Saint Peter bears the same witness to the Deposit of Morals: "Live for the rest of the time no longer by human passions but by the will of God . . . [not] doing what the Gentiles like to do, living in licentiousness, passions, drunkenness, revels, carousing, and lawless idolatry" (1 Pet. 4:3). "I intend always to remind you of these things" (2 Pet. 1:12). The entire Epistle of Saint James is devoted to this same conversion from sin to God, the doing of the good works of the new Way of Life.

The New Testament, therefore, bears abundant witness to the apostolic teaching of Gospel morality. It continues the doctrine of the Prophets on the two Ways, the Way of Life and the Way of Death. It teaches the Ten Commandments of Moses suffused with Jesus' new motive of love for God and neighbor: "I am the Way, and the Truth and the Life. . . . If you love me you will keep my commandments" (John 14:6, and 15). The teaching of the faith, summarized in the Apostles' Creed, leads directly to conversion, the *metanoía* of the new Way of Life in personal prayer, sacramental living, and Gospel morality. This structure of teaching abides in the Church as its catechetical tradition; it comes to us from Jesus and his Apostles. There is no sign in the apostolic witness of a conflict between doctrine and life, as if doctrine somehow interferes as something abstract with the rich, experiential immediacy of life as it is lived.[46] For Jesus and his Apostles, the doctrine of the faith is precisely that concrete teaching that results directly in putting on the new creation, the new Way of Life of Eucharistic communion with Jesus and union with God.[47]

The Apostolic Origin of the Creed and the New Testament

We may conclude this chapter briefly with two important results of Jesus' doctrine and its consequent apostolic *kērygma* and teaching. The first is the substance and pattern of the Apostles' Creed; the second is the set of writings that we call the New Testament.

The Apostles' Creed

Everything in these first three points results in the fact that the new converts persevered in "the Apostles' teaching" (Acts 2:42), "obedient from the heart to the standard of teaching, the *typos didachēs*" (Rom. 6:17). It was one and the same in all the churches founded by the Apostles: "All this presupposes a fixed and precise oral teaching, and this teaching was called the way of the Lord, the way of God, the way of salvation, or simply the Way."[48] It cannot be overstressed that this is the program of Jesus the Divine Teacher that his Apostles were continuing, making it the foundation of each church they founded.

The pattern or *typos* of this teaching is the Trinity of Divine Persons whom Jesus revealed as the inner life of God. They exist in the one unique, almighty, and eternal nature of Yahweh, the Lord God of both the Primitive and the Hebrew Revelation. This pattern, clear in the Gospels, is linked by Jesus himself with the teaching that prepares for the profession of faith in sacramental initiation.

This Revelation from the Triune God, made by Jesus when teaching his Apostles, is a set of truths diffused in the Bible. For the practical purposes of his teaching program intended for all nations, there was needed a syllabuslike summary of the most basic Articles of Faith made on the Trinitarian pattern. This Jesus did as the consummate Teacher: he provided both the content and the Trinitarian pattern or form. An authority, indeed a divine authority, over the teaching program was needed to gather the basic Articles of Faith into a teachable summary. This summary had thus a set pattern that served as the standard or model or type for the teaching. Jesus was this authority. He passed it on to his Apostles, sending them as the Father had sent him: "All authority in heaven and on earth has been given to me. Go therefore and make disciples of all nations, baptizing them in the name of the Father and of the Son and of the Holy Spirit, teaching them to observe all that I have commanded you; and lo, I am with you always, to the close of the age" (Matt. 28:18–20).

This passage in the Gospel suffices to show that Jesus the Divine Teacher stands at the origin of the Apostles' Creed. They learned its substance and its pattern from him. While the living authority of their Church supports the slight variations in the wording and especially the developed wording of the Nicene Creed in the Patristic Age and the Creed of the People of God in the present day, the substance and essential pattern are always the same. They express Jesus' teachable summary of the Divine Revelation diffused in the Hebrew Scriptures. In the last analysis, when we say that in substance the Apostles' Creed originates with Jesus and his Apostles, we have in mind its meaning and Trinitarian pattern, not the formulated words of the Apostles' Creed that we of the Latin Rite teach and pray today.[49] But when we teach and pray this venerable wording that has stood in the Latin West since the Fathers of the Church, it is indeed the Catholic faith that comes to us from the Apostles, which we pray and which we professed in one Baptism.

The New Testament

Biblical scholars by common consent recognize that the writings of the New Testament came forth from the catechetical teaching of the apostolic church. This may be considered even true of the majestic conclusion to the Bible as a whole, the Book of Revelation, for it resulted from the banishment of Saint John from his community and its teaching at Ephesus.

The Gospels, it has been noted already, reflect the pattern of Saint Peter's Jerusalem Kērygma. They were not texts, however, for that fixed elementary instruction for Christian initiation: they appear rather to be a part of that higher level of teaching to which Hebrews alludes (see Heb. 6:1–2). Saint Luke is quite clear on this at the outset of his Gospel: "Inasmuch as many have undertaken to compile a narrative of the things which have been accomplished among us, just as they were delivered to us by those who from the beginning were eyewitnesses and witnesses of the Word, it seemed good to me also, having followed all things closely for some time past, to write an orderly account for you, most excellent Theophilus, that you may know the truth concerning the things of which you have been informed" (Luke 1:1–4). The Greek word translated as "delivered" is in the root of *parádosis,* a "tradition" handed on by the teaching. Thus it bears witness to the elementary level of fixed and systematic instruction that was preparing converts for sacramental initiation. The Greek verb translated as "informed," furthermore, is in the root of *katechéo:* concerning which you have been "catechized." This golden introduction to the Gospel of Saint Luke, therefore, bears witness to the higher level of teaching in the apostolic parish communities and indeed to the theme of these present chapters on the Word of God, the teachable Deposit, and the actual teaching done by the Apostles.[50]

All four Gospels fit into this structure of the apostolic teaching. They result from it, come forth from it, and consolidate its elementary level. The same is true of the Acts of the Apostles and the Epistles, as we have seen. They presuppose that fixed and systematic catechetical instruction of the new converts, illuminate it indirectly, and in many instances implement the higher level of teaching in the Church of the Apostles.

Conclusion for Biblical Catechetics

The Catholic Church always and everywhere has taught that her Apostolicity is in the order of doctrine. Her Apostolicity abides as the foundation of her unity, holiness, and catholicity because she and her teachers from the Holy See through all the bishops, priests, and deacons, down to all the parents and catechists, are faithful to this catechetical tradition, which comes from Jesus and his Apostles.[51]

With this we conclude Biblical catechetics, the study of the Deposit of Faith and Morals in itself, in its sources, and in its transmission by teaching. At the death of the last Apostle, Saint John, around A.D. 100, the apostolic Church is always and everywhere a Teaching Church, in every apostolic center, whether at Jerusalem (now disrupted by the Jewish catastrophe of A.D. 70), Rome, Antioch, Ephesus, or Alexandria. The catechumenate of the Fathers of the Church is already clearly visible, functioning systematically and purposefully in the very writings of the New Testament. A scientific documentation of the biblical foundation of catechesis exists. It is the teaching program of the Apostles. It constitutes the ongoing dynamism and the doctrinal substance of the Apostolicity of the Church.

It remains to examine the Deposit of Faith and Morals in the Fathers of the Church and across the centuries to the present. This will require another book to follow this one.

References, Suggestions for Teaching, and Topics for Discussion

Part I. The Hebrew Revelation: Prophecy and Preparation

Chapter 1. Religion in the Life of Mankind

1. See John Courtney Murray, *The Problem of God* (New Haven: Yale University Press, 1964). This book by a well-known priest and professor of the twentieth century, is not without merit, but the title casts a false light upon the subject and illustrates the tendency to locate wrongly the problem upon Planet Earth. This mistake about God and mankind could well be a topic for further research and discussion in the light of the catechesis of sin and redemption. The *General Catechetical Directory* (hereafter cited as *GCD*) titles its part 1 "The Reality of the Problem." It offers teachers and those who train catechetical teachers the basic principles for approaching and discussing the problems and difficulties in teaching the Catholic faith today. Note especially par. 9, "The Work of Renewal," and the causes of the current "period of crisis."

2. In the preparation of Catechists this is an excellent topic for further discussion. It can be studied in connection with the first Encyclical of each contemporary pope, from Leo XIII to John Paul II. The first Encyclical is always an analysis of the problems that the pontificate will face and a projection of the way each pope intends to handle those problems. See especially the insightful *E Supremi Apostolatus* (October 4, 1903) of Saint Pius X, in Vincent A. Yzermans (ed.), *All Things in Christ: Encyclicals and Selected Documents of St. Pius X* (Westminster, MD: Newman, 1954), pp. 3–13. As an example of sociological analysis, see Jacques Ellul, *Prayer and Modern Man* (New York: Seabury, 1970). This French professor of sociology analyzes keenly the widespread disappearance of prayer under the pressure of modern conditions of life. "I believe that we have entered," he writes on p. viii, "upon a human condition which is new." There is a large literature on the secularization of modern Western society, which results in alienation from God and divine things. Social pressure mounts, causing people to live as if the purpose of human life is confined to this world. Perhaps Saint Pius X expressed this best in his document introducing his *Catechism of Christian Doctrine:*

> There is a special circumstance today. An atmosphere of unbelief has been created which is most harmful to the interior and spiritual life. This atmosphere wages war upon any idea of a higher authority, any idea of God, of revelation, of the life to come, and of mortification in this life. Hence parents and teachers must inculcate with the greatest care the basic truths found in the first questions given in the Catechism. Let them inspire in the children the Christian concept of life, and the sense

273

of responsibility in each human act toward the Supreme Judge who is everywhere, knows everything and sees everything.

This atmosphere has been created by the false philosophy that has arisen in educated circles during the last three centuries. This also affects the approach of modern man to the Bible and hence will be studied in coming chapters of this present work.

3. See John Henry Newman, *Apologia pro Vita sua* (New York: Doubleday Image, 1956), part 7, "General Answer to Mr. Kingsley," pp. 317–321. "What shall be said to this heart-piercing, reason-bewildering fact? I can only answer, that either there is no Creator, or this living society of men is in a true sense discarded from His presence" (p. 320). See also Max Picard, *The Flight from God* (Chicago: Regnery, 1951), a classic study of the "atmosphere" to which Saint Pius X refers in the previous footnote. Again a fruitful topic for discussion in the training of catechetical teachers.

4. The idea and practice of idolatry, the worship of false gods and their man-made images, is a fundamental of biblical Catechetics, for it is a theme that pervades the Bible from beginning to end. It offers the catechist a constantly recurring occasion for teaching and discussing the importance of achieving the true concept of God and placing in him one's personal purpose of life: "I am the Lord thy God. . . . Thou shalt not have strange Gods before me. . . . Thou shalt not adore them nor serve them" (Exod. 20:1–6). Moses and all the Prophets were constantly warning the Chosen People against the idol worship of their pagan neighbors. Saint Paul praises his first converts because they "turned to God from idols, to serve a living and true God" (1 Thess. 1:9). Idolatry pervades the modern post-Christian world, assuming new forms but in substance ever the same. For a profoundly helpful discussion see John Henry Newman, *A Grammar of Assent* (New York: Longmans, Green, 1930), "Natural Religion," pp. 389–408, and "Revealed Religion," pp. 409–492.

5. The conflict of Satan with the divine plan for the redemption of mankind is again a basic theme of the Bible from Genesis through the Book of Revelation. Teachers can pursue it readily in the concordances. The life of Christ can be studied in the Gospels from this point of view, beginning with the temptations in the desert at the outset of Jesus' public ministry when Satan sought to entice him to the program of the false Messianic Expectation, to be studied later in detail. Satan exists and has power; the Church bears witness to this across the ages with the ritual of exorcism, which indeed forms a part of the baptism of every Catholic. Again, this offers a fruitful point for catechetical teaching and a topic for further study and discussion.

6. The annual Gifford Lectures at the University of Edinburgh are devoted to Natural Theology. For one of the most lucid treatments of the Gifford theme, see the 1947 contribution of Christopher Dawson, *Religion and Culture* (London: Sheed and Ward, 1962). For an introduction to the concept see Chervin-Kevane, *Love of Wisdom: An Introduction to Christian Philosophy* (San Francisco: Ignatius, 1988).

7. See Werner Jaeger, *Paideia: The Ideals of Greek Culture,* vols. 1–3 (New York: Oxford University Press, 1939–44).

8. The moral failure of the classical civilization is one of the themes of Saint Augustine's early writings that document his thinking during his conversion. See especially his dialogue *On the True Religion* (1955).

9. Saint Augustine, *De Magistro,* chapter 14, *The Teacher,* Joseph Colleran (transl.), (Westminster: Newman, 1950), p. 185. See Augustine's *De doctrina christiana,* book 2, chapters 40–42, on the conversion of the heritage of philosophy, "converted to our use."

10. See Etienne Gilson, *The Spirit of Medieval Philosophy* (New York: Scribner's, 1940), the Gifford Lectures of 1931–32, in which he shows the relationship of Christian philosophy to the catechetical teaching of God's self-revelation in his divine Name: "I am who am."

11. Catechetical teachers find the questions and articles of Saint Thomas's *Summa Theologiae* (1964) a helpful resource, especially when teaching teenagers. See the *GCD,* no. 88, on the catechesis of adolescents, where reference is made to the contemporary renewal in the Catholic Church of this natural knowledge of God. For comprehensive commentaries on this Thomistic Natural Theology, see the works of R. Garrigou-Lagrange, O.P., now classic in this renewal.

12. Saint Pius X, essay on catechetical teaching in his *Catechism of Christian Doctrine* (Arlington, VA: Center for Family Catechetics, 1975). It is because of this atmosphere and its harmful effects for the pastoral care of souls that the Catholic Church called the First Vatican Council into session and enacted its Constitution *Dei Filius* (1870) on the basic philosophical truths that form the preambles of the Catholic Faith. This Constitution resulted in the program for the renewal of Christian philosophy in all Catholic schools, launched by Pope Leo XIII with the Encyclical *Aeterni Patris* (August 4, 1879) and sustained by each succeeding pope to the present. The pastoral dimension is clear in the *GCD,* no. 88, on the catechesis of adolescents, where reference is made to the Constitution *Dei Filius.*

13. See William James, *Varieties of Religious Experience: A Study in Human Nature* (New York: Modern Library, 1902), the Gifford Lectures for 1901–2.

14. See note 6. A fruitful topic for discussion and further study in classes for catechetical teachers is the relationship between religion and human cultural life in Dawson throughout his works. In addition to *Religion and Culture* (note 6), see his *The Age of the Gods* (London: Sheed and Ward, 1933) and *Progress and Religion: An Historical Enquiry* (New York: Sheed and Ward, 1938). For Dawson religion is the foundation of all human life and culture, in contrast with the nineteenth-century axiom, exemplified in such works as those of J. B. Bury and E. Gordon Childe ("Man Makes Himself"), where progress results from leaving the heritage of religion behind.

15. Dawson, *Religion and Culture,* p. 39.

16. *Ibid.,* pp. 38–39.

17. *Ibid.,* pp. 42–43; see "the authority of the Veda," p. 42, as an illustration of "the authority of revelation in the strict sense of the word," and his chapter on prophets and divination, pp. 65–84, with quotations from the North American Indians, on the religious ideals and ancestral practices of "the Men of the Great Spirit."

18. See Dawson, *Religion and Culture,* p. 16: "The publication of J. B. Taylor's *Primitive Culture* in 1871, which was the first important synthesis of the new anthropological knowledge, marks an epoch in this field." This new knowledge of mankind's religious past offers students of catechetical teaching a fruitful field for study and discussion. In addition to the synthetic writings of Dawson, there are the voluminous scientific and analytical works of Fr. Wilhelm Schmidt, S.V.D. See his *Primitive Revelation* (Saint Louis: B. Herder, 1939) and *The Origin and Growth of Religion: Facts and Theories* (London: Methven, 1935), his treatise on the comparative history of religion; especially noteworthy in chapter 13, "The Progressive Recognition of the Primitive High God during the Twentieth Century," pp. 185–218,

where one can study the essentials of this scientific discovery made in late nineteenth and early twentieth century. Above all, there is Schmidt's abiding masterwork, *Der Ursprung der Gottesidee* (Münster: 1913–52) in twelve large volumes. Selections of the substance have been translated by Ernest Brandwie in *Wilhelm Schmidt and the Origin of the Idea of God* (New York: University Press of America, 1985). For a comprehensive source of information and of reference to the literature of Comparative Religion, see Mircea Ehade (ed.), *The Encyclopedia of Religion* (New York: Macmillan, 1987).

19. Here again light shines from a different direction on "The Reality of the Problem" for Catechists today, as the *GCD* terms it. It is the Bible and its revealed view of mankind that is at stake. For the constant problem in recent times is the philosophical effort to see these facts without God and revealed religion, making them seem to support atheistic evolutionism. James G. Fraser's *Golden Bough* might be termed the "bible" of the evolutionist view, as if the first stage of man's religious history must necessarily be magic and animism arising out of nonreligious and subhuman beginnings. See *The Golden Bough: A Study of Magic and Religion* (New York: Macmillan, 1951). There are many editions of this seminal work of atheistic evolutionism. The atheistic worldview is constrained to see a degraded polytheism at human beginnings, with monotheism a much later development.

20. For an introduction to this body of new scientific information on mankind's worship by sacrifice, see Joseph Henninger, S.V.D., "Sacrifice," in Eliade, *The Encyclopedia of Religion,* vol. 12, pp. 544–57, with copious bibliography.

21. The discovery of this primitive monotheistic religion introduces a set of scientific facts that do not support the worldview of atheistic evolutionism. For seminal works on this discovery, see Edward Horace Man, *The Aboriginal Inhabitants of the Anadaman Islands* (London: Royal Anthropological Institute, 1885), and Andrew Lang, *The Making of Religion* (London: Longmans, Green, 1900). These works exemplify the discovery of the religion of the food-gathering primitives, free of animism and magic, and quite unlike the earliest stage imagined by the evolutionists. These seminal reports on the fact of this religion of the primitives antedate the work of the Catholic priests Wilhelm Schmidt, cited in note 18, Wilhelm Koppers, and their associates. Obviously both a large field of factual knowledge and an equally large philosophical question open up before students of biblical Catechetics. There was a challenge in the late twentieth century both to science and to catechetical studies: it was to unmask and disallow philosophical suppression of these facts on the religion of the primitives. The voice of the primitives is a clear witness to the Bible of educated Westerners, whether priests or scientists: for a synthetic overview, see Wilhelm Koppers, S.V.D., *Primitive Man and His World Picture* (London: Sheed and Ward, 1952).

22. See Schmidt, *The Origin and Growth of Religion,* chapter 13, "The Progressive Recognition of the Primitive High God during the Twentieth Century," pp. 185–218, already cited, and his other works in note 18. For a scientific recognition of the discovery of the primitive religion, see the English translation of "The Problem of Primitive Monotheism," a paper presented by Professor Herbert Kühn to a gathering of scientists in Germany, in Hastings and Nicholl (eds.), *Selection II* (New York: Sheed and Ward, 1954), pp. 63–86.

23. There was a definite and quite unscientific tendency in the universities of both Communist Russia and the secularized West across the late twentieth century to suppress these facts regarding the primitive High God. For a competent summary of this phenomenon, see the monograph of Franz Cardinal König, himself

formerly a professor of Ethnology at the University of Vienna, *Gibt es einen Wissenschaftlichen Atheismus?* (Freiburg: Herder, 1978). He answers his question "Does Scientific Atheism Exist?" with a flat negative. The sciences can no longer be made to appear in support of atheism—whether the physical and biological sciences—or those of Ethnology and Prehistory: "A science which serves political power as the handmaid of atheism loses all validity" (p. 20).

24. Koppers, *Primitive Man and His World Picture,* p. 180. See also Dawson, *Religion and Culture,* pp. 25–27.

25. This is the purpose of catechetical teaching given by the *GCD,* par. 22.

Chapter 2: The Bible and Biblical Catechetics

1. See Arnold J. Toynbee, *An Historical Approach to Religion* (London: 1956), p. 139, where he uses "The Age of the Civilizations" to name the relatively recent period in human history that began at about 4000 B.C. with the development of the city out of the agricultural village of prehistory and the invention of writing.

2. John Henry Newman, "Holy Scripture in Its Relation to the Catholic Creed," in *Discussions and Arguments on Various Subjects* (London: Longmans, Green, 1899), pp. 146–47. These eight lectures by Newman, pp. 109–253, offer perhaps the best and most lucid general introduction to the Bible in the English language, not least because it recognizes the need for the Catholic and Apostolic Creed as the necessary rule for interpretating the Bible in accordance with the unifying meaning that comes from its divine authorship. Other general introductions to the Bible are given in the bibliography.

3. One of the most important topics for discussion in training teachers of the Catholic faith is the fact that the *GCD* in par. 88 on the catechesis of adolescents cites the Constitution *Dei Filius* of Vatican I, which launched this program of metaphysical renewal in all Catholic institutions of higher education. This is at the very heart of the catechesis of adolescents, who need to be helped in fundamental religious thinking.

4. Augustine, *Serm. II,* M.L. 38, 30.

5. Thomas Aquinas, *Summa Contra Gentiles,* I, 22, "That in God Being and Essence are the same." See *ibid.,* III, 25, where Saint Thomas teaches that the entire purpose of the Seventh Liberal Art, which since the work of Saint Augustine has been First Philosophy on Metaphysics, is to know God by the cultivated power of natural reason. This is the natural preamble for divine faith.

6. Augustine, *Serm. XII,* M.L. 38, 102.

7. Saint Thomas Aquinas, *Summa Theologiae* (1964), II-II, q. 171, art. 2. There is a growing interest in Saint Thomas's treatise "On Prophecy" (*ibid.,* II-II, qq. 171–178), with *Summa Theologiae* III, 1. 7, art. 8; his *De veritate,* q. 12, art. 1; and his commentary on the Prophet Isaiah, chapter 1, on 1 Corinthians 14 (lect. 1), and on the Epistle to the Hebrews 11 (lect. 7). The reason is the direct connection between this concept, "the Prophetic Light," and the inspiration of Sacred Scripture, a matter that must be rediscovered at the present time because of the vicissitudes suffered by Natural Theology in the period of Modern Philosophy. See chapter 1.

8. Aquinas, *Summa Theologiae* II-II, q. 171, art. 3.

9. Saint Thomas devotes q. 175 of his treatise on prophecy to ecstasy and rapture, which sometimes accompany the prophetic light but do not constitute its inner nature.

10. *Ibid.*, q. 171, art. 1.

11. Vatican I, Constitution *Dei Filius*, chapter 4, D-S 3015, translated by John J. Broderick, S.J., in *Documents of Vatican Council I* (Collegeville, MN: Liturgical Press, 1971), p. 46. These passages of Saint Thomas and of the Supreme Magisterium should be elaborated and discussed fully in the training of catechists, for they eliminate the Modernist Heresy of recent times, since 1835, which reduces religious education to nothing but the first two kinds of light.

12. See John Henry Newman's classic "Natural Religion" and "Revealed Religion in his *Grammar of Assent* (New York: Longmans, Green, 1930), pp. 398–408 and 409–920.

13. Aquinas, *Summa Theologiae* II-II, q. 171, art. 2.

14. Without this true concept of God based on the natural foundation that is open to his personhood, deity, and almighty power one cannot see the unity of the Bible that results from its divine authorship. Catechetics will falter and at last the official catechism will be suppressed. This is a topic that needs thorough explanation and discussion in the preparation of catechists for their teaching. One cannot emphasize enough the importance of the renewal of Christian Philosophy in the present times of the Church. See Chervin and Kevane, *Love of Wisdom: An Introduction to Christian Philosophy* (San Francisco, Ignatius, 1988), part 4, "The Renewal of Christian Philosophy."

15. See Jesus' words in Matthew 23:1–12 and Saint Peter's in 1 Peter 1:10–12.

16. DS 1501. The Council then proceeds to list the books of the Holy Bible by name (DS 1502 and 1503) and to state the most basic principles for their correct exegesis and interpretation (DS 1506, 1507, and 1508). Here again a fruitful topic for discussion with catechists, going directly to these sources of defined doctrine.

17. DS 3006. This should be studied and discussed together with the entire document of Vatican II, *Dei Verbum*, On Divine Revelation.

18. DS 3007, English translation of John J. Broderick, S. J., in *Documents of Vatican Council I*, pp. 42–43.

19. Leo XIII, *Providentissimus Deus,* in John T. Wynne, S.J. (ed.), *The Great Encyclical Letters of Pope Leo XIII* (New York: Benziger, 1903), pp. 271–72.

20. Leo XIII, in Wynne, *The Great Encyclical Letters,* p. 273.

21. See his treatise *De doctrina Christiana,* in *Corpus Christianorum,* vol. 32 (Turnholt: Brepols, 1962), pp. 1–167; English translation by John J. Gavigan, in *Writings of St. Augustine,* vol. 4: in *Christian Instruction* (New York: CIMA, 1947). One of the most pressing tasks in biblical Catechetics at the present time is the recovery of the approach to the Bible by the Fathers of the Church. This work of Saint Augustine is without doubt the place to begin.

22. Thus the title of the Vatican II Dogmatic Constitution on the Church, *Lumen Gentium,* takes on a special significance from the viewpoint of biblical Catechetics.

23. See Aloisius Gramatica (ed.), *Bibliorum Sacrorum iuxta Vulgatam Clementinam,* Nova Editio (Rome: Typis Polyglottis Vaticanis, 1959). Pope John Paul II has continued this work on the Latin Vulgate (see the latest edition [Rome: Libreria Vaticana, 1979]) with his important Apostolic Constitution, pp. v–viii, on the care of the Church for the sacred text.

24. See his *De reductione artium ad theologiam,* translated by Sister Emma Thérése Healy (Saint Bonaventure, NY: Franciscan Institute, 1955), on "how the other

illuminations of knowledge are to be brought back to the light of Sacred Scripture" (p. 29).

25. *Ibid.*, p. 27. Perhaps no one in all the tradition of Christian learning has expressed the fact that Jesus Christ is the unity of the Bible better than the same Saint Bonaventure in his *Itinerarium Meritis in Deum* (translated by Philotheus Boehner, O.F.M., 1956), chapter 4:"All Sacred Scripture treats . . . of the one Spouse of the Church, Jesus Christ, who is at one and the same time our Neighbor and our Friend, Word Incarnate and uncreated Word, our Maker and our Re-maker, the *Alpha* and the *Omega* . . . , who purifies, enlightens and perfects his spouse, that is, the whole Church and every sanctified soul" (p. 77).

26. *General Catechetical Directory* (Washington, DC: U.S.C.C., 1971), par. 5.

27. *Ibid.*, par. 7, quoting Vatican II, *Gaudium et spes,* "The Church in the Modern World," par. 19.

28. See Chapter 1, note 12, on the renewal of Christian Philosophy, and Chervin and Kevane, *Love of Wisdom: An Introduction to Christian Philosophy* (San Francisco: Ignatius, 1988).

29. See the Encyclical of Pope Pius XII, *Divino afflante Spiritu,* "On the Most Opportune Way to Promote Biblical Studies" (September 30, 1943). This Encyclical on the human authorship must be studied as a whole in order to see its harmony with all the other documents of the Church on the divine authorship. Often quotations from it are presented out of this context in a slanted way.

30. Raymond E. Brown, "Catechetics in an Age of Theological Change," *Origins: NC Documentary Service* (April 19, 1973), p. 691.

31. See D-S 3462, where this opinion of the Modernist Heresy is condemned. See also the teaching of Vatican Council I, *Dei Filius,* c 4 and especially the Canon related to this point, D-S 3043.

32. *Ibid.*

33. *Ibid.*

34. *Ibid.*, p. 689.

35. For a convenient collection of the Papal Encyclicals on the Bible and of the decisions of the biblical commission, see *Rome and the Study of Scripture* (Saint Meinrad: Grail, 1962). Priests giving homilies and teaching religion and catechists in their classrooms are "Professors of Scripture" for their hearers. The study of this collection begets an openness to the guidance of the Holy See in questions of the human authorship, for it becomes clear that the intention of that guidance is the proper use of the sciences in relationship to the divine authorship of the Bible. All priests and other catechists can make their own, for example, the "Instruction" of May 13, 1950, pp. 154–67, on the proper way to teach Sacred Scripture. From beginning to end, the heart of the matter is the divine authorship that gives the Bible its special quality by which it is "Holy" and its writings "Sacred." It is deeply beneficial, furthermore, not to judge the biblical commission of the Holy See by hearsay but to be familiar with the letter and spirit of the Apostolic Letter of Leo XIII, *ibid.*, pp. 30–35, which established it on October 30, 1902.

36. *Ibid.*, p. 51.

37. For the text of *Providentissimus Deus,* see *ibid.*, pp. 1–29; for that of *Spiritus Paraclitus,* pp. 43–79; for that of *Divino afflante Spiritu,* pp. 80–107. These three Encyclicals should be studied comprehensively by every priest and catechetical teacher, for they expound the meaning of the catechetical approach to the Holy Bible, as distinct from the recent unsound approaches that concentrate exclusively on the human authorship.

38. For the text, see the reprint, *The Historicity of the Gospels* (Boston: St. Paul Editions, 1964).

39. *GCD* par. 40.

40. *Humani Generis* (August 12, 1950), pars. 39–40.

41. See John F. McCarthy, *The Science of Historical Theology* (Rome: Propaganda Mariana, 1976), and the periodical *Living Tradition*, organ of the Sedes Sapientiae Study Center in Rome, of which Monsignor McCarthy is the director. See his programmatic essay, "The Neo-Patristic Alternative to Form-Criticism," in the issue of February 1986, pp. 10–15, where he clarifies the essential difference between the modern natural and historical sciences and "Form-Criticism," which is a philosophical deformation or abuse of those sciences by defective hermeneutics. "Form-Criticism," he writes, "sees the Gospel text as a human writing in which expressions of the miraculous and the supernatural are regarded as mere manifestations of the naive outlook of the time and place. . . . The Neo-Patristic approach continues to read the text of the Gospels and the whole of Sacred Scripture as Sacred Writing from the hand of God" (p. 13). It is clear that Monsignor McCarthy and his collaborators at the Holy See represent a new generation of younger scholars who are postmodern in their thinking because, having recovered and renewed the metaphysics of openness to God, they have transcended the limitations of the atheistic hermeneutics deriving from its inner-cosmic metaphysics.

42. Card. Joseph Ratzinger, "Sources and Transmission of the Faith," *Communio* (Spring 1983), p. 21. This is his discourse delivered in Paris and Lyons, January 1983, on the contemporary crisis in Catechetics and on its remedy.

43. See Card. Joseph Ratzinger, "Foundations and Approaches of Biblical Exegesis," *Origins: NC Documentary Service* (February 11, 1988), pp. 594–602. These two lectures of 1983 and 1988 are basic for biblical Catechetics, for they liberate this ecclesiastical science from the dark cloud cast by the Spinozan inner-cosmic metaphysics and its atheistic hermeneutics of the Bible in the nineteenth century. See also René Laurentin, *Comment reconcilier Exégése et la foi* (Paris: OEIL, 1984), for a lucid analysis of the dependence of unsound exegesis on unsound philosophy.

44. *Ibid.*, pp. 594–95.

45. *Ibid.*, p. 595.

46. *Ibid.*, p. 596.

47. *Ibid.*, p. 599.

48. *Ibid.*, p. 599.

49. *Ibid.*, p. 600. It is significant that this period of time, "the last 100 years," is also the period of the philosophical renewal in Catholic higher education, launched by Vatican I (1869–70) and the Encyclical *Aeterni Patris* (August 4, 1879).

50. *Ibid.*, p. 601. Throughout his pontificate Pope John Paul II has exemplified the position in exegesis represented by Cardinal Ratzinger. This can be studied in his biblical catecheses at his weekly general audiences as reported in the English edition of *L'Osservatore Romano,* particularly his series on Genesis, the Creation, and the Elevation and Fall of mankind and his series on the Gospels that teach the baptismal profession of faith in Jesus the Messiah and Son of God, truly God and truly man, the redeemer of mankind. These audiences exhibit biblical Catechetics in action at the highest level of the apostolate.

51. This insight of the Prophet Isaiah into the vocation of the Hebrew people (see Is. 42:6) was taken for the title of the Dogmatic Constitution of Vatican II on the Church, *Lumen gentium.*

Chapter 3. The Hebrew Prophets and the Bible

1. Christopher Dawson, *Religion and Culture* (London: Sheed and Ward, 1962), p. 68. For further study and as a topic for discussion, see this entire chapter 4, "Prophets and Divination," among "The Sources of Religious Knowledge and the Religious Organs of Society," pp. 65–84. This study and discussion might well include chapter 1, "Natural Theology and the Study of Religion," pp. 3–22; chapter 2, "The Elements of Religion: God and the Supernatural," pp. 25–44, and chapter 3, "The Relation between Religion and Culture," pp. 47–62. These were the prestigious Gifford Lectures delivered at the University of Edinburgh in 1947. They place the Hebrew Revelation and its Prophets, who received the light of Revelation from God and taught it to their people, in the context of the modern discovery of the rest of mankind by Western exploration and missionary outreach. Dawson, an Oxford graduate and convert in the way of John Henry Newman, has produced an abiding contemporary classic in these Gifford Lectures, an illustration of the new Science of Comparative Religion at its best.

2. *Ibid.*, p. 72.

3. For further study of this point, and as a topic for discussion, see Saint Thomas Aquinas, *Summa Theologiae* II-II, q. 174, art. 4: "Whether Moses Was the Greatest of the Prophets." Michelangelo's statue of Moses in the Church of St. Peter in Chains at Rome captures this greatness in marble.

4. In these chapters of part 1 on the Hebrew Revelation, unless otherwise noted, all quotations from the Bible will be made from *The Holy Scriptures according to the Masoretic Text* (Chicago: Menorah Press, 1973), the official text of the Jewish Publication Society of America, edited by Rabbi Morris A. Gutstein, Ph.D., and others. The reason is the fact that the Catholic Church has accepted the work of the Jewish scholars who produced the Masoretic text. It is recommended that teachers and students make use of the Jerusalem Bible both for comparison and for its valuable footnotes, which offer the best detailed commentary on the text of the Old Testament, both from the viewpoint of the divine authorship and from the viewpoint of recent scholarship on the human authorship. The recognition given to the Jewish Masoretic text by the Catholic Church illustrates the fundamental basis for the relationship between Catholics and Jews that Vatican II addressed in *Nostra aetate* (October 28, 1965), the "Declaration on the Relation of the Church to Non-Christian Religions," no. 4. This fundamental document, which now has additional official guidelines and an extensive literature, can provide an important topic for study and discussion in biblical Catechetics. The Masoretic text is used in these present chapters in order to show what it is that Jews read and study in their synagogues to this day. The Masoretic text helps Catholic Christians realize better our union with the Jews through the Sacred Scriptures that we have from them. Our reception of the Masoretic text, furthermore, may help our brethren, the Jews of today, to take a fresh new look, without the Talmudic prejudices of the past two millennia, at the Sacred Scriptures of the New Testament as the fulfillment of their own Sacred Book. For they have the same Heavenly Father as their Author. Thus the full and complete Holy Bible, in the unity of its divine authorship, may well become the instrument for that reunion of which Saint Paul writes in Romans 9–11, chapters which are basic for further study and discussion in this connection.

5. "Upon this mountain": Mount Horeb had a second name in antiquity, Mount Sinai. This initial conversation or dialogue between the Prophet and the Supreme Being, Moses' first reception of the prophetic light, took place at the

very place that was to see the culmination of the Hebrew Revelation. The concept of "token," the sign that will authenticate his divine mission in final fashion, is based upon the Lordship of the Supreme Being over the course of contingent events: God promises to bring Moses back to this very mountain and with him the entire Chosen People of God. Moses is already understanding that the Creator has spoken to him, for the bush is preserved in being in a manner above the laws of nature, and he understands further that this Creator is the Lord of history, because his almighty power extends to the contingencies of human events. This mountain, over a mile high, is usually identified with the peak called by natives to this day the *Jebel Musa*, the Mountain of Moses, standing in the desert roughly halfway between Egypt and Palestine.

6. See Rabbi Gutstein's note *op. cit.,* The Masoretic text, at this point: "The ineffable name; read *Adonai,* which means *Lord."* The Hebrew Revelation was chiefly concerned with communicating the correct concept of God, to which the Divine Name, when rightly understood, bears witness and becomes the instrument of a teaching on the part of God and a learning on the part of the Hebrews. The Septuagint Greek translation of this verse (Exod. 6:3) uses simply the word *Kyrios:* "But I did not manifest to them My name, *Lord* [or *The Lord]".* The recent Jerusalem Bible translates: "I did not make myself known to them by my name Yahweh." The essential point for biblical Catechetics is the personal Reality of the Supreme Being who comes close to his people and speaks to them, not directly but by means of a certain man named Moses, chosen and set apart for this special purpose and mission. This Name of the Divine Reality, now used in human speech, is the instrument of a communication of meaning by explanation and didactic teaching on the part of the Prophets. This concept of God can be studied throughout the entire Bible and with vivid prayerful directness in the Book of Psalms.

7. Card. Jean Daniélou, *Advent* (New York: Sheed and Ward, 1951), p. 35.

8. In the New Testament, Luke 1:26–38 shows Mary as truly one of the authentic Prophets, and the same is true of Saint Paul in Acts 9:3–11. These instances of prophecy are in the service of the One like Moses, the One of whom Moses wrote, Jesus of Nazareth, the preeminent Prophet who stands at the end of the line as the fullness and completion of Divine Revelation. See the *GCD,* no. 12. For further study see *The Jerusalem Bible* (New York: Doubleday, 1966), "Introduction to the Prophets," pp. 1115–41, a competent and readily available resource for the training of catechists.

9. H. Haag, in Langsfeld-Haag-Hasenhüttl, *La Révélation dans l'Écriture et la Tradition* (Paris: Cerf, 1969), p. 79.

10. Many topics for further elaboration and discussion in the training of catechists. For example, "inerrancy," which follows from the divine authorship and which is best presented directly from the documents of the Supreme Magisterium of the Church; see chapter 1, note 37. Or again, the distinction between the academic and the catechetical orders of teaching: the former is concerned directly with the human sciences and the latter with the higher order of the Prophetic Word.

11. In volume 2 of this manual for catechists much attention will be given to the so-called Experience Approach in religious education, which became a common aberration in the late twentieth century. It suppresses the official catechisms of the Church and with them the teaching of the Deposit of Faith and Morals. It wants no part of the teaching of a definitely formulated doctrine. Much fruitful discussion of this matter can take place here with the nature and purpose of the

Bible, showing that the "Teaching Approach" belongs to the divine plan. See also the opening paragraphs of the following chapter.

Chapter 4. Divine Revelation and the Schools of the Prophets

1. The approach in religious education that is generated by the Modernist Heresy is a large subject and will be studied in detail in volume 2 of this manual in the chapter on the philosophical and theological foundations of Catechetics. In general, the disdain for the very idea of a Divine Deposit formulated by a divinely appointed teaching authority into propositions of human discourse is expressed in such popular clichés as "you can't give them propositions; you have to give them experiences." Biblical Catechetics analyzes the contrary approach in the Bible.

2. See John F. Broderick, S.J. (trans.), *Documents of Vatican Council I* (Collegeville: Liturgical Press, 1971), p. 46, the Constitution *Dei Filius*, chapter 4: "The constant consensus of the Catholic Church has also held and still holds that there is a twofold order of knowledge, distinct not only in origin but also in object." This is the charter of catechetical teaching because of the operating words "order of knowledge," which eliminate the so-called "experience approach" reflected in the religion textbooks produced under the auspices of the Modernist Heresy. For the original Latin of this fundamental dogma of the Church, see D-S 3015.

3. This summary is not intended to be a comprehensive and fully elaborated presentation of biblical doctrine such as the standard treatises on the theology of the Old Testament contain. This summary, with some of the texts that illustrate the prophetic doctrines, is a guide toward that direct and personal familiarity with the sacred text that the work of the catechist entails. The treatises on the Theology of the Old Testament are helpful in acquiring this Christian familiarity with the Hebrew Scriptures and can be consulted with profit by catechetical teachers according to their circumstances. See, for example, Paul Heinisch, *Theology of the Old Testament*, trans. William G. Heidt, O.S.B. (Collegeville: Liturgical Press, 1950), and P. F. Ceuppens, O.P., *Theologia Biblica* (Rome: Manetti, 1949), especially vol. 1, *De Deo Uno*.

4. Herbert Kühn, "The Problem of Primitive Monotheism," in Hastings-Nicholl (eds.), *Selection II* (New York: Sheed and Ward, 1954), p. 73; this is the English translation of a paper read originally at the Mainz Academy of Science in Germany. For a discussion of the meaning of Yahweh as the Eternal and Self-Subsisting Being, *ipsum esse*, presented in a popular way that is not technical from the philosophical point of view, see Ceuppens, *Theologia Biblica*, vol. 1, pp. 23–28 and 128–36. "The Pentateuch teaches," Ceuppens writes, "that monotheism in the strict sense was not a religious teaching that began with Moses, but one which had been held throughout the period of the Patriarchs and indeed by primitive mankind" (p. 97). "We conclude, therefore, that the monotheistic doctrine is not new with Moses, introduced into the Bible by the Prophets because of influence coming from cultural progress. Sacred Scripture teaches on the contrary that there is one unique God, Yahweh of the Israelites, existing from the first origin of mankind to this 8th century B.C., and that the beings which the Gentiles call "divinites" are man-made idols of gold and silver, empty of reality" (p. 101). Cf. also Heinisch, *Theology of the Old Testament*, pp. 50–57, on the meaning of the name Yahweh in the light of recent linguistic science and Semitic studies.

5. The advancing religious ignorance of Catholics in modern and contemporary times, lamented increasingly by the successors of Saint Peter, especially pope Saint Pius X, results in a loss of this true concept of God that begets reverence and awe in human minds before the Divine Mystery. Such secularized mentalities, even in children affected by the secularized culture, can hardly be catechized. Hence Saint Pius X in his *Catechism* places at the beginning twenty-seven "Basic Truths" as the instrument for reevangelization. They contain the prophetic truths of the Self-Revelation of God. Thus biblical Catechetics establishes the roots in the Bible for this apostolate of contemporary reevangelization.

6. For the defined doctrine of the Church on this point, see Vatican I, Constitution *Dei Filius,* chapter 1, with its canons. In certain levels and circumstances of catechetical teaching, and especially in the training of catechists, this body of doctrine should be explained in detail and discussed thoroughly in relation to the current religious ignorance. For the original Latin, see D-S 3001–3 and 3021–25; for the English translation, Broderick, *Documents of Vatican I,* pp. 40–41 and 49. In the catechesis of adolescents, see *GCD,* no. 88, where these passages are cited. The heart of this solemn definition on God our Lord, D-S 3001, and Broderick, p. 40, reads as follows: "The holy, Catholic, apostolic, Roman Church believes and professes that there is one true and living God, creator and lord of heaven and earth, omnipotent, eternal, immense, incomprehensible, infinite in intellect and will and every perfection. Since He is one unique spiritual substance that is completely simple and unchangeable, He must be declared distinct in reality and in essence from the world, perfectly happy in Himself and of Himself, and inexpressibly exalted above all things other than Himself that exist or can be conceived." Clearly this is defined against the Spinozan pantheism and the entire modern movement of philosophical atheism. It is this true concept of God that stands behind the divine authorship of the Bible as his unified message to mankind.

7. See Isaiah and the Constitution *Lumen Gentium* "On the Church"—the Light of the Gentiles, par. 1:"Christ is the Light of Humanity."

8. This identifies another biblical foundation of Catechetics: the authentic catechesis of children. See the first question of the Saint Pius X *Catechism:* who made you?

9. Heinisch, *Theology of the Old Testament,* p. 148.

10. See *ibid.,* p. 142.

11. This is still another biblical foundation of Catechetics. Catechists should rest the case on human origins on Moses' teaching out of the prophetic light. The human sciences do no more than point back toward human origins but do not themselves reach them. This is another important topic for explanation and discussion.

12. Heinisch, *Theology of the Old Testament,* p. 162.

13. *Ibid.,* p. 255.

14. See M. J. Scheeben, *The Mysteries of Christianity* (Saint Louis: B. Herder, 1946), part 3, "The Mystery of Sin," pp. 241–310. This is a classic and comprehensive treatment, helpful for all catechists and especially for those who train catechists.

15. See chapter 1 on the history of religions and mankind's decline.

16. One may say that the dominant theme of the Old Testament is sin with the promise of the Redeemer and that of the New Testament is the Redeemer and his redemption.

17. Heinisch, *Theology of the Old Testament,* p. 229.

18. This is the recurring theme of the prophetic message, and it runs through all the Hebrew Scriptures. For illustrations, see Numbers 14:9; Deuteronomy 28:15;

Isaiah 1:4, 24:5, 30:9; Ezechial 2:3, 2:8, 3:9, 21:16, 44:6; Jeremiah 2:5, 3:20, 9:1, 11:10; Obediah 4:12, 6:7; Malachi 2:10. This is the context of the New Testament and of he who said, "I am the way, and the truth, and the life; no one comes to the Father, but by me" (John 14:6).

19. Heinisch, *Theology of the Old Testament,* pp. 233–34.

20. This is the substance of Satan's suggestion to Adam and Eve, to Judas in his betrayal, and to modern man's idolatry of the human self.

21. The Roman Canon of the Catholic Mass calls Abraham "our Father in faith."

22. See Herbert Kühn, op. cit., pp. 63–73. The survey of primitives around the globe:

> yields one clear result: the first fruits of the hunt are offered in sacrifice . . . to a deity who is a single unique God. . . . Archaeology reveals [that] early man, the man of the last inter-glacial period, offered sacrifice. If he offered sacrifice, then he must have offered it to a God; and the clearest indication of the nature of this god is the persistence of the same approach to him, thousands of years later, among the hunting peoples around the North Pole. Among them that God is still alive today. We know his name [and] the ceremonies of sacrifice. . . . It is to the Supreme Being that this sacrifice is made, the primeval divinity, creator and sustainer of all things. As yet the concept of God was not splintered into a number of divinities. . . . The pattern of this primeval memory of man can be seen [likewise] in the pattern of Biblical tradition. (p. 72).

All four aspects of the doctrine of the Hebrew Revelation: its teaching about God and its threefold teaching, on prayer, on the commandments, and on the worship, constituting the way of life that is the fitting human response to the prophetic word, become visible in the light of recent scholarship as a renewal of the original religious condition of mankind.

23. *The Holy Scriptures according to the Masoretic Text* (Chicago: Menorah Press, 1973), p. 78.

24. Julius B. Maller, "The Role of Education in Jewish History," in Louis Finkelstein (ed.), *The Jews: Their History, Culture and Religion,* vol. 2 (New York: Harper and Row, 1960), p. 1234.

25. Thus there is no basis in the Bible for the present "Experience Approach" of the Modernist movement in religious education.

26. This emphasizes once again that biblical Catechetics identifies biblical foundations of Catechetics that have a special contemporary importance. When one notes that the Scriptures bear no witness to descriptions of individual experiencings to be emulated by the people generally but rather bear witness to insights and understandings communicated socially to the people by a teaching program, a large subject has been opened, one that agonized the twentieth century. For the moment, one can note that Divine Revelation does not fall from heaven among the Hebrews like stones. Truths are not emotional experiences, and neither are they stones. The prophetic light is quite different. It can shine in a special way upon a specially chosen mind, for God is everywhere. If he wishes, he can illuminate in a special way the mind of his Prophet who lives and moves and has his very being in God, as do all men. The Man of God can then formulate what he understands in human speech for his fellowmen to receive and to hand on socially, especially to the children of the oncoming generation. It is not correct to scorn *a priori* this

reception of truth and knowledge for communication among men by human discourse, as if these truths were then only inert stones fallen from heaven. They are far from inert, for they generate the entire living dynamism of this unique People of God and become its principle of formation unto its distinct and qualitatively superior Way of Life. This fundamental point will recur for more detailed analysis in connection with the philosophical and theological foundations of Catechetics.

27. This touches the very heart of catechesis in the Catholic Church, as the enemies of this Church know well. In earlier modern times, they did everything possible to prevent the Church from schooling her children in their Catholic faith. In the contemporary phase, when the enemies have penetrated within the Church, they propagate theories on new "psychological" views that Christian doctrine cannot be given to young children but must wait until their adolescence, when presumably they would receive it in the light of modern philosophizing. This is the significance of approaches such as that of the quite well known "Green Bay Plan" in the United States after Vatican II.

28. Flavius Josephus, *Against Apion* II, 18.

29. Philo Judaeus, *Leg. ad Caium*, no. 31, in William Barclay, *Educational ideals in the Ancient World*, (London: Collins, 1959), p. 12.

30. S. Schechter, *Studies in Judaism*, 1st Series, p. 300, quoted in Barclay, *Educational Ideals in the Ancient World*, p. 35.

31. Barclay, *Educational Ideals in the Ancient World*, p. 36.

32. Isidore Epstein, *The Jewish Way of Life*, op. cit., p. 196; see also pp. 196–99.

33. This is a fruitful topic for further discussion in the training of catechists. See Pope John Paul II Address to the Dutch Bishops (January 25, 1988): "It will certainly be necessary to give absolute priority to the family apostolate . . . , the first School of Faith. Encourage families to have times for prayer and Scripture reading in common."

34. Barclay, *Educational Ideals in the Ancient World*, p. 14.

35. For catechesis in Christian times, the Holy Family at Nazaareth is the model that passes this Hebrew heritage forward into the Christian era.

36. Here again is a basic scriptural foundation of Catechetics. Vatican II restates this constant teaching of the Church in its *Declaration on Christian Education*, no. 3, in Austin Flannery, A.P. (ed.), *Vatican Council II: The Conciliar and Post-Conciliar Documents* (1975), p. 728:"As it is the parents who have given life to their children, . . . it is above all in the family that children should be taught to know and worship God, and to love their neighbor, in accordance with the faith . . . received in baptism."

37. Simon Greenberg, "Jewish Educational Institutions," in Louis Finkelstein (ed.), *The Jews: Their History, Culture and Religion*, vol. 2 (New York: Harper and Row, 1960), p. 1257. Cf. A. R. S. Kennedy, "Education," in James Hastings (ed.), *Dictionary of the Bible*, vol. 1 (New York: Scribner's, 1903), p. 647: "The Synagogue . . . was not originally a place of worship but a place of religious instruction, and indeed was so named by . . . Philo of Alexandria in his *Vita Moysis* III, 27." On the Hebrew schools and schooling, see Barclay, *Educational Ideals in the Ancient World*, chapter 1, "Education among the Jews," pp. 11–48; Nathan Drazin, *History of Jewish Education from 515 B.C.E. to 220 C.E.* (Baltimore: 1940); and especially N. Morris, *The Jewish School* (London: 1937.

38. Henri Daniel-Rops, *Daily Life in the Time of Jesus* (New York: Hawthorn, 1962), p. 419.

39. Barclay, *Educational Ideals in the Ancient World*, p. 32.

40. Alfred Edersheim, *The Life and Times of Jesus the Messiah*, vol. 1 (London: Longman's Green, 1883), p. 436.

41. *Ibid.*, p. 77. This universality of the synagogues is a Providential preparation for the Christian Revelation: the Gospels will show Jesus teaching in the synagogues of the Holy Land, and the Acts of the Apostles will do the same for Saint Paul.

42. Julius B. Maller, "The Role of Education in Jewish History," in Finkelstein, op. cit., vol. 2, p. 1238.

43. Barclay, *Educational Ideals in the Ancient World*, p. 38.

44. These essentials have continued to live and perform their didactic function in the Liturgy of the Hours of the Catholic Church, where the Shema is professed and prayed each week and the entire Book of Psalms each month. Thus the true concept of God, the divine Self-Revelation to Moses, has been offered to the Gentile peoples of the entire world.

45. See Barclay, *Educational Ideals in the Ancient World*, p. 42, and A. C. Bouquet, *Everyday Life in New Testament Times* (New York: Scribner's, 1954), p. 156: "Many people still seem to think that in the days of Christ there were no schools, and indeed that universal education is something that was brought in during the 19th century. Nothing can be farther from the truth. Organized education of children is a most ancient thing." This religious education and formation is significant for understanding the New Testament. Mary and Joseph had this training in the Hebrew religion and were able to cooperate with the synagogue on behalf of Jesus. He of course attended the synagogue school at Nazareth. And this pattern of Jewish religious education was the basis for his work with his own disciples later on. They included fishermen of active outdoor life, but they were Hebrews who frequented their synagogue faithfully and who had been trained as boys in the synagogue school at Capernaum. They possessed the foundation for pursuing a program of higher study with a Rabbi—with John the Baptist or with Jesus himself. See Robert Aron, *The Jewish Jesus* (New York: Orbis, 1971), especially chapter 2, "In the Shadow of the Synagogue," pp. 41–91.

46. This concept of a "pattern of teaching" that relates doctrine to personal formation in the three chief practices that sustain the Way of Life is an important biblical foundation of Catechetics. It, too, will be fulfilled in the Christian Revelation. See Romans 6:17, where Saint Paul speaks of the *typos didaches*, "the pattern of the teaching." This "pattern or standard of teaching" was followed for fifteen centuries in the oral catechetical practice of the Catholic Church, when it became the structure in print of *The Roman Catechism*, "the four principal doctrinal headings . . . which comprise the whole substance and teaching of Holy Scripture"; see Bradley-Kevane (trans.), *The Roman Catechism* (Boston: St. Paul Editions, 1985), preface, p. 11.

47. See Isidore Epstein, *The Faith of Judaism* (Jerusalem: Soncino, 1980). And Barclay, *Educational Ideals of the Ancient World*, p. 47. The ideal of the Hebrew education is the transformation of the common and the ordinary in human life into the precious. This is the qualitative "quantum leap" that the Hebrew Fact represents historically, when the study of religion places it in the context of the surrounding pagan nations. It is a teaching that helps them choose the higher way effectively, the Way of Life.

48. This purpose is not changed in the catechetical teaching of the Catholic Church but fulfilled. Thus it is a prime instance of Jesus' stated principle that he came not to abolish but to fulfill the Prophets (see Matt. 5:17). This again is one

of the basic biblical foundations of Catechetics. See the *GCD*, no. 22: "Catechesis performs the function of disposing men to receive the action of the Holy Spirit and to deepen their conversion." Thus the purpose is holiness, for the Holy Spirit is the Sanctifier. Deeper conversion to God in faith, hope, and divine charity is the process by which the sanctification takes place.

49. Karl Heinrich Rengstorf, in Gerhard Kittel-Bromiley, *Theological Dictionary of the New Testament* (henceforth *TDNT*), vol. 2, trans. (Grand Rapids: Eerdmans, 1964–75), vol. II, p. 149. For Greek words in the root *didask-*, used throughout the New Testament, see pp. 135–65, on *didāsko, didāskalos, didascaliā* and *didachē*. Certain key concepts in Catechetics are linked once and for all with the Greek language, for the Early Church spoke Greek and Greek was the original language in which the inspired New Testament Scriptures were written. These words in the root *didask-* are among the most important of these key concepts and merit careful study for their bearing upon the two contrasting approaches in religious education in these two centuries since Rousseau and his *Émile,* the "teaching approach" and the "experience approach." In general, Gerhard Kittel's fundamental work of German scholarship, now available in this ten-volume English translation, is an indispensable aid for the study of the biblical fundamentals of Catechetics. For the lexicographical meaning of this and other key catechetical concepts reference will be made frequently to Kittel-Bromiley in the later chapters on the New Testament.

50. Rengstorf, *Ibid.*, p. 137.

51. *Ibid.*, p. 149.

52. Barclay, *Educational Ideals of the Ancient World,* p. 43. "The teacher was held in the very highest honor" (p. 45).

53. For the uses and meaning of the word *Rabbi* in the Scriptures, see Kittel, *TDNT,* vol. 6, pp. 961–65.

54. Cited in Barclay, *Educational Ideals of the Ancient World,* pp. 45–46.

55. See "*Mathetēs,* Disciple," in Kittel-Bromiley, *TDNT,* vol. 4, pp. 415–60. "The dominant position of the *Rabbi* in the educational system of the Hebrews resulted in the formation of 'schools' around each one. The circle of students that gathered about a *Rabbi* became under his leadership a closely-knit community of learners, undergoing by his influence both an external and an interior formation." See Karl Heinrich Rengstorf, in Kittel, *TDNT,* vol. 6, p. 962:

> The saying handed down. . . . "Get a Teacher *(Rabbi)* and find a fellow-student," shows that a student had to try to gain admittance into the circle of a respected teacher and to engage in the study of Scripture and Tradition in this fellowship. If the teacher acceded to his request, the disciple could enter the school and in daily contact with his master he could get to know the Torah. . . . The pupil followed his teacher with obedience and respect and expressed this by addressing him as . . . "my Rabbi"; "my Teacher." Since the student-teacher relation is determined by respect, and this is as great as that accorded to God . . . , the student was bound to his teacher for the rest of his life. When after several years of association with his master he had become familiar with the oral tradition, he would be . . . allowed to teach himself and be addressed as *Rabbi.*

Also Finkelstein (ed.) *The Jews: Their History, Culture and Religion,* (New York: Harper and Row, 1960) vol. 2, p. 1238: "The Scribes were scholars . . . who steeped themselves in the study of Sacred Wisdom and imparted their knowledge to disciples. This institution—the teacher and his circle of students—became the characteristic mark of Jewish life for centuries. . . . They were regarded as the elite of the nation, men who considered the learning of the Law as the very purpose of life."

56. Rengstorf, in Kittel, *TDNT*, vol. 4, p. 416. For a comprehensive discussion of the meaning of the Greek word *mathetēs* in the Hellenistic culture generally and in the original Greek writings of the New Testament, see Rengstorf's detailed study, pp. 390–461. See p. 413: *"Mathma* is found for an object of learning from the time of Aristophanes. It is later a special term for knowledge, esp. the mathematical sciences." The fact is evident that it is specifically the root of the English word *mathematics*. Generically, the fact that Jesus' twelve specially chosen followers are invariably called his *Mathetēs* emphasizes the fact that he was a Teacher, they learners, and that a content of knowledge was involved.

57. *Ibid.* The word *mathetēs,* Rengstorf continues, has a technical meaning, "which implies a direct dependence of the one under instruction upon an authority superior in knowledge, and which emphasizes the fact that this relation cannot be dissolved" (p. 416). Perhaps the closest modern counterpart to this educational system is the classical type of graduate seminar in the German universities, where the chosen students practically live with the professor, frequently taking room and board at his house, using his specialized library, and making their own his techniques of research and ideals in scholarship.

58. *Ibid.*, p. 423.

59. *Ibid.*, p. 424. Rengstorf's mention of the New Testament is a valid one and must be taken up again later in connection with the human side of Jesus Christ's work in training his *mathetēs* and sending them as "Apostles." Thus once again the Old Testament offers a biblical foundation of Christian Catechetics.

60. See *Ibid.*, p. 440: "The formal dependence of the Rabbinate on Hellenism in respect to *mathetēs* [disciples] may be taken as certain." For the fact that it was indeed "higher education" among the Hebrews, see *ibid.*, p. 441: "The *mathetēs* is a student who has already reached a certain ripeness, as distinct from a beginner." Rengstorf gathers copious evidence, pp. 439–40, for the introduction of the Greek concept *mathetēs* into the Hebrew vocabulary, in support of his conclusion: "We may finally venture to say that the Hebrew word for 'disciple' as such came into Judaism from the educative process of the Greek and Hellenistic philosophical schools" (p. 439). One cannot but think of Saint Justin Martyr and Eusebius's *Praeparatio Evangelii* in the expansion of Jesus Christ's teaching program into this same Hellenistic culture, to be studied in volume 2 of this manual.

61. *Ibid.*, pp. 440 and 437. It is clear that the Rabbis should not have allowed merely human interpretations to form, let alone "schools" like those of Hillel and Shammai, but should have transmitted unencumbered the original deposit of Hebrew Revelation as such. This question of merely human traditions added in an all-too-human way to the Divine Tradition will be a crucial issue in the human life of Jesus Christ as a Rabbi in Israel. For the formation of Rabbinical schools in Israel, see *ibid.*, pp. 435–37.

62. See *ibid.*, p. 402.

63. *Ibid.*, p. 435.

64. *Encyclopedia Judaica,* vol. 14, col. 637, s.v. "Sages." See also vol. 13, "Rabbi, Rabbinate," cols. 1445–58.

Chapter 5. The Promises of God, Teacher of Mankind

1. Cited from *The Holy Scriptures According to the Masoretic Text* (Chicago: Menorah Press, 1973), the official Jewish translation. This translation of the Hebrew

Bible will be used throughout this chapter unless otherwise noted. Students should compare and discuss the translations given in the Catholic Bibles, especially the Jerusalem Bible, the New American Bible, and the Catholic edition of the British Revised Standard Version of the Holy Bible.

2. This prohibition may be called a constantly recurring theme in the Old Testament. See Paul Heinisch, *Christ in Prophecy,* trans. William G. Heidt, O.S.B. (Collegeville: Liturgical Press, 1956), especially pp. 3–18 on the Gentile approach to magic and divination in contrast with the Hebrew Prophecies.

3. For the difference between the Old Testament and the New Testament in this matter, see St. John of the Cross, *The Ascent of Mount Carmel,* book 2, chapter 23.

4. See Psalm 139 (1.138).

5. See J. Salguero, O.P., *La Rivelazione Biblica o La Storia di Salvezza* (Rome: Angelicum University Press, 1971). This imperfect and unfulfilled state of the Hebrew Revelation is a theme in the works of Father Salguero.

6. Penance for infidelity is a constant theme of the Old Testament. It would be excessive to list references, which can be found in the standard concordances of the Bible.

7. See Genesis 12:1–2: "Now the Lord said unto Abram: 'Get thee out of thy country, and from thy kindred, and from thy father's house, unto the land that I will show thee. And I will make of thee a great nation, and I will bless thee, and make thy name great; and be thou a blessing.'" As time went on, the Prophets taught this purpose continually and in detail, for instance, Isaiah: "I will also give thee for a light of the nations, that My salvation may be unto the end of the earth" (Isa. 49:6, Masoretic).

8. Heinisch, *Christ in Prophecy,* p. 16.

9. See *ibid.* and especially pp. 198–211.

10. *GCD,* par. 40; see also pars. 44 and 52.

11. Thus *the Anointed One* becomes *the Christ* when translated into Greek and thence into Latin and English. Jesus himself accepts this name, as in Peter's confession, "You are the Christ" (Matt. 16:16) and indeed throughout the New Testament.

12. Heinisch, *Christ in Prophecy,* pp. 17–18.

13. Again the relevance of part 1 of the *GCD,* nos. 1–9, titled "The Reality of the Problem."

14. Heinisch, *Christ in Prophecy,* pp. 16–17.

15. This entire book is readily available: see the German work of Fr. Paul Heinisch, translated by William G. Heidt, O.S.B., *Christ in Prophecy.* The table of contents offers a panorama of forty-two prophecies in the various books of the Bible on "the Prophet like Moses," "King and Priest," "Son of God and ruler of the World," "The Innocent Sufferer," "The Pierced One," "Freed from the Bands of Death," "The Virgin's Son," "Emmanuel: The Prince of Peace," with many prophecies concerning his "Messianic Kingdom of God." This work has become an abiding classic of recent Catholic biblical scholarship: it can serve Biblical Catechetics well as a comprehensive introduction to further study of the Messianic Prophecies and as a source of particular topics for discussion. See also L. C. Fillion, *The Life of Christ,* vol. 1 (Saint Louis: B. Herder, 1931), the chapter on the Messiah gradually revealed to Israel by the Messianic Prophecies, pp. 209–24, and the condensed and informative article "Messia" in F. Spadafora (ed.), *Dizionario Biblico* (Rome: Editrice Studium, 1963), pp. 411–414. See also Alfred Edersheim, *The Life and Times of Jesus the Messiah,* vol. 2 (London: Longmans, Green, 1883), appendix

9, "List of Old Testament Passages Messianically Applied in Ancient Rabbinical Writings," pp. 707–38. Professor Edersheim, born and raised a Jew, received a full education in the writings of Talmudic Judaism. Later he was converted to Anglicanism in the British university world. He lists 456 passages of the Bible in this appendix and gives a short commentary on each one from the *Targumim,* the two *Talmuds,* and the most ancient *Midrashim"* (p. 707). This unusual work of immense scholarship provides leads for further study and discussion in the context of the *GCD,* nos. 40, 44–47, and 52. For the roots of the Catholic Tradition on the Messianic Prophecies, see Jesus' own explanation during the Forty Days after Easter; and then see St. Justin Martyr, *Dialogue with Trypho,* especially chapters 50–55, 66, and 108, and Saint Augustine, *De civitate Dei,* book 18, chapters 28–35.

16. These mysterious passages, so difficult to reconcile with those that describe the royalty and glory of the King-Messiah, evoke the Ethiopian's question that expresses the heart of catechetical teaching and its hermeneutics or interpretation of the Holy Bible: "Of whom is the prophet saying this, of himself or of someone else?" (Acts 8:34). In part 2 after the interpretation of the Scriptures that the Apostles were taught by Jesus, their Teacher, to use in their own teaching.

17. The interpretation of this passage is much disputed, as one would readily expect. The fact remains that the Hebrews themselves, when they produced their official translation of their Scriptures into Greek, the Septuagint Version, used the Greek word *parthenos,* which means what the English word *virgin* means. The Hebrews took no offense at this until later when Christians, indeed the Apostles, called to this passage in their catechetical teaching: "Isaiah saw that Virgin in spirit, through whom the marvel would be fulfilled" (Heinisch, *Christ in Prophecy,* p. 85).

18. It is a matter of practical importance for catechetical teachers to study these headings and at least the chief passages of the Hebrew Scriptures as indicated, in order to continue in the present day the method of catechesis that Christ himself taught his Apostles to use.

19. The Apostles will have definite ideas on all of this: cf. Romans 11, 25 26, and, indeed, chapters 9–12 as a whole. See the remarkable contemporary work on these matters by Father Elias Friedman, O.C.D., a mid-twentieth-century convert from Judaism, *Jewish Identity* (New York: Miriam Press, 1987); and Heinisch, *Christ in Prophecy,* p. 102: "The time will come when He will again raise His hand to lead back from exile the people He scattered over the whole earth in punishment for their sins." In this prediction Isaiah repeated what the Prophets Amos (9:14) and Osee (2:17–25 and 13:14) had already held out to the purified and cleansed people. "When the Gentiles turn to Yahweh, the whole Chosen People (both Israel and Judah) will come home from exile and enter the Messianic Kingdom. The punishment inflicted because of her obstinacy will have terminated. . . . As a people she then would enter Christ's Kingdom."

20. It is important to note that the Prophets do not foresee the Messianic Kingdom as a political world empire that smashes the natural growth of distinctive peoples on earth into a common unrelieved gray "masses" of humanity. The Gentile peoples will retain their natural identity and their political independence when they come to Yahweh and his revealed religion. For the Messianic Kingdom will be a religious one, a "Church," and not a political empire. From this the Hebrews, too, could know that they would not lose their national characteristics and cherished natural values when entering the worldwide rule of their own Messiah. This is the point of the work of Father Friedman, *Jewish Identity,* already cited.

21. A. Edersheim, *The Life and Times of Jesus the Messiah,* vol. 1, p. 160. The entire chapter 5, pp. 160–79, is a valuable scholarly resource for further study and

discussion of this deviation of the Messianic Expectation. See also Joseph Klausner, *The Messianic Idea in Israel: From the Beginning to the Completion of the Mishnah* (New York: Macmillan, 1955): "The Jewish Messianic idea . . . came forth from an essentially political aspiration—the longing to recover its lost political power and to see the revival of the Davidic kingdom. . . . This idea necessarily remained in its essence mundane and political" (p. 517). Jesus will contend against this all during his public life, even among his Twelve Apostles.

22. Edersheim, *The Life and Times of Jesus the Messiah*, p. 164.

23. *Ibid.*, p. 165.

24. *Ibid.*, p. 167.

25. See Matthew 4:1–11, the account of Jesus' temptations by Satan as he prepared for his public mission. As Satan's way of thinking is reflected in the false Messianic Expectation, so it is the substance of these temptations. Jesus is invited to think in an inner-cosmic manner, appearing as the Messiah whom the Jewish leadership wanted: "The devil took him to a very high mountain and showed him all the kingdoms of the world and the glory of them" (v. 8). A moment before, Satan had suggested Jesus cast himself down from "the pinnacle of the Temple," for so they expected the King-Messiah to appear, to take charge, to lead the victorious revolt against Rome, and to introduce Daniel's Fifth Empire, an empire in and of this world ruled by the Jewish nation. Jesus' replies to the solicitation of Satan are abiding biblical foundations of Catechetics and at no time more so than in the late twentieth century.

26. The Essenes are now much better known to us because of the discovery of the Dead Sea Scrolls. See Jean Carmignac, *Christ and the Teacher of Righteousness: The Evidence of the Dead Sea Scrolls* (Baltimore: Helicon, 1962), with its "Bibliography for the General Reader," pp. 159–64.

27. See Josef Pickl, *The Messias* (Saint Louis: B. Herder, 1946), chapter 1, "'The Internal Political Condition of Palestine," pp. 1–42; chapter 2, "Messianic Expectation," pp. 43–62; and chapter 3, "Struggles for Freedom," pp. 63–96. This translation of a scholarly German work is illuminating on the problems Jesus faced as a teacher, for these ideas were general among the crowds and even his own Twelve were variously infected by them, up to the extreme case of Judas, his betrayer. Professor Pickl's objective scientific analysis refutes the current misconceptions of Jesus as a partisan in these political and paramilitary movements.

28. See *ibid.*, for the distinction between the Zealots and the Pharisees, a distinction that gradually faded in the approach to the furious nationwide revolt that led to the destruction of the Temple in A.D. 70 and the consequent cessation of the sacrificial worship of Moses' Covenant.

29. See Friedman, *Jewish Identity*, for this "sin of infidelity." This is the work of a Catholic priest, a Carmelite at Stella Maris Monastery in Israel, who was born and raised in Judaism. Coming forth from the awesome Holocaust suffered by the Jews, Father Elias's book is Providentially helpful to Jews who are discovering their Messiah in the spiritual life of his Eucharistic Kingdom and to catechists who are called upon to help them.

30. Bradley and Kevane (trans.), *The Roman Catechism* (Boston: St. Paul Editions, 1985), p. 55.

31. *Ibid.*, p. 59.

32. *Ibid.*, p. 60.

33. Vatican II, *Nostra aetate* (October 28, 1965), "Declaration on the Relation of the Church to Non-Christian Religions," no. 4, in Austin Flannery, O.P. (ed.),

Vatican Council II: The Conciliar and Post-Conciliar Documents (New York: Coatello, 1975), pp. 741–42.

Part II. The Christian Revelation: Fulfillment and Teaching Mission to All Nations

Chapter 6. Jesus Christ and His Revealed Religion

1. The Fathers of the Church were unanimous in teaching the unity of the Old and the New Testaments in Jesus Christ first foretold and then actually present on this earth as *Emmanuel*, God-with-us. This unity witnesses to the divine authorship of the Bible. Saint Augustine's *Contra Faustum* defends this unity against the Gnostic heresy, offering an especially lucid example of the Patristic approach to the Bible. Return will be made to it in the text.

2. The *GCD*, mandated by Vatican Council II, was published by Pope Paul VI on April 11, 1971, after a process of preparation supervised by Cardinal John Wright. For the text, see Eugene Kevane (ed.), *Teaching the Catholic Faith Today: Twentieth Century Catechetical Documents of the Holy See* (Boston: St. Paul Editions, 1982), pp. 41–144. These guidelines should be studied in correlation with these other documents gathered in this volume, especially that of Pope John Paul II, *Catechesi tradendae*, pp. 209–70.

3. The word *tradition* derives from the Latin *tradere*, meaning "to hand on." Pope John Paul II puts the word and the concept in the title of his *Catechesi tradendae*, and he makes use of it in no. 22, where he notes that "the revelation that God has given of Himself to humanity in Christ Jesus . . . is constantly communicated from one generation to the next by a living, active *traditio.*" In no. 21, John Paul II makes it explicit that this *traditio*, this "handing on," is accomplished by "systematic instruction . . . , not improvised but programmed to reach a precise goal." Hence his conclusion in no. 22: "It is quite useless to campaign for the abandonment of serious and orderly study of the message of Christ in the name of a method concentrating on life experience."

4. Pope John Paul II in *Catechesi tradendae*, no. 6, confirms this principle and makes it quite specific: "Christocentricity in catechesis also means the intention to transmit not one's own teaching or that of some other matter, but the teaching of Jesus Christ. . . . In catechesis it is Christ, the Incarnate Word and Son of God, who is taught—everything else is taught with reference to Him—and it is Christ alone who teaches—anyone else teaches to the extent that he is Christ's spokesman, enabling Christ to teach with his lips." The next three sections of *Catechesi tradendae*, nos. 7–9, are devoted to "Christ the Teacher." It is clear that the catechetical study of the Gospels will have the task of providing the biblical foundations for this challenging didactic concept of Christocentrism.

5. For the Latin originals of Vatican I from which this paragraph is drawn see D-S 3015, 3020, 3041, 3042, 3043 and 3462. For the full English translation of the Constitution *Dei Filius* of Vatican I, see John J. Broderick, S.J. (trans.), *Documents of Vatican Council I* (Collegeville: Liturgical Press, 1971), pp. 37–52.

6. Pius XII, Encyclical *Humani generis* (August 12, 1950), no. 22.

7. Quoted in *Living Tradition* (November 1988), p. 6. Cardinals Ratzinger and Baum actually are supporting the approach of John Paul II in his weekly general

audiences at St. Peter's. Throughout his pontificate he has been giving a series of catechetical explanations of Scripture, which can be studied in *L'Osservatore Romano-English Edition,* where the text of each is given in full.

8. Quote in *ibid., Living Tradition,* (November 1988) p. 6. It should be noted that Pope John Paul II will have no part of this withholding of the Bible from the Catholic people, especially the parents. Addressing the Dutch bishops as reported in *L'Osservatore Romano, English Edition* (January 25, 1988), he gave them the following way of overcoming the ravages of the Modernist Heresy in Holland: "It will certainly be necessary to give absolute priority to the family apostolate.... Encourage families to have times for prayer and Scripture reading in common."

9. See, for example, the cover story of *Time* (August 15, 1988) headlined "Who Was Jesus?," reporting on the Scorsese movie, which caused widespread outrage among Christians, and, for further example, the report in the *Washington Post* (November 12, 1988) on "the national group of biblical scholars" headed by Robert W. Funk that is cooperating with the production of another Hollywood movie: "There will be no reference to a virgin birth nor any hint of a resurrection.... [It] will not show Jesus preaching the Sermon on the Mount. Seminar members have declared that the sermon is basically a collection of Jesus' 'table talk' compiled by early Christian writers." This illustrates again the outcome when the false approach is applied to the Gospels.

10. See Saint Augustine, *De vera religione,* 1(1)–4(7), his initial statement of the question and then the dialogue as a whole.

11. See St. Augustine, *Contra Faustum,* in Migne, *The Latin Fathers,* vol. 42, pp. 307–518. This is a major work that shows Augustine at his best, in his mastery of the Bible and in his personal involvement, having been for some years a member of the Manichean sect. Here one may draw attention to book 13, chapter 14 (M.L. 42, 290) for Augustine's own summary of the Patristic approach. When a Gentile comes to realize that the Jewish Scriptures contain many prophecies that now are fulfilled before our eyes, he will accept personally "the divinity of Christ," for this faith is the meaning of the entire unified panorama of prophecy and fulfillment.

12. St. Augustine, *De catechizandis rudibus,* chapter 3; see J. P. Christopher (trans.), *St. Augustine: The First Catechetical Instruction* (Westminster, MD: Newman, 1946), p. 18.

13. *Ibid.,* p. 18.

14. *Ibid.,* p. 19.

Chapter 7. Jesus Christ, Teacher and Prophet in Israel

1. Julius B. Maller, "The Role of Education in Jewish History," in Louis Finkelstein (ed.), *The Jews: Their History, Culture and Religion,* vol. 2 (New York: Harper and Row, 1960), p. 1238.

2. See chapter 4 for the origin, nature, and perversion of the Messianic Expectation, with its note 15.

3. The study of Jesus Christ as a Rabbi of His place and time, a teacher in Israel, is one of the most important principles and biblical foundations of Catechetics. More perhaps than any other single aspect of catechetical study, it enables catechists to acquire their objectively correct and subjectively strengthening self-image. Carpenters and workingmen generally have Jesus Christ as a model. But

the day came when he worked in his shop for the last time, locked it, and turned the key over to another. Then he took up the calling of a specialized Teacher of the Revealed Word of God, the work of a Rabbi in Israel. Catechetical teachers of the Word of God across the centuries to the present have Jesus as a model in a special way that deserves careful research in the sources and study in the secondary works that are available. For the comprehensive scholarly study, see Friedrich Normann, *Christos Didaskalos: Die Vorstellung von Christus als Lehrer in der Christlichen Literatur des ersten und zweiten Jahrhunderts* (Münster: Aschendorffsche Verlagsbuchhandlung, 1967). Normann analyzes each of the Gospels from this point of view: "Die Evangelientradition," pp. 1–66. Also see Luigi Civardi, *Gesú Educatore* (Torino: S.E.I., 1962); Clifford A. Wilson, *Jesus the Teacher* (Melbourne: Hill of Content, 1974); C. H. Dodd, "Jesus as Teacher and Prophet," in Bell-Deissmann (eds.), *Mysterium Christi* (London: Longmans, Green, 1930), pp. 54–65; and William H. Russell, *Jesus the Divine Teacher* (New York: Kenedy, 1944), abidingly helpful to catechists for its emphasis upon Jesus' teaching methods.

4. This catechetical point of view reveals the fact that Divine Revelation is handed on by teaching, a process to which both the Old Testament and the New Testament bear the strongest kind of witness. This is a fundamental theme of this manual and should be made a frequent topic for explanation, illustration, and discussion in the training of catechetical teachers. The reason is the presence of the Modernist Heresy in contemporary religious education programs. It induces ignorance of the Deposit of Faith and Morals and indifference, not to say hostility, to the idea of teaching a definite doctrine received from the past. It wishes to "give experiences," as they say, drawing on mere natural life and its natural religiosity. All of this becomes especially clear when Jesus is seen as the Teacher of the revealed Word of God.

5. His mother undoubtedly called him Jesus as Gabriel told her to do (Luke 1:30–31). But this familiar name in the Holy Family naturally would not be used by his disciples and much less by men in society at large. *Jesus* is the Greek, Latin, and now English form of the Hebrew-Aramaic *Jeshua*, meaning "The Lord is salvation." The name of the Hebrew leader Joshua is translated "Jesus" in the Greek of Acts 7:45, Hebrews 4:8, and Jude 5. Jesus was a name in use by the Hebrews and understood well by them. The fullness of its meaning emerged with Jesus of Nazareth. We Christians since Apostolic times customarily add "Christ" to his name. It is a title from the Greek *christos* (the same in root as the word *chrism*) translating the Hebrew *Mashiah*, hence "Messiah," the "Anointed One." The Jews used this word in a special sense, meaning the Coming One, the Prophet "like unto Moses" whom they expected. The Gospel according to Saint Matthew already uses Jesus Christ as the proper name of Jesus of Nazareth: "The Book of the origin of Jesus Christ, the Son of David, the son of Abraham" (Matt. 1:1). Also John 1:17: "Grace and truth came through Jesus Christ," and Philippians 2:11: "Every tongue should confess that the Lord Jesus Christ is in the glory of God the Father." See Lucien Cerfaux, *Aux Origines de la Tradition* (1968), p. 20: "The primitive formula . . . for profession of faith . . . , which has been kept for us in Romans 10:9, was *Kyrios Iesous* and not *Kyrios Christos*. The latter could only have been formula where 'Christos' was taken as a proper name, and this is not at all an early usage or custom, and it was only used by Christians in pagan lands." Thus the way Jesus of Nazareth was addressed by men generally as reflected in the Gospels, especially Mark and John, indicates the immediacy of their witness. In this chapter all quotations from the Gospels will be from the Revised Standard Version of the Bible

unless stated otherwise. Pronouns referring to Jesus Christ will not be capitalized in this chapter, following the usage which has become customary in contemporary English Bibles.

6. See Gerhard Kittel, *Theological Dictionary of the New Testament* (henceforth *op. cit.*), vol. 2, pp. 135–165, trans. Bromiley (Grand Rapids: Eerdmans, 1975), a comprehensive treatment of the meaning of this cluster of words for the Jews and the Greeks. It could well be a primary source for further explanation and discussion with catechists. For example, p. 164: "This review of the use of *didachē* leads to an important conclusion. Especially when it is linked with the name of Jesus, the term enables us to see to what extent the NT or its authors recognized that it is finally God who speaks in the teaching of Jesus and the Apostles." In volume 2 of this manual, this basic fact will be seen in its continuation in the teaching of the Apostolic Church under the authority of the successors of Saint Peter. This of course is fundamental for the self-image of catechists of the Catholic Church.

7. So the recent Revised Standard and New American versions; the Jerusalem Bible and the Knox render the Greek *Didáskalos* as "Master." Saint Jerome's Vulgate reads: "Magister," the Latin word for "Teacher" from which the English language has *Master* and *Mister*. When the word *Master* is in mind where the inspired Greek text has *Didáskalos,* English-speaking people tend to miss the real meaning, namely, that Jesus was an authorized Teacher in Israel and recognized as such. The newer tendency to translate as "Teacher" is to be welcomed.

8. The new American version likewise keeps the Jewish word *Rabbi.* Knox translates: "Master, it is well that we are here . . . ," as does the New Revised Standard. The King James translates it as "Master," not retaining the Jewish *Rabbi* from the inspired text. Interestingly enough, Saint Jerome's Latin Vulgate has the Hebrew word *Rabbi.*

9. Again the Revised Standard and the New American have "Teacher"; but the King James, the Knox, and the Jerusalem Bibles render *Didáskale* as "Master." Saint Jerome in the Vulgate translates it as "Magister."

10. The versions again render *didáskalos* as either "Teacher," "Master," or "Magister" as in the previous note.

11. The New American likewise retains *Rabbi* and also the Vulgate: "Rabbi, ecce ficus, cui maledixisti, aruit." But the King James, the Knox and the Authorized translate it as: "Master, look! the fig tree which you cursed has withered."

12. In both these instances the New American version renders *didáskalos* as "Teacher." Saint Jerome has "magister." The King James, Knox, Authorized, and Jerusalem Bibles all have "Master." See chapter 6 for the way in which Jesus' Finding in the Temple and its relation to his Bar Mitzvah solves the problem created by this universal recognition of Jesus as a Teacher, even by his official enemies of the government at Jerusalem.

13. Saint Jerome in the Vulgate does likewise: "Ave, Rabbi; et osculatus est eum," and also the New American and the Jerusalem Bibles. But again the King James, the Knox, and the Authorized have "Master" as the translation of *Rabbi.*

14. Friedrich Normann, *Christos Didaskalos: Die Vorstellung von Christos als Lehrer in der Christlichen Literatur des ersten und zweiten Jahrhunderts* (Münster: Aschendorffsche Verlagsbuchhandlung, 1966), p. 1. "One can recognize with certitude that this use of the word *Rabbi* or *Didáskalos* represents the generally-accepted mode of respectful address for a Teacher of the *Torah* in the lifetime of Jesus" (p. 2). "Jesus was generally accepted in his day as a *Rabbi*" (p. 3).

15. *Ibid.*, p. 25. *Rabbi* was the ordinary term of address within a Talmudim, and Judas up to that point was a member of Jesus' Talmudim, as Normann points out in the same place.

16. So Ignatius of Antioch, Irenaeus, Clement of Alexandria, and Augustine in his treatise *De magistro*.

17. In the Revised Standard and in the *New American* versions, *Didaskalos* in these passages is rendered consistently as "Teacher." The King James and Knox translate it as "Master." Saint Jerome in the Vulgate always uses *Magister,* the standard Latin term for a *Didāskalos,* an officially recognized professional teacher.

18. Normann, *Christos Didaskalos,* p. 49. "Luke portrays Jesus as a Rabbi with a group of students" (p. 51).

19. *Ibid.* (p. 49) speaks of "a remarkable set of instances in Luke which use the words formed from the root *didask-.*" See the Greek text of Luke 5:3, 19:47, 20:1, and 21:37–38.

20. See Lohse in Kittel *TDNT,* vol. 5, p. 964:"Following the Palestinian tradition, *Rabbi* appears more frequently in [the Greek text of] John' " and Normann, *Christos Didaskalos,* p. 54: "Likewise John, in agreement with the entire Synoptic tradition, recognizes the social presence of Jesus as that of a Teacher."

21. Saint Jerome in the Vulgate: "Rabbi (quod dicitur interpretatum Magister) ... "; the King James version: "Rabbi (which is to say, being interpreted, Master) ... "; the New American: "Rabbi (which means Teacher) ... " The Greek text of John gives the same translation in Mary Magdalen's recognition of Jesus on the first Easter morning: "She turned and said to him in Hebrew, 'Rabboni' (which means Teacher)" (John 20:16). Saint Jerome retains the Hebrew word in his Latin: "Conversa illa dicit ei: Rabboni (quod dicitur Magister)!"

22. The catechist, the nonspecialist in biblical studies who uses the Scriptures as the Church always has used them in her Ordinary and Universal Magisterium or teaching apostolate, will say that John's Gospel does indeed have the appearance of being the work of a man who participated in an earlier phase when Jesus was addressed as "Rabbi" and also in a later phase when his followers had come to realize that *Kyrie* was, after the Resurrection, the preferred way of addressing him.

23. Cf. E. Fascher, "Jesus der Lehrer," *Theol. Literaturzeitung* (1954), p. 332: "This is the highest possible type of recognition, and it represents the judgment of one of the Jewish Doctors of the Torah," quoted in Normann, *Christos Didaskalos,* p. 59.

24. "He *taught* them: edīdasken." The Greek original leaves no possible doubt: Jesus was a Teacher of the Torah. He was doing "My Father's business," completing Divine Revelation to mankind and preparing to mediate it to all nations by his teaching program for which he trained the Twelve and sent them forth with it as his Apostles. Thus the Apostolicity of the future Catholic Church is exactly and precisely this teaching program and its content, the Deposit of Faith and Morals.

25. Rengstorf, in Kittel *TDNT,* vol. 2, p. 153, with cross-reference to the article on *Mathetēs,* "Disciple," in *TDNT.* See Lucien Cerfaux, *Christ in the Theology of St. Paul* (New York: Herder and Herder, 1966), p. 478: "In antiquity, a name meant much more than it does today. It represents a being, exteriorizes it, and makes its activity present." And Cerfaux refers to the article on "Name," *honoma,* in Kittel, *TDNT,* vol. 5, pp. 242–83.

26. Rengstorf, in Kittel *TDNT,* p. 153. The Talmud recognizes Jesus in the Jewish tradition as a Rabbi of the tanaitisch epoch: Aboda Zara 16B-17a; Sanhedrin 43a (cited in Normann, *Christos Didaskalos,* p. 18).

27. This is usually an effective way for catechists to introduce and to explain the concept of the Magisterium, the technical term for the teaching authority and mission of the Catholic Church. Reflection on Jesus' position and status as a

Teacher leads readily to a new respect for his Church as the religious Teacher of mankind, sent by him to teach, authorized by him to teach, and indeed simply continuing to be Jesus Christ present on this planet, teaching in his Mystical Body, which is the Church. This again is the direct biblical refutation of the Modernist Heresy of the nineteenth century and its popular impact on religious education in the twentieth century.

28. In the preparation of catechetical teachers for their mission and work, this fact has special significance. It assists the catechist to come quickly and concretely to a mature concept of self-identity. Frequently it is more helpful in securing authentic content in catechetical teaching than theoretical studies of the Magisterium of the Catholic Church and of the nature of doctrine in catechesis. Furthermore, there is a dimension of the imitation of Christ that concerns the catechist in a particular way. Catechetical teaching continues to be the building of a Talmudim like his, a group of disciples where each is known personally and in which the teaching is a formation by means of the instruction, helping each to "deepen his conversion" to God through Jesus Christ and in his Church *(GCD,* no. 22). And see *Catechesi tradendae,* no. 30, "Integrity of Content": "The person who becomes a disciple of Christ has the right to receive 'the Word of Faith' (Rom. 10:8) not in a mutilated, falsified or diminished form, but whole and entire, in all its rigor and vigor. . . . No true catechist can lawfully make a selection . . . in the deposit of faith." The perception of Jesus the Teacher helps the catechist greatly in this regard, helping him to teach, as it were, *in Persona Christi.*

29. See, for example, F. Lemonnyer, O.P., *The Theology of the New Testament* (London: Sands, 1929); and Joseph Bonsirven, S.J., *Theology of the New Testament* (Westminster, MD: Newman, 1963). The standard lives of Christ, such as those of Prat, Fillion, De Grandmaison, and many others, offer much "theology of the New Testament."

30. The *TDNT* again is a most helpful resource for explaining the concept *didachē,* the doctrine that a teacher teaches. See note 25.

31. The idea that one could be a teacher without a content or body of truth to teach, structured into logical sequence for clarity and articulated with definitions and divisions, would have appeared quite ridiculous in all cultures and tongues and tribes of mankind since the beginning. It is only since Rousseau and his *Émile* in these last two centuries that other concepts have invaded the teaching profession, disparaging the arts, sciences, and disciplines of human culture and viewing the teacher as a mere companion or guide who arranges for the learner to have experiences. Dewey popularized the substance of Rosseauism to a quite special degree in the United States. This cultural phenomenon works its way into religious education as well, and as the twentieth century proceeded, Catholic catechists proclaimed, "You cannot teach them propositions. You have to give them experiences." It is but a short step to view teachers not as teachers any longer but as "therapists" who have a cure to effect—whether the therapy is sociologism or psychologism or some other philosophism, all ideologies of recent human invention. In the preparation of catechetical teachers, it is essential to be clear on this fundamental point, whether Jesus has a content of truth that he taught. The study of Jesus as a Teacher, analyzing the full import of the words in *didask-,* with the noun *didachē* that denotes his activity, is both practical and timely today.

32. Rengstorf in Kittel, *TDNT,* vol. 2, p. 164: "Didachē here means 'that which I teach.' "

33. *Ibid.*: Under question was "his whole *didaskein,* his proclamation of the will of God as regards both form and content." This is Jesus' *didachē* in the comprehensive sense: his *doctrina,* his content of truth communicated by his socially recognized activity of teaching. Today we call it simply Christian Doctrine.

34. These are: the Sermon on the Mount (Matt. 4:25–7:27); The Instruction of the Twelve for their first mission (Matt. 10:5–11:1); The Parables (Matt. 13:3–52); On Fraternal Behavior (Matt. 18:1–35); The Discourse in the Temple (Matt. 21:23–22:14); His Teaching of the Crowds about Pharisaism (Matt. 23:1–39); The Great Discourse on the Parousia, the End of the World and the Last Things of Man (Matt. 24:3–25:46). This emphasis on the content of Jesus' teaching gives Matthew's Gospel its greater length on the same Synoptic Gospel outline upon which Mark and Luke were written.

35. Normann, *Christos Didaskalos,* p. 26.

36. *Ibid.,* p. 28. It has been a particular interest and achievement of scholars using the German language to identify and clarify this catechetical character of the Gospels, the fact that they actually came out of the catechetical life of the Church of the Apostles and were written to meet the immediate practical needs of catechetical teaching. See the important work of Krister Stendhal, *The School of Matthew and Its Use of the Old Testament* (Lund: Gleerup, 1967).

37. Normann, *Christos Didaskalos,* p. 26.

38. Contemporary biblical scholarship, especially that of Europe, recognizes the catechetical teaching program of the earliest Church as the practical reason for including this content in what originated as a manual or handbook for catechetical teachers—which these written Gospels have continued to be across the centuries to the present. See *ibid.,* p. 27: "Within the Sermon on the Mount the thematic framework indicates that it has a catechetical purpose . . . ": "Prayer," 6:5–15; "Trust in Providence," 6, 19:34, "Leaving Judgment to God," 7:1–6, and "Prayer and the Golden Rule," 7:7–12.

39. *Ibid.,* p. 34. See also Matthew 23:1–2: "Then Jesus said to the crowds and to his disciples, 'The scribes and the Pharisees sit on Moses' seat; so practice and observe whatever they tell you, but not what they do; for they preach, but do not practise.' "

40. For scholarly research on this aspect of Jesus' teaching, see R. T. France, *Jesus and the Old Testament: His Application of Old Testament Passages to Himself and His Mission* (London: Tyndale, 1971); also René Aigrain and Omer Engelbert, *Prophecy Fulfilled: The Old Testament Realized in the New* (New York: McKay, 1958): "The closest link unites the New Testament with the Old. For from Genesis to the Apocalypse it is the same Spirit that inspires the divine message that is embodied in the pages of the Bible and gives them life. To lose sight of this spiritual unity of the Bible is a grave mistake, and hinders our understanding of the Scriptures" (p. 259). Likewise A. T. Maas, S.J., *Christ in Type and Prophecy* (2 vols.) (New York: Benziger, 1893) and C. Larcher, O.P., *L'actualité chrétienne de l'Ancien Testament d'après le Nouveau Testament* (Paris: Cerf, 1962); for the blinded synagogue's reading of the Hebrew Scriptures see pp. 20–24. These works show that Jesus in his teaching gave his own "hermeneutics" of the Bible, which he handed on to his Catholic Church through his Apostles.

41. See France, *Jesus and the Old Testament,* chapter 4, "Jesus' Use of Old Testament Prediction," pp. 83–171. It follows that Jesus teaches the divine authorship and unity of the Bible.

42. *Ibid.,* p. 151; see pp. 150–59, "The Assumption of the Role of Yahweh." Jesus is teaching his own divinity by the way he uses the Holy Bible.

43. See Aigrain and Engelbert, *Prophecy Fulfilled,* pp. 259–260.

44. Psalm 8.

45. See France, *Jesus and the Old Testament,* p. 153: "At least it is clear that here Jesus applies to himself an Old Testament description of Yahweh."

46. For Jesus' teaching, see Mark 7 and Matthew 11 and 25:31–32. For the Old Testament that Jesus is calling to the minds of his hearers, see Daniel 7, Joel 4:1–12, and Zechariah 14.

47. R. T. France, *Jesus and the Old Testament,* p. 159.

48. See Normann, *Christos Didaskalos,* p. 32: "Der Lehrer mit Macht" (A teacher with power): "This 'power' in Matthew's Gospel is first and foremost to be understood as a power inherent in the very teaching."

49. Apostolicity, the constitutive mark or quality of the Church, the most fundamental one, without which the other three marks of the Church cannot exist, finds here one of its most important scriptural foundations. Putting the matter plainly, the Church that preserves "Apostolicity" will teach with power and authority: it will exercise a "magisterium," to use the technical term for the living teaching authority of the Catholic Church that has come into use over the centuries. See Charles Jôurnet, *The Church of the Word Incarnate,* vol. 1: *The Apostolic Hierarchy* (London: Sheed and Ward, 1955), chapter 10, "Apostolicity, Property and Notes of the True Church," pp. 526–59: " 'Roman' is one of the names for the authentic Church. It is not her complete name. . . . The adequate name, naming the Church in the fullness of her reality, naming her by her efficient and conserving cause, is Apostolic" (p. 526). All perceptiveness regarding the Magisterium and fidelity to it in content and mode are bound up with insight into the nature of the Apostolicity of the Church. This is an important topic for further study and discussion with catechists. One can draw upon the theological distinction among the material and the formal object of divine faith, the content that is taught, and the motive for receiving it as the Word of God. Catechists are to teach in Jesus' way, with his authority. Thus the catechumens accept the content that is taught on the authority of God revealing and not merely on that of the catechist. This is especially true in family catechetics, where the parents so clearly represent the authority of God.

50. These Greek words deriving from *Keryx* as their root, the verb *keryssein* and the noun *Kērygma,* represent biblical fundamentals of Catechetics in a direct literal sense. There is a set of concepts and a dimension of meaning attaching to these words that need careful study. After World War II, in the 1950s and 1960s, when "False Americanism in Religion" (as the Holy See termed it in its document to the American bishops in 1899) was ripening on the vine of the Catholic Church in the United States as rust gathers on the stalks of wheat in the fields of the Great Plains, weakening them, it was not uncommon for some bishops to foster and protect priests and religious who were introducing a new so-called Kerygmatic approach in catechetics. Other bishops were perceived to become upset at the very hearing of the word *Kerygmatic.* Ideology can deviate the meaning of authentic and basic words of the Christian heritage. This interesting question, the meanings that the word *Kerygmatic* has come to have in Catechetics, will be taken up again in volume 2 of this manual for a careful sifting of wheat from chaff.

51. For a comprehensive discussion of the use and meaning of the words in *keryx-,* in Greek secular literature and in both Testaments of the Bible, see Gerhard Friedrich in Kittel, *TDNT,* vol. 3, pp. 683–718, summarized here. There is a set of characteristic words of the Greek-speaking Church of the Apostles that denote basic concepts expressing the meaning of the Christian Revelation in the New

Testament. These words offer an entry to the biblical foundations of catechetics. *Didāskalos* (with its Hebrew counterpart *Rabbi), didāskein,* and *didachē* have been encountered already. Others include *evaggelion, kyrios, pistis, metānoia, apostolos, ekklesia, eucharistia,* and *katechesis* itself. Gerhard Kittel's *TDNT* was a major achievement of biblical scholarship in the twentieth century, and the recent completion of Professor Bromiley's translation from the German into English, published in ten volumes by the Protestant firm Eerdmans in Grand Rapids, is an indispensable aid for students generally in this field, especially when personal mastery of the biblical languages has become the exception rather than the rule. Ethelbert Stauffer gives an appreciation of the value of Kittel in the preface of his *New Testament Theology* (London: SCM, 1955), p. 7: "The number of documents, discoveries and problems that ought to be considered in a theology of the New Testament has grown so much in the last thirty years that it would be easy enough to write a textbook of a thousand pages. But the present work has been kept down to a few hundred pages only. This is possible because the reader can now consult Kittel's *Wörterbuch* and its preliminary lexicographical work can be presupposed. This saves many pages." This work will depend upon *TDNT* in a similar way, referring students to it repeatedly. Only in rare instances will a particular philosophical or theological slant be encountered, and these are easily recognized, as for instance in the case of the article on *pistis,* faith, because it was done by Bultmann. Kittel's work represents modern philological science at its best, in the service of understanding key words of the New Testament in the sense in which the Apostolic Church understood and used them.

52. For example, Saint Jerome in the Vulgate translates Exodus 32 into Latin: "Aaron, *praeconis voce,* with the voice of a Herald . . . " Aaron was to head the priesthood of the Hebrew religion; he was also the herald for Moses, the ruler of the Chosen People on behalf of Yahweh. Vatican II *(Lay People* no. 11), using the same Latin, calls parents the *primi praecones,* the first heralds of the Catholic faith to their own children. This is perhaps one of the most significant passages in all the documents of Vatican II from the viewpoint of the catechetical situation of the latter decades of the twentieth century.

53. For *evaggelion,* see Kittel, *TDNT,* vol. 2, pp. 707–737. Saint Jerome translates in the Vulgate: "Initium Evangelii Jesu Christi, Filii Dei." The Greek *evaggelion* and Latin *evangelium* mean "Good News," hence the Old English "God-spel," which has become the word *Gospel.* This word is used in the New Testament to mean not a writing but the actual message or "Good News" of God's action for man's salvation. And Jesus Christ is himself both the messenger and its message. The four written Gospels find in this character and dimension the unique nature not at all incompatible with their historicity but rather, to the contrary, with their literary genre.

54. See C. H. Dodd, *According to the Scriptures* (London: Collins, 1965), p. 69: "Most striking of all perhaps is the allusion to Daniel 7:22 in the summary of the first proclamation of the Kingdom of God by Jesus in Galilee in Mark 1:15. . . . There is amply enough here to show how deeply this chapter of Daniel is embedded in the foundations of New Testament thought." This concept of Jesus' life and work as the fulfillment of all the Prophets, of the entire Hebrew religion, which prepared for his coming, is absolutely basic to Catechetics as to both content and as to method; it will be taken up further later.

55. On the Jewish Expectation, see chapter 5.

56. The word *preaching* today fails to convey the proclamation of an event done with the authority of God. The original Greek means the heralding of an

historical event, calling to action now in view of things that are going to take place. Catechists teach in this prophetic mode: they are God's heralds to their cate-chumens.

57. See Mark 1:14 ff; Matthew 3:1, 4:17, 4:23, 9:35; Luke 8:1; Matthew 10:2; Luke 9:2; Matthew 24:14; and Acts 20:25, 28:31. See Dodd, *According to the Scriptures*. A noted theologian of the late twentieth century, Emmanuel Doronzo, expresses all of this as follows: "The very proper name 'Church,' which etymologically means convocation, shows the Church as a herald ever calling through the desert of this world and preparing the path of the Lord (see John 1:23, from Is. 11:12), inviting to itself those who have not yet believed" *(The Church* [Middleburg, VA: Notre Dame Institute Press, 1976], p. 258). All of this merits discussion with cate-chists, for it helps them see their work in its proper light.

58. The words throughout the Gospels in the roots *keryx-* and *didask-* establish the biblical foundations for distinguishing Evangelization and Catechesis. See *GCD* 18, "Catechesis and Evangelization," and *CT*, nos. 19–26. "Since catechesis is a moment or aspect of evangelization, its content cannot be anything else but the content of evangelization as a whole" *(CT* no. 26). Catechetics therefore is a teach-ing that has a prophetic and messianic quality or dimension.

59. See note 50. There is an abusive use of the word *kerygmatic* that surfaced in the field of catechetics shortly after the mid–twentieth century when the Neo-Modernist movement in religious education was being prepared. This new and arbitrary meaning imposed upon a word that has its own original and important meaning in the Church of the Apostles will be analyzed in its proper place in volume 2 of this manual, when the nature of the Neo-Modernist movement is dis-cussed.

60. The lives of Christ point out Jesus' great physical endurance in his journeys on foot in Palestine. He was in no sense Nietzsche's imaginary "Pale Galilean."

61. See Luigi Civardi, *Gesú Educatore* (Torino: S.E.T., 1962), p. 72: "I discepoli sono una *turba*"; the *mathetai* are a *crowd*. See chapter 3, "A chi insegna," pp. 53–88. As Civardi points out, the use of the word *mathetēs*, "disciple," occurs practi-cally "on every page of the Gospels," but it is used in two senses: "In the strict sense it signifies the Twelve of the Apostolic College . . . while in the broad sense it designates together with the Twelve the large body of the rest of the disciples."

62. See Mark 1:27–33, Matthew 21:23–27, Luke 19:47–48 and 20:1–8, and John 4:1–3. Jesus' support from the population caused a stand-off until the betrayal took place.

63. This has been described in chapter 4. And see Rengstorf on *mathetēs* in Kittel, *TDNT.*

64. The confusion among the people due to the resistance to Jesus from the government at Jerusalem is clear throughout the Gospels. There is also the elevated and demanding nature of his teaching, as John 6 on the promise of the Eucharist describes: "After this many of his disciples drew back and no longer went about with him" (John 6:66).

65. How did Jesus Christ teach and train and form this special group, the Twelve? The Gospels, written from within this same group of Twelve, bear witness. One must turn to them, reading them simply as they were written and carried carefully across the centuries to this current moment. For a helpful study of the Gospels from the point of view of Jesus' training of his Twelve Apostles, see Felix Klein, *Jesus and His Apostles* (New York: Longmans, 1932); Antonio Ammassari, *I Dodici: Note e segetiche sulla vocazione degli Apostoli* (Rome: Città Nuova, 1982);

Karl Hermann Schelkle, *Jüngerschaft und Apostelamt* (Freiburg: Herder, 1957); and Marco Adinolfi, *L'apostolato dei Dodici nella vita di Gesù* (Milan: Edizioni Paoline, 1985). The present summary of Jesus' method and the content he communicated to his Twelve by means of his method is not intended to replace the Gospels but rather to lead further into the study of them from the catechetical point of view, from the perspective of Jesus as the Master Teacher in Israel.

66. See A. Dwight Culler, *The Imperial Intellect: A Study of Newman's Educational Ideal* (New Haven: Yale University Press, 1955).

67. Jesus' example of celibacy as a way of human life is closely connected with his priestly mediation and bears witness to the fact that human sexuality in its exercise is not the purpose of human life. Hence this aspect of Jesus' teaching by example is studied best in the many more recent documents of the Holy See on priestly celibacy and on the principles of sound formation of young men for the priesthood. For a penetrating short discussion of Jesus' example of celibacy in the context of contemporary problematic, see Cardinal Luigi Ciappi, "Il celibato sacerdotale nella luce trasfigurante di Cristo," *L'Osservatore Romano, Italian Edition* (July 30, 1967), p. 2. Jesus Christ's example of prayer as essential to human life is treated customarily in the lives of Christ that distinguished the decades of the twentieth century between the second and third manifestations of the Modernist Crisis. For an excellent treatment of Jesus' teaching of prayer to the Twelve, see Klein, *Jesus and His Apostles,* chapter 6, "Pray Thus," pp. 183–94.

68. The lives of Christ reconstruct these trips apart with the Twelve Apostles. And see Carlo M. Martini, *L'itinerario Spirituale dei Dodici* (Rome: Borla, 1983).

69. F. Prat, S.J., *La théologie de Saint Paul,* vol. 1 (Paris: Beauchesne, 1933), p. 35.

70. See Henri de Lubac, S.J., *The Christian Faith* (San Francisco: Ignatius 1987). Cardinal de Lubac calls his work "an essay on the structure of the Apostles' Creed" and states that he did it to help catechists in the confusion and chaos that beset religious education in the aftermath of Vatican II. It is a basic resource for all catechetical teachers.

71. This is a basic fundamental of Biblical Catechetics and a vital one for discussion with catechists. Jesus is the founder of the Seven Sacraments, as the Church has solemnly defined (D-S 1601). It follows that the Profession of Faith in Baptism comes from him. This Profession has been the interrogatory form of the Apostles' Creed since the Apostolic Church. Catechetics then becomes the teaching process in which this same Profession of Faith is first explained and then applied to life by the triple response of prayer, Gospel morality, and Eucharistic living. In other words, Jesus stands at the origin of the Apostolic Tradition, the Ordinary and Universal Magisterium of the Catholic Church, and of the catechesis that continues his own teaching program. All of this will be elaborated in volume 2 of this manual. It is likewise the operating principle of chapter 8 of this volume.

72. Dodd, *According to the Scriptures,* pp. 109–10; France, *Jesus and the Old Testament;* "The Originality and Influence of Jesus. Jesus saw the fulfillment of the predictions and foreshadowings of the Old Testament in himself and his work. From this sprang his constant emphasis on the true character of the Messiah not as a conqueror and ruler, in any worldly or political sense, whether violent or peaceful, but as one who through lowliness and suffering would achieve the spiritual restoration of his people" (pp. 223–224); "The school in which the writers of the early church learned to use the Old Testament was that of Jews. . . . The church did not create Jesus, but Jesus created the church" (pp. 225–26). Return will be

made to this fundamental point in volume 2 of this manual when the origin of the Apostolic writings of the New Testament is considered. Clearly the study of Jesus the Divine Teacher offers to catechists the solution to the contrast between the Jesus of history and the Christ of faith that agonizes a false type of Scripture scholarship in modern times.

Chapter 8. The Credal Summary of Jesus' Teaching

1. *DS* 3020 and 3043; John J. Broderick, S.J., (trans.), *Documents of Vatican Council I* (Collegeville: Liturgical Press, 1971), pp. 48 and 51.

2. The prophetic light is discussed in chapter 2. Since this Deposit of Faith and Morals is the content of catechetical teaching, this is a basic fundamental of biblical Catechetics and should be at the center of all catechists and the training of catechists. This is what enables the catechumen to receive this Deposit of Doctrine from parents or catechists as the very Word of God, on the authority of God revealing. "We thank God constantly for this," Saint Paul writes to his Thessalonians, "that when you received this word of God which you heard from us, you accepted it not as the word of men but as it really is, the word of God, which is at work in you believers" (1 Thess. 2:13). This is at the heart of all catechetical teaching, whether at Saint Paul's time or in the present day.

3. For the text of the Creed of the People of God (June 30, 1968), see Eugene Kevane, *Creed and Catechetics: A Catechetical Commentary on the Creed of the People of God* (Westminster, MD: Christian Classics, 1978), p. 9–27. This Creed, as Pope Paul VI says in his introduction, "repeats in substance, with some developments called for by the spiritual condition of our time, the Creed of Nicea, the Creed of the immortal Tradition of the Holy Church of God. In making this profession, we are aware of the disquiet which agitates certain groups of men with regard to the faith" (p. 11). And see Candido Pozo, S.J., *The Credo of the People of God: A Theological Commentary,* trans. Mark Pilon (Chicago: Franciscan Herald Press, 1980). The original Spanish edition of Pozo's work was used in the Catechetical Commentary earlier.

4. See Jules Lebreton, S.J., *The Spiritual Teaching of the New Testament* (London: Burns and Oates, 1960), chapter 1, "God, Our Creator and Father," pp. 3–26.

5. *Ibid.*, pp. 3–4.

6. For the training of catechists and for catechists in their teaching, this theism of Jesus is essential in the current atheistic and pantheistic age. Many topics for discussion are offered by the document of Pope Paul VI "Evangelization in the Modern World" (December 8, 1975), in Eugene Kevane (ed.), *Teaching the Catholic Faith Today: Twentieth Century Catechetical Documents of the Holy See* (Boston: St. Paul Editions, 1982), pp. 145–207; also see *The General Catechetical Directory,* nos. 47–49, on God and his genuine worship in a secularized world (pp. 79–81).

7. In the writings of the Old Testament the plural *Elohim* is often used in addressing Jahweh; God himself when speaking of himself frequently uses the word *we.* See P. F. Ceuppens O.P. *De Sanctissima Trinitate* (Rome: Marietti, 1949), volume 2 of his *Biblical Theology.*

8. Some in the times of the modern apostasy have attempted to derive the doctrine of the Trinity from the later influence of the pantheistic Greek environment, but to no avail. The Gospels present it clearly as the doctrine of Jesus the Divine Teacher.

9. When heard by a Jewish audience, Jesus' initial programmatic call in Mark 1:14–15 is already a theophany. It is the philosophical error of modern times to prejudge that such a revelation of God to mankind is impossible. In the current "Reality of the Problem" *(GCD,* part 1), this needs explanation and discussion with catechists and with catechumens. For the current crisis of faith derives from the pressure of this secularized and atheistic social environment.

10. The writings of the New Testament came out of this school, in which Jesus taught and formed the Twelve. In it the fulfillment and mediation of Divine Revelation were taught, seen, experienced, if one will: in a word, *learned* and *understood* in a way that could be handed on by them in their own teaching. Thus all catechesis continues to do the same thing, handing on an order of knowledge higher than the human natural sciences and philosophies.

11. Both the Creed and the catechetical teaching and explanation of its Articles come directly forth from Jesus' teaching, a teaching that is actually Divine Revelation taking place. Joseph De Ghellinck, S.J., makes this clear in his *Recherches sur l'origine du Symbole* (Paris: Desclée, 1949), p. 270:

> The Incarnation is at the basis of our knowledge of the Trinity. . . . The revelation of the trinitarian doctrine in the New Testament is accomplished by the mediation of the Son. . . . In this sense, it is exact to say that the Trinity is based on Christology, the Christology that Jesus himself accomplished and taught by his Self-revelation, and not on a Christology coming one knows not from where that wishes to take the Christ out of Jesus. The mystery of the Son of God is the center of the Faith and in particular of the trinitarian dogma: Jesus Christ *IS* the Son, whose coming by itself manifests the Father and gives us to know the Holy Spirit.

12. See Matthew 11:29: "Learn from me; for I am meek and humble of heart." The imitation and following of Christ has become an essential part of Christian spiritual life, as the classic *Imitation of Christ* by Thomas à Kempis bears witness. All human education from Homer through the ages has had the twofold process of instruction in doctrine and the holding up of models and examples for the young to imitate. Jesus the Divine Teacher retains this human process.

13. All catechetical teaching must necessarily contain instruction and formation in prayer and the practice of daily prayer. This teaching in order to be fruitful must be sustained by the prayer of both the catechist and the catechumens. Volume 2 of this manual will study the teaching of prayer in the writings of the Fathers, in Saint Teresa of Avila in her *Way of Perfection,* and especially in the *Roman Catechism.*

14. In recent times as part of the crisis of faith among some theologians a special problem has been created for catechists. It is the idea that Jesus only learned gradually in his life who he is. This is contrary to the credal rule of faith since the Apostles. Jesus was the Divine Teacher, not a learner. It was the Twelve who were learning. See William G. Most, *The Consciousness of Christ* (Front Royal, VA: Christendom College Press, 1980).

15. See John 8:57–59: "The Jews then said to him, 'You are not yet fifty years old, and have you seen Abraham?' Jesus said to them, 'Truly, truly. I say to you, before Abraham was, I am.' So they took up stones to throw at him." They recognized immediately that he was applying the Divine Name, Yahweh, *I AM,* to himself. There are many such *"I am"* passages in all four Gospels. The Twelve report his divine works and these verbal revelations of Jesus' divinity in the Gospels that were written later under their authority and supervision.

16. In a mysterious way the Holy Spirit proceeds from the Father and the Son: he is the divine love that unites the eternal Father and eternal Son. Christian prayer and prayerful thought will develop treatises on the Mystery of the Trinity, for example Saint Augustine's *De Trinitate*. For the classic work of the twentieth century, see Jules Lebreton, S.J., *History of the Dogma of the Trinity from its Origins to the Council of Nicaea* (2 vols.) (London: Burns, Oates and Wachbourne, 1939). The origins are in the Bible as a whole, fully revealed in the New Testament.

17. Lebreton, *History of the Dogma of the Trinity*, vol. 2 "Introduction," p. xxiii; and see vol. 1, pp. 252–58.

18. It is a fundamental of biblical Catechetics to recognize the substance of the Apostles' Creed in the New Testament, especially in the Gospels that report Jesus' teaching. Catechists need help to see the perfect consistency and harmony among the pattern, syllabus, and content of the teaching program of the catechumenate, in volume 2 of this manual, and this teaching by Jesus of the Trinitarian faith to which the Gospels bear witness. There has been much research in the twentieth century on the roots of the Apostles' Creed in the New Testament. See Lebreton, *History of the Dogma of the Trinity*, vol. 1, and the excellent Protestant work of Prof. Paul Feine, *Die Gestalt des apostolischen Glaubenshekenntnisses in der Zeit des Neuen Testaments* (Leipzig: 1925), on the form of the Apostles Creed at the time of the New Testament.

19. Meditative reflection on Mary and her privileges has been a part of Christian spiritual life across the centuries; see, for example, *The Glories of Mary* by Saint Alphonsus Liguori.

20. Jesus does not include his mother among the Twelve men whom he ordained into their kind of ministerial priesthood at the end of their course of training. As the new Eve she has a priestly ministry of love in the dimensions of her spiritual motherhood of her son's Church.

21. For a defense of the Infancy Gospel against the one-sided "purely rational exegesis," see René Laurentin, *The Truth of Christmas beyond the Myths* (Petersham, MA: St. Bede's Publications, 1986).

22. Lebreton, *The Spiritual Teaching of the New Testament*, pp. 37–38 and 51, and see all of chapter 2, "Men, the Slaves of Sin," pp. 27–54, especially pp. 51–54, "The Hatred of God," on the satanic quality of the opposition to Jesus' teaching and presence to which the gospel according to Saint John witness with special lucidity. For the abiding classic on this matter of sin, most helpful for catechetical teachers, see M. J. Scheeben, *The Mysteries of Christianity* (Saint Louis: B. Herder, 1946), part 3, "The Mystery of Sin," pp. 243–310.

23. This is of course the false Messianic Expectation, discussed earlier, especially in chapter 5. See in general Joseph Pickly, *The Messias* (Saint Louis: B. Herder, 1946), especially chapter 2, "Messianic Expectation," pp. 43–62, and chapter 3, "Struggles for Freedom," pp. 63–96.

24. Hoskyns and Davey, *The Riddle of the New Testament* (London: Faber and Faber, 1931), p. 165.

25. For the meaning of the Greek words *Apostle, Apostolicity, Catholic,* and *Catholicity,* see Gerhard Kittel, *Theological Dictionary of the New Testament,* trans. Bromiley (10 vols.) (Grand Rapids: Eerdmans, 1964–75). For the modern classic on the Apostolicity of the Catholic Church, see Charles Journet, *The Church of the Word Incarnate* (London: Sheed and Ward, 1955), Volume One, *The Apostolic Hierarchy.*

26. Charles Journet, *The Church of the Word Incarnate,* vol. 1: *The Apostolic Hierarchy* (London: Sheed and Ward, 1955), p. 131. Journet continues: "However,

Christ left it to the Apostles to promulgate, that is, authoritatively to notify and make obligatory the other sacraments. Thus Confirmation is only fully made known to us by the Acts of the Apostles (7:17 and 19:6), Extreme Unction by the Epistle of St. James (5:14); and the dignity of Matrimony by that of St. Paul to the Ephesians (5:21)" (*ibid.*, citing Denz. 844, 926, 969, 996, 2088 [older numeration]). "Christ instituted the chief sacraments, such as Baptism and the Eucharist, in detail," Journet concludes: "He could deal with the rest in a more general way, leaving the Church a certain latitude for the concrete determination, even modification, in the course of time." These basic positions on the founding of the Seven Sacraments by Christ, their new divine power to cause what they signify, namely, the giving of the Holy Spirit and his graces, the fact that they are therefore Sacraments of Faith, of the Catholic Faith in Jesus' Person and Natures, and the authority over his Sacraments that Jesus taught his Twelve to exercise (and through them their successors) are of course basic for catechists. These truths and principles belong to fundamental Catechetics in a special way. It is important when preparing catechetical teachers for their work to help them see the sacramental system of the Catholic Church as deriving directly from Jesus in and through his teaching of the Twelve to be the Founders and foundations of his Church.

27. It is fundamental in catechetical teaching to recognize the result of the continuing opposition of the authorities at Jerusalem to John the Baptist's announcement and Jesus' teaching mission. It led eventually to Peter's transfer of his office and function to Rome, the world capital of the Gentile nations, which thus became the New Jerusalem, the City of the Holy One of Israel in fulfillment of all the Prophets. In A.D. 70, as a matter of historical fact, the physical city of Jerusalem was utterly destroyed together with its Temple. From that time the animal sacrifices of the Old Law offered by the Levitical Priesthood have ceased. They have been replaced by the Eucharistic Sacrifice of the New Testament, offered in every place. All of this will be an important theme in volume 2 of this manual.

28. The liturgical feast of the Epiphany continues to celebrate in the Catholic Church this universal aspect of Jesus' teaching program in and through his extension of it to the Gentile people by the Church founded upon his Apostles, trained, mandated, and sent by himself.

29. These are the words professed by the Catholic Church in the Creed of the People of God. See Antonio Piolanti, *Dio nel mondo e nell'Uomo* (Rome: Desclée, 1959), p. 272: "In Sacred Scripture it is affirmed explicitly that the soul is a spirit completely distinct from the body, the subsisting form which preserves its reality also after the destruction of the material part of man; see Eccl. 12:7; and Mt. 10:28, 'Do not fear those who kill the body but cannot kill the soul.' See also John 5:17, Luke 23:46, Acts 7:59. In Saint Paul the parallelism is affirmed frequently between flesh and spirit (see Rom. 5:8; 1 Cor. 15:44)." This is a timely topic for discussion with catechists, both in general and especially because the Modernist movement in the twentieth century has been claiming that this dualism is not scriptural but a derivative from Greek philosophy.

30. Journet, *The Apostolic Hierarchy*, p. 134.

31. It is a hallmark of the Modernist approach that it wishes always to have Jesus ignorant of various things, just as it resists recognizing the dogmas of the Church Jesus sent to teach all nations as the proximate rule of faith in Divine Revelation. These are the two surest signs of the Modernist approach: what it holds about Jesus' knowledge when he was teaching his Twelve and what it holds about the dogmas of the Teaching Church that he built upon his Twelve. From these

signs, catechists can know whether a writer is a person of the Catholic Faith in the Divinity of Christ as the Catholic creed professes. See the reference to the work of William G. Most in note 14.

32. Emmanual Doronzo, *The Church* (Middleburg, VA: Notre Dame Institute Press, 1976), p. 258; the internal quotation is from Vatican I, *Const. Dei Filius*, chapter 3 (Denz. 3014); and the reference to the pilgrim Church is from Vatican II, *Decree on Ecumenism*, no. 2. For a compact and competent theological summary of the doctrine on the Last Things, see A. Piolanti, *De Novissimis* (Rome: Marietti, 1949).

Chapter 9. The Redemption: Jesus Our Divine Savior

1. St. Pius X, *Catechism of Christian Doctrine* (Arlington, VA: Center for Family Catechetics, 1980), p. 115.

2. The Fathers of the Church catechized in this manner, awakening the response of love, of conversion to God and aversion from sin, by instilling this double motivation, that of Jesus and that of the response of those for whom he suffered, died, and rose again to manifest the fact of the resurrection of the body and life everlasting. In volume 2 of this manual the *First Catechetical Instruction* will be analyzed in illustration.

3. It is noteworthy that the *GCD* cites Vatican II, *Gaudium et Spes*, no. 18, the paragraph that leads directly into the discussion of the Council on the kinds of Atheism and their causes: "Christ won this victory (over bodily death) when he rose to life, for by his death he freed man from death. Faith, therefore, with its solidly based teaching, provides every thoughtful man with an answer to his anxious queries about his future lot." By keeping catechesis in focus upon these realities of the human situation and the hope given by the Catholic faith, catechists become able to cope with the atheistic atmosphere described by Saint Pius X.

4. Papal Commission for Biblical Studies, *On Bible Research* (April 21, 1964) (Washington: NCWC, 1964), no. 11. Catechetical teachers are referred to this Document of the Magisterium as a whole, which when combined with the Constitution *Dei Filius* of Vatican I and the Constitution *Dei Verbum* of Vatican II makes clear the historicity of the Gospels and the reliability of their witness to the teaching of Jesus Christ.

5. See Pope Paul VI, "Apostolic Exhortation to All the Bishops" (December 8, 1970): "In fact it is not we who are judges of the Word of God. It is His Word which judges us and exposes our habit of conforming to this world. The weakness and insufficiency of Christians, even of those who have the function of preaching, will never be a reason for the Church to water down the absolute nature of the Word. The edge of the sword can never be dulled thereby. The Church can never speak otherwise than as Christ did of holiness, virginity, poverty and obedience" (in Eugene Kevane, *Creed and Catechetics: A Cathetical Commentary on the Creed of the People of God* (Westminster: Christian Classics, 1978), p. 199; see the document as a whole (*ibid.*, pp. 195–204) for a remarkable presentation of Jesus' teaching by one of his Vicars, a successor of Peter twenty centuries later. All of this is an apt topic for discussion in training catechists and for catechists in their teaching.

6. For the newer scholarship on the writings of the beloved disciple, see John A. T. Robinson, *Redating the New Testament* (Philadelphia: Westminster, 1976), pp. 254–311.

7. See Roman B. Halas, O.F.M., *Judas Iscariot: A Scriptural and Theological Study of His Person, His Deeds and His Eternal Lot* (Washington, DC: Catholic University Press, 1946), with the bibliography.

8. See R. B. Halas, op. cit., chapter 6, "The Betrayal," pp. 73–93. "The betrayal was no sudden act," Halas writes (pp. 71–72); "he had been slowly gravitating toward it." Judas Iscariot was "tired of hearing Jesus always announcing his kingdom without ever inaugurating it" (p. 82). Loss of faith was the substance of Judas's betrayal, and its chief motive, as Saint Augustine teaches, a dimension of misguided religiosity that will recur throughout the life of the Church across the centuries and not least in the "Crisis of Faith" experienced and suffered by the Church of the late twentieth century.

9. *Ibid.*, p. 61.

10. *Ibid.*, p. 64.

11. In the Latin Rite the name for this Sacrifice has been for centuries of popular usage the Holy Sacrifice of the Mass. It is taken from the *Ite, Missa est,* "Go, the Mass is ended," the dismissal of the congregation at the end of the celebration.

12. For Jesus' preparation, see Luke 22:7–13 (with Mark 14:12–16 and Matthew 26:17–19). "Then came the day of Unleavened Bread, on which the passover lamb had to be sacrificed. So Jesus sent Peter and John, saying, 'Go and prepare the passover. . . . The householder will show you a large upper room furnished; see Matthew 26:26–29, Mark 14:23–25, and Luke 22:19–20, with 1 Corinthians' " 11:23–27. Catechists should read these central passages of the Catholic faith carefully. The summary in the text only describes the setting, showing the way the Gospel of Saint John relates to the Synoptics. What Jesus said to his Twelve at the Last Supper (John 14–17) is the fountainhead of Christian doctrine and spirituality; it is basic in preparing catechists for their teaching.

13. See M. J. Lagrange, O.P., *Évangile selon Saint Jean* (Paris: Gabalda, 1925), p. 397; and Felix Klein, *Jesus and His Apostles* (New York: Longmans, 1932), pp. 295–297:

> With the most recent and most authoritative commentators, notably with Père Lagrange and Dom Paul DeLatte, we see in it rather the indication of a simple movement within the Cenacle itself. . . . What was this movement?. . . Between the end of the legal Pasch (of the Jews) and the departure for the Garden of the Agony what was it that happened?. . . It is here that we become conscious of a mysterious and holy calm which invades the Cenacle. . . . In concordant testimony, St. Matthew, St. Mark, St. Luke and St. Paul are about to tell us of the institution of the Eucharist and the essential function of the priesthood. . . . St. John does better than repeat the account of the others. . . . He relates, and is alone in doing so, the admirable prayer of thanksgiving with which Jesus, the Eternal Priest, concludes the first Mass and the first Communion (pp. 296–97).

14. This Upper Room, called the Cenacle, has been preserved across the centuries. It is in a complex owned by Mohammedans who with fine religious sensibility have preserved it intact and keep it open daily for a constant flow of Christian pilgrims. Catholics venerate it as the site of the Last Supper, the first Mass, the first Catholic Church, and the first Holy See of Saint Peter, the seat of his authority as the Vicar of Christ. Here the infant Church met in prayer in the days after the Resurrection. Here the Holy Spirit descended at Pentecost. Here the Church gathered to pray for Peter when he was in chains and under sentence of death. The Cenacle is indeed a spacious room: if equipped with seating it could

accommodate easily 150 persons. Well-to-do Jewish families kept their upper rooms, reached by an outside staircase, for festive occasions of family and friends. It has been handed down traditionally that this family, followers of Jesus, had a young son who became Saint Peter's associate and the author of the Gospel according to Saint Mark.

15. This reconstruction reflects the standard Christian altar across the centuries since the Apostles, essentially a table of wood or stone about forty-two inches high. This reconstruction at a separate location is supported by Luke 22:17 and 22:20, where it is clear that the chalice used for the Passover wine was different from the chalice for the Eucharist. So Klein, *Jesus and His Apostles*, p. 284: "The Gospel of St. Luke distinguishes very clearly the chalice served at the beginning of the supper from that which 'after he had supped' (Lk. 22:20) was used for the blood of Christ."

16. Catechists today are challenged by several current aberrations in the doctrine of the Holy Eucharist. One of the chief ones is the notion that the Eucharist and the Passover do not differ; another is the idea that the Mass is nothing but a continuation of the ordinary meals of Jesus with his disciples during his public life. See DS 1635–61 for the defined doctrine of the Church on the Eucharistic Sacrifice. And see the German Bishops' Conference, *The Church's Confession of Faith* (San Francisco: Ignatius, 1987), pp. 287–296, and above all *The Creed of the People of God*, nos. 24–26.

17. Klein, *Jesus and His Apostles*, p. 301.

18. For the solemnly defined doctrine of the Catholic Church on these points, see D-S 1635–42 and 1651–61. And see *The Creed of the People of God*, nos. 24–26, in Eugene Kevane (ed.), *Teaching the Catholic Faith Today: Twentieth Century Catechetical Documents of the Holy See.* (Boston: St. Paul Editions, 1982), pp. 37–38. Among the most damaging aberrations that face catechists today is the idea that the offering of the Sacrifice of the Mass takes place by the offertory procession. This misconceives the nature of the Eucharistic Sacrifice and of the Priesthood, opening the door to loss of reverence and mere noisy human togetherness. The doctrine of the faith teaches that the offering of the Sacrifice is accomplished by the separate consecration of the bread and wine, done by a priest who stands within the succession of priestly power from Jesus and his Apostles. "At the offertory and the offertory procession," to quote a leading theologian, Emmanuel Doronzo, "the Church offers the bread and wine not in sacrifice, but as the elements in which the transubstantiation will take place and the Eucharistic Sacrifice will be offered," *De Eucharistia* (Milwaukee: Bruce, 1948), p. 1032. See also the Congregation for the Doctrine of the Faith, *Letter concerning the Minister of the Eucharist* (Boston: St. Paul Editions, 1983).

19. See Herbert Haag, *Vom alten zum neuen Pascha* (Stuttgart: KBW, 1971), "Umstiftung," pp. 60–67. This German word expresses well the idea of a new institution or new foundation that preserves the nature and character of the old *Stiftung.* Here the *Stiftung* is the institution of worship of God by sacrifice among all tribes and peoples back to the earliest beginnings of mankind. It was a worship of the Lord God of Creation. Moses by the Passover Sacrifice reinstituted it as a worship of the Lord God of History. Jesus gave it its final reinstitution as the Eucharistic Sacrifice of the New Testament, the way of personal Passover to eternal life in heaven. This *Stiftung* is the basic institution of mankind, the worship of God the Creator by sacrifice. Always the sacrifice is constituted by the offering of a victim, which has been immolated. The victim must be really present: the primitives

in offering the first fruits of their gathering always immolate or set aside for God something gathered today. They never "offer" something to be gathered tomorrow. Jesus culminates the refoundation of this universal institution of mankind by making himself, the Victim immolated on the Cross, really present under the sacramental veils, whether that evening in the Cenacle or in every future place among the Gentiles when his priests "do this" in his Person and by his mandate and power. For the general concept of sacrifice as the offering of an immolated victim, see Doronzo, *De Eucharistia*, vol. 2, pp. 786–827. For the teaching of Saint Thomas Aquinas, see the *Summa Theologiae* (1964), II-II, q. 85 and q. 86, art. 1.

20. St. Pius X, *Catechism of Christian Doctrine, op. cit.*, p. 57. It is significant that this official catechism does not use the word *transubstantiation*. Since it is a catechism of the elements of Christian Doctrine intended for children and adult beginners, it teaches the same reality by using the words of ordinary speech.

21. The Sign of the Cross has been the hallmark of the Catholic Christian across the centuries since the Apostles. It is an outward profession of faith in the Holy Trinity and the Redemption on the Cross by the Sacred Person incarnate. Catechists give formation when they teach how to make this sign, for it is a summary of the entire Deposit of Faith.

22. The living catechetical tradition of the Earliest Church is witnessed at Acts 2:23, 32, 3:15, 4:10, and 5:30 and, indeed, throughout the Acts and the Epistles. "But we would not have you ignorant, brethren," Saint Paul writes, "concerning those who have fallen asleep, that you may not grieve as others do who have no hope. For since we believe that Jesus died and rose again, even so, through Jesus, God will bring with him those who have fallen asleep" (1 Thess. 4:13–14). This Christian hope casts its light over all catechetical teaching and forms the catechumens in love for the Redeemer and in thanksgiving for his Redemption.

23. Heinrich Schlier, *La Résurrection de Jésus-Christ* (Paris: Casterman, 1969), p. 10.

24. *Ibid.*, pp. 13–14. It has been pointed out many times across the centuries, and not least in the twentieth century, that discrepancies in the secondary facts surrounding a central fact are the hallmark of authentic eyewitness accounts. Auto accidents are a continuing illustration of the point.

25. The catechetical apostolate is basically a witnessing to the Resurrection of Jesus. All catechists bear this witness and teach joyfully in its light. The addresses of the popes at Eastertime reported in the *Osservatore Romano* give helpful examples of this witness. See, for one example, Paul VI, "We Are Witnesses" (to a General Audience, April 5, 1972):

> Note two things. First: Jesus rose again with the same body he had taken from the Blessed Virgin, but in new conditions, vivified by a new and immortal animation, which imposes on Christ's flesh the laws and energies of the Spirit. The wonder does not wipe out the reality; on the contrary it is the new reality. Second: this new reality, which has been documented in the invincible proofs of the Gospel and afterwards of the Church living by those testimonies, is so far above our capacities of knowledge and even of imagination, that it is necessary to make room for it in our minds through Faith (see John 20:9 and 20:27–28). Thus it was on Faith—on reasonable, credible Faith, but on Faith, not tangible, but tried, founded on the apostolic testimony and on Jesus' divine word—that the risen Christ founded his religious society, his Church, to which it is our fate to belong, thanks to his kindness and luckily for us.

26. See the *GCD*, no. 40: "Catechesis must necessarily be Christocentric." Clearly Jesus is continuing and confirming his way of teaching the divine authorship and unity of the Bible; see chapter 7.

27. This will be a basic theme of volume 2 of this manual. It is the very idea of the Apostolicity of the Catholic Church.

28. This is the definition of catechesis given in the *GCD*, no. 22: "Catechesis performs the function of disposing men to receive the action of the Holy Spirit and to deepen their conversion"; and see part 2 of the *GCD*, "The Ministry of the Word," nos. 10–35, as a whole.

29. A constant principle of catechetical teaching is the fact that Divine Revelation to mankind closed with the teaching that Jesus gave to his Apostles. After the Apostles comes the handing on of this revealed truth in its purity and integrity by teaching. The ordinary form of this teaching is chiefly Catechetics. This will be a principal theme of volume 2 of this manual. See D-S 3421, 3459, and 3462. The nature of the Modernist Heresy becomes clearly visible at this point, for it believes in what it calls "Ongoing Revelation," holding that "with the progress of human knowledge it is sometimes possible that dogmas proposed by the Church can be given a meaning different from the one that the Church has understood and still understands" (D-S 3043).

30. This will be a theme of volume 2 of this manual. Language is so basic to Catechetics that it becomes the very substance of its rationale and the burning issue between the Apostolic teaching approach of Catholics in Catechetics and the experience approach of Modernists in their religious education.

31. See Gerhard Kittel, *Theological Dictionary of the New Testament* (Henceforth *TDNT*), trans. Bromiley, vol. 3 (London: Sheed and Ward), pp. 1039–95, for *Kyrios*; pp. 1060–88; for *Kyrios* as the Greek translation of the ineffable divine Name, Yahweh; pp. 1088–95 for "Jesus as Lord," and vol. 4, pp. 466–72 for *Maranatha*.

32. See *ibid.*; also Spadafora-Romeo-Frangipane, *Il Libro Sacro* (Padova: Edizioni Messaggero, 1958), "Il testo" (by F. Spadafora), pp. 191–257; and Enrico Castelli (ed.), *L'analyse du langage theologique: Le Nom de Dieu* (Paris: Aubier, 1969).

33. The Jerusalem Bible notes: "These Aramaic words ('The Lord is coming') had passed into liturgical use: they expressed the hope that the *parousia* would not be long delayed. An alternative reading [in the manuscript tradition] is *Maranatha* (Lord, come!)"; with references to Apocalypse 22:20; see Roman 13:12, Philippians 4:5, James 5:8, and 1 Peter 4:7. Lucien Cerfaux comments on p. 466 of *Christ in the Theology of St. Paul* (New York: Herder and Herder, 1966): "The Aramaic *Maranatha* survived the early period as one of the acclamations used in the worship of Christ." (An echo survives to this day in the *Kyrie eleison* of the Latin Mass of the Roman Rite.) And p. 464:"The Aramaic *Marana*, which corresponds to *Kyrios*, has a technical sense of Royal Prerogative, and Jesus is true King in virtue of the enthronement that came about through his resurrection. . . . The decisive event is the resurrection, after which Christ becomes the Lord for his disciples." It is important to recognize with careful scholars, for example W. Foerster *(Herr ist Jesus* [Gutersloh: 1924]) that the use of *Lord* for Jesus is Aramaic in origin, for *Marana* is witnessed in the Gospels together with *Rabbi*. The concept comes to the Greek from the Aramaic, and not vice versa. See Cerfaux, *Christ in the Theology of St. Paul*, p. 465: "The custom of calling a ruler 'Lord' (Kyrios) was an oriental one and made its way into Greek language and custom under the influence of oriental ideas. Almost everywhere in the East we find that kings were called 'Lord.'. . . . Among the Arameans, in particular, *Marana, Maran,* is essentially a royal title, applied exclusively to a reigning king . . . and there is no necessary connotation of emperor worship in the title."

34. Cerfaux, *Christ in the Theology of St. Paul*, p. 475. For catechetical discussion, see the *GCD*, paragraphs 40 and 53: "Catechesis ought daily to defend and strengthen belief in the divinity of Jesus Christ."

35. Werner Foerster, "Kyrios," in Kittel *TDNT,* vol. 3, p. 1089.

36. Cerfaux, *Christ in the Theology of St. Paul,* p. 464, and particularly see the entire chapter, "The Lord," pp. 461–79.

37. See chapter 8, points 9, 10, and 11 of his teaching.

38. For the Greek word *apostolos,* see Kittel, *TDNT,* vol. 1, p. 398–447.

39. There are many theological treatises on the Church, its powers, and its mark or quality of Apostolicity. Most helpful to catechists is the classic treatise of Charles Journet, *The Church of the Word Incarnate,* vol. 1: *The Apostolic Hierarchy* (London: Sheed and Ward, 1955); see especially chapter 10, "Apostolicity: Property and Note of the True Church," pp. 526–559.

40. See *ibid.,* "The Two Powers of the Apostolic Hierarchy," pp. 21–27.

41. *Ibid.,* p. 79.

42. See Chervin and Kevane, *Love of Wisdom: An Introduction to Christian Philosophy* (San Francisco: Ignatius, 1988). For the importance of this fundamental thinking in the catechesis of teenagers, see the *GCD,* no. 88.

43. Journet, *The Apostolic Hierarchy,* p. 39.

44. The Church founded by Jesus is "One, Holy, Catholic and Apostolic" (the Nicene Creed). For the fact that Apostolicity is the constitutive mark or quality upon which the other three depend, see Journet as cited in note 39.

45. Both the *GCD* and *Catechesi tradendae* offer many helpful topics for teaching and discussing these points.

Chapter 10. The Word of God

1. In the use of this manual for the training of parish catechists this aspect of the study should be explored and discussed with them, for it defines the self-image of the catechist today and specifies the nature of both Evangelization and Catechetics. When a catechist teaches what the Apostolic Church teaches in her official catechisms, the Word of God is being handed on to the catechumens.

2. Pope St. Pius X in his *Catechism of Christian Doctrine* (Arlington, VA: Center for Family Catechetics, 1975) is the prophet of reevangelization in the twentieth century. He writes there is a special circumstance today:

> An atmosphere of unbelief has been created which is most harmful to the interior and spiritual life. This atmosphere wages war upon any idea of a higher authority, any idea of God, of revelation, of the life to come, and of mortification in this life. Hence parents and teachers must inculcate with the greatest care the basic truths found in the first questions given in the catechism. Let them inspire in the children the Christian concept of life, and the sense of responsibility in each human act toward the Supreme Judge who is everywhere, knows everything and sees everything. Let them develop in the learner, together with the holy fear of God, the love of Christ and of the Church, a task for charity and for solid piety. Let them cultivate in the children a love for the virtues and for Christian practices. Only thus will the formation of children be founded on the rock of supernatural connections not to be overturned throughout their entire life, regardless of the storms that will come. Any other approach is an attempt to build the Christian formation of children on the sand of changeable ideas and mere human respect. (p. 115)

Saint Pius X gives these "basic truths," the true and real concept of God, in the first twenty-seven questions of his *Catechism.* They are actually the instrument for

Evangelization and should be used with any group of catechumens who indicate by their attitude that they have been infected with "the atmosphere of unbelief" described by the Saint. Catechists who turn to them whenever the atmosphere betrays its presence, often today even among children, let alone adolescents, find an extraordinary success. First Evangelization, then catechesis.

3. In the Heresy of Modernism since 1835 this very concept is denied; hence the Deposit of Faith is suppressed.

4. For catechists today, this is fundamental because it establishes the teaching approach and eliminates the so-called experience approach.

5. For the training of catechists and the teaching of catechumens it is important to clarify this true idea of God for them which is found in the Bible and defined by the Constitution *Dei Filius* of Vatican I. For the study of it see Chervin and Kevane, *Love of Wisdom: An Introduction to Christian Philosophy* (San Francisco: Ignatius, 1989).

6. See Heinrich Schlier, *Wort Gottes* (Wurzburg: Werkbund, 1962), pp. 9–10.

7. See 1 Thessalonians 2:13, Hebrews 12:25 ff, 1 Thessalonians 1:8, 2 Thessalonians 3:1, Colossians 3:16, and others.

8. Schlier, *Wort Gottes*, p. 10.

9. See the chapter on Moses and the Prophets in this manual for the idea of prophetic religion.

10. See Matthew 9:35–38, 10:1–33; Mark 6:7–13, 30; and Luke 9:1–6, 10:1–24.

11. Schlier, *Wort Gottes*, p. 13. This is basic for the self-image of catechists today. If I teach as a Minister of the Word in the Church according to the official catechisms that explain the Apostles' Creed and the triple response to it, I am handing on the Word of God. This applies above all to parents.

12. *Ibid.* Obviously, all this bears upon Evangelization and catechetical teaching today, in a way that remains to be analyzed in detail.

13. *Ibid.*, p. 14.

14. *Ibid.*, p. 13. Renewal of faith today and of the role and self-image of the priest and his catechists depends on recovering this basic fact—again in a way that remains to be studied in detail. It is essential to recover the official catechisms of the Church from the suppression they are currently suffering.

15. See also Acts 9:3–6, 17–20; 22:7–16; and 26:16–20.

16. See note 9.

17. This is vital for developing an authentic self-image in catechists today. It should be a part of the training of all catechists.

18. The *GCD*, no. 13, quoting the *Dei Verbum*, no. 8, of Vatican II.

19. See D-S 3011; see also *Catechesi tradendae*, no. 52.

20. *GCD*, no. 13, in Eugene Kevane (ed.), *Teaching the Catholic Faith Today: Twentieth Century Cathetical Documents of the Holy See* (Boston: St. Paul Editions, 1982), pp. 56–57.

21. *Ibid.*, Kevane (ed.), *Teaching the Catholic Faith Today*, p. 57.

22. *GCD*, no. 15, in Kevane (ed.), *Teaching the Catholic Faith Today*, p. 58.

23. *GCD*, no. 17, in Kevane (ed.), *Teaching the Catholic Faith Today*, p. 60.

24. *GCD*, no. 22, in Kevane (ed.), *Teaching the Catholic Faith Today*, pp. 62–63.

25. *GCD*, no. 24, in Kevane (ed.), *Teaching the Catholic Faith Today*, pp. 63–64. This is the false "experience approach" that results from the Heresy of Modernism to be studied later.

26. See *Catechesi tradendae*, no. 6, with nos. 7–9 and 30. No authentic catechist indulges in personal opinions.

27. Schlier, *Wort Gottes,* p. 17.

28. See Vatican I, *Dei Filius,* chapter 4, D-S 3020, in John J. Broderick, S.J. (trans.), *Documents of Vatican Council I* (Collegeville: Liturgical Press, 1971), p. 48. It is important for catechists to note this concept of "the Deposit of Faith"; it is the Word of God as handed on by teaching.

29. See *Catechesi tradendae,* no. 30; also note 26 and indeed *Catechesi tradendae* as a whole.

30. See the whole of chapter 9 in First Corinthians.

31. This is the essential message of *Catechesi tradendae:* that catechists be clear and complete on the objective meaning of that doctrine of the faith that the Church gives them to teach. Only so does the catechist give authentic personal witness to Jesus in his Lordship.

32. It goes without saying that this understanding of Jesus' intention and work is essential in the training of parents and catechists. For only this gives them their consciousness as teachers of the Word of God.

33. See John Paul II, *Letter concerning the Minister of the Eucharist* (August 6, 1983), citing Vatican II, *Lumen Gentium,* nos. 20 and 28.

34. See Schlier, *Wort Gottes,* chapter 3, "Das Evangelium in der Kirche," pp. 49–64; L. Cerfaux, *La Communaute Apostolique* (Paris: Cerf, 1953); and Karl Hermann Schelkle, *Jüngerschaft und Apostelamt* (Freiburg: Herder, 1957).

35. The phrase of Paul VI in the introduction to the Creed of the People of God.

36. See D-S 3011.

37. In teaching and training of seminarians and catechists, this should be a central concern; it is at the very heart of the ecclesiastical Science of Catechetics.

38. St. Augustine, *De vera religione,* 1(1), translated by J. H. S. Burleigh in *St. Augustine, of True Religion* (Chicago: Regnery, 1959), p. 1; for the Latin, see K. D. Daur (ed.), Vol. 3, *De vera religione* (Turnholt: Corpus Christianorum, 1962), p. 187. In Saint Augustine's time, the pantheistic polytheism was the prevalent error. Today it is the secularism and atheism of the once-Christian culture. But the metaphysical substrate of the errors is one and the same: it is a defective concept of God.

39. St. Augustine, *De vera religione,* 1(1), p. 4; for the Latin *ibid.* vol. 3, p. 3.

Chapter 11. The Evangelization and Catechetical Teaching of the Apostles

1. See Vatican I, *Dei Filius,* chapter 4, in John J. Broderick, S.J. (trans.), *The Documents of Vatican Council I* (Collegeville: Liturgical Press, 1971), p. 48.

2. Karl Hermann Schelkle, *Jüngerschaft und Apostelamt* (Freiburg: Herder, 1957), p. 133.

3. In the teaching and training of catechists today these questions and their answers are of fundamental importance. They give the catechist of today the self-image proper to a teacher of the Deposit of Faith in the present day and the sense of continuity of contemporary catechetical teaching with that of the Apostles. This establishes the Apostolicity of the Church as an ongoing process or tradition from the Apostles through the present. In programs for parish volunteer catechists, their priests and lay directors can draw upon these chapters as time and the nature of each group indicate, always linking the course with Jesus the Divine Teacher. For

the general background and remote preparation for such training courses, see the documents of the two Synods after Vatican II on Evangelization and catechesis in Eugene Kevane (ed.), *Teaching the Catholic Faith Today: Twentieth Century Catechetical Documents of the Holy See,* (Boston: St. Paul Editions, 1982), pp. 145–207 and 209–70. Always it should be stressed that the Catholic Church has had a doctrine since Jesus and his apostles; priests and catechists must continue this teaching in the same meaning it had for the Apostles.

4. Biblical scholarship notes that in the first ten chapters of Acts the Greek of Saint Luke indicates translation from Aramaic sources.

5. For *keryx* see chapter 7.

6. The current relevance is of course the primacy of the successors of Saint Peter. The Jerusalem Bible in its footnote on p. 203 gives the following instances of the *kerygma* as "prehistory" of the tradition of the teaching: Acts 2:14–36, 3:12–26, 4:8–12, 5:29–32 (Peter to the Sanhedrin), and 10:34–43 and Saint Paul's discourse at Antioch of Pisidia, Acts 13:16–41.

7. F. J. Badcock, *The History of the Creeds* (London: 1938), p. 123. He notes with Cerfaux that Christ as a proper name is only used in Greek Gentile circles. In the Jerusalem Kerygma, Jesus is the proper name, while "Messiah" ("Christ" in Greek) names the office of Jesus of Nazareth. Relevant to this credal meaning of the Jerusalem Kerygma is the literature of the *Symbolforschung,* the research on the Apostles' Creed. See also Lucien Cerfaux, *Christ in the Theology of St. Paul* (New York: 1966), p. 21: "This teaching (in 1 Cor. 15:1–8) has become the basis for the faith of the Church, and Paul speaks of it as a *paradosis,* a 'tradition' received from the community at Jerusalem, . . . already seen as a kind of 'symbol' or creed."

8. See Lucien Cerfaux, *The Spiritual Journey of St. Paul* (London: 1968), pp. 20–22, commenting on Acts 9, 22, and 26, where Saint Paul describes the revelation he received: "He *knew,* at once in a flash of thought which was not his own, that Jesus had risen and who Jesus really was. . . . The meaning of the vision was contained in the vision itself. God had revealed his Son in Paul (Gal. 1:16). The Son of God was the person of Jesus. . . . The lines of the only true Christology were fixed in his mind from the beginning of the vision . . . beyond human time . . . - where God alone is and where Christ was already present (see 1 Thess. 1:9–10, Rom. 1:3–4, and Gal. 4:4). No other Christology entered into his mind." This Christology of the preexistent Logos, the only true concept of Jesus, is the one given by the faith that comes from the Apostles and is proclaimed by the Jerusalem Kērygma of Saint Peter. It is important in the training of parish catechists that they see the primacy of Saint Peter manifested in the Jerusalem Kērygma and that they recognize two things about Saint Paul: he received his revelation from God about the person of Jesus, but he received the facts about Jesus and his redemption by being taught the faith that comes from the Apostles. For a comprehensive study of this matter, see Paul-Émile Langevin, S.J., *Jésus Seigneur et l'Eschatologie* (Paris: 1967).

9. Already one can see in Jesus' prophecy the coming structure of the Christian era. There will be a time of the Gentiles, and it will end, fulfilled somehow. This structure is important for catechists today and will be studied in volume 2 of this manual.

10. This "Rule of Faith" will emerge explicitly in the life of the Early Church and will be studied in volume 2 in the apostolic Fathers, especially Saint Irenaeus.

11. Saint Paul's self-image is properly that of each priest and catechist to this day. His declarations of this identity could well conclude each lesson of all courses of training for catechists. See the *GCD,* part 2, nos. 10–35, "The Ministry of the

Word." Saint Paul's self-concept is the animating principle of this ministry for catechists to this day.

12. See Pope Paul VI at Manila in 1970 and Liturgy of the Hours III 334–35, his address to the United Nations in New York. It has been brought several times to the reader's attention that "preach" usually translates a Greek word rooted in *keryx* in Saint Paul's inspired text. The *heralding* of the message or Word of God is in a far more powerful and meaningful concept than the word *preach* has come to mean. In the training of catechists, one should refer to the use of *keryx*, "herald," in Jesus' life and work, in chapter 70.

13. The catechist today has the same obligation, that of giving the teaching of the Church and not personal opinions. See *Catechesi tradendae,* nos. 6 and 30.

14. Cerfaux, *The Spiritual Journey of St. Paul,* p. 439. See, pp. 95–97; after giving a set of such statements by Saint Paul, Cerfaux comments: "These are relics of the formulas of the earliest Christians at Jerusalem." See also pp. 76–77 and 499–508.

15. *Ibid.,* p. 500.

16. *Ibid.,* p. 20. Note the recurrence of the fact of the teaching. There is no sign in the documents of earliest Christianity of a mere effervescence of experience as imagined by Hamack and his Liberal Protestantism and by Catholic Modernism.

17. The mostly German research in the last two centuries has made it clear that the substance of the Apostles' Creed is already in the New Testament. See J. N. D. Kelly, *Early Christian Creeds* (London: Longman, 1972).

18. Here one should recall the earlier discussions of the Bultmann School, which imagines a hiatus between the Jesus of history and the Christ of postcrucifixion faith. Jesus the Divine Teacher is the refutation of this modern philosophical imagination, for he taught his Apostles their faith.

19. This fact establishes the truth that the Early Church in the very New Testament itself was a *Teaching* Church. This is important for catechists today, who are solicited by the "experience approach" of the Heresy of Modernism in its religious education.

20. The Scandinavian school of exegesis has done much research on this. See Krister Stendahl, *The School of St. Matthew* (Lund: Gleerup, 1967). Saint Matthew was the Apostle most versed in literary and educational background, indeed, but Peter was in charge and all the Apostles participated in this program of teaching.

21. See Rengstorf in Gerhard Kittel, *Theological Dictionary of the New Testament,* (henceforth *TDNT*), trans. Bromiley, vol. 2 (Grand Rapids: Eerdmans, 1964–78), pp. 157–159: "The *didaskalei* of the Early Christian Community."

22. See Rengstorf in Kittel *TDNT,* vol. 2, p. 158:"We must be on our watch against the idea that there is an order of rank in the lists in 1 Cor. 12:28 ff. and Eph. 4:11. The order is purely material. The activity of the *didáskalos* (teacher) is needed only when that of the *apóstolos* and *prophétes* has laid the foundation for the Christian outlook and manner of life. . . . Once we understand 1 Cor. 12 and Eph. 4 in this way, 1 Tim. 2:7 and 2 Tim. 1:11 become plain. *Keryx* takes the place of *evangelistés,* and with *didáskalos* describes the twofold function of the *apóstolos.*" Rengstorf points out the similarity with Jesus, the *Keryx* in Matthew 4, the Evangelist who awakens the Faith; after this he emerges as the *didáskalos* in Matthew 5. It is the same today: Evangelization, then catechetical instruction.

23. Fernand Prat, S.J. *The Theology of St. Paul,* vol. 2 (Westminster: Newman, 1927), p. 30. Prat elaborates upon and stresses the fact that there was a system of instruction. See "The Apostolic Catechesis," pp. 28–35.

24. Again, the Church is a *Teaching* Church; it does not "give experiences." See note 19. Catechists today need to rediscover the Church's definite content and method in catechetical teaching.

25. See Jean Daniélou, *La catechesi nei primi secoli* (Torino: Elle Di Ci, 1969), p. 61.

26. Hermann Wolfgang Beyer, "Catechéo," in Kittel, *TDNT*, vol. 3, p. 638: "It means to impart instruction. . . . This is a late and rare word in secular Greek, which is not found at all in the Septuagint. Its basic meaning is 'to sound from above.' "

27. *Ibid.*

28. See Prat, *The Theology of St. Paul*, vol. 2, p. 28, also Cerfaux, *The Spiritual Journey of St. Paul*, p. 451: "The apostolic community treasured the teaching of the Master, without developing it very much."

29. Prat, *The Theology of St. Paul*, vol. 2, p. 28. See Cerfaux, *The Spiritual Journey of St. Paul*, p. 439: "In 1 Thess. 1:9 ff. we have the summary of the discourse of instruction which Paul preached to the pagans."

30. Prat, *The Theology of St. Paul*, p. 35. Professor Kittel agrees; see *TDNT*, vol. 2, p. 164: "Didache in Heb. 6:2 means an established and formulated doctrine."

31. See A. Seeberg, *Der Katechismus der Urchristenheit* (Leipzig: 1905). On p. 85, Seeberg gives his idea of "The Catechism of Earliest Christianity": "The living God, Creator of all things, sent his Son, born of the race of David, Jesus Christ, who died for us according to the Scriptures, was buried and rose again on the third day according to the Scriptures, sitteth at the right hand of God in heaven, having subjected to himself principalities, powers and dominions, and will return in the clouds of heaven invested with power and glory."

32. Prat, *The Theology of St. Paul*, vol. 2, p. 33.

33. For a comprehensive study of this tradition, see Robert I. Bradley, S.J., *The Roman Catechism as Illustrative of the "Classic Catechesis"* (New York: University Press of America, 1990). Also see Card. Joseph Ratzinger, "Sources and Transmission of the Faith," *Communio* (Spring 1983), p. 29.

34. Ratzinger, "Sources and Transmission of the Faith," p. 29.

35. Prat, *The Theology of St. Paul*, vol. 2, p. 31.

36. J. N. D. Kelly, *Early Christian Creeds* (London: 1950), pp. 7–8 and 10.

37. In training cadres of parish catechists, and for the self-study of parents and teachers of the Catholic faith, this point is of special practical value today, when the very idea of a Christian doctrine to be handed on has been largely lost in some parts of the world. This is because the very idea of a Word of God, given by Jesus as a sacred and teachable Deposit of Faith and Morals, has been weakened or has vanished among members of the Church. For this reason, the biblical truths discussed in these chapters, the concluding part of biblical Catechetics, should become part of the preparation of all catechists for their apostolate.

38. Prat, *The Theology of St. Paul*, vol. 2, p. 30. See Cerfaux, *The Spiritual Journey of St. Paul*, pp. 34–35: "Paul . . . never makes his conversion experience the basis for doctrine . . . but rather the *kerygma* illuminated by the prophecies of the Old Testament. . . . [Doctrine] is not a rationalizing of Christian experience." In other words, the Heresy of Modernism finds no support in the Bible.

39. See the first twenty-nine questions of the *Catechism of St. Pius X*, the "Basic Truths of the Christian Faith."

40. For the training of catechists today, see Pope John Paul II, *Catechesi tradendae* no. 55, on memorization on the elementary level of the teaching, in Kevane, *Teaching the Catholic Faith Today*, pp. 252–53.

41. See the *GCD,* no. 40: "Catechesis must necessarily be Christocentric." Again, therefore, the need for a biblical foundation for the training of catechists today. And see *Catechesi tradendae,* nos. 6, 20, 21, and 22.

42. See Rendel Harris, *Testimonies* (London: 1916) and especially C. H. Dodd, *According to the Scriptures* (2 vols.) (London: Collins, 1965). "The evidence suggests," Dodd writes (p. 126), "that at a very early date a certain method of biblical study was established and became a part of the equipment of Christian evangelists and teachers. This method was largely applied orally, and found literary expression only sporadically and incompletely, but it is presupposed in our earliest sources." It is the merit of the Scandinavian exegetes to call attention to the "School" that the Apostles, under the authority of St. Peter, conducted at the Cenacle after the crucifixion. See Krister Stendahl, *The School of St. Matthew and Its Use of the Old Testament* (Lund: Gleerup, 1967). Saint Matthew's Gospel is a direct result of this "Apostles' teaching" *(didachē* in the Greek) (Acts 2:42).

43. This positive and encouraging method is reflected in the very order of the four parts of the *Roman Catechism.* This is basic in the preparation of catechetical teachers and will be studied in detail in volume 2 of this manual.

44. The *GCD,* no. 22, defines the purpose of catechetical teaching in identical terms: "Catechesis performs the function of disposing men to receive the action of the Holy Spirit and to deepen their conversion." It goes without saying that this consciousness of purpose is essential for all catechists. The study of the Apostles helps to develop this purposefulness.

45. This is a point essential for catechists and parents today and their training courses. There is nothing in the Bible about the current notion that acts make no difference but only the fundamental option that is imagined to perdure through any and all actions contrary to the law of God.

46. In the training of catechists today, this biblical fact needs to be stressed, for this is the characteristic teaching of the Heresy of Modernism.

47. Hence the admonition of Jesus to pray, to watch and pray always, lest temptation pull the catechumens back into the sins of the old nature, is a part of catechetical teaching on all levels, especially the elementary level of children.

48. Prat, *The Theology of St. Paul,* vol. 2, p. 35. See Acts 13:10, 16:17, 18:25, 22:4, and 24:22. Saint Paul says the same to the Corinthians: "Therefore I sent to you Timothy . . . to remind you of my ways in Christ, as I teach [verb in *didask-]* them everywhere in every church" (1 Cor. 4:17).

49. In the later Patristic Age and confined to the Latin West, a pious legend grew up that imagined that the Apostles on Pentecost Day composed our Latin Rite Creed, each contributing one of its twelve Articles of Faith. Rightly called a preacher's device, it witnesses in its own way to the apostolic origin of the Apostles' Creed. It should be noted that the Greek East, which produced the Nicene Creed, amplified but in the same substance of meaning and on the Trinitarian pattern, knew nothing of this legend. See Henri de Lubac, *The Christian Faith* (San Francisco: Ignatius, 1987), chapter 1, "History of a Legend."

50. Contemporary catechists and parents and those who train volunteer catechists will need to have an eye on the New Age movement of pantheistic religiosity and mysticism that is rampant today. It rushes into the void created by religious ignorance of the Deposit of Faith and Morals. Catechists are challenged to teach the Catholic faith, which rests on the historical facts regarding Jesus and his Redemption. One may say that biblical Catechetics, which the present chapter concludes, provides the antidote for this poisonous new atmosphere.

51. See *The Roman Catechism,* part 1, no. 17, "The Fourth Mark: The True Church Is Apostolic."

Bibliography

Adinolfi, Marco. *L'Apostolato dei Dodici nella vita de Gesù*. Milan: Edizioni Paoline, 1985.

Aigrain, René, and Omer Engelbert. *Prophecy Fulfilled: The Old Testament Realized in the New*. New York: McKay, 1958.

Ammassari, Antonio. *I Dodici: Note e segetiche sulla vocazione degli Apostoli*. Rome: Città Nuova, 1982.

Aquinas, Saint Thomas. *Summa Theologiae*, 1964.

Aquinas, Saint Thomas. *Summa Contra Gentiles*, 1970.

Aron, Robert. *The Jewish Jesus*, 1971.

Augustine, Saint. *The First Catechetical Instruction*, 1946.

———. *On the True Religion*, 1955.

———. *The Teacher, Trans.* Joseph Colleran (transl.). Westminster: Newman, 1950.

———. *Writings of St. Augustine*, vol. 4: *Christian Instruction*. John J. Gavigan (transl.) New York: CIMA, 1947.

Bonsirven, Joseph, S.J. *Theology of the New Testament*. Westminster, MD: Newman, 1963.

Brandwie, Ernest. *Wilhelm Schmidt and the Origin of the Idea of God*. New York: University Press of America, 1963.

Broderick, John J., S.J. (trans.). *Documents of Vatican Council I*. Collegeville: Liturgical Press, 1971.

Carmignac, Jean. *La naissance des Evangiles synoptiques*, 1984.

Cerfaux, Lucien. *Aux Origines de la Tradition*, 1968.

Ceuppens, P. F., O.P. *Theologia Biblica*, 1949.

Chervin and Kevane. *Love of Wisdom: An Introduction to Christian Philosophy*. San Francisco: Ignatius, 1988.

Civardi, Luigi. *Gesù Educatore*. Torino: S.E.I., 1962.

Daniélou, Card. Jean. *Advent*. New York: Sheed and Ward, 1951.

Dawson, Christopher. *Progress and Religion: An Historical Enquiry*. New York: Sheed and Ward, 1938.

———. *Religion and Culture*. London: Sheed and Ward, 1962.

Denzinger-Schönmetzer (eds). *Enchiridion Symbolorum,* 1975.

Dodd, C. H. *According to the Scriptures.* London: Collins, 1965.

Edersheim, Alfred. *The Life and Times of Jesus the Messiah* (2 vols.). London: Longman's Green, 1883.

Flannery, Austin, O.P. (ed). *Vatican Council II: The Conciliar and Post-Conciliar Documents.* New York: Coatello, 1975.

France, R. T., *Jesus and the Old Testament: His Application of Old Testament Passages to Himself and His Mission.* London: Tyndale, 1971.

Friedman, Father Elias, O.C.D. *Jewish Identity.* New York: Miriam Press, 1987.

Gilson, Etienne. *The Spirit of Medieval Philosophy.* New York: Scribner's, 1940.

Grail Publications (eds.). *Rome and the Study of Scripture,* 1962.

Heinisch, Paul. *Theology of the Old Testament.* (Trans. William G. Heidt, O.S.B.) Collegeville: Liturgical Press, 1950.

——. *Christ in Prophecy.* Collegeville: Liturgical Press, 1956.

Henninger, Joseph, S.V.D. "Sacrifice," in M. Eliade, *The Encyclopedia of Religion.* 1987, pp. 544–57.

Jaeger, Werner. *Paideia: The Ideals of Greek Culture,* vols. 1–3. New York: Oxford University Press, 1939–44.

James, William. *Varieties of Religious Experience: A Study in Human Nature.* New York: Modern Library, 1902.

Journet, Charles. *The Church of the Word Incarnate,* vol. 1: *The Apostolic Hierarchy.* London: Sheed and Ward, 1955.

Kevane, Eugene. *Creed and Catechetics: A Catechetical Commentary on the Creed of the People of God.* Trans. Bromiley. Westminster, MD: Christian Classics, 1978.

—— (ed.) *Teaching the Catholic Faith Today: Twentieth Century Catechetical Documents of the Holy See.* Boston: St. Paul Editions, 1982: This contains the *Acerbo nimis* of pope Saint Pius X; *Provido Sane* of Pope Pius XI; the Creed of the People of God; the *GCD,* and the *Catechesi tradendae* of Pope John Paul II.

Kittel, Gerhard. *Theological Dictionary of the New Testament* (10 vols.). Grand Rapids: Eerdmans, 1964–75.

Klein, Felix. *Jesus and His Apostles.* New York: Longmans, 1932.

Koppers, Wilhelm, S.V.D. *Primitive Man and His World Picture.* London: Sheed and Ward, 1952.

Labreton, Jules, S.J. *History of the Dogma of the Trinity from Its Origins to the Council of Nicaea.* (2 vols.) London: Burns, Oates and Wachbourne, 1939.

————. *The Spiritual Teaching of the New Testament.* London: Burns and Oates, 1960.

Langsfeld-Haag-Hasenhüttl. *La Révélation dans l'Écriture et la Tradition.* Paris: Cerf, 1969.

Larcher, C., O.P. *L'Actualité chrétienne de l'Ancien Testament d'après le Nouveau Testament.* Paris: Cerf, 1962.

Laurentin, René. *Comment reconcilier l'Exégése et la foi.* Paris: OEIL, 1984.

————. *The Truth of Christmas beyond the Myths.* Petersham, MA: St. Bede's Publications, 1986.

Lemonnyer, F., O.P. *The Theology of the New Testament.* London: Sands, 1929.

Lubac, Henri de. *The Christian Faith.* San Francisco: Ignatius, 1987.

Maas, A. J., S.J. *Christ in Type and Prophecy* (2 vols.). New York: Benziger, 1893.

McCarthy, John F. *The Science of Historical Theology.* Rome: Propaganda Mariana, 1976.

Morris, N. *The Jewish School.* London: 1937.

Newman, John Henry. *Apologia pro Vita Sua.* New York: Doubleday Image, 1956.

————. *A Grammar of Assent.* New York: Longmans, Green, 1930.

————. "Holy Scripture in its Relation to the Catholic Creed," in *Discussions and Arguments on Various Subjects.* London: Longmans, Green, 1899.

Norman, Friedrich. *Christos Didaskalos: Die Vorstellung von Christus als Lehrer in der Christlichen Literatur des ersten und zweiten Jahrhunderts,* 1967.

Picard, Max. *The Flight from God.* Chicago: Regnery, 1951.

Pickl, Josef. *The Messias.* Saint Louis: B. Herder, 1946.

Ratzinger, Card. Joseph. "Sources and Transmission of the Faith," *Communio* (Spring 1983), p. 21.

————. "Foundations and Approaches of Biblical Exegesis," *Origins: NC Documentary Service* (February 11, 1988), pp. 594–602.

————. *The Ratzinger Report.* San Francisco: Ignatius, 1985.